THE FLOOD MYTHS
OF EARLY CHINA

SUNY series in
CHINESE PHILOSOPHY AND CULTURE

Roger T. Ames, *editor*

THE FLOOD MYTHS

OF EARLY CHINA

Mark Edward Lewis

STATE UNIVERSITY OF NEW YORK PRESS

Published by

STATE UNIVERSITY OF NEW YORK PRESS, ALBANY

© 2006 State University of New York

For information, address
State University of New York Press,
194 Washington Ave, Suite 305, Albany, NY 12210-2384

Production, Laurie Searl
Marketing, Susan Petrie

Library of Congress Cataloging-in-Publication Data

Lewis, Mark Edward, 1954–
    The flood myths of early China / Mark Edward Lewis.
        p. cm. —(SUNY series in Chinese philosophy and culture)
    Includes bibliographical references and index.
    ISBN 0-7914-6663-9 (alk. paper)
    ISBN 0-7914-6664-7 (pbk. :alk. paper)
    1. Floods—China—Folklore.   2. Floods—China—Religious aspects.
I. Title. II. Series.
GR685.L49 2006
398'.363—dc22

                                                                    2005007315

ISBN-13: 978-0-7914-6663-6 (alk. paper)
ISBN-13: 978-0-7914-6664-3 (pbk. : alk. paper)

10 9 8 7 6 5 4 3 2 1

CONTENTS

ACKNOWLEDGMENTS

My greatest debt is to all the scholars whose research has been incorporated into my own. Their names are listed in the notes and bibliography. I would also like to thank my wife, Kristin Ingrid Fryklund, for all of her work in the preparation of the manuscript.

INTRODUCTION

Among the remnants of early Chinese mythology, tales of the taming of a great flood figure prominently. These stories of the creation of an ordered world out of chaos provided a rich ground for reflecting on the nature and components of human society. Among the aspects of society whose roles and origins were depicted in these tales were the ruler, the lineage, the household, and even the human body. The institutional background and philosophical or literary aspects to many of the ideas dramatized in these stories are dealt with in a separate book, *The Construction of Space in Early China*. This volume on the flood myths examines the manner in which the early Chinese read the origins of many Warring States and early imperial institutions or practices into high antiquity. As such it forms a companion volume to *The Construction of Space*, but it can also be read independently as a study of a major topos of early Chinese mythology. This introduction places the Chinese myths within a larger context by examining stories of a great flood that appear in different parts of the world. These stories provide a useful background for understanding the Chinese flood myths by showing how they both resemble and are distinct from related myths found in other civilizations.

COMPARATIVE FLOOD MYTHS

In this book, "myth" refers to any "traditional tale with secondary, partial reference to something of collective importance," in which the vexed word "traditional" means that it has no identifiable author but appears in several sources and develops over time. These stories "express dramatically the ideology under which a society lives," reflect on the elements and tensions that form a society, and "justify the rules and traditional practices without which everything in a society would disintegrate."[1] Myths thus belong to and serve to define particular groups, and both their form and significance will entirely depend on the uses to which they are put by those groups. As the groups change across time, the form of the myths and their uses will likewise change, or the stories will simply be forgotten.

1

Myths are always to be understood in context

This account of myths means that they cannot be defined as an objective "substance" that exists outside or apart from the people who create and employ them. The impossibility of any "substantial" definition of myth has been pointed out in recent years by scholars who have shown that myths are not a distinctive mode or genre of narrative that can be distinguished from other stories by any substantive trait or linguistic mark. They have usually concluded that the category "myth" is an illusion or a modern construct used to fetishize or deride certain stories in the service of some rival program that claims to transcend "primitive" myths, for example, philosophy, dogmatic religion, science, or history.[2] Alternatively, rival intellectual programs, such as Gnosticism or some forms of Romanticism, embraced the same hypostasized concept of "myth" as a weapon against the all-encompassing claims of dogma or reason.[3] However, this dismissal of the category of "myth" can be challenged in several ways.

First, while myths are not distinguished from other stories by any definitive attributes, they can be operationally defined in terms of who told them, on what occasion, and for what purposes. Thus Lowell Edmunds, in his introduction to *Approaches to Greek Myth*, examines various discussions of stories and storytelling in ancient Greece, and is able to show how a certain set of stories that we would call myths were distinguished by the Greeks on the basis of their subject matter (supernatural or heroic), their variable forms of transmission (poetry for pan-Hellenic or oral for local), the motives for telling them, and their constant reappearance in new versions depending on their range (pan-Hellenic or local) or context.[4] While the formal theory of a category of stories called myths was not formulated until Plato created it as a negative term to valorize his own definition of "philosophy," Edmunds shows how an incipient category already operated in the writings of Pindar, Aristophanes, and Herodotus.

Second, it is striking that the critics who constituted the category of myth as a negative term used to set off the glories of their own programs elaborated their own stories that performed the sanctioning role of myths. Plato's use of stories about the afterlife, Atlantis, the origins of the world, and other clearly "mythic" themes has been the object of considerable study. The traditional myths condemned by Plato were in turn interpreted as poetic truths by Aristotle, or as veridical allegories by the Hellenistic philosophers.[5] Paul contrasted the "godless and silly myths" of the Greeks with the Christian logos (adopting Plato's categories), Clement of Alexandria and Irenaeus attacked classical mythology as the work of demons, and the rejection of Gnosticism hinged in part on the criticism of its reliance on an elaborate mythology. Nevertheless, elaborate tales spun out from the New Testament and later lives of saints formed a "Christian mythology" as analyzed at length by scholars of the Enlightenment and the early Romantic movement.[6] Similarly, propagandists proclaimed that modern science supplanted the errors of myth, which Francis Bacon and others described as a primitive attempt to answer the questions that true science would resolve.[7] Nevertheless, science elaborated mythic

Those who deride the category use it for their own purposes

accounts of its own heroic origins, for example, the misrepresented trial of Galileo, and as Kurt Hübner has shown at length, the tale of science supplanting myth is only one version of numerous mythicizing accounts of the end of mythology.[8] Finally, whereas historians from the time of Thucydides have defined themselves in opposition to myth, and modern positivist historiography made the supplanting of earlier myths one of its chief tasks, increasing numbers of modern historians have incorporated myths into their work, studying the work of mythology as a central topic of their research.[9] This constant resurgence of mythic tales within the works of those who demonize mythology suggests that it is not purely the invention of those critics.

Finally, the operative definition of myth refutes the criticism that the category of myth is an illusion or invention precisely by defining it not through the nature of the tale but through the attitudes of its tellers and listeners. This point is made most clearly in Hans Blumenberg's *Work on Myth* (*Arbeit am Mythos*). As the title itself indicates, this book elaborates its theory of mythology in terms of what is done *to* or *with* the stories, rather than some quality of the stories themselves. In a sense, Blumenberg applies to myth the same sort of ideas as those applied to literature in the "reception" theories elaborated by Ingarden, Iser, and Jauss, in which the assumptions, questions, and rules of reading provided by the audience constantly shape and reshape the meaning of the text.[10] The primary difference is that, unlike literature, in which new readings are applied to a given text, in the case of a myth the story itself will be constantly adapted and rewritten as the concerns of its tellers and its audience change. It is for this reason that, as Blumenberg points out, myths are "stories that are distinguished by a high degree of constancy in their narrative core" but by an equally pronounced capacity for variation. These correlate attributes allow myths to be transmitted over centuries; their constancy produces the attraction and the authority due to familiarity, while their variability allows for constant adaptation to new intellectual needs.[11] This combination helps account for the power of myths, which, as Blumenberg argues, are the product of a "Darwinism of words" in which stories that seize attention and help people cope with their world are selected for repetition, and in which these same stories are adapted over time to changing circumstances.

This variability of myths, in which new versions are constantly elaborated to explain or supplant old ones, also helps to explain why mythology is routinely theorized by those who claim to refute it, only to fashion new myths in their own turn. As Lowell Edmunds has pointed out, even before "myth" was theoretically formulated by Plato as a negative category, the term was often applied to stories that the author chose to reject in favor of some other version or tale. Thus, in Aristophanes's *Wasps*, Bdelycleon tells his father not to tell "myths [*mythoi*]" about supernatural creatures, but "stories of the human kind." Likewise, Pindar prefaces his version of the story of Pelops by repudiating a version of the myth that he claims was started by "malicious neighbors" of Pelops's family. Edmunds concludes that, for many Greeks, "My version is the truth, but yours is a *mythos*."[12] Given that the coining of variants and competition between these different versions was a feature of the tales that emerged as myths, the repeated theorization of mythology as a target of criticism is not a proof of the illusory character of the category, but rather of its mode of generation and perpetuation.

Tales of a world-destroying flood are one of the most widespread and continuously evolving categories of stories in the world, and probably the most exhaustively studied by scholars over the centuries. The most thorough collections of such tales have described more than 300 examples drawn from every continent.[13] Western studies of the flood across the centuries were dominated by the biblical tale of Noah, although versions of the myth were also known from ancient Greece and Rome.[14] The true beginning of comparative studies on flood tales, however, was the publication in 1872 by George Smith of a fragment of the flood story from what is now identified as chapter eleven of the Gilgamesh epic. This version, supplemented by Smith's discovery in the next year of much of what is now known as the *Atrahasis*, showed the world that the biblical account was based on, or closely related to, earlier accounts that had circulated in the Middle East.[15] The rise of comparative folklore and anthropology in the final decades of the nineteenth century produced evidence of flood tales from many other areas. Some scholars argued that such widespread accounts were evidence of the historicity of a universal flood, and even in recent decades people have written books seeking to demonstrate the veracity of these stories.[16] However, for scholars not religiously committed to a belief in the absolute veracity of the biblical account, the multiplicity of versions across the globe was treated as an interesting phenomenon for analysis through the methods of comparative folklore or mythology. Thus, the first great summation of comparative flood myths by James Frazer—who collected evidence of tales from Mesopotamia, the Bible, ancient Greece and Rome, South Asia (both ancient and modern), Southeast Asia (both continental and the islands), Australia, New Guinea, Melanesia, South America, and North America—was published in a book entitled *Folklore in the Old Testament: Studies in Comparative Religion, Legend, and Law*. The biblical account, once a central element of belief in Western culture, was reduced to the role of being a single case, and apparently a derivative one, in a worldwide phenomenon.

The sheer breadth and diversity of flood legends also mean that it is impossible to speak in any meaningful sense of *the* flood myth or to derive any useful generalizations that would apply to all cases. No interesting statement can be made that is true of all accounts of the flood. This point is made by Dorothy Vitaliano:

> However, there is not *one* deluge legend, but rather a collection of traditions which are so diverse that they can be explained neither by one general catastrophe alone, nor by the dissemination of one local tradition alone. Some are highly imaginative but very wide-of-the-mark attempts to explain local topographic features or the presence

of fossil shells high above sea level. A large number are recollection—vastly distorted and exaggerated, as is the rule in folklore—of real local disasters, often demonstrably consistent with special local geologic conditions. . . . Flood traditions are nearly universal . . . mainly because floods *in the plural* are the most universal of geologic catastrophes.[17]

Although the prevalence of floods is certainly a necessary condition for the frequency of flood myths, it is not sufficient as an explanation. Not all widespread phenomena become the subject of stories, much less of fundamental myths. Furthermore, it provides no insight into the wide ranges of meanings attributed to the flood in different versions.

Floods become the recurring topic of stories because, like animals, they are "good to think." Although there is no *single* feature or meaning common to all versions, certain topoi or ideas to which floods lend themselves do recur in many contexts. In the balance of this introduction I will examine several major recurrent themes in flood myths, emphasizing those that provide insights into the Chinese case. These themes are: (1) the flood as a re-creation of the world within the human era, in which the world's enduring survival is made possible by new institutions or practices; (2) the flood as a form of punishment or revenge by some powerful spirit; (3) the repopulation of the earth after the flood as a means of dramatizing kinship structures, incest taboos, or the origins of the different peoples of the earth; (4) the relations of people and animals, who collaborate or compete for the purposes of rescue or repopulation; and (5) water as an image of formlessness and fertility.

One of the most important points about flood myths is that they are often closely linked to creation myths that they either repeat or modify. Thus, the flood story is frequently, as Alan Dundes notes, a *re-creation* myth.[18] Dundes, on the basis of a single example, argues that the original creation is always feminine and that the tales of a re-creation all express male womb envy. While male–female tensions do figure in some versions of the flood myth, as will be discussed, they are far from a universal feature. Much more striking is the fact that the world re-created after the flood, particularly in the myths preserved in literary traditions, is often altered through the imposition of new laws or institutions. Thus the flood myth, a tale of origins that are subsequent to human creation, regularly becomes a sanction for the existence of a particular body of practices that are central to the people who created the myth.[19] This feature of the flood stories is central to the biblical and the Mesopotamian versions, as well as those from China.

In the story in Genesis, the flood ends with the establishment of a new relationship between God and his creation, and the institution of new rules for the human race. At the end of Chapter 8, Noah emerges from the ark and makes a sacrifice of every clean animal and bird, which leads God to say that he will never again curse the earth because of man or destroy all living creatures. In the next chapter, he announces a new order, in which humans are granted lordship over all creatures whom they are allowed to eat. God bans only the eating of an animal's blood. This is followed immediately by the statement that any animal or human who kills a human being will likewise be slain. As Tikva Frymer-Kensky has pointed out, this marks a new legal order based on the absolute sanctity of human life, for in the pre-deluge world murderers such as Cain and Lamech were not slain but marked with a sign of God's protection and then exiled. The spilling of the blood of unavenged innocents had consequently polluted the earth and made it sterile, so that the flood at least in part was a means of cleansing the earth prior to the imposition of the principle of a life for a life.[20] This is followed by God's proclamation of a covenant with Noah, all his descendants, and all the creatures of the earth, in which He pledges to never again destroy the earth through a flood and places the rainbow in the sky as a sign. This tradition of a covenant with the entire human race that preceded the establishment of the covenant with the Jews alone was developed in rabbinic theology in the tradition of the "seven Noahide commandments" that supposedly bound all men, unlike the later ten Mosaic commandments that applied only to the Jews. Early Christian writers also elaborated this theme, as in the case of Irènaeus who argued that this covenant introduced the practice of eating meat, for prior to the flood humans had been vegetarian.[21]

While the biblical account presents the flood as the occasion for the imposition of the first laws and first covenant—an intermediate step between Adam, the full covenant with Abraham, and the Mosaic ten commandments—the earlier Mesopotamian version as best represented in the *Atrahasis* emphasized the question of population control and the shifting relation between humans and gods. In this account, the lesser gods were originally burdened with the labor of digging channels and carrying heavy loads, so they rebelled. In response, the high gods created humans to do the work. However, with the passage of time, people, who were apparently in this initial period immortal, grew too numerous and their clamor prevented the gods from sleeping. As a consequence the latter decided to destroy the human race. They first attempted to cause a drought, but sacrifices to the rain god instituted on the advice of the god Enki (a Prometheus figure) to his favorite, Atrahasis, brought an end to this threat. Soon the people were again too numerous, so the gods brought on a plague, but once again the institution of a sacrifice to the proper deity ended the disease. The third and final attempt to destroy the burgeoning human race took the form of a flood, which only Atrahasis and his family survived by building a boat at the urging of Enki. However, with all people now gone, the gods discovered that they missed the fruits of regular sacrifice. When the offerings of Atrahasis alerted them that one family had survived the flood, they allowed the human race to endure. However, they introduced sterility, miscarriages, and the institution of attaching virgin female devotees to temples in order to restrict population growth. Judging from a recently discovered Sumerian text, the story closed with the imposition of death as the fate of all humans.[22] The *Atrahasis* myth thus provides a just-so account of how death, in all its forms, entered the world, but it also serves to justify key practices related to temple cults as well as the central role of temples themselves. In particular, it explains the introduction of regular sacrifices to the gods, and the practice of removing women from the household to serve as dedicated attendants of the gods at the temple.

In the Tamil versions of the myth from south India there is no single flood but a series of recurring deluges that destroy the world at intervals. In these stories the equivalent of the legal or ritual innovations that prevent future floods are the institutions that survive the flood and provide a fixed point from which the world could be re-created. In some versions of the myths, this institution is the Caṅkam, literary academies in which the compositions of the poets were gathered and judged. In other tales that grew up around specific shrines, the institution was the shrine itself, which magically survived the flood and provided the place from which the god, usually Śiva, could restore the land.[23] Thus, the myths are once again about the re-creation of the world and the institutions that guarantee its survival, but this re-creation—like the destruction that precedes it—is a recurrent phenomenon rather than a unique event.

A second recurring topos of flood myths, closely related to the first, is the idea that the flood was a form of punishment or revenge. In an extreme formulation, Hans Kelsen argued that virtually all flood myths were about retribution, and although this is certainly not true in all cases, it highlights a feature of many versions.[24] Thus, in the biblical account God creates the flood to destroy all life because of mankind's evil. In the Mesopotamian version the gods create the flood because people are too noisy, and while this does not strike all readers as morally serious, it certainly falls within the category of retribution or revenge.[25] In the two main surviving versions of the flood myth from classical antiquity—the tale of Deucalion and Pyrrha, and that of Philemon and Baucis—Zeus resolves to destroy humanity by a flood for violations of the laws of hospitality of which he is the patron deity. Kelsen also has gathered tales from Persia, Southeast Asia, Australia, New Zealand, the Pacific Islands, Africa, South America, and North America of floods unleashed by gods for unspecified wickedness or particular offenses. Sometimes these appear as moral failings, and sometimes as personal insults to the god, such as an Australian tale in which the world was inundated because one man did not lend his boomerangs and opossum bags to the moon god. In many cases the flood occurs as one step in a series of acts of vengeance, as in the Algonquin myth in which some water lynxes kill the nephew of a medicine man who in turn wounds one of the lynxes and thus unleashes a great flood. There are also versions, such as that found in the *Popol Vuh*, in which earlier races of creatures are destroyed by the gods because they lacked certain necessary features. These are yet further examples of the flood legends as tales of *re-creation*, but in these cases a series of physical creations are necessary to attain the desired result.[26]

In some versions the flood appears not as punishment for some crime(s), but is itself a criminal act. Thus, the Acawaoios in British Guiana told how the flood was unleashed by a mischievous monkey who removed the lid from a basket in which the waters of the world were enclosed. The Arawaks from the same region told how a wicked woman caused a river to swell up so as to cover the entire plateau. Her husband exiled her to become the moon, and opened up a great waterfall to drain the plateau so that agriculture could be resumed there. Again the Chirguanos of Bolivia tell how the flood was created by an evil supernatural being who rebelled against the true god and sought to destroy humanity. The south Indian myths tell not of the punishing of criminality, but of a battle between the inchoate and violent forces that periodically submerge the world, and the creative powers of the gods who time and again must conquer the forces of chaos.[27] As we will see, these themes of criminality as the origin of floods and proper drainage as its cure figure prominently in the Chinese myths.

The third recurring aspect of flood myths is their frequent linkage to accounts of male–female relations, the origins of families, and the process of reproduction. In a few cases—as in the Arawak myth or a tale of the Narrinyeri in South Australia, where the flood is unleashed by a man to punish his two wives for deserting him—the flood is produced by failures in marital relations. The Mandingo in the Ivory Coast tell of a generous man who distributed all his goods to animals and, ultimately, to a god. His wife and children deserted him, and were consequently destroyed in a flood from which the man was rescued. A tale of the Basonge relates how several animals wooed the granddaughter of the high god, who accepted the zebra. However, the animal broke its pledge not to allow his wife to work, and she poured forth a great flood that covered the earth.[28] Improper marriages figure also in one element of the biblical account, which precedes God's decision to destroy the human race by describing the mating of the "sons of God" with the "daughters of men" to produce a race of "mighty men" or giants.

However, the primary focus on marriages in the flood myths figures in accounts of the survivors. Thus, in the biblical version, the *Atrahasis*, the Greek versions, and many other flood myths, a single family survives the deluge and goes on to repopulate the world. However, many versions insist on the unusual character of the surviving pair, their manner of reproduction, or their relation to their children. Some are marked by criminality or the violation of fundamental taboos. In this way myths on the restoration of the world after the flood, a restoration based on the formation of a single household, often provide modes for thinking about the characteristics, tensions, or taboos that form the household.

A classic example is the biblical account. This version follows the story of the flood and the covenant with an account of Noah's inventing wine and consequently becoming drunk. Ham, the father of Canaan, sees his father's genitals and reports this to his two brothers, who back into their father's presence and cover him without looking. As a consequence Noah curses Canaan and his descendants to be slaves of the other two. This account overtly provides a just-so story about the origins of ethnic tensions in the Middle East, but it also hints at the theme of rivalry, explicitly sexual rivalry, between father and son. Later Jewish commentary on this story elaborated the theme of sexual rivalry between Noah and Ham, describing how Ham attempted to castrate Noah. In a highly speculative essay Eleanor Follansbee argues that the story of Noah—in its account of him as cultivator and inventor of wine—is a version of myths of the castration, death, and rebirth of a vegetation spirit, in which case the father–son tension would become even more graphic.[29] Although Noah's relation to his wife does not play any role in the biblical account, it became important in later developments of the tale, such as the Eastern European version in which the devil seduces Noah's wife and with her aid either destroys a first version of the ark or enters the completed ark and attempts to sink the ship to destroy all life.[30] In this version, she replays the role of Eve in the biblical creation myth.

Another recurring topos of reproduction in the flood myths that figured in the tale of Noah and his sons was the identification of the different peoples that populate the earth as each being the descendants of one of the sons of the survivor of the flood. Thus, the Lolos in northern Myanmar and southern China had a tradition that the literate peoples, such as themselves and the Chinese, were each descended from one of the four sons of the flood survivor Du-mu, while the illiterate peoples were descendants of wooden figures carved by Du-mu after the flood in order to repopulate the earth. The Kammu of northern Thailand told how a brother and sister survived the flood sealed in a drum and, at the urging of a bird, became husband and wife. The sister gave birth to a dried gourd, from which they constantly heard the sound of talking. Finally they heated a long iron rod to bore open the gourd, from which emerged in sequence the Rəmeet (whose skin turned brown from the ash that lined the hole), the Kammu, the Thai, the Westerners, and the Chinese. The full version of the myth also narrates how these people acquired different languages, writing systems, and levels of economic development. In a myth among the Brazilian Indians around Cape Frio, the flood was triggered by a fight between two brothers who alone survived it, and the different tribes traced their ancestry to one or the other brother. In a gruesome version of this myth from Myanmar, a brother and sister who survive the flood take refuge in a cave inhabited by two elves (nats) where they give birth to a child. The child's squalling disturbs the female nat who chops up the baby, strews its blood and flesh at the meeting place of nine roads, and serves the remnants to the unsuspecting parents. On learning the truth, the mother goes to the crossroads and calls on the Great Spirit to restore her child. The Great Spirit confesses that it cannot put the child back together, but in recompense it makes the woman the mother of all nations, with each of the nine roads among which the child was distributed corresponding to one people.[31] As we will see in chapter four, there are also versions of the flood myth from the south of China preserved in later texts in which the sibling pair who marry to repopulate the earth produce an undefined blob that is carved up and distributed throughout the world to form the different peoples of the earth. Thus, in each of these stories the account of the repopulating of the earth becomes a just-so story on the division of mankind, a division based on the struggles between brothers or the carving up of a single ancestor who is often the product of an incestuous union.

While the Atrahasis myth does not have any narrative elements overtly reflecting tensions within the household, it does problematize families and the male–female bond in two ways. First, the theme of human reproduction is central to the story (as it also is in the biblical account, which highlights the theme of people's "multiplication" both before and after the flood). Second, the great reform that ends the problem that had led to the flood is the introduction of a pivotal role in the temple for women who will never marry. This practice, which challenged or limited the institution of the household, becomes the basis of the future survival of the human race.

The theme of couples and reproduction is also central to the Greek myth of Deucalion and Pyrrha. This is another version of the story in which a single couple survives the flood and must repopulate the earth. However, rather than reproducing by conventional means, Deucalion and Pyrrha repopulated the earth by picking up rocks (the "bones" of their "mother" the Earth) and throwing them over their shoulders. Those that Deucalion threw became men, and those that Pyrrha threw became women. Apart from its nonsexual mode, the striking feature of this form of reproduction is that women produce women and men produce men, so the two genders form distinct races. This notion of women and men as separate races or species is a recurrent theme in Greek mythology, most notably in the story of Pandora, the first woman, who was manufactured by Hephaestus as a trap for men. As has been demonstrated by Nicole Loraux in a series of works, the myths of men and women as separate races, and their original reproduction from the Earth without sex, figure prominently in the claims of Athens to unique, autochthonous origins.[32] However, while the insistence on autochthony was distinctively Athenian, the radical division between men and women implicit in the myths of Pandora, and of Deucalion and Pyrrha, was part of a much broader Hellenistic phenomenon.

In several cases repopulation after the flood involves incest. Sometimes this entails the joining of father and daughter, most notably in the classic Indian flood myth of Manu. In this story Manu alone survived the flood. Desiring offspring, he performed austerities and cast offerings of clarified butter, sour milk, whey, and curds into the water. In a year these offerings congealed to become a woman. When the woman encountered the gods Mitra and Varuna, they asked who she was, and she replied that she was Manu's daughter. Despite their demands that she acknowledge herself to be theirs, she insisted on her paternity from Manu. When she met the sage, she presented herself as the offspring generated by his offerings and insisted that if he would use her as the benediction in the middle of the sacrifice (where the sacrificial food is eaten) he would be rich in offspring and cattle. He used her repeatedly in his offerings, and thus generated the human race. Although the whole account is mediated through the mechanism of sacrifice, for which it provides an origin tale, the theme of the joining of father and daughter to repopulate the earth remains explicit. As J. C. Heesterman has elaborated in several places, in this earliest version of the Indian flood myth the themes of cosmogony, incest, and the origins of sacrifice are all intertwined.[33] A similar story among the Muratos in Ecuador told how only a single man survived the flood, and to repopulate the earth he cut off a piece of his own flesh that he planted in the ground. A woman grew up from this, whom he married. The Dyaks in Borneo related how the flood survivor created multiple wives from stones, logs, and other objects and thereby repopulated the earth. A few other flood myths from South America and insular Southeast Asia recount how the world was repopulated through the incestuous union of father and daughter or mother and son.[34]

Far more common than tales of incest between parent and child are those of the marriage of siblings. Frazer's collection of flood myths includes versions from India, continental Southeast Asia, and South America in which a brother and sister form the primal couple who repopulate the earth, and Baumann has collected examples from Africa.[35] Versions involving sibling incest are particularly frequent in Southeast Asia, southern China, and Taiwan, where over fifty examples have been collected.[36] These tales, sometimes linked with accounts of a cosmic egg or gourd from which the world emerged (related to accounts of the shapeless primal offspring), offer an embodied form of myths of the generation of the world through the union of the two sexual principles, or rather of a complementary pair of generative principles that are sexual when manifested in animal life. Thus, once again these are flood myths that reenact in human time with human actors the cosmological processes of primal creation. A few versions of the myth also contain explicit references to the origins of the incest taboo.[37] Some modern scholars have attempted to read these traditions back into early Chinese mythology, an argument that will be discussed in chapter four.[38]

A final form of irregular marriage that often figures in flood myths is the union of humans (usually men) and animals. The Cañaris of Ecuador tell how two brothers who alone survived the flood discovered that food had been mysteriously prepared for them. After this had recurred for ten days, they hid and discovered that the food was being prepared by two macaws who had the faces of beautiful women and wore clothing like the Cañaris. They managed to capture one of the birds, and with her they sired six children from whom all the Cañaris are descended. In a story told by the Huichol people of western Mexico, the earth goddess instructs a man how to survive the flood by making a box and placing in it five grains of corn of each color, five beans of each color, five squash stems, fire, and a black bitch. After surviving the flood the man planted the crops and lived with the bitch. As in the other story, the survivor regularly came home to find that food had been mysteriously prepared, and on hiding he discovered that the bitch removed her skin to become a human woman who cooked his food. Throwing the dogskin into the fire he forced her to permanently become a woman with whom he sired a large family that repopulated the world. The Montagnais in Canada described how the world was repopulated by the marriage of a man with a muskrat who had fetched the soil for the rebuilding of the earth. The Haida of Queen Charlotte Island reversed the standard gender arrangement, telling how a being that was half-human and half-crow repopulated the world through marriage to a human woman that it had sired on a cockle shell through pure desire. Some tribes in British Columbia relate how all the different peoples of the region were sired by a coyote who mated with diverse trees.[39] As we will see in chapter four, the early Chinese also had a version of the flood myth that entailed the generation of offspring through the mating of a human with an animal.

These tales of the joining of people and animals to repopulate the earth after the flood relate to a much broader range of topoi in which animals figure in every aspect of the myths of the deluge. First, animals are often responsible for causing the flood. In some cases the killing of a particular animal apparently causes god(s) to unleash a deluge. In other cases the flood is created by the animal kin of a slain creature, for example, the mother of a crocodile killed by some people or by a wounded creature itself. Mischievous animals, such as a monkey, also trigger the flood through curiosity or carelessness.[40] Second, animals often warn a chosen person of the imminent coming of the flood. Thus, Manu is warned of the flood, and ultimately saved, by a small fish whom he rescues, rears, and finally releases. In other stories the survivor of the flood is warned by a dog, a llama, a coyote, or a water rat, who also provide instructions on how the survivor can escape from the water's ravages.[41] Again, certain versions describe how the human survivors took a few animals, or examples of all animals, onto their raft either before the flood struck or as the water was rising. The most elaborate example of this is the biblical account, but the rescue of key animals figures in stories found throughout the world. Some of these stories account for the physical features of certain animals by describing what happened to them during the flood.[42]

Such animals, in turn, often play a major role in detecting the end of the flood, rescuing the survivors, or bringing the survivors fire or some other necessary object. In versions of the Mesopotamian myth, the biblical account, and stories influenced by it, the use of animals to detect the end of the flood takes the form of sending out first the raven and then the dove. In a version common throughout much of North America, known to folklorists as the "Earth-Diver myth," a list of animals—often including the beaver, otter, types of aquatic fowl, and muskrat—attempt sequentially to bring up mud from beneath the flood. This mud, usually recovered by the muskrat, is breathed on or magically manipulated by the human to create a new earth.[43] In other versions a human ghost having taken on the form of a king-fisher tricks the high god into restoring fire to the survivors, a frog preserves fire in his belly and gives it to the surviving brother–sister pair who have incestuously wed, a pelican rescues the people out of lust for one woman, a frog or a bittern swallows up the flood, birds fetch the lumps of soil that people need to restore the earth, a turtle carries the survivors on its back, and a dove teaches the surviving children how to speak.[44] In some African versions, people turn into animals in order to escape the flood or as a punishment.[45] In one myth from the Native Americans of California, all animals perished in the flood, but the ghosts of the ancestors of the human survivors became every species of animal.[46] Finally, as we have seen above, the repopulation of the earth often involved human–animal cooperation or mating.

There are several reasons for this prominence of animals in every aspect of the flood myths from around the world. First, animals function as markers of the universality of the catastrophe, which included not only humans but all living things. Second, in what could loosely be described as their "totemic" role, the animals were necessarily involved in the reestablishment of the human order because they defined the social structure by becoming the ancestors or the insignia of the human groups. Third, the flood collapses distinctions between formerly separate zones or substances: the worlds of water, land, and air. Many of the animals who figure in these stories are those who can move from one zone to the other, particularly from land to water such as the beaver, muskrat, and aquatic birds. Fourth, in some cases the mixing of people and animals marked a stage in the evolution of the world, a stage that in certain versions ended with the flood. Thus, some South American Indians described the prediluvian world as one in which wild beasts mingled freely with men, while in a North American version early animals and men shared a common language.[47] Elements of the story of Noah's flood are related to this idea, although in inverted form, as Noah in the new covenant receives lordship over all animals and the right to eat them. It is possible that the absence of boundaries between men and animals was linked to the idea of the flood itself, which drowned all divisions in universal nondistinction. This last point is yet another version of the flood myths serving as charters for fundamental fea-tures of the world known to the tellers of the myth, in this case the separa-tion of men and animals.

A final recurring element in the flood myths is the pivotal role of water. This is not a trivial point, for at least two reasons. First, flooding is not the only means by which the world could be destroyed. The most common alternative is fire or the closely related drought. In several stories, floods follow or alternate with cataclysmic fires. However, the universal flood is mythically far more common than tales of a universal fire. The Chinese materials also occasionally pair fire and water, but once again the theme of the flood is much more frequent. Disaster by water, as opposed to disaster by fire, produces many of the characteristic recurring features of the flood myths, such as the reliance on boats to survive, the taking of refuge on high mountains or trees, or the importance of amphibians and aquatic birds or mammals in rescuing humans or repopulating the earth.

The power & peril of water

More important, the watery nature of floods allows for the elaboration of myths around the contrast of contained or channeled water that is beneficial, and rampant water that is destructive.[48] In analyses of non-Chinese materials, the clearest demonstration of the importance of this contrast between conflicting modes of water as a theme of flood myths appears in *The Origin of Table Manners* by Claude Lévi-Strauss. As he points out, in both North and South America certain myths are structured around the contrast between the "two extreme modes" of water: the voyage up and down stream by canoe that regulates the passage of time (as linked to the motions of the sun and the moon, or the seasonal moving of settlements), versus the floods or storms that upset the natural course of things. While Lévi-Strauss embeds this contrast between the contrasting modes of water within analyses dealing with the seasonal cycle and seasonal migration, his collected material provides considerable detail showing how water functions as an alternating image of order and chaos.[49] As will be discussed throughout this book, this contrast is prominent in the Chinese flood myths.

Water as necessary for recreation

Furthermore, destruction of the human race through water allows flood myths to recapitulate stories of creation. Because it has the three attributes of formlessness, dynamism, and fructification, water frequently figures in the human imagination as the source of life and of all things. Mircea Eliade has pointed out how water is a recurring element in many cosmogonic myths.[50] Although not explicitly cosmogonic, many myths also relate how specific plants or creatures, including the human race, emerged from water.[51]

The link of flood myths to tales of creation through their shared reliance on water as a major image is shown by the fact that in many cosmogonies or creation myths the chaos that precedes the emergence of the world is described in terms of water. Thus, the account in Genesis states that at the time of creation "darkness was upon the face of the deep. And the Spirit of God moved upon the face of the waters." Furthermore, on the second day God created a firmament (Heaven) that "divided the waters which were under the firmament from the waters which were above the firmament." On the next day God then concentrated the lower waters to allow the emergence of dry land. Thus, the original state of the world was a watery chaos, from which the structured cosmos was created through sequential steps of division and concentration. Consequently, the onset of the flood essentially restored the world to its original state prior to creation. Indeed, this link of creation and flood played a fundamental role in early modern scientific thought, when a series of authors appealed to the biblical account of a vast "abyss" of waters stored up beneath the earth at the time of the first separation in order to resolve the question of where the waters of the flood had come from and to where they had departed.[52] These authors thus read the flood as the reversal of the process of creation, and the ending of the flood as a reenactment of the world's origins.

The same is true of other flood myths. In the Akkadian origin myth, *Enuma elish*, the primal chaos of the waters formed by the pair Apsu (fresh waters) and Tiamat (the all-engendering ocean) is defeated in battle and the body of the ocean carved up to form the heavens and earth.[53] Thus, the flood abolishes the division that had made possible the world's existence, and overcoming the flood replays the process of creation. That Mesopotamia's creation myth parallels its flood myth is marked by the fact that just as in the latter the gods decided to destroy humankind because their clamor prevented sleep, so Ansu and his followers originally decided to destroy the gods for the same reason.

Similarly, in Hesiod's *Theogony*, the world is progressively carved out of its primal state through a series of spontaneous divisions, acts of violence, and ultimately war between the forces of order and chaos. While in this version the primal chaos is explicitly distinguished from the ocean, which appears only in the course of the divisions, the earlier *Iliad* described the ocean, Okéanos, and his wife Tythus as the primordial couple from which all things emerged. Moreover, these passages from Homer were interpreted as a cosmography by Plato and Aristotle, the same idea appears in a cosmogonic poem by Alcman, and Thalés argued that all life emerged from water. The links between the Akkadian and the Greek myths are particularly strong, because both connect the emergence of ordered space from chaos to the establishment of social order on the basis of political sovereignty.[54] This link, as we will see, was also central in the case of early China.

In summary, while there is no single flood myth, the flood regularly figures as an image of the collapse of the distinctions and boundaries that had defined the world. Consequently, accounts of the ending of the flood constitute a second creation of the world in which humans and other creatures take an active part. On the one hand, the flood itself can be provoked by people or animals, often through some act of crime or rebellion. On the other hand, the world re-created after the flood is often marked by the imposition of some new regime or institutions, and the purpose of many flood myths is to explain or justify such institutions. Among the institutions created, altered, or restored in the flood, particular prominence is often given to the marital and kin relations that constitute the family. In addition, because the flood myths deal with the dissolution and re-creation of boundaries, the crossing of major boundaries such as that between people and animals or water and land figures prominently in these myths.

CHINESE FLOOD MYTHS

In China during Warring States period (481–221 B.C.) and the early empires (220 B.C.–A.D. 220) the myths through which literate people dramatized their self-understanding took the form of accounts of the creation of human civilization by the sage-kings. These superhuman beings recognized the patterns implicit in the natural order, and from these brought forth the tools, technical procedures, virtues, and institutions that separated men from beasts.[55] In the case of the flood, most of the tales center on the work of the sage-king Yu, sometimes in association with the earlier sages Yao and Shun. A small number focus on the female divinity Nü Gua. As is now generally recognized, these tales were developed from earlier myths dealing with supernatural beings who figured in shamanic rituals, cosmogonic tales, or stories of the origins of various tribes or clans.[56] Thus, these tales already exemplified the variability and dynamism that characterize myths in other cultures. As will be shown in the course of the book, the tales also varied considerably in their details depending on the argument or idea that they were being used to justify. They also continued to evolve in later periods, as new religious or philosophical movements adapted existing accounts of antiquity to their own uses.[57]

The Chinese flood myths exhibit all the features previously described in accounts of flood myths from other parts of the world. First, they were tales of the re-creation of the world that provided origin myths and thus justifications for major political institutions, particularly those associated with the role of the monarch or emperor and his servants.[58] Second, they employed water as an image for the dissolution of all distinctions, and thus presented the taming of the flood as a process that recapitulated in the age of men, and, through human action, the creation of the world. Several versions of the myth also explicitly contrasted channeled water that flowed properly and thus was beneficial with the rampant waters of the flood. Third, those versions that touched on the origins of the flood attributed it to rebellion, and several versions identified the taming of the flood with the punishment of criminals. Fourth, many of the stories associated with the flood dealt with the question of the emergence of a properly constructed lineage, in the relations of father and son, or a household, in the joining of husband and wife to generate offspring. Fifth, the issues of man–animal relations, notably in the importance of metamorphoses and hybrids in taming the flood, figure in many versions of the myths, as does the theme of animal assistants. Thus, while many of the particular forms of these myths were distinctive to China, as were their political and social messages, the major topoi and themes through which these tales of the flood were employed to think about human society were common with those of many other societies.

This book is organized around these themes and topoi. The first point, the myths as sanctions of political authority, is fundamental to the entire book, and thus does not figure as the topic of a distinct chapter. Each of the other points forms the topic of one chapter. Chapter one examines how early Chinese cosmogonic myths and accounts of the origins of human society were organized around the image of the sequential carving up of a primal chaos. Against the background of these images and theories, tales of the flood and its taming provided narratives that graphically dramatized both the creation of a structured spatial order and a regulated human society. Thus, many stories described the watery chaos of the flood, and presented the ruler's or officials' dredging and channeling as the sole means of establishing fixed courses for the water and thereby defining the land. The classic late Warring States account of this process in the "Tribute of Yu" also explicitly links the proper flowing of water to the movement of tribute that spatially defined the state by distinguishing periphery and center. These tales thus constituted a mythology of origins that justified the state through literally demonstrating its role in water control in the period, and figuratively dramatizing the role of the ruler as the one who maintained the crucial distinctions that defined human society. The earliest versions of these stories in the *Shang shu* dealt with the fashioning of world order, but later accounts also developed them into stories of the creation of distinctive regional cultures.

Chapter two deals with a second set of tales, in which the flood appears as the work of malefactors and its taming thus becomes a process of punishing evil. In some versions of these tales, a numbered set of criminals is expelled to the edges of the earth, which gives dramatic form to cosmological accounts of a world defined by establishing a center and the four cardinal directions. As will be discussed in this chapter and further in chapter three, in many versions these numbered sets of criminals are sons of a ruler. In other versions the criminality that leads to the collapse of order is linked with the invasion of the human realm by animals. This is another case of using man–animal relations to dramatize the themes of the flood stories. Other tales focus on named rebels, usually Gong Gong or Gun, who embody destructive aspects of the flood that is tamed through the process of punishing them. Stories of Gun, like those of the criminal sons mentioned earlier, also deal with the tensions between fathers and sons that figure prominently in the myths. Finally in the *Shan hai jing* (*Classic of the Mountains and Seas*), or more accurately in the *Hai jing* (*Classic of the Seas*) that forms the second half of this text, such tales become part of an encompassing world model in which the physical traces of the battles between rulers and rebels provide key visual signs marking out the structure of space.

Chapter three deals with tales of the flood as stories of the emergence of the human lineage, dramatized in tales of the tensions between fathers and sons, and how these tensions were resolved. Aspects of this problem, as already noted, figure in chapter two. Chapter three begins with a discussion of the mythology of the emergence of the dynastic state, which presupposes the establishment of proper relations between fathers and sons as the basis of the transmission of political power from the former to the latter. A central element of this mythology was a cluster of tales, largely dealing with the ante-diluvian world, in which good fathers inevitably had bad sons and good sons bad fathers. This state of affairs came to an end as the culmination of the process of taming the flood. The significance of these myths will be analyzed as elements in the narrative of the creation of an ordered world through proper division, as well as a meditation on the contradictions created within the Chinese household through the emergence of the doctrine that the house-hold was a microcosm of the state. Given such a belief, the normal replace-ment of the father—identified as the ruler—by the son—identified as the minister—became associated with rebellion and regicide. This theme is high-lighted in myths that insist on the radical distinction of the father and son, one treated as a human and the other as a monster, and in complementary myths that emphasize the overly close identity of father and son, who thus necessarily become rivals.

Chapter four examines those versions of the flood myth that link the control of the flood to the formation of married couples, and to the associ-ated manipulation of the human body. This manipulation included the theme of childbirth, but also involved transformation from or into animals or hybridization with them. This theme of hybridization, and the joining of men and animals in a common enterprise, reflects the issue of the disappearance of boundaries that was central to the flood myth in China as in other parts of the world, but also marks that absence of boundaries as an essential precondition to the structuring of the world. In these tales, the blurring or collapse of boundaries that figures as a threat in the form of the flood is also a source of potential energies out of which a structured world could be fashioned. Such a model reflects the twin vision of chaos in China as threat and as potential, a vision discussed in the introduction to *The Construction of Space in Early China*.

Some of these flood myths relating to couples and the transformations of the body attribute the restoration of world order to the goddess Nü Gua, who in other myths is the fashioner of the human race and the patron goddess of fetal development. These myths insist on her use of organic materials to control the flood, and also invoke her reliance on aspects of metallurgy that were mythically patterned on human sexual intercourse. Significantly, Nü Gua is herself iconographically a hybrid creature, half-human and half-snake, a being whose own body manifested the abolition of physical boundaries marked by the flood, as well as the central role of the element water. In Han art she formed a primal couple with Fu Xi, and their coiling bodies served to define the structure of the cosmos as divided into the registers of Heaven, Earth, and the human realm. They also often acted as guardian figures placed on doorways that defended the structured world within the tomb by clearly separating it from the outside world. In this way the role of Nü Gua in the myths of her ending the flood found thematic echoes in the role that she and her consort played within the tomb. In later Chinese tales, the two of them appeared as the original sibling pair who physically mated to repopulate the earth after the flood.

Related myths deal with the birth of the flood-taming Yu from stone, his marriage to Nü Gua, and the birth of Yu's own heir from stone. These stories about the fertility of stones are linked to accounts of Yu's work in taming the flood, but also tied to the role of stone in major cults of fertility for which he and Nü Gua served as the mythic prototypes. Related stories describe how Yu's body was deformed through his brutal labors in taming the flood, and how these provided the model for a form of bodily movement patterned on Yu's gait that generated power in medical and magical traditions. These traditions, as will be discussed in chapter three, are closely related to other myths that indicate Yu was the physical transformation of a fish. There are also myths in which Yu's taming of the flood involved the assistance of various animals, as well as his own transformation into a bear. These versions of the myth overtly or in veiled form relate the flood to the theme of the shifting relations between humans and animals, a central theme of early Chinese mythology, but also link the taming of the flood with the ordering or constitution of the human body.

All these themes converge in the role of the flood myths as origin tales and sanctions of the new political order forged in the Warring State period and early empires around the figure of the supreme ruler.[59] Unlike versions of the flood myth in other cultures in which the deluge is created and ended by a god, or begins and ends spontaneously through an unspecified natural process or fate, the Chinese myths insist that the flood began through rebellion, or some other criminality, and was ended through the successful actions of the ruler and his servants. The manner in which the flood was conquered in the tales of Yu, the bringing of water back into channels where its course could be guided for the benefit of humankind, was directly adapted from one of the major roles of the government in the period. More important, the broader theme of the creation of an orderly space through the maintenance of proper divisions was the primary task of the ruler in those philosophical traditions that discussed this issue. Again, the theme of the emergence of proper lineage ties in association with the taming of the flood focuses specifically on the problem of the dynastic state, that is, the relation of son to father as a political heir. The broader tensions in the family that these myths dramatize and mediate were also a direct outgrowth of the idea that the family was patterned on the state. Consequently, these myths about creating proper relations between fathers and sons were also myths about the nature of the ruler and his dynasty. Finally, tales of taming the flood through forming hybrid couples and manipulating the human body, which were also myths about the shifting relations of men and animals, also dealt with the nature of the ruler. This is true not only in the overt morals offered in several versions, in which the body-altering toils of Yu were offered as models to present rulers, but also in the whole question of the relation of men to animals. The central act of

the ancient sages, the mythic prototypes of the Warring States and early imperial rulers, was to divide men from animals, so tales about the appearance and
disappearance of such divisions were inevitably at least in part myths of sovereignty. Thus, every aspect of the Chinese flood myths, in contrast with the
similar topoi from most other cultures, converged in meditations on the nature
of the ruler and the justification of his authority.

CHAPTER ONE

FLOOD TAMING AND COSMOGONY

As noted in the introduction, flood myths are accounts of the *re-creation* of
the world, so they are often closely linked to the creation myths. While there
is no surviving evidence of a creation myth in early China, in a handful of
accounts the world emerges out of a primal, undifferentiated chaos through
the process of division. These accounts in turn are part of a broader range of
ideas and models in which every aspect of the human world depended on
the maintenance of divisions. Theoreticians of physical cultivation argued that
the embodied self was menaced by the collapse of the division between inner
and outer, theoreticians of kinship and ritual argued that the social order could
be maintained only by preserving fundamental divisions—primarily those
between men and women, and theoreticians of the state argued that the political order endured only through the preservation of divisions between ruler
and ruled. Even ideas about the afterlife were drawn into this complex,
because in the Warring States and early empires the cult of the dead came to
be devoted to the task of maintaining the *separation* between the living and
the deceased. At every level, the early Chinese perceived the threat of a
looming chaos, and argued for the necessity of maintaining clear lines of division to prevent a collapse back into this void.[1] The tales of the flood can only
be understood against the background of these broader concerns, for the flood
was the image par excellence of the collapse of divisions into chaos, and tales
of taming the flood provided models for the maintenance of order through
the reimposition of vanished distinctions or the repeated drawing of lines.
Consequently, this study of the flood myths must first briefly examine the
broader complex of theories and practices devoted to the avoidance of or
escape from chaos through the imposition of division.

COSMOGONIES AND SOCIAL DIVISIONS

The earliest surviving Chinese account of the origins of the world from chaos
is the Chu silk manuscript.[2] Although this text was stolen from a tomb, the
tomb was later systematically excavated and dated to the middle of the Warring

States period.[3] Around the edges are twelve figures, largely human–animal hybrids, distributed three on each side. Each figure at its side has a three-character name. Since the first character of each name is one of the twelve months recorded in the *Er ya*, Li Xueqin argued that they represent the gods of the months.[4] Each god is accompanied by a brief passage describing what one should and should not do in that month. As the instructions are addressed exclusively to the ruler, the document clearly anticipates the "monthly ordinances" texts that dictated the actions of the ruler in accord with the seasons, and described the disastrous consequences of failure to observe their prescriptions.[5] At each corner of the silk is also the image of a tree, and perhaps one intended in the center.

Account of the initial ordering of the world

In the center are two passages of text that read in opposite directions. One tells the story of the creation of the world out of the primal chaos by Fu Xi, his wife, and their four sons. They first established the proper order of the mountains and the waters. This pairing of mountains with water, and the emphasis on the placing of each in their proper positions, is routinely attributed to Yu in accounts of his taming the flood. Fu Xi and his family then fixed the celestial lights. Following this, the directional spirits or the sons paced out the four seasons. It is important to note this identification of the sons with the four cardinal directions and the edges, for as we will see, several myths of taming the flood entailed the expulsion of four criminal sons to the edges of the earth. When the sons were pacing out the seasons, there was no sun or moon, and the seasons remain fixed only by the pacing of footsteps. At this point, Heaven fell off balance and obscured the five trees that corresponded to the Five Phases. These are presumably the trees depicted on the manuscript. Then the Fiery Thearch commanded Zhurong, another fire deity and divine ancestor of the Chu ruling house, to lead the spirits of the four seasons to restore the Heavens. It was only then that the seasons fixed by the movement of the sun, moon, and stars came into existence.[6] This account forms a cosmogony in which the establishment of a regulated space through its division into four directions preceded and made possible the introduction of time divided into four seasons and Five Phases. This cosmogony figures in the illustration, with its four sides corresponding to the four directions and seasons, and its trees indicating the Five Phases (assuming that a central tree mentioned in the narrative should be found in the place where the two passages are located). The final establishment of order in the world is credited to the ancestor of Chu, where the manuscript was presumably created.

Relation of astral phenomena & the seasons

The second passage in the center of the manuscript reads in the opposite direction, probably to indicate that the passages form a cycle like the months and seasons in the outer illustrations and in the narrative. This text is longer than the other and deals with astral phenomena in a seasonal context. Although the relation of the two is disputed, this seems to follow the other passage, for it deals with the situation established in the earlier cosmogony. The first section discusses how the moon, which appeared only near the end of the cosmogony, must follow a fixed pace. If it is too quick or too slow, then the normal attributes of the seasons would be lost. Moreover, all the asterisms would lose their order, and calamities—such as the fall of comets, the collapse of mountains, the death of vegetation, the descent of untimely frost and snow, and the outbreak of wars—would take place. The second section speaks of the Sui cycle and the need of people to match their actions with the cycle to avoid Heaven's punishment. The passage concludes that people must make regular seasonal offerings to Heaven, Earth, the mountains, and the rivers. Failure to offer sacrifices, like the failure to observe the taboos, will result in disaster.[7]

Although not dealing explicitly with a flood, this manuscript does presuppose a state of primal nondifferentiation brought to an end through the initial division between mountains and waters. This is followed by the imposition of a series of procedures to create an ordered space and time through dividing both into regular units. Moreover, it includes a tale in which the initial order—represented by Fu Xi and his pacing sons—collapses back into chaos, only to be replaced by a new dispensation based on regular astral phenomena that provide a structure for time and a model for human action. This new dispensation entails the activity of a ruler whose failure to observe the routines imposed by the cosmic order would lead to the resumption of chaos. In this way, the story structurally parallels the themes of several flood myths discussed in the introduction, and employs several of the themes and images that figure in Chinese flood myths.

The early Chinese themselves had already developed discourses dealing with the historical construction of ordered human space. These began from the image of a primal state of undifferentiated chaos out of which all objects and ultimately human society emerged. Perhaps the most influential was a cosmogonic discourse preserved as a complete narrative in four texts, as well as in references scattered through the *Dao de jing*, the *Huainanzi*, and other texts.[8] These describe a formless, watery chaos at the beginning of time, and then depict the emergence of objects through a process of sequential division. This is sometimes described in mathematical terms as the division of an original unity into two parts, then three or four, ending in the formation of all things. While these divisions are not the work of men, the texts repeatedly insist that only the sage could understand the principles underlying this emergence of ordered space and use that understanding to regulate the world.

The earliest of these cosmogonies appear somewhat later than the Chu silk manuscript in a handful of cosmogonic accounts in texts associated with what came to be called the Daoist tradition. The opening section of the received version of the *Dao de jing* states: "The nameless is the beginning of Heaven and Earth; the named is the mother of the myriad things." Other passages refer to "the gate of the primal female, which is known as the root of Heaven and Earth" or to "the ancestor of the myriad things" that "seems to be prior to God-on-High." Even closer to a full cosmogony is the following passage: "There was something formed in chaos, born prior to Heaven and Earth. Isolated! Still! Independent and unchanging, endlessly revolving, one can take it to be the world's mother. I do not know its name, but one might style it the 'Way.'" The passage that comes closest to describing the actual process of origins states: "The Way produced the One, the One produced the Two, the Two produced the Three, and Three produced the myriad things." This makes explicit what is suggested in many of the other passages, that the world began in an undifferentiated chaos that through the imposition of sequential divisions—above all, that between Heaven and Earth—gradually formed a complete cosmos.[9]

Cosmogonies also appear in several texts discovered in association with the *Dao de jing* in an early Western Han tomb at Mawangdui. In the section "Observations (*guan* 觀)" from the so-called Sixteen Classics (*shi liu jing* 十六經), the Yellow Thearch gives a long account of the primal chaos, the initial division into *yin* and *yang*, and the subsequent emergence of the four seasons. From this he develops a theory of government through the imitation of natural principle. In four other sections of the same work, either the Yellow Thearch or one of his ministers describes the origins of the cosmos through the emergence of Heaven and Earth out of chaos and then uses this account to ground a theory of government. The text that modern editors have entitled "The Origin of the Way (*dao yuan* 道原)" consists of two parts. The first is a description of the primeval chaos and the attributes of the Way that preceded Heaven and Earth. This section has several watery epithets, suggesting the flood-like nature of the primal state, as well as terms for stillness and void. It also describes how the primal Way existed prior to the division of Heaven and Earth, permeates all things, is the source of all existence, and how all things can collapse back into it. The second is devoted to the unique capacity of the sage to perceive the actions and attributes of the Way and thereby to bring order to the world.[10]

More elaborate versions of this account of the origins of the world and the powers of the sage figure in chapters entitled "Yuan dao" or "Dao yuan" in two texts, the *Huainanzi* and the *Wenzi*, which are probably slightly later than the Mawangdui materials.[11] In addition to their other differences from the Mawangdui text, both these chapters add long passages on water as the image of the Way. Indeed the *Huainanzi* applies identical epithets to water and the Way.[12] In addition to the "Yuan dao" chapter that begins the *Huainanzi*, chapters 2, 3, 7, and 14 open with accounts of the original state of the universe as watery, formless, and lacking all divisions.[13] All of these further describe the processes of division or separation that culminate in the world experienced by people, but in the form of the Way the initial chaos remains as a permanent background condition of existence. Thus, while the primal chaos was an original state that had since vanished, it also survived as a permanent background condition to human existence in two ways. First, it formed a constant reservoir of infinite potentiality accessible only to the sage who thereby obtained the power to alter the spatially structured present. Second, it remained as a constant menace of universal dissolution and chaos should the principles that had forged order out of nondistinction ever be aban-

doned. This is the source of the specter of "chaos (*luan* 亂)" that has haunted
the Chinese imagination through the centuries.

While accounts of the physical emergence of the world from a primal
chaos that prefigures the flood are largely characteristic of the traditions that
formed Han Daoism, the other traditions articulated social versions of the
same schema. In these accounts, the primal chaos took the form of a world
in which humans lived intermixed with animals, dwelling in caves or trees,
wearing furs, and eating raw meat. This free intermixing of the human and
the animal, as discussed in the introduction, figures in many versions of flood
myths found around the world as well as in several Chinese versions. In these
stories of primal nondistinction, the human world was progressively separated
from the animal realm through a series of technological and moral innovations introduced by the sage-kings. These accounts were employed polemi-
cally by rival traditions, for each identified the key factors that separated people
from animals with their own teachings.[14] Consequently, as we will see, rival
philosophies could be equated with the flood or with wild animals as that
which destroyed proper distinctions and reduced the world to savagery and
chaos. These stories of the sages' invention of human society, more clearly
than the cosmogonies, present a model of the *construction* of human society
through the imposition of divisions. Several Warring States accounts linked
the cosmogonies and the separation from animals as either two steps in a larger
process or as parallel recurrences of a single category of event.[15]

In addition to these early Chinese accounts of the original formation of
space and society out of chaos through the process of division, several texts
insisted on the importance of continued action in their own day to ward off
the threat of nondifferentiation. First, early discussions of ritual repeatedly
asserted that it maintained order through imposing divisions, which thus
became its defining role. It was through separating men from women, senior
from junior, ruler from subject, or civilized from barbarian that ritual constituted social roles and groups. Without ritual's constant guidance to create and
maintain these divisions, society would collapse back into undifferentiated
chaos or animal savagery. These divisions were part of a broader schema
running through the philosophical and ritual texts, which repeatedly insisted
that the role of ritual was to separate people into their respective social categories and thereby maintain social order. This idea is most clearly articulated
in remarks that pair the roles of ritual and music. These routinely assign to
ritual the task of creating distinctions, while music then serves to forge a harmonious unity from the disparate units:

> Music creates identity [*tong* 同] while ritual creates difference [*yi* 異].
> When there is identity, then there will be mutual kinship [*qin* 親,
> or "closeness"]. When there is difference, then there will be mutual
> respect. If music conquers, then things flow together [*liu* 流]; if
> ritual conquers, then they fall apart [*li* 離]. To join feelings and deco-
> rate appearances are the tasks of ritual and music. When ritual duties

are established, then noble and base will be ranked. When musical patterns are shared [*tong*], then superiors and inferiors will be in harmony.[16]

These general remarks take on specific forms in dozens of passage that insist, as in the *Xunzi*, that the purpose of ritual is to maintain social divisions (*fen* 分). These divisions create human society and distinguish humans from beasts. Among the divisions, the ritual texts place particular importance on maintaining the separation (*bie* 別) between men and women.[17] The formula that the role of ritual was to separate (*bie*) also figures in texts that criticize it, such as chapter 14 of the *Huainanzi*.[18]

Ritual leading for separation [handwritten margin note]

Just as the exponents of ritual, and even its critics, insisted that its role was to divide or separate people in order to preserve social order, the advocates of the new state order argued that its legal codes, systems of rank, and administrative practices served to maintain appropriate divisions and thereby preserve society. Only through maintaining the distinction between ruler and ruled, and through establishing a carefully regulated hierarchy encompassing the entire population, could natural human propensities be contained, social order preserved, and people kept separate from animals.[19] Thus, all major early Chinese theories of society and the physical world assumed an original undifferentiated chaos that remained in the background both as a source of potential power and as the threatening consequence of improper actions.

Legal codes maintaining division [handwritten margin note]

This model was extended from the world of nature and of humans to include the realm of the spirits. As Lothar von Falkenhausen has argued, the clear division that appeared by the middle of the Eastern Zhou between the ritual vessels of the living and those buried with the dead marks an early stage in the shift away from a Western Zhou world based on the shared existence of the living and the deceased to a world in which the *separation* of the living and the dead had become the ultimate aim of funerary ritual. In place of the costly assemblages of ritual vessels that had defined Western Zhou funerary practice, the grave goods of the late Warring States, Qin, and Han were dominated by objects of daily use (clothing, lacquer bowls and plates, other pottery, food) or by models or images of such objects and other aspects of worldly life (houses, granaries, animals, and tools). Replicas and images also depicted human beings, both those buried in the tomb and all the servants, entertainers, cooks, agricultural laborers, and other people necessary to their leisured existence.[20] All this was intended to provide the dead with a happy existence in the tomb, but an existence based on objects that were only miniature replicas or images of the world of the living. Thus, the *Xunzi* and several chapters in the *Li ji* argued that the objects buried with the dead, while imitating those of the living, had to be distinct. Although they were analogous, the two world had to be clearly separated.[21]

Creation of the division b/w living + dead [handwritten margin note]

While these classicist texts on ritual do not usually discuss the reasons for separating the dead from the living, one passage in the *Li ji* makes the motive explicit: "When a ruler attended the funeral of an official, he brought with him a shaman carrying a peach branch and reed broom [objects to expel evil spirits], as well as a soldier with a lance. This is because they dread [spirits]. It is the reason why they distinguish them from the living."[22] Here the dead must be kept separate from the living because those who have died are a menace. Anna Seidel traced the emergence of this idea that the dead were potentially demonic figures who if not kept carefully sequestered in the tomb would return to wreak havoc on the living. As she remarked, the dead as depicted in texts in Eastern Han tombs are "terrifying revenants" who could inflict disease or misfortune, and who consequently "have to be securely locked away."[23] Thus, one "grave ordinance" inscribed on a jar in the year A.D. 175 uses rigorous parallelism to insist on the separation of the living and the dead:

High Heaven is blue [cang cang],
The underworld is limitless [mang mang].
The dead return to the shadows [yin],
The living return to the light [yang].
The living have their villages [li],
The dead have their hamlets [xiang].
The living are subordinate to the western Chang'an [an],
The dead are subordinate to the eastern Mt. Tai [shan].
In joy they do not remember one another,
In bitterness they do not long for one another.[24]

Other texts call for expelling the deceased by any means necessary:

The subject who died on the day yi si has the ghost name "Heavenly Brightness." This name has already been reported to the Spirit Master [shen shi 神師] of the Heavenly Emperor [tian di 天帝, who ruled the realm of the dead]. Instantly remove yourself three thousand leagues. If you do not immediately depart, the [. . .] of the Southern Mountain will be ordered to come and devour you. Act promptly, in accord with the ordinances and statutes.[25]

Even the lengthy "funeral narrative" found at Cangshan, which asks the deceased to grant prosperity and longevity to his descendants and describes all the pleasures depicted in the tomb's imagery, ends with a chilling insistence on the need for absolute separation:

Having entered the dark world,
You are completely separated from the living,
After the tomb is sealed,
It will never be opened again.[26]

This threat of the dead also figured in stories in the *Han shu*, in which the skeletons of the deceased were pulverized and boiled in poisonous substances to prevent them from intruding into the dreams of the living.[27] Burial was one method of removing the threat posed by the dead, but should this fail people could employ the more drastic measures depicted in these stories.

All these models—the early cosmogonies, the accounts of the primitive state of man and the inventions of the sage-kings, the discussions of the role of ritual or the state, and the depictions of the relations of the living and the dead—shared a common model in which order and intelligibility depend on separation or division. The chief threat was the disappearance of distinctions that would result in a collapse back into the original state of chaos. Accounts of a great flood provided a vivid dramatization of such a possibility. Furthermore, the tales of how this flood was brought to an end depicted numerous ideas about the necessary distinctions that constituted human society: water/land, criminal/law-abiding, man/woman, father/son, human/animal, and so on. The balance of this chapter will examine the earliest versions of the flood myth and trace their relation to the political ideas and practices of the period.

SOCIAL DIVISIONS AND THE FLOOD

Like all surviving myths from early China, accounts of the flood are scattered through numerous works that each touch on only selected events or themes. Over the course of the twentieth century, several leading scholars have brought together many of these dispersed accounts to try to reconstruct a hypothetical original form of the myth and to trace its development in later periods.[28] Some of these scholars have pointed out that the Chinese myths of the flood, like stories of the taming of floods in many cultures, provide an account of the fashioning of order from primal chaos. As previously discussed, early Chinese stories of the origins of the world largely focus on the way in which order emerged through progressive divisions that extracted defined entities from a chaos of formless energies. Consequently, tales of the channeling of flood waters into rivers so as to divide the land into fixed units form a human version of the accounts of creation that existed in early China.[29] As in all such early Chinese tales, the imposition or extraction of order was attributed to the early sages, primarily to Yu but also, as discussed at length in the final chapter, to Nü Gua.

Yu is the central figure in most accounts of the flood, the one noted in the earliest texts, and the tamer of the flood in the first extended accounts. As Gu Jiegang has pointed out, there are no less than six references to Yu in Zhou odes that date from between ca. 1000 and 600 B.C. These poems praise Yu as the figure who ordered the fields so as to make agriculture possible, established the foundations from which Hou Ji later developed agriculture, channeled rivers to flow to the east and thus regulated the four directions, and fixed the foundations on which all later rulers founded their capitals. One poem refers explicitly to the "endless flood waters" in response to which Yu laid out the dry land. Similar ideas and phrases, such as references to all dry land as the "traces of Yu," also appear in a small number of bronzes. Recently, a bronze acquired in Hong Kong that some scholars date to the Western Zhou but others think much later, contained a lengthy inscription that describes Yu's work in ending the flood by dredging out the rivers and thereby dividing the world into its natural provinces.[30] Since these references assume knowledge of the achievements of Yu in ending the flood and thereby establishing a delimited expanse of dry land, there was clearly already by the late Western Zhou a well-known story of his taming the flood. This is of use in showing that the flood myth in some version existed from a fairly early date, and that even then its hero was the same Yu who figured as the central figure in later accounts. It is also noteworthy that Yu's work was cited as the origin of an ordered human space that made possible both agriculture and city building. His achievements thus figure in the songs as the prototype for those of the Zhou's founding ancestors and dynastic heros.

These songs, however, merely *refer* to the story of Yu, but provide no connected narrative or incidents. The fullest early recounting of the story appears in several chapters that are clustered near the beginning of the *Shang shu*, but are almost certainly of Warring States composition. Taken as a group, these chapters narrate the fashioning of an orderly human realm out of chaos. Ordered time emerges through the introduction of the calendar, ordered space through the taming of the flood, and ordered society through the expulsion of animals and the introduction of punishments. The first chapter, the "Yao dian," retells as historical events a set of early myths dealing with both the movement of the sun and with the flood.[31] In the first half of the chapter, the sovereign Yao, who according to arguments elaborated by some scholars was probably originally a sun god, stationed four brothers at the cardinal points of the earth to supervise the movement of the sun from its rising to its settings and its shifting positions over the course of the year.[32] Having described the introduction of the basic units of time—day, season, and year—by means of the fixing of the directions, the text proceeds to the regulation of space through an account of the taming of the flood. In this section Yao seeks for a man who can subdue the flood that was raging in the world at that time. His officials, including one who is named "Four (Directional) Peaks (*si yue* 四岳)" and thus an extension of the theme of the preceding section of the "Yao dian," suggest two men: first Gong Gong and then Gun. The former is rejected, and the latter for nine years attempts to tame the flood but in the end fails. At the conclusion Yao fixes upon Yu, to whom he grants his two daughters in marriage as a form of test of his ability to order a household and, by extension, the world.[33]

The second chapter deals with the work of Shun, to whom Yao yielded the throne, and it touches on the theme of the flood only briefly. However, it is noteworthy that the theme of the creation of an orderly space through the fixing of the directions is once again central to the text. After assuming

sovereignty on the first day of the first month, Shun gives audience to the
minister "Four Peaks." Over the course of the year Shun makes a tour of
inspection to each of the four great directional peaks, where he assembles the
lords of each region to fix the seasons, months, and days. After this ritual constitution of time and space, he divides the world into twelve provinces, per-
forms a sacrifice on the central peak of each province, and dredges their rivers.
Finally, he publicly proclaims his laws and expels four ministers, including
those previously charged with the regulation of the flood, to mountains at the
edges of the earth. As a consequence, all the world is brought to order.[34] This
theme of the ritual expulsion of a numbered set of malefactors to the edges
of the earth as a means of creating order will be discussed at length in chapter
two.

At this point in the narrative Yu appears as the first in a series of appoint-
ments. He is named minister of works for having "stabilized the water and
land." This clear reference to the taming of the flood is followed by the
appointment of an official who will teach the people agriculture, one to establish proper social relations, one to introduce punishments to control the barbarians and criminals, one to create all crafts, one to regulate the affairs of the
plants and animals that grow in the wilderness, one to introduce ritual ceremonies, one to create music, and one to guarantee truthful speech.[35] Thus,
while Yu and the flood figure only briefly in the chapter, their placement indicates their significance within the broader process of creating an ordered time
and space out of chaos. Moreover, the themes of the invention of agriculture
and of the regulation of the plants and animals that lie beyond the human
realm figure prominently in several versions of the flood myth.

The next chapter, entitled "The Counsels of the Great Yu (da Yu mo
大禹謨)", again touches on the flood only in passing. The extended discussion of the construction of order from watery chaos appears in the "Yu gong,"
which provides the fullest account in the Shang shu of the works of Yu.[36]
This chapter, probably composed in the middle of the Warring States
period, describes in detail how Yu brought an end to the flood through
opening passages in the mountains and guiding rivers into their courses.[37]
The lines of mountains and rivers that he traced out divided China into the
"Nine Provinces," a magical number that played a significant role in later
Chinese models of the world.[38] Yu himself then sketched out the lineaments
of this newly structured world with a journey along the rivers that he had
fixed and the establishment of the tribute that each region would send to the
center.

Several features of the account in the "Yu gong" merit notice. First, the
chapter begins with an echo of the description of Yu's work in the Shi jing
to the effect that Yu "laid out (fu 敷)" the land. The early commentators gloss
the character fu as fen 分 "to divide," thus emphasizing the critical importance
of the idea that the central act in taming the flood was the division of the
water and land. This is followed immediately by the statement that he "fol-

lowed the mountains and cut down the trees, to establish the highest mountains and the greatest rivers." This emphasis on mountains recurs throughout
the chapter, in the descriptions of how Yu's work allowed the people to *山 as dividers*
"descend from the hills and dwell in the fields," and the fact that the limits
of several provinces are defined by mountains.[39] The same theme is marked
by the fact that restoring a particular region to order from the chaos of the
flood was marked by sacrifices to the surrounding mountains, as they were in
some sense responsible for the ending of the flood.[40] After the pattern of
tribute is described, the chapter even provides an inventory of the mountains
that Yu crossed or surveyed in the course of taming the flood.[41] This opposition between mountains and rivers figures prominently in many accounts of
Yu's taming of the flood, and indeed is a feature of flood myths from all over
the world, including the biblical account of Mt. Ararat.[42] Here it clearly carries
forward the theme of the laying out of the land by the separation of the water,
for mountain ranges are the feature of landscape that most readily rose above
the flood and that in the ordered world divided the major rivers into their
respective drainage channels. Thus, they could be used to define boundaries
and, as discussed earlier, the establishment of boundaries was a major theme
of accounts of ending the flood.

Second, the account emphasizes that the core of the work was to cause
the rivers to "follow (*cong* 從)," be "guided in (*dao* 道 = 導)," "gathered in
(*zhu* 豬)," or "enter (*ru* 入)" their channels, a point that will be discussed as
a major attribute of the work of Yu.[43] It also emphasized how the work of
Yu made possible agriculture in each region, a theme already noted, and
describes the quality of the soil in each region. This theme even forms the
substance of semantic parallels, as in the sentence, "The Huai and Yi [rivers]
being regulated [*yi* 乂], Meng and Yu [regions] were cultivated [*yi* 藝]."[44] The
emphasis on agriculture, as the natural outgrowth of land that has now been
separated from the water, also runs throughout the theme of tribute.

This theme of tribute forms yet another key aspect of the structuring of
the world through the process of division. While tribute was a movement of *Tribute*
goods, it was a movement that served to define the structure of space. The *marks the*
arrival of tribute marked the capital as the center of the world, while the *capital as the*
sending of tribute identified each region as a periphery. Moreover, the dif- *center of the*
ferent types of tribute defined the character of each region, thus distinguish- *world...*
ing southern regions from those in the north, or coastal regions from those
in the interior. In this way the lists of tribute in the chapter on Yu were a *...also divides*
direct outgrowth of his work in taming the flood, for they served to distin- *the world according*
guish the regions one from another and thereby marked the divisions that his *to what is*
work had restored.[45] This linkage between the theme of tribute and the struc- *produced where*
ture of the world is emphasized by the addition at the end of the chapter
of the earliest surviving version of the "Five Zones of Submission (*wu fu*
五服)" model of the world. In this model the center of the world is the royal
or imperial capital, and the rest of the world is divided into successive zones

in which the level of civilization declines as one moves away from the capital. Each zone is marked by reduced obligations of tribute and weakened political control.[46]

Another aspect of the theme of tribute in the "Yu gong" that links it to the flood is the emphasis on moving from place to place along rivers. Thus, after each discussion of the limits of a region, the character of its soil, and the nature of its tribute, the chapter narrates how they "floated (fu 浮)" down certain rivers until they "reached (da 達)" a specific location, at which point the account of the next region begins.[47] Commentators over the centuries have debated whether those who were floating were Yu or the later bearers of tribute. In either case, the important point is that the end of the flood is marked by the transformation of formless water as a destructive force to controlled water as a positive one. As noted in the introduction, some flood myths in both North and South America are built around the opposition between the deluge and controlled movements up or down rivers that mark out seasonal changes. The movements along the rivers of Yu or the tribute bearers described in the "Yu gong" play an identical role in the Chinese flood myths, which is why the chapter contains a complete inventory of all the major rivers of China and their interlinkages.[48]

The culmination of Yu's work in transforming the chaos of the flood into an ordered, human space is summarized in a rhyming panegyric passage that follows the comprehensive accounts of the mountains and rivers and precedes the description of the Five Zones:

> The nine provinces formed a unity, with the usable land to the four edges of the earth all having been made into habitations. The nine mountains had roads carved through their forests and offerings presented to them. The nine rivers were dredged and flowing, while the nine marches had all been embanked. Everything within the four seas converged [at the capital]. The six treasuries [all natural resources] were all completely put in order. The myriad soils [of the different regions] had all been correctly evaluated, so as to scrupulously impose a levy on resources. He had completely modeled the three soil types, to perfect the levies of the central states.[49]

With its repetition of the number "nine," which indicates totality, its pairing of mountains and rivers; its insistence on the carving of lines—the chopping of forests in the mountains, the channeling of rivers, the banking of marshes; its emphasis on the creation of land as a space of habitation; its description of the structuring of the world through the fixing of the four directions and the convergence of them all in the capital; and its elaboration of the theme of surveying the newly created land to fix the amounts and forms of tributes, this passage gives a complete summary of how the work of Yu converted the flooded world into a distinctively human space. It is crucial to note, moreover, that his work in establishing this space consisted essentially in perform-

ing the administrative tasks that defined the states of early China. Particularly
important in this regard are discussions of the proper methods of water
control, a question that reflects not only the technology but the moral philosophy of the period.

A final reference in the *Shang shu* to the flood occurs at the opening of
the "Hong fan," a chapter placed much later in the text than those previously
mentioned but probably composed at about the same time. This chapter details
a comprehensive model of government supposedly presented to King Wu of
the Zhou by a virtuous Shang noble.[50] The chapter states that the high god
had originally presented this model to Yu after the latter had inherited the
work of his father Gun. While the account in the "Yao dian" simply stated
that Gun had not succeeded, the "Hong fan" asserts that he failed because he
had sought to control the waters by blocking them up.[51] This implicitly marks
a contrast with Yu, who as described in the "Yu gong" had ended the flood
not by blocking water but by causing it to flow along channels to the sea.
Moreover, as noted earlier, in the "Yu gong" the use of properly flowing water
as a mode of transportation defines the structure of the world that Yu shaped.
This opposition between Gun and Yu based on their contrary techniques of
water control figures in several other texts that will be discussed later.

THE FLOOD AND THE HUMAN–ANIMAL DIVIDE

Another Warring States text presenting substantial narratives about Yu and the
flood is the *Mencius*, probably compiled from the late fourth century down
into the third century. This text contains two major narratives dealing with
the flood. One of these that describes the question of Yu's art for the control
of water links the flood to the collapse of distinctions between humans and
animals:

> In the time of Yao the waters reversed their course and overflowed
> the middle kingdoms so that snakes and dragons dwelt there. The
> people had no fixed dwellings, so those in lower regions made nests
> in trees, while those in higher ones lived in mountain caves. The
> *Documents'* saying, "The floods are a warning to me," refers to this
> inundation. [Yao] had Yu put it in order. Yu dredged out the land
> and channeled the rivers to the sea. He expelled the snakes and
> dragons to the grassy swamps. The movement of the water outward
> from the land formed the Jiang, Huai, Han, and Yellow Rivers. As
> the dangers were removed to the distant regions, the harm of the
> snakes and dragons vanished. Only then were people able to obtain
> level land to dwell on.[52]

This passage echoes the "Yu gong"'s references to Yu's guiding or channeling
water to lead it to the sea. This theme will be discussed in the next section
of this chapter. What is significant here is its identification of the flood with

the confusion of humans and beasts, and its consequent emphasis on the issue
of creating human habitations.

Although the *Mencius's* discussions of the unconstrained mingling of
people and animals, discussions that also figure in passages that will be discussed in chapter two, appear primarily in its accounts of the flood and of
human criminality, they also figure in a discussion of the sage Shun. This is
significant because Shun was the ruler during the period of the flood and the
man who appointed Yu to reimpose order and distinctions in the world. The
mythic association of Shun with the collapse of distinctions between men and
animals runs through many texts, indicating that the theme was not an invention of the *Mencius* but part of a broader and earlier mythic topos in which
the ruler at the time of the flood was in fact an embodiment of the flood
itself. This is clearly demonstrated in the passage from the *Mencius*, which not
only describes Shun's life in the wilds, but also through the choice of epithets
and the account of his character that treat him explicitly as an embodiment
of the flood:

> When Shun dwelt in the deep mountains, he lived together with
> trees and rocks and wandered freely with the deer and wild boars.
> He was scarcely different from a wild man of the mountains. But
> when he heard a single good word or witnessed a single good deed,
> then it was as if one had opened up the Yangzi or the Yellow River.
> As he poured out with great force (*pei ran* 沛然), nothing could
> check him.[53]

Here Shun is described first as a man of the wilds whose life was marked
precisely by the free intermingling with forests and wild animals that characterized the moralizing versions of the flood. This is followed by a description of Shun's character that compares him to unstoppable, flooding water,
who, when properly guided, acted like the waters of the flood that became
rivers channeled into the sea. Moreover, several passages in the *Mencius*
that touch on the topos of the fragility of the boundaries between men and
animals cite Shun as the exemplary figure associated with these boundaries.[54]
Thus, it appears that in certain traditions Shun, as a man who lived with wild
animals and whose character was like that of a raging flood, embodied the
state of the world that was overcome by the labors of Yu. This would provide
a mythic substratum to later accounts of the political transition from Shun to
Yu.

Nor are these links between Shun, wilderness, and the abolished boundaries between humans and animals limited to a few passages in the *Mencius*.
The title of Shun's "kingdom" or reign, which routinely precedes his name,
was *yu* 虞, a word whose most common meaning was "forester." This term
appears as early as the "Shun dian" chapter of the *Shang shu* as the title given
to Yi, the figure who in one of the versions of the flood myth in the *Mencius*
previously cited used fire to drive animals out of the human realm. In the

"Shun dian" this figure is charged with the duty of "putting in order the grasses, trees, birds, and beasts of above [mountains] and below [marshes]."[55] In the *Zhou li*, Yi's office as forester is divided between two officials, one who is charged with the supervision of the mountains and the other who bears responsibility for controlling the marshes or wastes.[56] According to the account given in the *Zhou li*, these officials, whose divided responsibilities echo the oppositions of mountain/river and marshland/waste that structured Yu's labors, controlled the times at which people could enter the wild places and the sorts of materials, largely plants and animals, that they could remove. Thus, the title of Shun's reign, which was inherited by the states that claimed descent from him, was "forester" and marked his links to the classic realms of the non-human, that is, the mountains and the wastes. This title consequently supports the remarks made in the *Mencius* about Shun's conduct and character.

While some have argued that the graph *yu* 虞 "forester" is a loan for some other word, there is plentiful material, apart from these passages, to show that Shun was in fact associated with the mountains and wastes. A story in the "Shun dian" relates that when Yao was considering employing Shun: "He placed him in a great forest [*lu* 麓, also glossed "mountain forest"]. Amid violent wind, lightning, and rain he did not lose his way."[57] When this story was incorporated into a *Shi ji* passage translated below, the links of Shun with the realms administered by the forester official were made even more explicit. In this account Shun's entering the wilderness is the final and most difficult test by which he proved himself fit to become Son of Heaven. It is also significant that, according to several texts, Shun's many exertions culminated with his "death in the wilds [*ye si* 野死]."[58] Shun's links to forests are also revealed in his policy of setting up a *tree* into which criticisms could be inserted so that he could judge the quality of his own reign.[59]

The identification of Shun as a man of the wilds in the *Shi ji* forms part of an extended narrative relating a series of achievements by which he progressively imposed order on ever widening spatial units:

> Then Yao gave his two daughters [to Shun] as wives to observe his virtuous power in relation to the two women. Shun commanded the two women and kept them modest at Weina, so they acted in accord with the rituals of wives. Yao regarded this as good, so he had Shun carefully harmonize the five teachings [on basic kin and political ties], so the five teachings were all followed. He then had him successively enter all the offices, and the offices were ordered in accord with the seasons. He was made to perform the rituals of welcome at the gates of the four directions. The four gates became truly solemn, so the feudal lords and guests from distant lands were all respectful. Yao had Shun enter the mountain forests and the riverside marshes. In violent wind, lightning, and rain Shun did not lose his way. Yao thought he was a sage.[60]

Here Shun is asked to successively put in order the nuclear household, the broader kin ties that form the lineage, the offices of government, relations with foreign peoples, and finally the savage world of the forests and wastes.[61] Proving himself capable in all of them, he is clearly a sage and receives his charge as Son of Heaven. While Shun's links with the wilds are here incorporated into a much larger spatial schema, they still reveal his older, more exclusive links to the realm of wild plants and animals as revealed in the *Shang shu* and the *Mencius*.

Shun's ties to the animal kingdom are also revealed in a set of passages dealing with the incorporation of beasts into the human world.[62] In the *Shan hai jing* several passages describe peoples descended from Shun who eat wild animals and the produce of forest trees, and who command "the four birds, tigers, leopards, bears, and dragons." Two passages describe magical birds that accompanied Shun alone as their companion or gathered in the lands of his descendants. Still another passage tells of a giant bamboo forest and a marsh that are associated with Shun. This theme of commanding animals also figures in the "Shun dian" account of Shun's appointing Yi as forester. Yi unsuccessfully attempts to yield the office to two officials named "Red Tiger (*zhu hu* 朱虎)" and "Bear (*xiong pi* 熊羆)." While in the story these are presented as human officials, just as Four Peaks is, their names reveal their animal nature. Moreover, in a celebrated story that appeared in several texts and was quoted repeatedly down through the centuries, Shun's music master Kui struck musical stones and caused the myriad animals to join in a dance. Thus, it is clear that like the Yellow Thearch, who trained an army of wild animals to defeat his enemies, Shun drew animals from their native wilds into his realm where he commanded them as his minions.[63] Shun was thus not only a man who prior to appointment lived in the wilds amid animals and forest plants, but who, after attaining sovereignty, drew these animals into his court.

Humans who were originally animals appear not only in Shun's court but even in his family. In early texts Shun had a brother named Xiang 象 who attempted to kill him. However, several texts also refer to "elephants (*xiang* 象)" who work the fields next to Shun's tomb, just like the birds in the Hangzhou region who were taught by Yu to engage in agriculture.[64] As the Tang scholar Zhang Shoujie pointed out in his commentary to the *Shi ji*, several early texts beginning with the *Di wang shi ji* note that Shun's brother Xiang was enfeoffed in the state "Nose (*youbi* 有鼻)," and that he received sacrifice under the title "Spirit of the Nose Pavilion (*bi ting shen* 鼻亭神)."[65] The twentieth-century scholar Wen Yiduo collected further examples to demonstrate that Xiang's identifying feature was his nose, which was almost certainly a reference to an elephant's trunk.[66] Thus, Shun's links to the collapse of distinctions between men and animals extended so far that an animal was a member of his own family.

Finally, there is one striking, if relatively late, story that shows that Shun saved himself from his parents' attempts to murder him by himself becoming animals:

Gu Sou [Shun's father] ordered Shun to clean out the granary. Shun told Yao's two daughters [his wives]. They said, "This time he will burn you. You must make your clothing into a magpie, and depart with this bird art [*niao gong* 鳥工]." Shun then ascended into the granary, put on the bird art clothing, and flew away. . . . Shun was to dig a well, and again told his wives. They said, "Remove your clothing and depart with the dragon art [*long gong* 龍工]." When he entered the well Gu Sou and Xiang dumped down the earth to fill up the well, but Shun was able to get out through another well.[67]

[margin note: Shun becoming an animal?]

Here through the clever advice of his wives Shun was able to manipulate his clothing to turn himself into a bird to escape from a burning building, and into a dragon to move through the watery underworld where his father and brother had buried him. While this story of Shun adopting animal characteristics is not recorded until the fifth century A.D., the Han dynasty *Lie nü zhuan* already records the tradition that Shun consulted his two wives prior to undertaking the tasks set by his parents. Moreover, the role of wives and other women as prescient counselors figures prominently in this book.[68] Thus, the story clearly has ancient roots, although we cannot be certain when it took on its present form.

Shun was thus associated with the blurring or elimination of the boundary between humans and animals, to the extent of turning himself into animals in order to use their powers. This blurring of boundaries marked the flood as the replaying during the period of human existence of the original condition from the which the physical world had first emerged. It also became the defining characteristic of the flood as an image of social chaos in the *Mencius* and other texts that employed the flood as an image of criminality or social deviance.

Shun was also associated with the water of the flood itself. This was already demonstrated in the *Mencius*'s description cited above of Shun's character as *pei ran* 沛然 "pouring with force, voluminous." It also figures explicitly in several other texts. Thus, the *Mozi* records that Yao raised Shun from the banks of a marsh, where the latter was engaging in fishing.[69] A couple of passages in the *Shan hai jing* describe countries whose origins are traced back to Shun. One is ringed by deep bodies of water (*yuan* 淵) on all sides, and it is said that Shun bathed in the southern pool. The other state has a raised platform called "Shun's Altar" surrounded on all sides by water.[70] Interestingly, both the *Shan hai jing* and the *Guo yu* state that Shun's tomb was completely ringed by water, confirming that these water-ringed states or altars were indeed images of Shun.[71] Several Japanese scholars have noted this association between Shun and water. They argue that he was originally a water spirit, and that his association with wild vegetation and animals derives ultimately from the association of these wilderness creatures with water and, above all, marshlands.[72] Stories of his divine birth also indicate that his mother was

[margin note: Shun + 水]

impregnated by a rainbow and that he had the face of a dragon, both associated with water.[73] This overlap in the mythical attributes of Shun between
the flood waters and wild beasts also appears in tales of the origins of Qin
state. Qin's legendary ancestor Da Fei first quelled the flood together with Yu
and then assisted Shun in taming the birds and wild animals.[74]

It is clear that the *Mencius*'s use of the flood as an image for the collapse
of social distinctions and thus for rampant criminality was based on a broader
set of myths in which the era of the flood was associated with Shun. As a
spirit linked with water, marshes, and wastelands, and with the forest vegetation and wild creatures that flourished in such places, Shun embodied the
flood in its aspects both as rampant water and obliterator of distinctions.
The ultimate distinction that underlay early Chinese thought on morality was
the separation of men from beasts. As spirit of the wilds, or later patron sage
of the incorporation of wilderness and wild animals into the human realm,
Shun both signaled the original absence of that fundamental distinction and
presided over its appearance. It is thus worthy of note that in the myths Shun
lives amid water and animals, and rules in the midst of the flood, while it is
servants under his control—Yu, Yi, and Kui—who do the actual work of
bringing order to the world and either expelling or domesticating the creatures of the wild. Shun himself appears as a positive figure in the moralizing
uses of the myths presented by the Warring States philosophers, but abundant
traces remain of his liminal role as patron of the wilderness and embodiment
of the flood. In this way, the myths around him underlie and inform the
Mencius's use of the flood as the image of the collapse of the primal distinction between human and animal, and thus as the prototype for social collapse
and criminality (see chapter three).

THE FLOOD AND HUMAN NATURE

The passage from the *Mencius* cited at the beginning of the previous section
noted that Yu tamed the flood by "dredging out the land and channeling the
rivers to the sea." The idea that the flood was ended by allowing the waters
to flow naturally through reestablished channels is reiterated in another passage
in which Mencius criticizes a contemporary minister who dared to compare
his own irrigation works to the achievements of Yu:

> You are mistaken. Yu's method of controlling water was the natural
> Way [*dao* 道, a word regularly applied in the "Yu gong" to Yu's chan-
> neling of water] of water. So Yu used the Four Seas as the ditches
> into which he channeled the water. You only use the neighboring
> states as such ditches. When the water reverses its course this is called
> a flood, which refers to an inundation.[75]

The authors mark the close link between this passage and the preceding one
by paraphrasing part of the first at the end of the second. Both passages assert

that Yu's art was to avail himself of the spontaneous tendencies of water, which for unspecified reasons had been diverted from its natural course. The other account of the great flood in the *Mencius*, which will be discussed in the next chapter, also describes Yu's technique as involving "dredging (*shu* 疏)" the Nine Rivers, "opening up (決)" the Ru and Han rivers, and "clearing out (*pai* 排)" the Huai and the Si so that they can all be "channeled (*zhu* 注)" into the seas.[76] This fashioning of order through following the natural tendency of things is specifically contrasted with the practices of the rulers of his day, just as the "Hong fan" had contrasted Yu's technique of following the tendencies of water with that of Gun who did not. This contrast between Yu and the other tamers of the flood proposed in the "Yao dian"—Gun and Gong Gong—will be discussed in more detail in chapter two.

[margin handwritten note: Yu succeeds by using the natural properties of water in his attempt to control it]

This emphasis on the importance of following the natural tendencies of water might well have figured prominently in the *Mencius*'s account of the flood because the same issue played a major role in the debates on human nature between Mencius and Gaozi. The relevant passage of Mencius's argument says:

> Water truly makes no distinction between east and west, but does it make no distinction between up and down? The goodness of human nature is like water's flowing downward. There is no human who is not good, as there is no water that does not flow downward. Now as for water, if you slap it and cause it to leap up, you can cause it to go over your forehead. If you stir it up and make it flow, you can cause it to ascend a mountain. But how could this be the nature of water? The force of circumstances makes it thus.[77]

Yu's technique for controlling water exactly parallels the Mencian idea of the goodness of human nature, while Gun's practice would be lumped together with those who, according to Mencius, believed that people could become good only by doing violence to people's innate tendencies. Thus, the debate in myth over methods of water control was also about broader questions that preoccupied some philosophers of the day.

The aforementioned contrast between Yu's method of following the natural course of things and the others' attempts to constrain the floods through force, a contrast that also figured in contemporary debates on human nature, became a common theme that appeared in several texts in addition to the *Shang shu* and the *Mencius*. Without specifying the exact nature of the contrast, a set of questions in the "Tian wen," a lengthy poem written in the middle to late Warring States period, posits such a distinction between the methods of Yu and Gun:

> When Lord Yu came from the belly of Gun,
> How did he transform?
> Forcibly seizing his predecessor's task,

He completed his father's work.
How did he carry on the earlier task with different plans?
The flooding springs were supremely deep.
How did he fill them in?
The earth's square divided into nine,
How did he shore them up?
The Responding Dragon of the rivers and seas,
What did it completely pass through?
What did Gun contrive?
How did Yu succeed?[78]

This entire set of questions highlights Yu's success by contrasting it with the failure of his father Gun, and at least two questions specifically posit their reliance on different plans and methods. While we cannot be certain how the author of the "Tian wen" would have answered his own questions, in all other texts from the period the distinction is between Gun's blocking up rivers with dams to halt their flow and Yu's dredging and channeling them.

A final text from roughly the same period that insists on this contrast in methods of controlling the flood is the *Guo yu*. In one anecdote King Ling of Zhou wished to block up a river that threatened his palace. The heir-apparent remonstrated:

> This is not permissible. I have heard that those in antiquity who nourished their people did not topple mountains, raise up lowland wastes, block rivers, nor drain swamps. Mountains are the gathering of earth. Lowland wastes are where creatures take shelter. Rivers are where energy [*qi* 氣] is guided. Swamps are the amassing of water. When Heaven and Earth took shape they gathered [earth] on high to form mountains and gave shelter to creatures in the lowlands. They dredged out river valleys to guide the flow of energy, and ringed the stagnant pools in low places in order to amass moisture. Therefore the gathered earth did not collapse and the creatures had a place to take shelter. The energies did not stagnate, but also did not overflow. So in life the people had material resources and in death a place for burial. There were no worries about premature deaths, madness, plagues, or disease. There were no calamities of starvation, cold, or want. Thus the superiors and inferiors could find security together and be prepared against the unexpected. The ancient sages paid attention entirely to this.
>
> In the past Gong Gong renounced this Way. He took his ease in lascivious music and in dissipation destroyed his body. He desired to block up the hundred rivers, and to topple the mountains to fill

up the lowlands. Thereby he harmed the world. August Heaven *Blocking up it* did not bless him, and the common people did not assist him. *harms the world* Calamities and desires arose together, and Gong Gong was thereby destroyed.

In the court of Shun there was Gun, the lord of Chong. He gave free rein to his dissipated mind, and declared that he would finish what Gong Gong had erroneously begun. Yao therefore executed him at Feather Mountain. His son Yu meditated on the earlier lack of due measure, corrected the system of measures, made images of all the creatures in the world, made comparisons to divide all things into their categories, measured things in terms of the people, and brought affairs into accord with all living things. Gong Gong's descendant, Four Peaks, assisted him. Above and below they dredged out the rivers, guided what had become stagnant, and amassed water to enrich the creatures. They made lofty mounds of the nine mountains, dredged out the nine rivers, ringed the nine swamps, richly nourished the nine lowland wastes, opened and brought forth the nine springs, inhabited the nine interiors [of the provinces], and thus linked up with the passages to the four seas.[79]

This account begins with what is effectively a cosmogony in which the sage-kings fashion the earth through imposing the divisions between mountains and lowlands, rivers and marshes, and other categories of terrain. Proper flow of energy, here equated with the flow of rivers, is also central to this early account of the world. The passage interestingly makes no reference to the flood. It instead treats Gong Gong and Gun, the figures who preceded Yu as suggested tamers of the flood and were exiled or executed in the first two chapters of the *Shang shu*, as crazed, pharaonic engineers who for unspecified reasons attempted to block up the rivers, hence conflating them with marshes, and to abolish the distinction of mountains and lowlands. Both are also accused of a moral licentiousness that is manifested in an inability to follow the natural course of things, again linking techniques of water control to questions of morality as in the *Mencius*. Indeed, their improper manipulation of the landscape seems to be a direct manifestation of their moral depravity. Interestingly, their depravity manifests itself in harm to the body as well as to the world. This link is anticipated in the passage's reference to rivers as the flow of *qi*, which specifically assimilates the structure of the world to that of the human body animated by *qi*.[80]

Notable among the errors attributed to Gong Gong and Gun is the attempt to block up rivers. This again is contrasted with the methods of Yu, who not only relied on the method of dredging in order to allow the rivers to flow along their courses to the sea, but also preceded his work with a comprehensive division of existing things into their appropriate categories.[81] The account concludes with a complete typology of the categories of terrain and describes Yu's work as restoring their proper and complete form. The fact that this work consisted of reimposing divisions is marked by the pairing of opposed entities: rivers against mountains, swamps against lowland wastes, and the interior states against the edges of the earth. The theme of completeness is marked again by the recurrent use of the number "nine." Yu thus restored the divisions fixed by the earlier sages, and as in the "Yu gong" made the land suitable for human habitation.

While the theme of Yu's according with the nature of water and other objects figures prominently in the philosophical uses of the flood myth, Mitarai Masaru has pointed out that not all accounts of his work insist on Yu's practice of dredging channels to allow water to follow its own tendencies. He cites three counterexamples. First, when listing Yu's taming of the flood together with the Zhou conquest of the Shang, the expulsion of wild beasts from the human world, and Confucius's inspiring fear among the evil feudal lords through writing the *Spring and Autumn Annals*, the *Mencius* describes Yu's work with the character *yi* 抑 "to repress, to stop, to block." Second, a late section of the *Shan hai jing* states: "Yu blocked up [*yin* 湮] the flood and killed Xiang You [a nine-headed serpent minister of Gong Gong discussed in the next chapter]. Xiang You's blood stank, and [where it fell] could not produce grain. This land became largely water, and people could not dwell on it. Yu blocked it up [*yin*]."

Finally the early Han *Huainanzi* states: "Yu then used the swelling earth to fill in [*tian* 填] the flood and make it into the great mountains. He dug out [*jue* 掘] the wastes of Kunlun to make level ground. . . . The waters of the Yellow River flowed out from the northeast corner of Kunlun and bored through to the ocean, following the stone mountains piled up by Yu."[82] This last example, however, is not at odds with the conventional accounts of Yu's techniques. It refers not to "blocking" but to "filling in," and identifies this with the creation of the mountains that are essential to Yu's work as recounted in the "Yu gong" and *Guo yu*. Moreover, the work culminates in "digging out" land to allow water to flow. The mountains that Yu erects in this passage serve not as barriers but as the sides of channels. Moreover, at least ten passages in the *Huainanzi* explicitly refer to Yu's dredging out channels or according with the nature of water.

Thus, in two cases, Yu was described as using the same methods as those for which Gun and Gong Gong were treated as criminals. However, the huge preponderance of accounts of Yu "dredging" and "guiding," in contrast to only two references to his "blocking," is not to be ignored. Even the texts cited by Mitarai that refer to Yu's blocking up rivers also contain passages, some quite extensive, that describe his work as "dredging" or "opening."[83] Thus, a second version of the story of Xiang You in the *Shan hai jing* does not mention blocking the flood or the pond, but only refers to dredging out the pond. Indeed the reference to blocking the flood may well be a confusion induced by the description of blocking the water to form the pond, since building embankments around swamps or ponds is routinely attributed to Yu as a form of correct hydrology. Elsewhere he is credited with establishing all the high mountains and the rivers that flow from them.[84] Moreover, the frequent asser- tions that Yu accorded with the nature of water usually appear in passages in which the authors are criticizing some contemporary practice or policy. In such contexts the explicit contrast of Yu with Gun or Gong Gong thus serves a polemical purpose. When the story is invoked not for polemics but as an informative narrative, then the precise methods are not stressed, although ref- erences to dredging and guiding still predominate. Finally, in the two passages previously cited, the actions of blocking or stopping are attributed to Yu when the ending of the flood is either identified with or treated as parallel to the suppression of savage or criminal behavior. The links of the flood myth to tales of imposing world order through the exemplary suppression of criminals or rebels will be discussed in the next chapter.

Before proceeding to this second aspect of the flood myth, however, it is useful to note that the tale of Yu as a story about controlling a flood was rou- tinely invoked as a mythic prototype for all those who carried out hydrologic works in the service of the political order. This was shown in the *Mencius*, where the Warring States minister cited Yu as a model for his own irrigation projects. The authors of the *Mencius* rejected this claim by invoking the recur- ring theme of the superiority of whole to part.[85] They treated Yu as exemplary because his work structured the entire world, whereas the Warring States minister could only physically order his own state. Yu's channeling of the rivers culminated in their flowing into the four seas that ringed the entire world, while the minister could only guide the water to his own borders. Within a neighbor's state the flow could be reversed. Indeed in this period there are accounts of blocking up rivers in the course of a military campaign to alter their course in order to flood an enemy's capital.[86] The inclusion of this passage in the *Mencius* shows that already by the middle of the Warring States period Yu's hydrologic work had become a mythic ground of debate between rival visions of political action as well as moral philosophy.

[margin handwritten note: Later appeals to Yu to justify public works projects]

THE FLOOD AND LOCAL CULTURES

The *Mencius's* attempt to use Yu exclusively as an image of the sage who brought order to the *entire* world ended in failure. Indeed, because of the identification of Yu as the sage who *divided* China into its distinctive regions and established the items of tribute that served as markers of local culture, he from the beginning had strong mythic links to the various regions. With the rise of the regional literary traditions that celebrated the topographies and cul- tures of specific regions, Yu was regularly claimed as a model by those who contributed to water control in any locality.[87] The clearest examples of this come from Han stone inscriptions. One mountain inscription, erected at Songgao Mountain in A.D. 123, is dedicated to a temple for one of Yu's wives and consequently includes a detailed account of Yu's career. This inscription follows the literary accounts cited earlier, telling how Gong Gong and Gun

[margin handwritten note: Yu as establisher of regional diversity]

blocked up the rivers and thus aggravated the flood, while Yu engaged in
dredging and thereby drained off the waters. He thus was able to establish
the Nine Provinces and their nine sacred peaks.[88] It was in his capacity as
founder of the sacred peaks that he became a significant topic for mountain
inscriptions. Thus, as the sage who established the sacred peaks for each
province, Yu became a patron for those seeking recognition for cults established at the level of the province or indeed any locality. While this inscription commemorates the actions of the imperial state, and hence links Yu to
world rule, it is specifically devoted to a local cult that sought prestige and
financial support through imperial recognition. Thus, in this inscription, and
presumably in others that have not survived, Yu's achievements were invoked
to sanction local organizations and activities.[89]

Another mountain inscription that speaks of Yu's dredging out the
major waterways to fashion order from chaos was written for the renewal of
a temple on the western marchmount, Mt. Hua, near the imperial capital.[90]
While this inscription likewise ultimately celebrates imperial power, the
immediate focus of praise was a distant relative of the Han imperial house
who had served as a local official and took the initiative in restoring the rites
to Mt. Hua. Interestingly, the poem at the end of the inscription moves
directly from Yu's dredging out the rivers to the later establishment of the
sacrificial canon in which rivers were paired with Earth and mountains with
Heaven. Here the work of Yu as the sage who fixed the river channels and
established the mountain peaks became the ultimate foundation for the establishment of proper sacrifices. These sacrifices in turn provide the central theme
of the inscription. Other mountain inscriptions also cite Yu, or indirectly indicate his work through references to the "nine mountains" that are linked to
him in the "Yu gong," and to the *Shan jing* that was attributed to him and
his agents.[91]

In addition to figuring in mountain inscriptions, references to Yu appear
in inscriptions dedicated to exemplary local officials and worthies, particularly
those whose achievements included work on controlling rivers or improving
irrigation. Such men were sometimes described as "carrying on the work of
Yu" or "being an heir of Yu." In such contexts, Yu was often paired with the
inventor of agriculture, Hou Ji, as one of the twin patrons of the peasantry
and their toils.[92] As we saw, this pairing already figured in the early chapters
of the *Shang shu* where Yu and Hou Ji appear in a list of officials, and the
emphasis on Yu's work as the foundation of agriculture is a major theme of
the "Yu gong" and related accounts. Thus, Yu's work had become a general
model for any person involved in water control and the extension of agriculture. In this guise he was frequently cited as a patron of their activities by
local officials or powerful families who took an interest in water control.

There is also textual evidence for the importance of Yu as a local deity
in the region occupied by the Yue people, to the south of modern Hangzhou
Bay. Both the *Wu Yue chun qiu* and the *Yue jue shu*, works probably largely
compiled in the Eastern Han although later modified, trace the origins of the

region's culture to Yu.[93] This is elaborated at the greatest length in the *Yue jue shu*:

> Long ago, Yue's first ruler Wuyu lived in the time of Yu. He was
> sent off to a fief in Yue to care for Yu's tomb. . . . The people of Yue
> live along the seacoast. They alone have birds work in their fields.
> Great and small have their ranks, and in advancing or withdrawing
> they keep straight lines. None act arbitrarily for themselves. Why is
> this? I say, "At the beginning of Yu's career he worried over the
> people and rescued them from the flood. He arrived in Yue, ascended
> Mt. Mao, had a great assembly and reckoning [*hui ji* 會計], gave ranks
> to the virtuous, enfeoffed those with achievements, and changed the
> name of Mt. Mao to Kuaiji [會稽]. When he became king he made
> a tour of inspection to Yue where he had an audience with the elders,
> received poems and letters, examined the weights, and evened out
> the measures of volume. He fell ill and died and was buried at Kuaiji.
> He had an outer coffin of reeds and an inner coffin of tung-tree
> wood. They dug his grave seven feet deep. Above it had no leaks, so
> below there was no accumulated water. The altar was three feet high,
> with three levels of earthen steps. The courtyard was one acre. Yu
> thought that to dwell in it would be a joy, but to build it was bitter.
> He had no way to repay the people's work, so he taught the people
> to employ birds for agriculture."[94]

This account makes Yu the king who established Yue as a state, describes him
as a visitor to the region, presents the culminating act of his construction of
world order as taking place in Yue, lists his grave as Yue's first sacred site, and
explains local mores and distinctive practices as a result of his work. Moreover, the account of no water accumulated in his grave could well be a
reference to his work in draining away the flood, and as discussed in the introduction the theme of animals crossing into the human realm (as in the labor-
ing birds) is a frequent feature of flood lore in China and elsewhere. A later
passage in the same chapter also gives the location of a temple and an altar
of grain dedicated to Yu.[95]

   Probably the most widespread story that links Yu to the Yue region, a
story already sketched, is the one pertaining to the great assembly of the spirits
that he gathered at Kuaiji and from which that placename was said to derive.
One version of the story appears in the *Guo yu*, perhaps as early as the late
fourth century B.C. This tells how Confucius identified a giant bone discovered at Kuaiji as coming from the giant Fangfeng [防風 "guard against wind,"
perhaps a reference to quelling storms or waves/floods] who arrived late for
Yu's assembly and was executed as a warning to all other participants.[96] This
story is of considerable significance, because a series of texts dating back to
Ren Fang's (A.D. 460–508) *Shu yi ji* describe an active cult to Fangfeng in

the Hangzhou Bay region.[97] A major variant of this story appeared already in the fourth century B.C. *Zuo zhuan*, which stated that Yu assembled the feudal lords at Mt. Tu.[98] This is significant because Mt. Tu was the place of origin of Yu's wife, a figure who plays a major role in several stories that will be discussed in chapter four. Here it is important to note that not only Yu's grave and the physical traces of his career as a ruler, but also the origins of his wife linked him to the Yue region.[99] The *Han shu* also makes a passing reference to the fact that Yue state was established through the actions of Yu.[100] The flood tamer thus in these texts is treated as the patron divinity of the southeast region, a figure who both established Yue as a distinct region and initiated its defining mores and religious practices.

Yu + 四川

There is also evidence of Yu as a patron sage of local culture in Sichuan. First, a fragment of a *Chronicle of the Kings of Shu* written at the end of the Western Han by Yang Xiong gives a detailed account of Yu's miraculous birth.[101] Since the old Shu state had been in what is now called Sichuan, the land of Yang Xiong's birth, the inclusion of such a myth in a chronicle of that state clearly shows that this eminent native scholar traced the history of his home region back to Yu. Moreover the earliest surviving Chinese local history, the *Huayang guo zhi*, is devoted to Sichuan. It begins with an account of Yu's fashioning of the Nine Provinces and then focuses on his unique relation to Sichuan. This text even locates the scene of Yu's marriage on a mountain in this region. Like the sites in the Hangzhou Bay area associated with Yu's story, this mountain became the site of temples dedicated to him and his wife. Also like those in the area around Hangzhou Bay, these temples were treated as among the most important in their region. In a general purge of shrines in Sichuan during the Jin dynasty in the third century A.D., only the temples to Yu and Han Emperor Wu were left untouched.[102]

More important for their local significance than the myths of Yu were a derivative set of stories set in Sichuan that were patterned on his work as a flood tamer. These deal with the achievements of the historical figure Li Bing and his mythic son Er Lang as tamers of floods. Li Bing was an actual man, a Qin administrator who in the third century B.C. had built the great Dujiangyan water diversion and irrigation system that had turned the Chengdu plain into one of the most productive regions in China.[103] However, at least as early as the Han he had become a legendary being who was depicted in sculpture, received regular offerings in a temple, and figured as the hero of a set of tales in which he tamed the river through defeating its god in armed combat.[104] As several scholars have pointed out, there are numerous common points between these stories dealing with Li Bing and the earlier myths of Yu.[105] Thus, the role of Yu as the founder of Sichuanese culture and the tremendous cultic importance attributed to Li Bing in Sichuan clearly express their shared mythic attributes.

The theme of taming floods through defeating hostile gods of nature developed even further in Sichuan in stories of a local god, Er Lang, who was eventually identified as the son of Li Bing and received sacrifices together with him. In the later versions of these stories, which are preserved in local histories as well as oral tales collected in this century, it is Er Lang who in his travels discovers the wicked dragon that causes the floods in Sichuan, defeats the miscreant in armed combat, and imprisons him in a deep pond beneath a stone pillar. Li Bing, the hero of the earlier tales, plays no role in these later versions.[106] While these local Sichuan flood-taming myths lie largely outside the temporal range of this monograph, they demonstrate how flood myths throughout Chinese history link the three themes of water control as a means of constructing ordered space, flood taming as an extension of the punishment of criminals, and floods as a framework within which the relations of fathers and sons are elaborated. These two latter themes also figure prominently in the tales of Yu and the taming of the primal flood.

CONCLUSION

Like flood myths in many cultures, which are tales of the re-creation of the world, those in China were closely linked to the stories of how the world had first come into existence. In the case of China, the earliest cosmogonies depict a primal chaos out of which an ordered world emerged through repeated steps of division. The flood followed the same pattern, beginning with the realm of nondistinction created by the deluge and then portraying how an ordered world was restored through the division of water from dry land, rivers from mountains, marshes from lowlands, and ultimately a central realm from peripheral regions. However, unlike the cosmogonic tales (with the exception of the Chu silk manuscript), stories of the flood depicted it as a *human* achievement, usually the heroic work of the sage Yu. Moreover, the toils of this sage were directly assimilated to the work and administrative methods employed by the governments of the Warring States period and the early empires. In this way the myths became charter foundations for the political order of the period.

A further feature of the earliest extended accounts of Yu's work was that his taming of the flood was linked directly to the dividing up of China into regions, and the linking of those regions to the political center through the institution of tribute. Thus, the chapter in the *Shang shu* devoted to Yu's work was entitled the "Tribute of Yu (*Yu gong*)." With only indirect references to the flood in the opening passages, the work was devoted entirely to the accounts of the positions of the different regions of China, their suitability for agriculture, and the distinctive local products that were sent as tribute to the capital. Significantly, the chapter also insists that all this tribute proceeded along the rivers in which the waters of the flood now flowed in an orderly fashion to the sea. These links between Yu, tribute, and regional cultures emerged to prominence during the Han as the distinctive regional cultures of both Sichuan and the southeast came to claim cultural descent from the works of Yu and developed elaborate local mythologies and cults either devoted to Yu or to local gods patterned on his work.

Broder influence
of the flood
myth

The theme of creating order out of chaos, moreover, was not limited to cosmogonic accounts of the emergence of the physical world. Theories of the human body, human nature, the family, the broader social order, and even the relations of the living and the dead were all elaborated in terms of a homologous model in which *separation* or *division* were the keys to order and success, and where the disappearance of appropriate distinctions entailed chaos, calamity, and death. For this reason, the myths of the flood and the works of Yu were also invoked in discussions of the moral character of human nature or, as we will see in later chapters, the preservation of social order from criminals, the structure of the family, and even the proper working of the human body.

Chapter Two

FLOOD TAMING AND CRIMINALITY

As discussed in the introduction, flood myths in many cultures treat the flood either as the punishment of a god for some human criminality or as a rebellion by some negative power against a high god. Such myths employ the flood as an image of universal social disorder, so that the account of the ending of the flood can serve as a charter for the new regime that is proclaimed as necessary to maintain order in the world. In the Chinese context, all stories that explain the flood in terms of criminality employ the latter model, in which some rebellious man or monster triggers the flood and is finally defeated by the forces of political order. In this way the flood myths provide a sanction for the claims to power of the rulers of the Warring States and early imperial polities, whose authority was justified through the model of the punishments inflicted by the tamers of the flood.

Such stories in early China took at least two forms. In one type, the flood is treated not simply as uncontrolled water that swept away all physical distinctions, but also as the collapse of all divisions that preserved social order. Central among such divisions were the boundaries between men and animals or the closely related ones between the domestic and the wild. The collapse of such divisions, which were fundamental to a fully human existence, was explicitly linked with human criminality. In the second type, the flood itself appears as the work of rebels or criminals. As in the later stories of Li Bing and Er Lang discussed at the end of chapter one, taming the deluge requires the defeat or expulsion of the rebel. These versions of the myth show that by the Warring States period tales of the flood were employed as a means of thinking about the threat of a general collapse of the distinctions or hierarchy that constituted an orderly *social* space. In such stories the rampant waters served as the image or embodiment of the more general problem of resistance to the state order. This chapter will sequentially examine both these types of myth.

CRIMINALITY AND THE COLLAPSE OF
SOCIAL DIVISIONS

used against
Flood methods
correspondered
the collapse of
the division of
labor

The two earliest extended accounts that identified the flood with the collapse
of social divisions appear in the *Mencius* and thus date from the late fourth
century B.C. The first is introduced specifically as a refutation of the program of
the "School of the Tillers," who argued that all people, including the ruler,
should grow their own grain. This attack on the social division of labor and the
political division between rulers and ruled challenged two fundamental political principles advocated in the *Mencius*. The *Mencius* thus attempts to refute this
challenge first by an appeal to the benefits of economic specialization and the
necessity of having full-time rulers, and then by a presentation of the flood as
the image of the total collapse of the distinctions that defined human society:

> In the time of Yao the world was not yet in balance. The flood
> waters ran rampant and overflowed the world. Grasses and trees
> flourished, and the wild animals multiplied. The five grains did not
> grow, and the animals impinged on people. The tracks of wild animals
> and birds crisscrossed through the middle kingdoms. Yao alone
> worried (*you* 憂) over this, so he raised up Shun and bestowed power
> on him. Shun had Yi take fire to scorch the mountains and wilds
> and burn them. The birds and wild animals fled and hid. Yu dredged
> out the Nine Rivers. He caused the Ji and Luo Rivers to flow down
> and channeled them into the sea. He opened up the Ru and Han
> Rivers, arranged the Huai and the Si, and channeled them into the
> Yangzi. Only then were the middle kingdoms able to obtain food
> and eat it. At this time Yu spent eight years on the outside. Three
> times he passed the gate to his house but did not enter. Even if he
> had wanted to plow, how could he have been able to do so?
>
> Hou Ji taught the people agriculture, to plant and cultivate the
> five grains. The five grains ripened and the people were nourished.
> The way of people is that if they have sufficient food and warm
> clothing, but live at ease without instruction, then they are close to
> the birds and beasts. The sages worried (*you* 憂) over this, and had
> Qie serve as Minister of the Masses. He instructed them in human
> relations. There was kinship between fathers and sons, duty between
> rulers and ministers, distinction between husbands and wives, proper
> order between elder and younger, and good faith among friends.
> . . . The sages worrying over the people being like this, how could
> they have the free time to plow?[1]

Here the flood is announced as an initial condition of chaos, but the
detailed description does not indicate that water at that time covered the
surface of the earth. Instead, the world of the flood is marked by the flour-
ishing of wild grasses and forests, in contrast with the domestic crops that did
not grow, and the multiplication of birds and wild animals who swarmed

through the world of men. This suggests the invasion of the human realm by a threatening, endlessly fertile wilderness that overwhelmed the boundaries between the natural and the human. Nor did the remedy for this situation begin with the controlling of the flood, but instead with the burning of the wilds and the expulsion of the animals. Yu's work of dredging and channeling, central in any account of water control, figures only as the first step in the introduction of agriculture that is completed by Hou Ji. (This identification of Yu's work as the foundation of agriculture and his pairing with Hou Ji, as noted earlier, figured in several early texts and Han stone inscriptions.)

Yu laying the groundwork for Hou Ji's innovations

Moreover, the work of Yi, Yu, and Hou Ji does not introduce proper divisions between men and animals, for the moral state of people who were merely fed and clothed was "close to animals" just as they were physically close in the initial chaos. This identity of the two conditions is also marked by the repeated references to the sage's "worry." The true work of separation was achieved only by the introduction of proper divisions and hierarchies among people, which was precisely the state of affairs threatened by the teachings of the "Tillers." It is also noteworthy, as discussed in chapters three and four, that the account of the construction of order in the wake of the flood emphasizes the introduction of the relations that constituted a proper family. In short, the mythic flood here serves as a historical occasion for and a physical image of a *social* chaos produced by the collapse of *social* distinctions. Yu's fashioning of an ordered physical space through dredging the rivers and guiding them into the sea is only one step in the larger process of constructing an ordered and hierarchically divided human realm in which the central role is played by the family as a social unit.

The second account of the flood in the *Mencius* uses a similar rhetorical strategy in which the mythic account of a primal flood is invoked as the prototype for the periodic collapses of social order that had recurred through ancient history under the impact of evil rulers or deviant doctrines. Defending himself against the accusation of being fond of argument, Mencius justifies his activities as the natural succession to the earlier work of Yu, the Zhou founders, and Confucius:

> In the time of Yao the waters reversed their course and overflowed the middle kingdoms so that snakes and dragons dwelt there. The people had no fixed dwellings, so those in lower regions made nests in trees, while those in higher ones lived in mountain caves. . . . Yao had Yu impose order on it. Yu dredged out the land and channeled the rivers to the sea. He expelled the snakes and dragons to the grassy swamps. The movement of the water outward from the land formed the Jiang, Huai, Han, and Yellow Rivers. As the dangers were removed to the distant regions, the harm of the snakes and dragons vanished. Only then were people able to obtain level land to dwell on.
>
> When Yao and Shun died, the Way of the sages declined, and violent rulers arose in succession. They destroyed houses to make

(chaos renewed)

them into pools and ponds, so the people had no place to rest. They eliminated agricultural fields to make them into gardens and orchards, so that the people had no clothes or food. Heterodox doctrines and violent conduct also arose. Since pools, ponds, gardens, orchards, and marshes were numerous, the birds and wild animals arrived. When it reached the time of King Zhou [of Shang], the whole world was again chaotic. The Duke of Zhou assisted King Wu to execute Zhou. He attacked Yin and after three years punished its ruler. He expelled Fei Lian to the edge of the sea and executed him. He destroyed fifty states. He drove the tigers, leopards, rhinoceroses, and elephants out to the distant lands, and the whole world was happy. . . .

Order reestablished (margin note)

The generations degenerated and the Way declined. Heterodox theories and violent conduct again arose. There were ministers who assassinated their rulers and sons who killed their fathers. Confucius was afraid, so he wrote the *Spring and Autumn Annals*. This is the task of the Son of Heaven. Therefore Confucius said, "Will those who appreciate me do it only through the *Annals*? Will those who regard me as a criminal do it only because of the *Annals*?"

Chaos ascendant (margin note)

A sage king does not now arise, the feudal lords are unrestrained, and unemployed scholars engage in wild criticism. The words of Yang Zhu and Mo Di fill the world. All discourse in the world that does not tend towards Yang tends towards Mo. Master Yang's advocacy of being for oneself means having no ruler. Master Mo's advocacy of caring equally for all means having no father. To have no ruler and no father means to be a bird or beast. Gongming Yi said, "If the ruler's kitchens have fat meat and his stables sleek horses, while the people appear hungry and there are bodies of those who have starved in the fields, this is leading the animals to eat people." If the Way of Yang and Mo does not cease and the Way of Confucius does not become well-known, then heterodox theories and slanderous people will block up the teachings of humanity and duty. If the teachings of humanity and duty are blocked up, then you will lead the animals to eat people, and people will also eat one another. I for this reason am afraid. I study the former sages, block Yang and Mo, and reject excessive phrases, so that heterodox theories cannot arise. . . .

Long ago Yu suppressed the flood and the world became level. The Duke of Zhou conquered the barbarians, expelled the wild beasts, and the peasants were at peace. Confucius completed the *Annals*, and rebellious ministers and criminal sons became afraid. . . . I also desire to correct people's minds, halt heterodox theories, block disputatious conduct, expel excessive phrases, and thereby be heir to the three sages. How could it be that I love disputation? I have no alternative. One who through words can block Yang and Mo is the disciple of the sages.[2]

In this account the flood is only the earliest and most graphic form of a regularly repeated social collapse. As in the preceding passage, the recurrent image that epitomizes this collapse is the disappearance of the distinction between men and beasts. Yu ends the flood, but he is celebrated above all for expelling the snakes and dragons from the world of men to the edges of the earth. In the same way the Duke of Zhou ends the succession of evil kings through defeating King Zhou of Shang, but this achievement is once again paired with the expulsion of harmful wild animals who had been allowed back into the human realm by the rulers' crimes. Finally, the chaos triggered by rejecting Confucius and embracing rival schools is also marked by animals eating people, and even by people becoming animals through the crime of cannibalism. Thus, both of the *Mencius*'s accounts of the flood are not about the control of water or its separation from dry land, but about finding in the original construction of an ordered, human space a mythic prototype for his own social and intellectual program. In this schema the flood, and the primal chaos with which it is linked, stand for all the criminality, bad government, and intellectual deviance that threatened the social order.

While these lengthy passages in the *Mencius* present in its most developed form the idea that the taming of the flood provided a prototype for punishing rebellion or criminality, they borrow some of their ideas and structure from the opening chapters of the *Shang shu* that were discussed in chapter one. As noted there, these chapters narrate the fashioning of ordered time, space, and society. Like the *Mencius*, they present this process as the result of the successive labors of a series of ministers who each introduced some new technique or expelled some noxious power. Yu's taming of the flood thus figures as a single element in a broader process of constructing order through acts of demarcation, division, and expulsion.

These chapters of the *Shang shu* also link the flood to the theme of rebellion or criminality through introducing in a negative light the figure of Gong Gong, who will be discussed later, and through the account of Yu's suppression of the Miao.[3] The Miao figure in several chapters of the *Shang shu* as the origins of criminality and the archetypal rebels. In the "Counsels of Great Yu" the task of restoring them to obedience is assigned by Shun to Yu.[4] The *Shang shu* account of this deed presents it in the form of a parable on the proper techniques of government, in which Yu first relies on military force that fails to restore order. He finally succeeds only through using virtuous power and ritual performance.

In other Warring States accounts, however, Yu suppresses the rebellion of the Miao through a combination of violence and divine support. Thus, one of the chapters in the *Mozi* that criticize aggressive warfare describes Yu's combat with the Miao as follows:

Long ago the three Miao tribes created great chaos, so Heaven commanded him [Yu] to destroy them. The sun came out at night, and for three days it rained blood. A dragon was born in the ancestral

temple, and dogs howled in the marketplace. Ice formed in the
summer, so the earth cracked and springs gushed forth. All types of
grain grew in unnatural forms, so the people were terrified. Gao Yang
gave a command in the Dark Palace [*xuan gong* 玄宮] that Yu should
personally take Heaven's jade staff of authority in order to launch an
expedition against the Miao. As lightning flashed all around, a spirit
with the face of a man and the body of a bird came down bearing
a jade staff in order to wait upon Yu. An arrow struck the com-
mander of the Miao, so their army was plunged into chaos. They
thereupon were eliminated. Having conquered the three Miao tribes,
Yu then separated out the mountains and rivers, divided above from
below, and clearly laid out the four directional extremities of the
world. Consequently neither spirits nor people violated the laws, and
the whole world was at peace.[5]

Here the character who in the *Shang shu* and elsewhere figures above all as
the tamer of the flood appears as the minister who through force of arms
punished the rebels who first introduced armed violence and criminality into
the world. Significantly, his military suppression of the rebels leads directly
into his work in separating the water from the land, that is, taming the flood,
and laying out an ordered space marked by the fixing of the four directions
and the separation of above from below. This again shows the close links in
early China between myths of taming the flood and those relating to suppressing criminality or rebellion.

A final passage that depicts Yu suppressing deviance, and links this action
against criminality with his work in structuring the world, is the celebrated
account of his casting the Nine Tripods that became the embodiment of world
sovereignty:

In the past when the Xia had virtuous potency, the distant regions
made illustrations of their strange beings [*wu* 物] and paid a tribute
of metal to their Nine Shepherds. [Yu] cast tripods with images of
the strange beings. These completely depicted all the strange beings,
so that the people could recognize the spirits. Thus when the people
went through rivers and marshes, or mountains and forests, they
would encounter nothing untoward, and nothing could block their
way. Jie [the last Xia ruler] had benighted virtue, so the tripods passed
to the Shang dynasty. Zhou of the Shang was cruel and violent, so
the tripods passed to Zhou.[6]

Here the Nine Shepherds, corresponding to the regions of the earth in the
geographic schema of the "Tribute of Yu," send in a tribute of metal to be
cast into tripods that give an exhaustive visual inventory of all the harmful
spirits on the earth. These images become the means of suppressing the malevolent actions of such spirits, and serve to open up the rivers and the moun-

tains whose separation marks the completion of Yu's flood-quelling labors in other accounts. Thus, the suppression of miscreants and the flood-quelling structuring of space form two aspects of a single process.

Another form of evidence, not connected with Yu, on the links between the suppression of rebellion and quelling of floods appears in the military titles awarded in the Han and the immediate post-Han period. When commanded to suppress the rebellion of the non-Chinese peoples of Nanyue—which included what is now Guangdong, Guangxi, and parts of North Vietnam— the early Eastern Han general Ma Yuan was awarded the title of "Wave-Quelling General [*fu bo jiang jun* 伏波將軍]." The same title was bestowed upon Ge Hong, the author of the *Baopuzi*, for defeating a rebellion in the years 303–304.[7] Here the "waves" of the flood stand for the violence and chaotic nature of the rebels, although it might also refer to the importance of naval combat in these southern campaigns.

In the previous passages, as in the traditions pertaining to Shun that were discussed in chapter one, the flood served as an image of the collapse of all distinctions, particularly that between humans and beasts, and thus as the dramatic prototype for all forms of deviance and social disorder. In later centuries, the flood as an image of deviance or breakdown was extended to the realm of psychology, so that in the writings of Zhu Xi and other Song philosophers excessive and hence dangerous emotions were described as acting like a destructive flood.[8] These ideas found expression in a substantial body of traditions that the flood itself was the product of rebellion or criminality. Such traditions cluster around two figures: Gong Gong and Gun. These men were discussed in chapter one as figures whose water control techniques were opposed to those of Yu, but they were also treated—as shown in the passage from the *Guo yu*—as criminals.

GONG GONG AS A CRIMINAL

Gong Gong as a malefactor first appears in the "Yao dian."[9] In response to a request from Yao for a man who can deal with the urgent tasks of the day, Huan Dou recommends Gong Gong. Yao replies: "'Ah, quiet in words but his acts are contrary. He seems respectful but floods rampant to Heaven [*tao tian* 滔天].' Thearch [Yao] said, 'Alas, Four Peaks, swishing and swirling, the great flood now destroys. Surging and shaking, it enfolds mountains and sur-mounts hills. Rushing and limitless, it floods rampant to Heaven [*tao tian*].'"[10] Thus, as William Boltz has pointed out, Gong Gong is described here in the very words that are immediately afterwards applied to the flood. A rampant flooding that rises up to Heaven describes the physical state of affairs in the world and at the same time provides an image for the arrogance of Gong Gong.[11] Seemingly for this reason Gong Gong is rejected, and in the next chapter of the *Shang shu* both he and Huan Dou are exiled.[12]

While Yao's speech merely suggests Gong Gong's nature as a rebel or criminal, other accounts are more explicit. Thus, the passage in the *Guo yu* translated in chapter one, a passage that could well be earlier than the

"Yao dian," includes a discussion between King Ling of Zhou and his heir apparent on the best methods of flood control. When King Ling proposes blocking up a river, the technique for which Yu was routinely invoked as the classic counterexample, the heir apparent delivers a long address denouncing the practice of blocking rivers. In this speech rivers are described as the means of guiding the fundamental energies (*qi* 氣) of the world so that they circulate properly without either stagnating or completely dispersing. Maintaining such flows guaranteed that the people suffered no calamities such as early death, plagues, famine, cold, or poverty. The passage then brings in the figure of Gong Gong as a minatory example:

> The ancient sages thus were attentive only to this. But long ago Gong Gong renounced this Way. Taking pleasure in self-indulgent [*dan* 湛=耽] joys and losing himself in excess [*yin* 淫], he desired to block up all the rivers, lower the high ground to fill in the low places, and thereby ruin the world. August Heaven did not bless him, the common people did not help him, calamities arose on all sides, and so Gong Gong was destroyed.[13]

Once again the faults of Gong Gong's character are those of an excess marked by the recurring water signific in the graphs that describe him, graphs that suggest he is an embodiment of the flood or that the rampant waters of the flood express his criminal nature. The crime explicitly attributed to him is to go against the natural order of flowing energies and the separation of high and low.[14] In this he is linked to Gun, who will be discussed shortly, and contrasted with the "natural" techniques of dredging and channeling that are assigned to Yu. In the conclusion of the story, the narrator recounts that King Ling ignored his son and that the Zhou house consequently went into a protracted decline.

While here Gong Gong appears as a corrupt official who employed destructive techniques that expressed his wanton character, in early Han accounts in the *Huainanzi* he had become a rebel against the divinely ordained ruler and an enemy of the structure of the world:

> Long ago Gong Gong battled with Zhuan Xu to become Thearch. In his anger he butted against Mt. Buzhou. Heaven's pillar broke and Earth's cord snapped. Heaven tilted toward the northwest, so the sun, moon, stars, and planets move in that direction. Earth was left unfilled in the southeast, so the watery floods and the silted soil tend in that direction.[15]

This etiological myth that explains both the course of the celestial bodies and the hydrological structure of China invokes Gong Gong as a destructive rebel without any specific reference to the flood, which is only hinted at in the reference to the courses of the rivers. However, other chapters in the same work explicitly announce that Gong Gong's rebellious actions were the cause of the flood: "Long ago Gong Gong's strength butted against Mt. Buzhou, which caused Earth to tip to the southeast. He was battling with Gao Xin [Thearch Ku] to be Thearch. He then was submerged in the depths [*yuan* 淵], his kin were annihilated, and his succession cut off."[16] Here Gong Gong's rebellion and the consequent tilting of the earth led directly to his drowning in watery depths that are almost certainly a reference to the flood. This link is even clearer in a third passage:

> In the time of Shun, Gong Gong stirred up the waters into a rampant flood [*tao hong shui* 滔洪水] that ran against the Hollow Mulberry [a polyvalent mythic image associated here with the sun and sky]. Dragon Gate Pass had not yet been opened and Lü Bridge not cleared, so the Yellow River and the Yangzi flowed together and the seas were limitless. The people all ascended hills or climbed trees. Shun then sent Yu to dredge out the three rivers and five lakes. . . . He evened out the water channels and land, so the rivers flowed east into the sea. The flood drained away, and the nine provinces became dry.[17]

This passage specifically names Gong Gong as the instigator of the flood, and his crime is followed by the conventional account of the desperate actions of the people and the saving work of Yu. The description of the flood here closely resembles that in *Lü shi chun qiu* and in the *Shizi*, which demonstrates that the mythic account of a flood created by Gong Gong's rebellion existed in the pre-imperial period.[18]

A final passage in the *Huainanzi* also clearly casts Gong Gong in the role of rebel and author of the flood: "The origins of weapons are very ancient. The Yellow Thearch battled with the Fiery Thearch, and Zhuan Xu battled with Gong Gong. . . . The Fiery Thearch created calamities of fire, so the Yellow Thearch slew him. Gong Gong created calamities of water, so Zhuan Xu executed him."[19] This discussion of the mythic origins of warfare invokes a set of stories in which the appearance of organized violence in the service of the state is linked with tales of drought and flood.[20] Apart from the references to his water weapons, Gong Gong is twice cited in passages on the antiquity of warfare that assert he was attacked by Yu. In these passages, the battle between the flood and the flood tamer is translated into ordinary cases of warfare.[21]

In these references to "water weapons," the flood caused by Gong Gong forms a correlate pair with the droughts caused by the Fiery Thearch, both being described as primitive weapons. While the term "flood" is not specifically used in this discussion of early warfare, the reference to "calamities of water" in association with the explicit accounts of the flood elsewhere in the same text makes the sense clear. Moreover, in Warring States and Han China the correlate pairing of floods with droughts, usually associated with Yu and the founder of the Shang, King Tang, was an extremely common trope. The use here is simply one example out of at least eighteen.[22] A variant from Chu state of the story of a conflict between water and fire tells of a struggle between the fire god Zhu Rong, the Chu ancestral deity who figured prominently in the silk manuscript discussed in chapter one, and Gong Gong:

> Zhongli occupied the post of Minister of Fire [*huo zheng* 火正] for the Thearch Ku, Gaoxin. He achieved great merit and was able to illuminate and heat [*guang rong* 光融] the whole world. Thearch Ku gave him the title "Blessed Heat [*zhu rong* 祝融]." Gong Gong rebelled, and Thearch Ku sent Zhongli to execute him, but he did not complete the task. So on the *gengyin* day the Thearch executed Zhongli.[23]

While the account says nothing about the flood, the fact that the ruler/deity entrusts the task of suppressing Gong Gong to his minister of fire and heat shows clearly that this story is another version of those traced in the *Huainanzi* that attribute the origins of the flood to Gong Gong and link it to a battle between water and fire.

In addition to the accounts in the *Shang shu*, *Huainanzi*, and the *Shan hai jing*, a final version of the story of Gong Gong as a rebel who shattered the world in producing the flood was recorded in the Eastern Han by Wang Chong. He quotes the *Huainanzi* or a related account, tacks on the separate tradition of Nü Gua's restoring the world (see chapter four), and then subjects the two stories to critical questioning.[24] While his version adds nothing to the other accounts, it is noteworthy that he describes the story of Gong Gong as something to which the people of the world all assent, while men of refined erudition regard it as bizarre but for fear of being subject to attack do not dare to openly criticize it. This indicates that by the middle of the Eastern Han the tale of Gong Gong's rebellion causing the flood had become widespread and generally accepted.

Although this portrayal of Gong Gong as a villainous rebel who created the world-threatening flood became the most common version of his career, several passages treat him as an ancient ruler. This has led certain scholars to argue that there was an earlier or an independent tradition in which Gong Gong was not a rebel or a criminal, but an early ruler or even a sage. The passage from the *Guo yu* quoted in chapter one might well suggest such an idea, since Gong Gong seems to be acting entirely as a free agent in carrying out his plans to transform the surface of the earth. Nevertheless, in that account he is still clearly a rebel against the natural order, if not the political. A clearer expression of the belief that Gong Gong had been a ruler, although still associated with the covering of the earth in a great flood, appears in the *Guanzi*:

> Duke Huan of Qi asked Guan Zhong, "May I hear about the great calculation since the time of Suiren?" Master Guan replied, "Since the time of Suiren all have ruled the world through 'the light and heavy [*qing zhong* 輕重, a system of manipulating coinage that is the

subject of the last seven chapters of the *Guanzi*]'. When Gong Gong *[Gong Gong as ruler]* was king, water occupied seven-tenths of the world and land three-tenths. Taking advantage of these natural circumstances, he used this exiguous and adverse [*ai* 隘 "confined"] situation to control the world. When the Yellow Thearch became king he only avoided [the beasts'] claws and teeth, but did not make his weapons sharp. He burned the mountain forests, destroyed the layered thickets of vegetation, and set torch to the marshes. He drove away the birds and beasts and thereby truly benefitted people. Only then could the world be possessed and husbanded."[25]

This passage clearly describes Gong Gong as a king who used the flood to impose his rule on the world.

However, while Gong Gong appears as a king in this account, his rule is still treated as criminal, or at least destructive of order. This is suggested by the indication that his authority was based on the fact that the world of his day was "confined" or "exiguous," but it is demonstrated more clearly in the account of the career of the subsequent ruler, the Yellow Thearch. The actions of this ruler exactly recapitulate those by which Yu or the other officers of Shun restored order to the world in the *Mencius*'s account of the flood. The *[Equation of Gong Gong's rule w/the chaos that overcame]* reign of Gong Gong, marked by the predominance of water, overabundance of vegetation, and mingling of humans and beasts, is thus in this account the primal chaos that in the *Mencius* served as the prototype for all criminality. The Yellow Thearch's actions consequently appear as an act of rescue that "benefits" all people and for the first time fashioned an ordered world suitable for husbandry and the extraction of wealth. In this his role again parallels that of Yu in other accounts, which regularly note how his taming of the flood made human settlement of the land possible and provided the foundation for the introduction of agriculture by Hou Ji. Thus, even as a ruler, Gong Gong remains an embodiment of the flood that is presented as an original state of nondifferentiation and implicit criminality from which only the toils of subsequent sages could save the human race.

Another passage that treats Gong Gong as a king appears in the fourth-century B.C. *Zuo zhuan*. It also situates him as one ruler within a sequence of early monarchs: "Long ago the Yellow Thearch used clouds to keep records [or "fix his calendar" *ji* 紀], so he created cloud officers and gave them cloud titles. The Fiery Thearch used fire to keep records, so he created fire officers and gave them fire titles. Gong Gong used water to keep records, so he created water officers and gave them water titles."[26]

In an early example of the sort of schema that would later be organized under the Five Phases, Gong Gong is associated with water in contrast to *[Gong Gong + water]* earlier rulers linked with clouds and fire, and with later ones tied to dragons and birds. The theme of the flood does not explicitly appear, although it is clear that his identification with the flood led to his being classed under water, just as the "element" of the Fiery Thearch derives from his association with drought and that of the Yellow Thearch from his association with storms and fog. This passage is also linked to the common theme noted earlier of the opposition between drought and flood, a theme that often relates to the introduction of weapons or organized violence to the human world. Thus, although there is no suggestion of Gong Gong's criminality, he is clearly linked to the flood and implicitly to the problem of human violence.

Finally, there are several passages that do not refer to Gong Gong but rather to his son Hou Tu (後土 "Lord Earth"). According to these writers, the merits of Hou Tu allowed him to receive sacrifice as the mythic origin or embodiment of the altar to the earth (*she* 社). These passages on the achievements of Hou Tu begin by stating that Gong Gong "was ruler of the Nine Provinces [*bo jiu you* 伯九有]," that is, he controlled the entire world.[27] However, it is worth noting that the verb applied to his rule indicates that he was a hegemon, not a true king, and it was his son who received sacrifice. This suggests that his reign was without merit. Thus, even here, the traces of his image as rebel or malefactor have not entirely disappeared, although they are not made explicit.

This survey of the references to Gong Gong shows that he was a figure invariably linked to the flood, and the flood when evoked was invariably negative. Thus, he appeared alternatively as a savage rebel who triggered the flood through an act of cosmic violence, or in a few cases as a ruler who presided over the flood and ruled through its power, but from whom people had to be rescued by the true sages who came after him. In short, throughout all the surviving texts Gong Gong appears as an embodiment of the attributes of the flood, the author of the flood, or a ruler who presided over the flood and whose actions expressed its turbulent and destructive character. As William Boltz has demonstrated, the graphs that make up the name "Gong Gong" belong to a word group with the sense "bellicose" or "wanton." This word group also has associated derivatives meaning "waters out of control" or "floods."[28] This derivation of his name fits exactly with the observed facts of the Gong Gong mythology from the Warring States and Han periods, in which he figures as the cause, patron, or embodiment of an all-consuming flood that is the prototype of all human disorder and criminality.[29] Thus, he provides the clearest mythic image of the flood as the result of criminality and of its taming being the result of the imposition of punishment by an early king.

GUN AS A CRIMINAL

Phonetically related to Gong Gong, but not in the same word group, was Gun, the second great malefactor of the flood myths.[30] In fact, the careers of the two figures in most accounts follow such a closely parallel course that Yang Kuan has argued they were originally the same mythic character.[31] After Gong Gong was rejected in the "Yao dian," Gun was proposed, criticized by

Yao, ultimately accepted, but proved wanting. In the "Shun dian" his execution forms a cluster with the exile of Gong Gong and Huan Dou, as well as the imprisonment of the San Miao. In the "Hong fan" he is criticized for using techniques of water control that violated the course of nature, a criticism also leveled at Gong Gong. The passage cited in the *Guo yu* follows its account of Gong Gong with an account of Gun. His character is described with the same adjective as Gong Gong (*yin* 淫 "excessive, lascivious") and the *Guo yu* states that he claimed he would "carry out to the end Gong Gong's error [or 'fault'; *sui Gong Gong zhi guo* 遂共工之過]." Moreover, the ruin of the two figures is explicitly paired shortly later in the same text.[32] In the *Mozi*, as part of an argument against the institution of hereditary offices, Gun is described as the eldest son of a Thearch. This passage states that Gun abandoned his father's virtue and hence was punished.[33] This would assign him if not the status of a ruler, like Gong Gong, at least that of an heir. The two are again paired in an anecdote in the *Han Feizi*, where both appear as evil or rebellious ministers who opposed Yao's decision to yield the world to Shun.[34] Finally, both undergo nearly identical physical transformations into animals, generally either a bear or a dragon.[35]

However, while Gong Gong and Gun share many points in common, and may indeed be derived from a common mythic ancestor, they diverge in several significant ways in the Warring States and early imperial accounts. Most significant, Gun appears in several versions of his story as a potentially positive figure who attempts to end the flood. While the improper technique that he used of blocking up water exacerbated the flooding and thus caused great damage, unlike Gong Gong he was not described as the instigator of the flood. Moreover, in most accounts he appears as the father of Yu as well as his unsuccessful predecessor. Several of these stories treat the two as the beginning and end of a single process or course of labor that ultimately brought the flood to an end. I will discuss each of these aspects in turn.

The scholars who produced *Gu shi bian* have argued that the identification of Gun as Yu's father was a late development and that the two were originally independent figures who were only gradually drawn into a single narrative by inserting them into a genealogy. In some of their articles they argue that Gun, and the closely related Gong Gong, were heroes in distinct regional flood traditions that they associate with the South and the Southeast.[36] This position remains disputed, and it suffers from the weakness that we have no texts in which Gong Gong appears as a positive figure, or in which Gun appears independently. However, the handful of passages in which Gun appears in a more positive light than in most of the received tradition highlights the points at which he diverges most clearly from Gong Gong.

First, there are two passages that indicate a positive valuation of Gun without providing any narrative justification. Both the "Ji fa" chapter of *Li ji* and the "Lu yu shang" chapter of *Guo yu* contain long lists of the early sages and the types of sacrifices that they received from Shun, the Xia, the Shang, and the Zhou. While these accounts differ in detail, they both state that Gun received sacrifice from the Xia.[37] These clearly indicate that Gun was not viewed entirely as a wicked figure, if only because he was the father of Yu and hence the ultimate progenitor of the Xia dynasty.

The handful of passages that use narrative to hint at a positive view of Gun appear in the *Chu ci* and the *Shan hai jing*. The first reads:

> Since he was not up to taking charge of stilling the flood
> Why did they recommend him?
> They all said, "What is the worry,
> Why not test him and have him act?"
> When owl and turtle linked tail and beak [?]
> Why did he obey them?[38]
> He obediently desired to complete the work,
> Why did the Thearch punish him?[39]
> For a long time imprisoned at Feather Mountain,
> Why was he not released for three years?[40]

Apart from the cryptic reference to the owl and turtle, which most scholars assume offered some sort of omens to guide him, the questions closely follow the account in the "Yao dian." Gun was given the task of taming the flood on the basis of general recommendation, he attempted the task without success, and for some unexplained reason this failure was severely punished by the Thearch. Similar remarks to the effect that Gun was an honest and stubborn man who suffered for his failure appear in both the "Li sao" and one of the poems in the "Jiu zhang."[41] However, the latter passage suggests that Gun's straightforward stubbornness in some manner led to his failure, so this is clearly not an entirely positive trait of character. Indeed, the texts hint that his stubbornness was a form of defiance that consequently led to his execution.

In contrast with the idea of a steadfast man punished by an arbitrary or cruel ruler for unsatisfactory performance, a passage in the *Shan hai jing* sometimes cited by those seeking traces of a heroic Gun portrays him as a reckless figure whose devotion to his task leads to insubordination and treason:

> The flood ran rampant to Heaven [*tao tian* 滔天]. Gun stole the Thearch's "swelling soil [*xi rang* 息壤]" to block off [*yin* 堙] the flood waters. He did not wait for the Thearch's command, so the Thearch commanded Zhurong to kill Gun at the side of Feather Mountain. Gun's belly gave birth to Yu. The Thearch commanded Yu to finally apply the soil in order to fix the Nine Provinces.[42]

Here Gun appears as a trickster figure, who errs in his desire to end the flood as rapidly as possible. This desire leads him into theft and defiance of the ruler's orders. His son Yu, born directly from Gun's belly in a story that will be analyzed later, uses what is apparently the very soil stolen by Gun to finally end the ravages of the flood.

However, even in this single passage that suggests a heroic if misguided Gun, there are lingering suggestions of the negative figure. First, he plans to use the soil to "block" the flood, the very error or crime of which he and Gong Gong were accused in the texts cited earlier. This would contrast with Yu who used mountain heights, and hence the "swelling" soil, to form ranges that channeled the flood waters into the sea. Second, the execution by Zhurong at the command of the Thearch is the scenario that appeared in the Chu version of the myth preserved in *Shi ji*, except that in the latter it was Gong Gong rather than Gun who was slain. Thus, once again Gun blurs into the figure of Gong Gong, the embodiment of the flood who never appears as a hero or positive figure, and is placed in opposition to his offspring Yu.

A final set of passages that could indicate a more positive reading of Gun attribute to him the invention of the defensive wall (*cheng* 城) and by extension of the city (*cheng* 城).[43] However, in these passages the invention of the city is treated in a negative manner as an extension of the rebellious spirit or defiance of nature that figure in other hostile treatments of Gun. In this way it indicates a certain hostility to the notion of the city, or at least of the city as a community surrounded by walls, much in the manner of the biblical account that attributes the creation of the city to the arch-criminal Cain. In the *Huainanzi*'s account, Gun's building of the wall causes all the feudal lords to rebel and everyone in the world to develop treacherous thoughts. Yu, by contrast, levels the wall to fill in moats, distributes his treasures, and burns his weapons. As a result, the whole world submits to him and sends in tribute. In this way the two men's relations to city walls parallel their relations to the dams that control rivers. Gun tries to seal things up by building walls and thereby blocks the flow of that which should be in motion (water or tribute). Yu by contrast tears the walls down in order to allow goods (or water) to flow through proper channels and hence to create order. Gun's wall in this story is one of the corrupting inventions that creates villainy and disorder in the proto-Daoist accounts synthesized in the *Huainanzi* by shattering the original simplicity of the world.[44]

An account in the *Lü shi chun qiu* of Gun's invention of the walled city is even more explicit in treating the act as treason. When Yao proposes to yield his kingdom to Shun, Gun in a jealous fury assembles wild animals to launch a rebellion:

> Thinking that Yao had lost his sense of judgment, he desired to attain a rank among the Three Lords. He stirred up the savage beasts in hopes of launching a rebellion. Putting together the beasts' horns he made a wall, and raising their tails he made banners. He called [the people] but they did not come, so he wandered in the wilderness to inflict a calamity on the Thearch. Shun then imprisoned him on Feather Mountain and carved up his body with a dagger from Wu.[45]

Here the wall first fashioned by Gun is a mark of his rebellion. Moreover, it is composed from the horns of the wild beasts whose presence in the human world was so often linked with the flood as an image of social breakdown. Thus, his introduction of the wall and the city once again marked him as a rebel and linked him to the flood. Moreover, Gun's animal followers in this story hint at his own animal nature, which will be discussed in chapter four.

Consequently, in the surviving corpus Gun is never a truly positive figure. In certain texts he is conflated with Gong Gong as the embodiment of the flood or the purveyor of a faulty technology that only increases the calamity. In others he appears as a well-intentioned but fatally stubborn and insubordinate failure whose work could be completed only by his offspring Yu.[46] This is true even of the sacrificial lists, in which he receives offerings only from the dynasty founded by his son. Within the mythological system that operates through all known texts he is never a figure in his own right, but only a middle element in a triad that he forms with Gong Gong and Yu. At one pole there is the criminal author or embodiment of the flood, at the other the hero who brings order to the world, and in the middle Gun who oscillates between the two. Sometimes he is conflated with Gong Gong as a criminal or rebel, sometimes he is paired with his son as a minister who struggled to end the flood, but there is no trace of him acting as the hero of his own story. To fully explain this mediating role played by Gun, it will be necessary to examine the relation of the myths of the flood to Chinese ideas about the family and the body, for it is precisely his status as the *father* of Yu that is the key to his role in the myths. The significance of this will be discussed in chapter three.

CRIMINALITY AND FLOOD IN THE *SHAN HAI JING*

One of the most important sources for early accounts of the flood as a consequence of criminality associated with Gong Gong or Gun was the *Shan hai jing*, the "Classic of the Mountains and the Seas." This work was identified in the Han dynasty as the creation of Yu, and, as we have seen, the pairing of mountains and bodies of water was a recurring characteristic of early Chinese accounts of Yu. The *Shan hai jing* depicts a mythic geography of the whole of the Chinese world organized around the theme of mountains and seas, and its later sections contain several important accounts of the origins of the flood and Yu's work in bringing it to an end. The *Shan hai jing* consisted of two parts. The first, the "Classic of Mountains," was structured as a set of travels from one range of mountains to another, with each mountain being identified by its distinctive products or inhabitants and the types of offerings to be made there. Most scholars agree that these five chapters form the original core of a work that evolved over several centuries during the Warring States period and the Han.[47] The later sections, which present a vision of the world quite different from the core, consist of the "Classic of the Seas (*hai jing* 海經)" and the "Classic of the Great Waste (or 'Wilderness' *da huang jing*

大荒經)." These are treated by some scholars as a single work and by others
as two distinct strata. The "Classic of Seas" shifted to the horizontal dimension with accounts of ever more remote regions of the earth. These later
sections also introduced the principle familiar to modern anthropology of discovering traces of high antiquity at the edges of the earth. In the "Classic of
Seas" the antiquity discovered was the existing traces of the battles by means
of which the sages had imposed spatial order on the world.

The *Shan jing* is divided into twenty-six subsections formed from lists of
mountains, describing a total of 447 mountains found in the central land.
These mountains are linked as a journey or a procession. It thus uses the same
method as Renaissance cosmographies and *insulaires* that organized lists of
marvels and curiosities under the place where they were found and structured
the presentation by moving from place to place while locating each site only
in terms of the direction and distance from the preceding one.[48] Each entry
consists of the name of the mountain and information about its flora, fauna,
and minerals. Some also note prodigies, miraculous or divine beings that dwell
on the mountain, and mythological events. Rivers are mentioned only in association with the mountains from which they emerge. Twenty-four of the
twenty-six sections end with an account of the characteristics of the divinities of the region and the offerings that should be made to them. Many entries
also discuss the medicinal uses of plants and the events presaged by the appearance of some divine being or prodigy. I will here discuss the significance of
organizing the text as a procession, the import of focusing on mountains, and
the principles underlying the selection and categorization of contents.

As to organizing the text as a journey, Dorofeeva-Lichtmann has pointed
out that the *Shan jing* provides not just a model of the world, but rather "a
process-oriented scheme." By specifying a series of movements as its ground,
the text indicates the possibility of its repetition and thus provides both a prescription and a model for the performance of actions that organize space.[49]
The text of the *Shan hai jing* thus provides a world model within which the
reader can situate him or her self and actions in order to secure power or
efficacy. The theme of establishing authority by moving through the world
also echoes the account of Yu in the "Yu gong" and related texts discussed
in chapter one, in which the work of taming the flood consists of moving
along the major mountain ridges that would ultimately delimit the channels
of the rivers. This progress along the mountains likewise culminates in a procession through the world by Yu or the tribute bearers who follow his path
along the courses of the newly stabilized rivers. Thus, the organizing principle of the first part of the *Shan hai jing* recapitulates the labors of Yu as these
are recounted in earlier texts.

This link was not accidental, for within the text and in the memorial
presented to the court by its first editor, Liu Xin, this model of organizing
space for the purposes of imposing one's authority on the earth was attributed to Yu. The work is described as a by-product of his labors to tame the
flood. These labors followed the account in the "Yu gong" not only in taking

the form of a journey across the length and breadth of the subcelestial realm, but also in their account of the key flora, fauna, and minerals found at each mountain. According to Liu Xin, the very journey described in the "Yu gong," although with a different focus, produced the *Shan hai jing*. In his postface at the end of the work he wrote:

> The *Shan hai jing* appeared in the time of Yao and Shun. Long ago the great flood raged and swept through the Middle Kingdoms. The people lacked any foundation, perilously perched on hilltops or in nests in trees. Gun having failed, Emperor Yao had Yu carry on the work. Yu traveled for four years, following the mountains to cut down their trees and thereby fixing the high mountains and the great rivers. Yi and Bo Yi were in charge of driving away the animals [who lived mixed with the people], naming the mountains and rivers, classifying the plants, and distinguishing the quality of water and soil. The gods of the four sacred mountains [here a reference to the character "Four Peaks" who figured prominently in the *Shang shu*] assisted them to make a complete tour of the four quadrates, reaching to places where the tracks of men were rare, and where boats and chariots seldom came. On the inside [the *Shan jing*] they distinguished the mountains of the four quadrates and the center, and on the outside [the *Hai jing*] they separated the seas of the eight directions. They recorded the treasures and strange objects; the products of different regions; the places where waters, soils, plants, animals, insects, scaly creatures, and birds were found; where auspicious portents were concealed; and, beyond the four seas in isolated states, the unusual kinds of people. Yu divided the Nine Provinces and created tribute in accord with the quality of their soil, while Yi rated the quality of the different categories of things and thus wrote the *Shan hai jing*.[50]

Another reference to the text as the product of the work of Yu and his followers appears at the end of the *Shan jing*. Here Yu states he has passed through 5,370 mountains, gives the dimensions of the world, describes some of the products of mountains and their importance, and rehearses a common formula on the centrality of the *feng* and *shan* sacrifices at Mt. Tai.[51] The idea that the work was produced by Yu is also indicated by the fact that the complete text ends with the announcement: "The emperor then commanded Yu to apply soil in order to fix the Nine Provinces."[52] The significance of this last passage will be discussed in more detail.

Liu Xin's remarks about going along mountains to cut down trees, rating soils to establish tribute, and dividing the Nine Provinces refer to the "Yu gong," and his remarks about Yu's assistants derive from the other chapters in the *Shang shu*. However, these classical references are embedded in matters that figure only in the *Shan hai jing*. Thus, like other accounts of the world that developed in the late Warring States and the early empires—the model of Zou Yan, that of the *Huainanzi*, the *Mu Tianzi zhuan*—the *Shan hai jing* begins with the canonical model of the "Yu gong" and then extends it, insisting that the classic is too restricted in its geography and interests to account for the entire world.[53] The discussion of "naming" and "classifying" also directly echoes the accounts of Yu's work in the *Guo yu*. Thus, the first section of the *Shan hai jing* was clearly recognized in the early imperial period as a distillation of earlier accounts of Yu's taming the flood, while developing these in a new direction.

Although the first section of the work develops many of the themes laid out in earlier accounts of Yu's ending the flood, such as the "Yu gong," in the "Classic of the Seas" we find actual stories pertaining to the flood and the efforts of Yu to bring it to an end. This is part of a broader pattern, in which the geographic account of the "Classic of the Seas" is littered with references to the physical traces of battles in which early godlike rulers had established an orderly world through defeating rebels and monsters in battle. Many of these accounts culminate in the execution and mutilation of the criminals, whose bodies become permanent signs in the world of the ordering work of the early sages. Some accounts of such corpses that remain in the world are brief and lack all context, such as the statement that the archer Yi killed Zuochi.[54] However, there are several more detailed accounts of rebels who challenged the gods and were defeated in battle: "Xingtian [形天 "taking the form of Heaven"] battled for spirit power with the thearch [*yu di zheng shen* 與帝爭神]. The thearch cut off his head and buried him at Mt. Changyang. Then Xingtian made his nipples into eyes, his navel into a mouth, and took up his axe and shield to dance."[55] This posthumous defiance is not unique, for the text is full of transformed corpses (*shi* 尸). Some are the mutilated remains of criminals who transformed into sources of malevolent spirit power and continued to wield their weapons. Another such corpse is not itself a rebel but, as a victim of the simultaneous appearance of ten suns in the sky, became a physical trace of the earlier disorders produced by cosmic rebellion.[56] Thus, the world of the outer sections of the *Shan hai jing* is filled with mutated corpses that are the bloody inverse of the sages' tombs and towers described in other passages, the still potent traces of the sages' work.[57]

The two most important sets of tales deal with the Yellow Thearch's battle with Chi You and Yu's battles to control the flood. The former are part of a larger set of narratives using stories about the battle between drought and storm to develop a mythology of the introduction of combat into the human world as a form of political control.[58] In one story the Yellow Thearch kills Kui and the Thunder Beast to produce a drum, the chief means of giving signals in battle, with which he intimidates the world. In a more detailed account of the battle with Chi You, the Thearch sent down the Responding

Dragon and woman Ba who both serve to halt the rain and allow the Thearch
to kill Chi You. Both of these agents, however, could not reascend to Heaven,
so they remained in the world as producers of drought who figured in drought
prevention rituals in the period.[59] These agents of divine action that linger in
the world as threatening figures of drought and famine resemble the rebels'
corpses in being powerful and dangerous traces of the ancient work of the
sages left in the contemporary world. It is perhaps of significance that several
of the myths pertaining to the Yellow Thearch pertain to drought, just as those
dealing with Yu deal with the flood. As noted, the pairing of drought and
flood figures frequently in the rhetoric of the Warring States and the early
empires.

The last and largest body of references to sagely combat in the later sections of the *Shan hai jing* deal with Yu, who was also the mythic progenitor
of the first part of the text. These tales provide further examples of the early
sages creating order through killing rebels and leaving visible traces of their
work at the edges of the earth. They thus exemplify the discourse that explains
the flood as the consequence of rebellion or criminality and depicts the ending
of the flood as the consequence of the execution or exile of the rebels.

The stories in the *Shan hai jing* pertaining to the flood all deal with Yu's
struggles against Gong Gong and the flood that the latter had triggered
through his rebellion. They, and in a sense all the stories of battles between
gods and rebels in the text, present the structure of the world as the result of
a long process of conflict ultimately leading to the final imposition of proper
distinctions by a sage ruler. The first and most dramatic of these narratives is
as follows:

> Gong Gong's servant was named Xiangliu. He had nine heads in
> order to eat at all Nine Mountains. Whatever Xiangliu touched
> became marshes and valleys. Yu killed Xiangliu, but his blood putre-
> fied, so no seeds could be planted [in land touched by the blood].
> Yu dug it out to a depth of 3 *ren* [about 4.8 meters], flushed it out
> three times, and then took it [the dug up soil] and made the towers
> of all the thearchs [*zhu di zhi tai* 諸帝之臺] which lay to the north
> of Kunlun. . . . Xiangliu had nine heads with human faces, and the
> body of a blue-green snake.

In another version of the story, the bodies of water produced by the creature's leveling touch are bitter and nothing can dwell near them. Moreover,
Yu's slaying of Xiangliu is linked directly to his blocking the flood, and the
soil tainted by Xiangliu's blood grows no crops.[60]

What is noteworthy in these stories is the image of an enemy who
negated all elevation, devouring mountains and turning everything it touched
into lowlands. The figure of Xiangliu also echoes the account in the *Guo yu*
of Gong Gong and Gun, who both attempted "to topple the mountains to
fill up the lowlands." As noted in the *Shuo wen* passage quoted in chapter one,

note 38, Yu combatted the flood in part by having people dwell on higher land that survived as islands; the "provinces" that he created were originally such raised land. Moreover, in the "Tribute of Yu," he relied on moving through the mountains while toiling to channel the flood waters, and in the "Mountains" section of the *Shan hai jing* he appeared as the patron sage of travels through mountains and sacrifices to their spirits. Xiangliu, by contrast, is a spirit of lowlands, marshes, and flood, and thus the exact opposite of Yu and his mortal enemy. To mark his triumph, Yu reasserts the power of heights by erecting the towers of the Thearchs over the land rendered sterile by his adversary. In a striking image he constructs these towers with "cement" made from a mixture of earth and the blood of his vanquished foe. Thus, the towers of the Thearchs, like the corpses and drought spirits, are physical traces of a battle in which the defeated rebel forces are imperfectly absorbed into the landscape.

Although Gong Gong does not appear as an actor in the *Shan hai jing*, as he did in the *Huainanzi*, he figures through the agency of his "servant" (or "minister" *chen* 臣) Xiangliu. Each of this creature's nine heads ate at one of the mountains that formed the centers of each of the nine provinces, which indicates that it wreaked its havoc throughout the full expanse of China. Moreover, wherever it touched turned to swamps or rivers, so the harm inflicted by the monster would have taken the form of a universal flood in which the dry land throughout China was transformed into swamps and streams. Not surprisingly, it is Yu who slays the creature, directly in association with halting the flood. Here Xiangliu, and through him Gong Gong, are depicted as rebels who dissolve the world into a formless, watery mass. Their defeat and the containment of the water they have unleashed is marked by the erection of a tower or towers that recall the image of the tomb of Shun discussed in chapter one. This idea that Gong Gong triggered the flood as an act of rebellion but was defeated by Yu also appears explicitly in the "Cheng xiang" chapter that appears near the end of the *Xunzi*:

> Yu achieved merit and suppressed the flood.
>
> He eliminated what harmed the people, expelling Gong Gong.[61]

The *Xunzi* and the *Shan hai jing* thus both concur with the *Huainanzi* in attributing ultimate responsibility for the flood to the criminal acts of Gong Gong.

In addition to these lurid accounts of killings, putrefied blood, and sterile earth, the *Shan hai jing* also contains two names of mountains that refer to Yu's assault on the clouds and rain, and to his attack on Gong Gong.[62] Here once again the battles of the sages are translated into elements of the landscape, permanently visible traces of ancient struggles that created an orderly world. Finally, two passages near the end of the text deal with Yu's "spreading out soil [*bu tu* 布土]" to halt the flood and fix the Nine Provinces. The first of these simply mentions Yu with his father Gun, as though they worked together or were part of a single process, but the second treats Gun as a rebel whose death was essential to quelling the flood:

> The vast flood waters filled the heavens. Gun stole God-on-High's "swelling soil [xi rang 息壤]" to block up the floodwaters. He did not wait for God-on-High's command [ming 命, also "mandate"]. God-on-High ordered Zhurong to kill Gun at the side of Mt. Yu. Gun's [stomach] produced Yu. God-on-High then ordered Yu to spread out the soil in order to fix the Nine Provinces.[63]

The *Shan hai jing* ends with this line, presenting as the culmination of a sequence of rebellion and combat the shaping of the world whose structure was delineated in the first part of the book. The appearance in this narrative of Zhurong is of interest, for he had appeared in the fourth-century B.C. Chu silk manuscript as the god who restored the world by ordering the Heavens after it collapsed into chaos due to unspecified violations of taboos. The birth of Yu from the body of Gun by a process of metamorphosis offers yet another example of how the bodies of defeated rebels survive as traces in the later order. This bodily link of Gun and Yu will be further analyzed in chapter four.

Before proceeding with other texts it is useful to our study of the flood myths to examine why the *Shan hai jing* locates the ancient sages, their tombs, their battles, and their enemies in accounts of monstrous peoples and landscapes at the edges of the earth, or in an area "Within the Seas" that is a thematic extension of the distant lands. Why do the founding heroes of Chinese civilization, including the queller of the flood, appear as progenitors of the most distant peoples (on this see chapter four) and as actors at the remote periphery? There are at least four reasons for this phenomenon. First, distant realms can be equivalent to the ancient times when the sages lived. The equivalence of distance in space and in time, the vision of remote realms as a still present antiquity, is familiar to the modern West. Some early accounts of the New World suggested that its inhabitants still lived in the Golden Age, or even had escaped the Fall. Hostile versions placed them at the bottom of a scale of societies, corresponding to the early stages of men in the Old World.[64] Later tales of noble savages sometimes linked them with the warrior peoples of antiquity. Modern anthropology provided a complete discourse based on the assumption that tribal peoples in distant lands were "primitive" or "stone age" men, versions of our own remote ancestors still living in our world but not in our time. The conflation of remoteness in time and space thus became part of an ideology of power in which the "other" was assigned to the developmental status of infancy from which we had long escaped.[65]

For the authors of the *Shan hai jing* to write antiquity into their images of distant places is not dissimilar to this Western ethnology. Some early Chinese, in an idea related to the aforementioned theme of the separation of men from beasts through the cultural innovations of the sages, elaborated an evolutionary model that classified non-Chinese as more primitive and thus closer to the original human condition. Distant places and distant times had the common benefit of being unobservable, and hence open to imaginative projection. As one moved away from the familiar world into distant lands and ancient times, the constraints of direct knowledge fell away and familiar creatures were replaced by beings that were ever more bizarre and monstrous or ever closer to the perfect and the divine. Just as the ancient Greeks invented Ethiopians or Hyperboreans, and improvised freely on Scythians, as images of alterity, so they imagined people in antiquity who were radically different from themselves. The heroes of the Homeric epic were stronger than any modern man, and the people of the Golden and Silver ages even more alien. High antiquity and the earth's peripheries were alike as lands of fantasy and myth, so the creatures of one could slip easily into the other.[66] The ancient Chinese similarly attempted to define themselves through accounts of earlier or more distant peoples who were alternatively closer to the beasts or closer to the gods, and whose struggles provided a dramatic form in accounts of the elimination of the hybrid, chaotic, and bestial to the idea of an ordered world fashioned through the progressive drawing of ever clearer distinctions.

The second reason for locating sages amid the monstrous peoples at the edges of the earth is that the former were often man–animal hybrids or marked by bizarre physical features. Early texts tell how the Yellow Emperor had four faces or four eyes, others give him the features or body of a dragon, and still others call him a bear.[67] Fu Xi, the first of the sages in several accounts, and his consort Nü Gua were depicted in Han art with the lower bodies of snakes and the upper bodies of humans. Scattered passages in early texts also refer to physical deformities of sages, such as Shun's having four pupils in his eyes.[68] Finally, and most important, the idea of sages as hybrids and monsters had become sufficiently common that the Xunzi and other texts presented lists of virtually all the sages and their respective deformities, arguing that physical abnormality was a condition of sagehood.[69] These ideas were closely linked to the practice of physiognomy in early China, a doctrine suggesting that beings with extraordinary destinies would have extraordinary physical features.[70] There are several reasons for this belief: the nonhuman paternity of sages, their superhuman status, or their close links to the natural world. Whatever the reasons, there is no doubt that in the late Warring States and the early empires any discussion of hybrids or monstrosities could include reflections on sages. The role in accounts of taming the flood of hybrids, beasts, and the physical metamorphosis of men into animals or vice versa will be discussed at length in chapter four.

Physical deformities of sagehood

Third, the historical work of the sages in early Chinese accounts had been to separate humans from the animal domain. Virtually all the philosophical traditions spoke of a primitive age when humans had lived both physically and morally unseparated from animals. The sages had created the tools and introduced the moral and ritual practices that rescued people from their animal condition and created distinctions where none had existed before.[71] Given this model as a background, a model that provided the philosophical background to the tales of the flood, it was natural to find the sages at work in distant realms where both the cultural and physical separation of men from animals was blurred. This is particularly true in a text like the Shan hai jing, which takes as its ultimate theme the order underlying the cosmos and the manner in which that order came into being. The thematic importance of the sages' inventions is demonstrated by the fact that the work concludes with a series of entries enumerating many of them, from the invention of boats and char- iots (related to the text's interest in travel), through that of bows, to the cre- ation of musical instruments and dancing, and on to the introduction of crafts, agriculture, and the political state. Yu's taming the flood and thereby fixing the Nine Provinces concludes the last of these lists, demonstrating that for the authors of the Shan hai jing the ending of the flood was the final step in the sages' work of creating an orderly world.[72]

The final reason for finding the sages at the periphery is the idea that the ultimate demonstration of a ruler's power was the submission of distant peoples. This became a commonplace in the texts of the period, which repeat- edly note the geographic range of a ruler's pacifying power as the highest mark of his success.[73] This idea also manifested itself in the Han fascination with rare goods from distant places, the arrival of which showed that the ruler's power reached all corners of the earth. The clearest demonstrations of this are in the writings of Sima Xiangru, but it also figures in hymns for the Han ancestral temple from the reign of Emperor Wu, particularly those dealing with obtaining rare horses from Central Asia.[74] Thus, placing the early sages amid the monstrous peoples at the edges of the earth was related to emerging rep- resentations of power within the imperial state. Once again this theme is related to the tales of Yu and the flood, for the earliest systematic account of Yu's taming the flood takes the form of an account of his physical travels in the course of his toils and the manner in which these establish a model for the flow of tribute from the periphery to the center. This literal "flow" that moves along the rivers established by Yu's channeling of the flood established the relations of center and periphery that defined the structure of the newly ordered world. As will be discussed in the final section, the establishing of core and periphery is also mythically linked to the punishment of criminal- ity, specifically that of criminal offspring.

CRIMINALITY, FLOODS, AND THE EXILE OF SONS

Before turning in chapter three to the central role played by fathers and sons in the tales of the flood, it is essential to discuss a final aspect of the flood myths as tales of criminality or social disorder, an aspect that deals specifically with the question of creating an ordered world through the process of sepa- ration. The second section of Marcel Granet's classic Danses et légendes de la Chine ancienne is devoted to the study of myths and rituals dealing with the reconstruction of ordered time and space as an element in the establishment of a new regime. This analysis first focuses on the theme of the banishment of monsters or criminals to the four edges of the earth that correspond to the cardinal directions as a means of reestablishing order at the center.[75] The contents of Granet's discussion are too rich to be summarized here, but the model he develops provides crucial insights into certain aspects of the accounts of Gong Gong and Gun and thus to situating the mythology of the flood within the broader question of early Chinese ideas about the creation of spatial order.

The earliest version of the myth of the expulsion of four criminals to the edges of the earth as a means of re-creating order in the human world appears in the *Zuo zhuan*. The story first recounts how two early thearchs each had eight sons, whose great moral virtues were passed from one generation to another down to the time of Yao. While Yao for reasons that remain unexplained did not employ the descendants of the sixteen virtuous sons, Shun was able to do so. The story then proceeds:

> Long ago Thearch Hong had a worthless son who obstructed the dutiful and covered up for criminals, loved to exercise a maleficent power [*xiong de* 凶德], assimilated himself to wicked things, and associated with the recalcitrant, ill-spoken, and friendless. Everybody called him, "Chaos [*hun dun* 渾敦]." Shaohao had a worthless son who destroyed trust and rejected loyalty, was skilled at ornamenting wicked speech, was at ease with slanderers and employed the disobedient, practiced libels and assembled villains, and thereby insulted flourishing virtue. Everybody called him "Qiongqi [窮奇 'Completely Devious']." Zhuanxu had a worthless son who was unteachable, was incapable of all proper speech, rejected all advice, remained ill-spoken in the face of any pardon, and ignored all brilliant virtue, holding it in contempt. He thereby disturbed all natural constancy. Everybody called him "Taowu [檮杌 'Benighted Trouble']".
> These three clans transmitted their maleficence [*xiong* 凶] across the generations, increasing their ill repute, down to the time of Yao. Yao could not eliminate them. Jinyun had a worthless son who was greedy for food and drink and craved bribes. His desires grew ever more extravagant, so he could never be satisfied. He amassed grain and fruits, knowing no restraint or limit, sharing nothing with the orphans and solitaries, and showing no pity for the impoverished. Everybody compared him with the above "Three Maleficences [*san xiong* 三凶]" and called him "Taotie [Glutton]." Shun became Yao's minister, performed the guest ritual at the gates of the four directions [an action which figured prominently in the *Shi ji*'s account of Shun's career], and exiled the four maleficent clans. He expelled them to the four edges of the earth, so they could ward off sprites and demons. So when Yao died the entire world united as one with a

single mind to support Shun to be Son of Heaven, because he had
employed the sixteen ministers [the descendants of the virtuous sons
of the early Thearchs] and expelled the Four Maleficences.[76]

This story divides the offspring of earlier sage rulers and the descendants of
those offspring into two classes, those descended from two groups identified
by the magic number eight and those descended from a single son. The former
are virtuous and promoted to be ministers, while the latter are evil and are
expelled to the four edges of the earth. At the edges they serve as "converted"
demons used to ward off other demons, and their expulsion results in a united
and orderly world.[77] Raising the first group of descendants to high office and
expelling the second are the decisive acts that cause the people to rally around
Shun and thus transform him into a ruler. A similar, though less elaborate,
story in the *Zuo zhuan* describes how Thearch Ku had two wicked sons who
dwelt in the forest and continually fought. The subsequent thearch despatched
them to different places on the earth's surface where they became the regulating spirits of specified asterisms.[78]

As Granet has suggested, this story suggests a schema in which the establishment of a new regime entailed the ritual expulsion of the lingering influences of earlier rulers that through the process of decay over time had become
polluting or malevolent. Thus, it is the descendants, and in mythic terms the
sons, of earlier rulers who are the target of expulsion. The fixing of the
number at four and their assignment to the four edges of the world shows
that this is a ritual reconstruction of ordered space, a fact emphasized by the
naming of the first wicked son "Chaos." In a celebrated story in the *Zhuangzi*,
this name applies to a formless being who embodied the primal state of non-
division that is recapitulated in the flood, and who is slain by spirits of the
directions who bore a set of orifices into his undifferentiated body.[79] Finally,
the beings exiled to the four edges of the earth, as formerly evil beings sub-
jected by the power of the new ruler, are converted into protective powers
who guard against the very malevolent forces which they had previously
embodied.

One interesting problem in this narrative is the distinction between the
good sons who appear in groups of eight and the bad ones who appear as
individuals. While this feature is not explained, it is significant that in the
myths of Yao and Shun there is a parallel division between a group of nine
good sons and one wicked individual: "Thereupon Yao gave his two daughters to Shun as wives in order to observe his inner government, and then had
his nine sons live with Shun in order to observe his outer government. . . .
Yao's two daughters did not dare because of their nobility to be arrogant
towards Shun's parents. They truly developed the way of wives. Yao's nine sons
all became increasingly sincere."[80] In contrast with this collective group of
nameless sons who become Shun's virtuous followers, the single heir of Yao,
Dan Zhu, is portrayed in virtually all texts as a villain whose failings rendered
him unsuitable for kingship and led all the people of the world to reject him.
Two passages in the *Lü shi chun qiu* similarly tell of Yao's entrusting his ten

sons to Shun. One also refers to Shun's nine sons, but as we will see it is only the wicked heir Shang Jun who is cited.[81] This recurring pattern that contrasts multiple junior sons who remain good with the single heir who becomes wicked indicates that it is the fact of being the heir, the single true successor of the father, that results in a figure being treated as evil or unsuitable. A collective group of junior sons who cannot take the father's place are regularly described as virtuous servants or ministers. This pattern will be discussed further in chapter three.

A related tradition preserved in several Han texts tells how the deceased sons of Thearch Zhuan Xu became disease demons who, like the Four Maleficences described earlier, were scattered to key locations throughout the world:

> Thearch Zhuan Xu had three sons who died at birth and departed to become plague demons. One lived on the Yangzi and became the malaria demon. One lived on the Ruo River and became the *wangliang* demon [a malevolent spirit targeted in exorcism rituals]. One lived in the corners of houses and controlled plagues that inflicted disease on people. So at the end of the year when the agricultural work was done they expelled the plague demon in order to see off the old, welcome the new, and bring good fortune into the house. Generation after generation imitated this, and it evolved into the exorcism ritual used when building a house.[82]

The sons who become demons in this account are examples of the broader pattern in which people who die premature or violent deaths consequently turn into malevolent forces that attack humanity. It is noteworthy, however, because it shows how one version of the story of the dispersal of the offspring of sage rulers to the different regions of the world provided an origin myth for major diseases and baleful forces that threatened the Han Chinese and how this in turn provided an account of the origins of major rituals of exorcism. It is also significant that in the story of Thearch Ku's two wicked sons, one of them is described as the cause of a disease, although this explanation is ultimately rejected.

While the *Zuo zhuan* offers the most complete version of the schema of the ritual dispersal of wicked sons to the edges of the earth as a means of restoring order, the restoration of the world through the ritual expulsion of four villains to each of the cardinal directions became a central feature of several flood narratives. We have already seen one example of this in the "Shun dian" in which the expulsions of Gong Gong, Gun, Huan Dou, and the San Miao played a major role in Shun's establishment of his power. This story also figured in many Warring States and Han texts.[83] As we have seen, the first three figures appear as the destructive villains or embodiments of chaos in the myths of the flood, with Huan Dou in a peripheral role. The last appear as the malefactors who introduced violent punishments into the human realm without also introducing justice. In the major mythic account of this story in the "Lü xing" chapter of the *Shang shu*, their action leads to a collapse into chaos of random violence that is ended only by the restoration of the world through the Yellow Thearch's domestication of violence in the form of warfare and punishments for the sake of order.[84] Thus, in the accounts of the flood the schema of establishing a new regime through the expulsion of the lingering, malevolent influences of earlier ones was transformed into a narrative of the restoration of an ordered space through the expulsion of those figures who embodied the total social collapse that was given graphic form in the deluge.

The flood version of the expulsion schema also repeatedly speaks of laying out the four directions as a central step in the restoration of order. Thus, in the *Shi ji* and *Da Dai li ji* versions cited in note 79 each of the malefactors is responsible for the moral transformation of the barbarians associated with the direction to which he is exiled. Shun's role as the sage who exiles the Four Maleficences is also specifically linked in the account to his service at the four gates. As we have seen, this service figured in the *Shang shu* and *Shi ji* accounts of Shun as part of an expanding series of spaces that he brought to order, beginning with his own household and extending outward to the limits of the world. In these same accounts, the expulsion is also closely paired with the incipient ruler's triumphal tour of the four quarters of the earth, the positive form of his negative expulsions as a means of demarcating and ordering space through completing a directional mandala.[85]

The chief difference between the *Zuo zhuan* account of the directional ritual expulsion and the flood version of the same myth is that the exiled evils in the former are sons rather than rebellious ministers or alien peoples. However, while the versions of the expulsion linked to the flood do not discuss the question of sons, the relations of father to son, and their treatment of one another as criminals or malefactors, figure repeatedly in the myths of the flood. Thus, to fully understand the significance of the flood myths in early China, and the significance of criminality in those myths, we must turn to the issue of the role within the myths of family relations, particularly those of father and son.

CONCLUSION

The flood myths in China not only provided a dramatic depiction of general ideas about the founding of social order through the imposition of hierarchical divisions, but also served as origin myths of the political order. They did this by portraying the flood that destroyed all boundaries and distinctions as the works of rebels or criminals, and thus transforming the act of taming the flood into a question of suppressing violence or insurrection. The earliest versions of this political reading of the flood, those in the *Mencius* and the *Shang shu*, did not tell of rebels who caused the flood, but rather linked the deluge with the collapse of the separation of men from beasts that was the foundation of civilization. This collapse, in turn, was described as the prototype for the wanton criminality of later evil kings, usurpers, rebels, and deviant philosophers.

It was only such late Warring States and early imperial texts as the *Xunzi*, *Shan hai jing*, and *Huainanzi* that first present tales of monstrous rebels whose defiance of the early kings created the flood and whose defeat and punishment became the primary method of restoring distinctions and order to the world. The most elaborate work on this theme is the *Shan hai jing*, which in many ways is an encyclopedic work structured around the mythical themes associated with the flood. The entire work, which presents a mythic geography of the world, is attributed to Yu, or rather to ministers of Yu who accompanied him on his travels while he was channeling the flood and recorded the world that he shaped. The first part, the "Canon of the Mountains," gives an account of the Chinese world as a set of mountain ranges each defined by their particular flora, fauna, minerals, and gods. This emphasis on mountains as a structuring element of the world is basic to accounts of Yu's work in taming the flood, and the theme of the distinctive local characteristics is part of the theme of tribute, the establishment of which is also attributed to Yu in the earliest texts on his work.

More important for the study of the myths of the flood is the second part of the text, the "Canon of the Seas." This work, which describes the distant reaches of the earth and the strange beings who dwell there, is littered with accounts of the physical traces of battles between the early sages or thearchs and malevolent rebels. The most important of these are tales of the Yellow Thearch's battle with Chi You, an early Chinese myth of the origins of warfare that is closely linked to tales of drought and storm, and the tales of Yu's taming of the flood. The latter tales include references not only to his hydrological work, but also to his battles with and execution of the monster Xiangliu and the monster's master Gong Gong.

The latter is the most frequently cited malefactor, a figure whose very name indicated that he was an embodiment of violence and the flood. In some accounts he was a monstrous rebel who battled with the early sage-kings or thearchs, in others he was the lord of a monstrous servant who devoured the mountains and turned all land to swamps, while in still others he was an early king who either sought to level the mountains and dam up the rivers or imposed his rule through the power of the flood waters. In all cases, the defeat and execution of Gong Gong or his servant were necessary to make the earth once again habitable and suitable for agriculture.

Another figure associated with the origins of the flood, whose name and mythic attributes overlapped closely with those of Gong Gong, was Gun. However, while many texts treated him as a mythic double or follower of Gong Gong, others treated him as a servant of the early sages who unsuccessfully attempted to tame the flood and was consequently executed. In these latter versions of his myth he was identified as the father of Yu and his predecessor in the battle against the deluge, and his failure was attributed to his stubbornness, insubordination, or insistence on using faulty techniques of

water control. While certain modern scholars have speculated on the existence of early deluge myths in which Gun was the flood-taming hero, no real
evidence of these has survived. Instead he figures as a mediating figure in
a triad formed with Gong Gong and Yu. The former is the embodiment of
the flood and its criminality, the latter the tamer of the flood, and Gun in the
middle associated alternatively with one or the other. However, even when
linked to Yu, he remains a failure and a dark shadow that sets off the glory
of the flood-taming sage. The significance of his role as the father of Yu, and
of father and son relations in general within the myths of the flood, will be
discussed in chapter three.

A final set of myths that treat the flood as the result of criminality are
the references in the *Shang shu* to the execution of several criminals and the
exile of others to the four edges of the earth. As Marcel Granet has shown,
these tales are versions of more wide-ranging myths in which a new regime
imposes order by exiling the noxious traces of its predecessors to the edges
of the earth. These noxious traces are depicted as the sons or descendants of
previous rulers, and their exile not only serves to cleanse the center but transform these evil beings into servants of the new order, potent demons who
impose order on the demonic forces that dwell in the far reaches of the world.
A curious pattern of several forms of this myth is that numbered clusters of
sons of earlier rulers figure as ministers and forces of order, while the single
heirs of the rulers are invariably evil and are consequently expelled. The
reasons for this pattern, and its links to Chinese myths of the flood, will be
discussed in the next chapter.

CHAPTER THREE

FLOOD TAMING AND LINEAGES

The largest and ritually most important familial unit of this period, as discussed in chapter two of *The Construction of Space in Early China*, was the lineage, which was defined by the generational transmission of status and property from fathers to sons. Even within the individual household, where the centrality of the marriage that introduced a female outsider challenged the purely masculine nature of the lineage, the links of father to son remained of central importance. Consequently, the relation of father to son was a major defining element of kin structure in the period. As the myths of the flood depicted the characteristics of regulated spaces through a narrative of the transition from chaos to order, they also depicted the transition from improper or nonexistent ties between fathers and sons to fully formed links that allowed the transmission of character, property, and rank. This transition is marked in the stories by the fact that in the original human condition neither character nor status was successfully transmitted from father to son, while the appearance of the regulated household finally made possible the inheritance of the father's moral character and worldly status by his offspring. Thus, the emergence of proper ties between father and son, that is, lineage as a form of kinship organization, became a central theme of the tales of the flood in early China.

THE SAGES AS BAD FATHERS AND SONS

The definitive form of this change, and one that is central to the stories, is the introduction of the dynastic state in the act of transferring kingship from Yu to his son Qi. In this context the prior period, marked by the transmission of supreme authority from the king to a chosen minister, was an age in which the proper bonds between father and son had not yet been established. By the middle of the Warring States period the narrative of the flood had come to span the reigns of Yao, Shun, and Yu.[1] This period in early Chinese myths is distinguished by the fact that kingship was transmitted not from father to son but by the king selecting the best man in the world as his minister and ultimately his successor. Modern scholars have generally agreed that these myths arose to justify the principle of granting office on the basis of merit rather than heredity or to deal with the tensions between the principle of heredity that defined the dynastic state and the principle of Heaven's appointment of the best man as ruler, which justified the transition from dynasty to dynasty within a larger cycle.[2]

While this political reading of the myths is certainly correct as far as it goes, it is noteworthy that these tales of a world prior to the existence of the dynastic state are also accounts of a world in which the true family and the virtues that underpinned it did not yet exist. The family in Warring States and early imperial China, like those in most times and places, was a social unit that was constituted across time. It fully performed its functions and was capable of perpetuating itself only to the extent that property and status were transmitted across the generations from fathers to sons or, in some cases, to daughters. Without such transmission, groups based on kin ties could not cohere for more than a single generation. Thus, the inability of rulers to transmit their positions to their sons indicated either that these rulers were failed fathers who could not form a family or that the conditions for the formation of a family did not yet exist in their time. This state of affairs in antiquity is suggested by Sima Qian near the end of the first chapter of his *Shi ji*:

> From the Yellow Thearch to the time of Shun and Yu they all had the same surname but varied the names of their states in order to make clear their respective brilliant powers/virtues [*de* 德]. Thus the Yellow Thearch's state name was "Bear," that of Thearch Zhuan Xu was "Gaoyang," that of Thearch Ku was "Gaoxin," that of Thearch Yao was "Tang," and that of Thearch Shun was "Yu [Forester]." Thearch Yu's state was "Xia," but he took a separate family name, using the surname Si. Qie's state was named "Shang," and he had the surname Zi. Qi's state was "Zhou," and he had the surname Ji.[3]

Here all the rulers prior to Yu have state names without family surnames, while those after him have both states and surnames. Thus, in drawing together the myths of Yao, Shun, and Yu to form a single system, the writers of Warring States and early imperial China posited a parallel between, on the one hand, the transition from a universal flood to an ordered landscape and, on the other, the shift from a world without lineages (as marked by the possession of surnames) and one in which lineages existed. The collapse of all physical boundaries that had characterized the age of the flood was mirrored by the absence of those social divisions that constituted proper relations within the household and in the encompassing lineage. In such a schema the emergence of an ordered world and an ordered household realm were two parallel processes of fashioning regulated spaces out of chaos. For this reason the tale of Yu was also a tale about the relations of fathers and sons, as was that of Yao and Shun to a lesser extent.

During Warring States and early imperial China, the inability of Yao and Shun to transmit the kingdom to their sons was part of a much broader pattern in which fathers and sons were placed in regular opposition to one another both in moral and ritual terms. One aspect of this is the widespread belief that sages were the product of the mating of mortal women with gods or spirits and hence that no sage or dynastic founder was actually the son of his putative human father. Such beliefs are attested in the origin myths of the Zhou and Shang lineages, and by the time of the Han such beliefs were applied to all earlier sage-rulers, Confucius, and the founder of their own dynasty. Indeed, in the case of Confucius the spirit paternity of the sage is linked directly to the fact that he did not even know the site of his father's tomb.[4] Another example of this radical tension between fathers and sons is the *Zuo zhuan* passage previously cited in which the "Four Maleficences" who must be expelled to establish order are themselves the sons of sage-rulers, or the Han version in which plagues and major diseases are produced by the dead sons of a ruler.

More significant is the recurring pattern in early Chinese myths in which exemplary men have wicked fathers and themselves produce evil offspring. Throughout the tales of the sages preserved from this period it is virtually a rule that wherever the transition between generations is noted in the text it is marked by an inversion of moral character or worth. A supremely worthy man or sage invariably has a bad father, if the father is mentioned, and the son of the sage in turn is a bad man. This pattern has been pointed out by several modern Japanese scholars, who have collected numerous examples of such moral inversions between the generations.[5] Even more notable is the fact that this pattern was already pointed out in several Chinese texts written as early as the middle of the Warring States period. Thus, one story in the *Guo yu* relates how an official charged with educating the heir apparent declined the task by stating that he could do no good by working at such a task:

> The king said, "If you rely on the son's own goodness, then you can make him good." [The official] replied, "If there is goodness in the heir, then he will desire goodness, and good people will come to him. If he does not desire goodness, then the good will not be employed. Thus Yao had Dan Zhu, Shun had Shang Jun, Qi had Wu Guan, Tang had Tai Jia, King Wen had Guan and Cai. These five kings all possessed the highest primal virtuous power [*yuan de* 元德], but they had villainous sons. How could it be that the fathers did not desire them to be good? It was because the sons were not capable of it."[6]

This discussion appears in a text associated with the *ru* tradition that routinely celebrated the virtues of the early sages beginning with Yao. Nevertheless, the

speaker posits as an undeniable principle that the supreme sages routinely produced villainous sons, and he provides an exhaustive list of examples to
demonstrate his case. This clearly indicates that the idea of the sages as failed
fathers was already widespread among Warring States scholars and that this
theory was ultimately grounded in the now canonical examples of Yao and
Shun as kings who could not pass the kingship to their sons because of the
wickedness of the latter.

An identical list is given in the late Warring States or early Han period
text *Han Feizi* in order to demonstrate that the sage kings were those
who punished their own closest kin for the good of the state. The same argument, without reference to specific sages, is suggested in a model of history
proposed in the *Shang Jun shu*. In this model, exclusive concern for
immediate kin is held to typify the most primitive state of primal chaos.
A well-ordered society then progressively emerges through worthy men's
initial introduction of the transitional principle of honoring the worthy (i.e.,
themselves), followed by the sages' establishment of a public realm formed
by appointed officials who put into practice the laws and punishments
established by the ruler.[7] Here the unmentioned empirical fact of the sages'
sons invariably being the moral inversion of their fathers is turned into the
general legalist principle that proper government depends on the negation of
kin ties.

It is an interesting feature of these lists that Qi, Yu's son, is listed as a sage
whose own son Wu Guan is unworthy. This position appears in several early
texts.[8] Moreover, there is a tradition of a major war between Qi as king of
the Xia dynasty and an enemy people, the Guan Hu, who in some texts were
described as offshoots of the Xia line and phonetically are a simple inversion
of the sounds of Wu Guan.[9] This is significant because in many texts Qi is
treated as a deviant or criminal, acting as the moral inversion of his father
Yu.[10] Thus, he figures either as the unworthy son whose moral perversity
marks his father Yu as a sage or as a worthy king in his own right who consequently must be provided with an unworthy son of his own to demonstrate
his moral character and status as a sage.[11] In short, so prevalent was the idea
that the early sages had criminal sons that it had become a necessary attribute or hallmark of sagely status. To have had a virtuous heir in this mythic
age would have suggested the moral weakness of the father. This is all the
more striking because in some texts the kin enemies who are defeated by Qi
in texts that celebrate him as a sage are instead conquered by Yu.[12] Thus, there
was some disagreement between the Chinese of the late Warring States and
the early empires as to who was the true sage who founded the Xia dynasty,
but, whoever it was, he had to have a villainous son and engage in war with
rebellious kin.

While by the Warring States it had become a conventional idea that all
early sages had criminal sons, the standard figures who epitomized this topos,
and who were the ultimate malefactors, were Dan Zhu and Shang Jun, the

sons of Yao and Shun. The latter two were the classic models of those who transferred their position to a man selected as the most worthy. Some texts demonstrate the high degree of their public spirit and virtue by noting that they did not transmit their position to their sons.[13] Still other texts, primarily those outside the *ru* tradition, even stated that sages such as Yao had a "rep- utation for being unloving (*bu ci zhi ming* 不慈之名)," that they were poor fathers who could not teach their sons, or in the case of Shun that they were unfilial.[14] Since Yao and Shun defined themselves as sages in part by rejecting their sons and transferring their status and power to non-kin, yet at the same time were to be treated as the highest moral exemplars, it was necessary that their heirs had to become classic figures of those who were unworthy.

The role of Dan Zhu and Shang Jun as definitive figures of villainy, placed in exact opposition to their fathers who were the types of moral excellence, is clearly articulated in the *Huainanzi*:

> There are those whose persons are correct and natures good, who in firm resolve perfect their excellence, who in righteous indigna- tion carry out their duty, who by nature are open to persuasion, and without study accord with the Way. Such are Yao, Shun, and King Wen. There are those who sink into drunkenness and licentiousness, who cannot be taught with the Way nor enlightened through virtu- ous power. A severe father cannot correct them, nor a worthy teacher transform them. Such are Dan Zhu and Shang Jun. . . . There are those who above do not attain the excellence of Yao and Shun and below do not reach the baseness of Shang Jun. They are not so beau- tiful as Xi Shi nor so ugly as Mo Mu. These are those who can be enlightened through education, and upon whom fine blessings can be bestowed.[15]

Here Yao and Shun on the one hand, and Dan Zhu and Shang Jun on the other, define the two extreme positions that delimit the complete moral range of humanity. No one could be better than Yao and Shun, or worse than their two sons. Just as the legendary beauty Xi Shi and the supremely ugly Mo Mu marked out the full range of possibilities for physical attractiveness, the sages and their sons mark the apogee and the nadir of human character. The former accord with the Way without any teaching, and their emotions are fully mobilized in the pursuit of good. The latter are impervious to all edu- cation and are sunk in complete depravity. Here the moral inversions that mark generational shifts in the pre-dynastic era is worked out with mathe- matical rigor, taking the form of a swing from one absolute extreme to the other.

By the Eastern Han, texts such as the *Lun heng* repeatedly used the paired figures of Dan Zhu and Shang Jun as markers of the lowest possible point of

human character, of an absolute wickedness that was fixed in nature and
beyond the reach of any moderating influence:

> When Yangshe Shiwo was first born, his cry resembled a wild dog
> or wolf, and when he grew up his nature was wicked. He suffered
> calamity and died. He received this nature while still in his mother's
> womb. Dan Zhu and Shang Jun are in the same category.

> Zhou's [evil last king of the Shang dynasty] evil was present when
> he was a child. [Yangshe] Shiwo's rebellion was perceived in the
> sound he made when just born. When children are just born and
> have not yet come into contact with objects, who causes them to be
> perverse? Dan Zhu was born in Yao's palace, and Shang Jun was born
> in Shun's dwelling. At that time even neighboring houses were enfe-
> offed, so those with whom one came in contact were mostly good,
> and those at the side of the two thearchs were certainly mostly wor-
> thies. But Dan Zhu was arrogant and Shang Jun cruel. They both
> lost the thearch's power, and have served as a warning for successive
> generations.

> Dan Zhu and Shang Jun had already been influenced [literally
> "dyed" ran 染] by the moral transformations worked by Yao and Shun,
> but Dan Zhu was arrogant and Shang Jun cruel. They were of
> supremely wicked substance [zhi e zhi zhi 至惡之質], and received
> no change from [being dyed] indigo or vermilion.[16]

A similar idea appears in the Warring States text Shizi, which states that at the
time of Yao and Shun the entire world was well governed, and that Dan Zhu
and Shang Jun alone did not participate in this universal moral transformation.[17]

Dan Zhu is also marked as a violent figure by the fact that in several
texts Yao presents him with a game of chess or go. Both games served as substitutes for warfare that were given to bellicose people whom one wished to
lead into more peaceful pursuits.[18] As a result of Dan Zhu's misconduct, he
was exiled to the Dan River in the south, a river for which he apparently
served as an eponym. This theme of exile to a remote region links his story
to the aforementioned tales about the earlier malefactors who were expelled
to the four directions in the mythology of the flood.[19]

In reciprocal relation to Dan Zhu and Shang Jun, the wicked sons of sage
fathers, were Gun and Gu Sou, the wicked fathers of sage sons. The crimes
of Gun and his relation to Yu have already been discussed, and they will be
the topic of further analysis later and in the final chapter. The story of Gu
Sou and his repeated attempts in alliance with his second wife and Shun's
brother Xiang to murder Shun, along with other discussions of Gu Sou's hostility and Shun's attempts to placate him, were elaborated in their greatest
detail in the Mencius and then carried forward into later texts.[20]

Apart from these stories of Gu Sou's attempts to murder Shun, another mythical element that highlights the opposition between the two figures is the tradition preserved in several early texts that Shun had two pupils in his eyes. He hence was named "Double Flower (*chong hua* 重華)," while Gu Sou was blind and hence named or entitled "Blind Man (*gu* 瞽, or 'Blind Musician')."[21] Since several of the texts that referred to Shun's double pupils state explicitly that they indicated that he possessed "double acuity [*chong ming* 重明]," the contrast between the blindness of the father and the clear vision of the son provided a physical expression of their opposed moral natures.

This pattern of opposition between fathers and sons can be explained in several ways. First, it was a necessary condition of a world in which the father's status, in this case political authority, was not to be transmitted to the son. Such an explicit rejection of the son by the father entailed that if the latter was a sage, then the former had to be a criminal. This idea underlies the formulaic observations cited in note 14 that Yao had a reputation for not being loving, that is, that he lacked the virtue of the true father. At the same time, in agreeing to become the heir of the ruler rather than of his own father, the sage rejected the latter and inverted the familial hierarchy by placing himself above his own parent. This underlies the idea cited in the same note that Shun was unfilial, as well as the tradition that celebrated Yao's daughters who despite their higher status were able to serve Shun's parents (see chapter two, note 76). Indeed, the emphatic insistence on Shun's filial piety in the *Mencius* and texts derived from its account almost certainly reflect the need to defend the sage from these widespread accusations of betraying his father.

THE DEMON CHILD

If the significance of these stories as an exploration of the ties between fathers and sons was limited to the portrayal of an absence of true lineages in ancient times that were associated with the antediluvian chaos, a chaos that ended with the imposition of proper divisions, then it would have had little importance for our understanding of Warring States and Han Chinese. It would in such a case have been nothing more than an antiquarian account of the origin of the lineage in high antiquity and a reservoir of classical precedents for attacks on the hereditary transmission of status.[22] However, these accounts of the radical opposition between fathers and sons in fact express a basic structural principle of the Chinese kin system that persisted throughout the imperial period. This principle is already suggested in the *Zuo zhuan* account that opposed single heirs, who were treated as vicious criminals, with collective groups of sons who were regarded as virtuous. It is the fact of being an heir, the son who becomes a *duplicate* of the father in order to replace him, that turned the single son into a threat to his parent and consequently in the terms of the values underlying the lineage, a villain. Showing the significance of this principle requires first an extended detour into Chinese beliefs about children who threatened the lives of their parents or otherwise cursed them. It will be shown that such offspring were distinguished by being both too distant from their parents and too close. This will be followed by a demonstration that the wicked sons or fathers of sages possessed features or performed acts that made them duplicates of these exemplary figures (i.e., too close) as well as their moral opposites (i.e., too distant).

The idea that certain children were destined to destroy their families appears as early as the *Zuo zhuan*. This text tells stories of "wolf children," infants whose howls indicated that they possessed an animal nature that would lead them to destroy their families; consequently, they should be killed.[23] It is significant that one such child, Yangshe Shiwo, is cited twice in passages by Wang Chong quoted earlier in association with Dan Zhu as the image of the child who is irremediably evil by his very nature. This belief in animal children has parallels with the later doctrine of the divine conception of sages. Both groups of children are the product of a break in familial transmission that introduces a distinction in kind between the father and his son. In fact, the wolf child is only one of several types of children in early Chinese literature whose actions or circumstances at birth indicated that they would harm their parents. Here I will examine these types of children, suggest basic principles underlying their inauspicious nature, and link these principles to ideas about the nature of childhood and the family. I will focus on the Warring States and Han periods, but also show how these ideas and attitudes survived into late imperial China as constant features of the idea of "family" in China.

References to children who should not be reared because the circumstances of their birth indicated that they would harm or destroy their parents are scattered throughout the texts of the early period. They are usefully summarized in the late Eastern Han *Feng su tong yi* by Ying Shao. Since Ying Shao, like Wang Chong before him, criticizes these ideas as "popular" or "vulgar" theories, it is clear that they were widespread among all levels of the population. Ying Shao lists at least five types of threatening offspring in addition to the wolf children. Since these instances survive not in the transmitted text, but in quotations preserved in Tang and Song florilegia, we cannot be sure that there were not other categories that have vanished entirely.[24]

First, Ying Shao notes the widespread belief that children born on the fifth day of the fifth month, close to the summer solstice, would harm their parents and thus should not be reared. This also applies to children born in the first month. The belief in such dangerous dates appears in the *Shi ji*, as early as stories said to take place in the fourth century B.C. In later times the danger was explained by the fact that those born at the solstice were "owl children," once again animal spirits who in this case shared the unfilial character of that bird. We have no explicit evidence that this belief in dangerous owl children already existed in the Han. However, the common practice in that period of protecting houses at the solstice with talismans or figures made of peach wood and other apotropaic plants, as well as a taboo on climbing onto roofs in order to repair them out of fear of encountering ghosts there, clearly demonstrate the belief that hostile spirits would attack at this time. Bans in the calendrical literature on sexual relations on this date also indicate the belief that children *conceived* at this time, like those *born* then, would be possessed or corrupted by demonic forces.[25]

The third category of dangerous births was triplets and, presumably, any larger number of children who entered the world in a collective birth. The "popular theory" explaining this taboo states that in births of three or more "the children resemble domesticated animals," that is, they form an animal litter rather than a normal human birth. Fear of multiple births and consequent infanticide appear in many cultures, although it is interesting that in early China twins were still considered human, and only births of three or more were taken as proof of an animal nature. Later collections of stories pertaining to uncanny events or beings contain accounts of human mothers giving birth to mixed litters of human and animal infants.[26] These were clearly later versions of the beliefs demonstrated in the *Feng su tong yi.*

A fourth category of offspring that should not be reared was sons born in the same month as the father. In refuting the belief that such sons would kill their fathers, Ying Shao pointed out that Duke Huan of Lu was born in the same month as his father, yet did him no harm. Interestingly, as Ying Shao notes, Duke Huan's personal name was Zitong (子同) "identical" or "the son is identical." I will return to this issue of the problematic nature of too close an identity between the son and the father.

A fifth category that should not be reared was infants born with mustaches and a beard. The popular theory behind this belief asserted that only in their mid-forties did men develop full beards, so a child who had facial hair at birth would harm its parents.

The last category is the *wu sheng zi* (寤生子, literally "children born awake"), a disputed term whose earliest surviving use is in the *Zuo zhuan.* Ying Shao, the first scholar to provide an explicit gloss, states that popular belief in his time held that children were normally born with their eyes closed, but *wu sheng* children arrived with their eyes open. Consequently, they would harm their parents and should not be reared. The story in the *Zuo zhuan* narrates how the mother of Lord Zhuan of Zheng was frightened by the fact that he was *wu sheng.* She consequently named him "Wusheng" and favored his younger brother. The first major commentary to the *Zuo zhuan,* that by Du Yu in the third century A.D., follows Ying Shao's reading that the term indicated being born with the eyes open.[27]

This idea continued into the Age of Disunion. A fragment of the *History of the Southern Yan* (one of the sixteen kingdoms of the fourth century A.D.) recounts how a son of the ruler was born with his eyes open, and the father cited the story in the *Zuo zhuan* as a precedent for the event.[28] Finally, an anecdote in the *Lie xian zhuan,* perhaps of Eastern Han date, although possibly a later addition, tells how the mother of the immortal Muyu worked as a midwife. Once a child was born with its eyes open, which greatly frightened her. That evening a figure appeared to her in a dream holding the infant. This spirit visitor announced that the newborn child was an incarnation of the Master of Lifespans (*si ming jun* 司命君). In recompense for the midwife's assistance with his entry into the world, the Master promised to make her son an immortal.[29] This story not only reiterates the idea that a newborn infant with open eyes was a cause for alarm, but explains the event as evidence that the child was not a normal being, but rather a powerful spirit.

However, even while many early and medieval sources demonstrate the belief that *wu sheng* children were identified as those who were born with their eyes open because of their nonhuman nature, a more skeptical tradition also developed over the course of the centuries. Sima Qian's early Han retelling of the *Zuo zhuan* story simply states that "the birth [of Lord Zhuan] was difficult." Late imperial commentators on the *Zuo zhuan*, probably on the basis of Sima Qian's sentence, rejected the idea that *wu sheng* meant to be born with the eyes open. They argued instead that *wu* was used for a homophonous character (*wu* 悟) that meant "contrary" and that this term indicated a breech birth in which the infant's position was the inversion or "contrary" of a normal child's. However, the earlier gloss is clearly supported by the bulk of the evidence. The later reading reflects little more than a general suspicion of "superstition" that was also shared by Sima Qian.

These six types of children who threatened their parents can be divided into two categories: those who are dangerous because they are too far removed from the parents, that is, animals or spirits in the form of children (wolf children, children born on the summer solstice, triplets), and those who are dangerous because they are too close, that is, those who appear with adult traits (facial hair, open eyes) or are "identical" to the father (same month of birth).[30] The apparent opposition between these categories may be illusory for, as in the case of *wu sheng* children, premature adult features could be proof that the infant was not human but rather a spirit. However, for purposes of exposition I will divide the analysis into examining evidence for the beliefs that a child was dangerous because he or she was (1) not fully human or (2) an overly close replica of the parent. I will also point out major aspects of the orthodox Chinese model of the universe and of the kinship system that made the threat posed by certain children into a recurrent theme.

The belief that the child was not fully human was an extension of the conventional Chinese idea that humanity was not given at birth but fashioned through education and ritual practice.[31] In a society where people *became* human through education, the newborn remained far from full humanity. Consequently, the period of childhood consisted of a process of gradual humanization. This was clearly marked out in mourning regulations. Children who died in the first month were to receive no formal mourning at all. Children who died under the age of three months were likewise in no mourn-

ing category, but according to the *Yi li* and the Eastern Han commentator
Zheng Xuan (A.D. 127–200) parents could mourn one day for each month
of the child's life. Children who died under the age of six were categorized
as "early deaths for whom no mourning garments are worn" but were entitled to a stipulated type of coffin. Deaths between the age of six and the
attainment of full-blown humanity with the capping ceremony were divided
into three categories of "early death (*shang* 殤)." Children, moreover, could
not participate in the funerals of others because, as explained by Zheng Xuan,
they were not yet fully human (*wei cheng ren zhe* 未成人者). Moreover, in
the Qin code a handicapped child could be killed without legal penalty.[32] All
these are clear evidence that in both ritual and law the child in early China
was not a full human being.

In Qin and Han law, the crucial division seems to have been at age six.
Those below this age were, after the reign of the Emperor Yuan, exempt from
poll tax. Disaster relief edicts in the Eastern Han specified that aid would go
to all those above the age of six, but younger children received no assistance.
Some Han texts argue that it was around the age of six that children first
began to develop understanding and could enter school.[33] An Eastern Han
funerary stele for an adult by the name of Zheng Gu includes the words "Alas!
The eldest son, the bud that never blossomed." The images of a bloom with-
ered by an early frost or a flower that bore no fruit were often employed to
describe a child's death. However, what is significant here is that the boy, aged
six years, is never mentioned by name, nor does he warrant his own funerary inscription or even a stone. Instead he appears only as an incident in the
funerary account of his younger brother.[34] An inscription to a named five-
year-old dead child, one of only five known examples devoted to a young
child, describes him as "wandering alone in eternal darkness underground"
and "not recognizing his ancestors."[35]

Another indication of the less than human status of children is their hair
styles. As discussed in chapter one of *The Construction of Space in Early China*,
hair was a crucial insignia in marking social status. It played a particularly
prominent role in demarcating adulthood and thus full humanity. The binding
of one's hair marked membership in civilized society and variations in style
indicated differences in status. Numerous texts mention the wearing of hair
unbound (*pi fa* 被髮), which invariably denotes figures outside the human
community: barbarians, madmen, ghosts, and immortals. The transition to
adulthood in China was marked by the tying up of the hair and its capping,
in the case of men, or pinning, in the case of women.

The less than fully human status of infants was consequently marked in
the arrangement of their hair. An infant's hair during the Han dynasty was
left untouched for the first three months (those during which the child was
still outside all mourning categories), and then coiled into what is described
as "horns" for a male and "buns" for a female. Such horns on the heads of
children are confirmed by a Warring States figurine of a child excavated from
a tomb in Hui District in Henan.[36] A Han commentary to the *Li ji* indicates

that some hair was also to be crossed over the head to cover the fontanelle. In this period, horns figure prominently in tomb-guardian monsters found in southern tombs and in the iconography of such demon-quelling monsters as Chi You.[37] Both the coiled horns and the hair crossed over the fontanelle are clearly intended to protect the child from demonic assault. (As discussed in chapter one of *The Construction of Space*, the skull is described in several early Chinese texts as the dwelling place of the *shen* (神) spirit, and in Han apocryphal literature the *hun* (魂) soul moves in and out through the top of the skull.[38]) The practice of putting horns on children led to the custom in late imperial China of giving them animal hoods, often with protruding ears or horns, to protect them from spirits. Consequently, both in ancient China and more recent times the child was protected from potential attacks by hostile spirits by assimilating it to the status of an animal and thus placing it once again outside the realm of the fully human.

Vulnerability of children to animals/[...] spirits

While ritual texts, legal practices, and hair styles all marked the child as not fully human, they did not indicate that it was threatening to adults. However, this belief in threatening children or childlike beings *does* appear in several early texts. The "Spellbinding" text or "Demonography" from Yunmeng tells of child spirits that threaten or harass householders, and two recipes in the Mawangdui *Wushier bing fang* offer remedies against a malevolent child sprite called *qi* 魃.[39] This case is significant to the present argument because the *qi* with its predilection for attacking children has been linked by modern scholars with the aforementioned deceased son of Zhuan Xu who died and became a demon who dwelt in the interior spaces of houses and was inclined to attack children.

The Yunmeng cases are simply unhappy spirits who did not receive proper interment or died violent deaths. Hence, they are no different in kind from adult ghosts who for similar reasons would have been driven to violently intrude into the world of the living. The *qi* sprite, however, is identified in later sources as the product of a fetus still in the womb that is induced by a malevolent spirit to attack a living child.[40] The phenomenon of the fetus or pregnant woman as a destructive force will be discussed at length. Here it is important simply to note that several early texts link infants to man-killing spirits and thereby suggest the potential menace of the former.

This idea also figures in the *Shan hai jing*. This text includes at least ten different spirits that are described as having a cry or wail like that of a human infant, and eight of these are creatures that kill or eat human beings.[41] Similar dangerous creatures who sound like or physically resemble human infants are also mentioned in Gao You's Eastern Han commentary to the *Huainanzi*. Modern Japanese scholars have noted this phenomenon and suggested that the infant's cry produced by these malevolent spirits was a form of bait used to attract their human prey. This is a possible interpretation, but it is worth noting that spirits that do not eat men also have the cry of an infant. It is also significant that several passages in the *Shan hai jing* state that a spirit "names itself," that is, that the sound produced by the spirit serves as its name and thus announces what it is.[42] In light of this repeated formula, it is likely that the infant's wail of the man-eating spirits in the *Shan hai jing* similarly announced their true nature. Moreover, in post-Han literature, one increasingly finds accounts of malevolent spirits that had the form of a human infant. The fourth-century A.D. *Bao pu zi* described a mountain spirit (*shan jing* 山精) that had the shape of a human infant but only one leg. Its wail in the night announced its coming, and it would attack men who entered the mountains unless they could call out its name.[43] Such creatures also appear in the transmitted fragments and the Dunhuang version of the Six Dynasties *Bai ze tu* (白澤圖).[44]

The *Bao pu zi* links young children to dangerous spirits and animals in another context:

> All small mountains lack proper spirits as their masters, for their masters are mostly energetically refined spirits of wood and stone, thousand-year old creatures, and blood-drinking ghosts. They are all deviant and harmful. They never think of blessing people but only of wreaking calamities. They love to test Daoist masters, who must be able to protect themselves through their arts and to guide their disciples. But still some are able to ruin men's elixirs. Now whenever doctors brew efficacious medicines or salves, they never allow them to be seen by chickens, dogs, small children, or women. If they are encroached upon by any of these creatures, then the potions will not work when used. Moreover, those who dye colored cloth loathe to have such evil-eyed ones look at them, for the cloth will always lose its beautiful color. How much more so the great elixirs of spirits and immortals?[45]

Here women, children, and animals are the domestic version of blood-drinking ghosts and ancient nature spirits that menace the work of Daoist masters in the mountains. Their presence, like that of the spirits of wood and stone, destroys virtually any form of chemical concoction, whether it is medicine, elixir of immortality, or humble dye stuffs. Interestingly, it is the *eyes* of women or small children that destroy the effectiveness of medicine or the beauty of the colored cloth. This emphasis on eyes figured in the account of *wu sheng* children, and it will appear also in the case of pregnant women and fetuses.

Although the *Baopuzi* is a later work, and falls outside our immediate scope, its ideas on the menace of small children or women were already developing in the Han. Thus, in the first century A.D., Wang Chong wrote:

> People taboo a mother nursing a newborn child, and regard them as inauspicious. Anyone who is going to undertake any auspicious task,

enter mountains or forests, or take a long journey past rivers and marshes will have no contact with them. The family of the nursing child also taboos and loathes [*ji wu* 忌惡] them. The family has the mother dwell [in a hut] by the side of a tomb or at the side of a road. Only after a month do they allow them to enter [the household]. This is the extremity of their loathing.[46]

This passage anticipates the *Baopuzi* not only in its suspicion of women and small children, but also in particularly linking the harm that they inflict with mountains or with projects that involve going out into the wilds.

There is also evidence from late imperial China that dead infants were particularly liable to become harmful zombies. The *Zhonghua quan guo fengsu zhi*, compiled in the era of the Chinese republic, relates that in some regions dead infants were buried with special talismans or peach wood implements to prevent their return in the form of monsters. Elsewhere people hacked off the limbs of dead children, incinerated them, or peeled off their faces.[47] These practices closely resemble the mutilation of corpses described in chapter one of *The Construction of Space in Early China*, in which the bodies of victims were chopped up by their killers and buried with poisonous substances to prevent the unjustly murdered from returning as vengeful spirits.

It is not surprising that children were closely linked to spirits and often malevolent, or that harmful spirits often had the attributes of children, since infants had just arrived in the world and were not yet fully humanized. In China, the world of the spirits and that of men were thought to be closely related, with constant movement from one to the other. A newborn child was in some ways the mirror image of a newly deceased corpse. Both stood at the boundary between the *yin* world of the dead and the *yang* world of the living, both required extended ritual procedures to secure a successful transition from one to the other, both were generally in the care of women, and both were potentially dangerous if the transition for any reason failed. In the case of the recently deceased, all the stages of the funeral, the post-funerary rituals for its spirit, and the later processing of the corpse were essential to turn a dead body, which was itself dangerous and polluting, into a powerful ancestor who could provide benefits for the lineage. Failures could result in the corpse's becoming a destructive monster or the deceased wreaking havoc on the descendants. In the case of the child, a series of rituals and an extended education were required to turn a being that was part spirit or animal into a full member of the household, the lineage, the state, and ultimately of the human community. Failures in this process likewise produced a malevolent being who would wreak destruction.

This line of reasoning suggests that the child would have been most dangerous while in the womb, still more in the spirit world than the human. There is evidence that Chinese people in many times and places attributed just such dangerous powers to the fetus. Thus, the aforementioned *qi* spirit, attested from the Qin dynasty, was described as the product of a malevolent fetus. A story in the fifth-century A.D. *Yi yuan* (異苑 "Garden of Marvels") records the belief that when a pregnant woman died, the fetus had to be carved out of the body and separately disposed of; otherwise, the fetus interred in its mother's body would produce misfortune. In this story, set in what is now Anhui, the desperate prayer of a devoted wet nurse saves the woman's corpse from mutilation by miraculously bringing it back to life long enough to give birth to a living child before again collapsing. It is perhaps significant that the story immediately follows a series of tales in which women give birth to mixed "litters" of human and animal offspring and that in one of these tales the mother kills the human member of such a brood.[48] In *The Inner Quarters* Patricia Ebrey has noted the continued insistence many centuries later in the Song dynasty on removing any fetus from a dead woman, as evidenced by a story in Hong Mai's *Yi jian zhi*. By this time the belief was explained in Buddhist terms that a woman who died carrying a child was so unclean that she could not be reborn but would remain in purgatory forever.[49] However, the evidence from the Han and Age of Disunion shows that the belief had developed in China quite independently of its later Buddhist interpretation.

Hong Mai's story also tells of an unborn child that was in fact an evil spirit and sought to kill its mother. Ebrey notes that in the Song and later imperial China many people believed that certain infants were not ordinary children but evil spirits sent to cause their parents grief, usually as retribution for sins committed in an earlier existence. In his classic article "Gods, Ghosts, and Ancestors," Arthur Wolf noted that in his twentieth-century fieldwork the standard explanation for infant deaths was that the child was just such an evil spirit.[50] Given the high rate of infant mortality in the period, this suggests that the world of late imperial and Republican China would have been full of demon children. Indeed, every child was potentially a demon until he or she had survived long enough to prove itself human.

The fetus was dangerous and polluting not only in a corpse but also in a living woman. The *Bao pu zi* passage cited earlier argued that if a young child, woman, or domestic animal looked on medicine being mixed or cloth being dyed, then the attempt to produce the useful substance would fail. The same destructive power is attributed specifically to pregnant women. A sixth-century A.D. manual of agriculture and household management, *Qi min yao shu*, also cites such a taboo on allowing pregnant women to witness certain procedures for producing potent liquids. It notes specifically that the production of vinegars and sauces (*jiang* 醬) would be ruined by the presence of a pregnant woman. This taboo is also recorded in the late-Tang dynasty *Si shi zuan yao*.[51]

While the role of the fetus in these taboos on pregnant women is not clearly articulated in these early texts, it is indicated in later records of this taboo by the regular reference to the pregnant woman as the "four-eyed person" (referring to the two of the woman plus the two of the fetus). The earliest application I have found of this phrase to a pregnant woman is the Ming-dynasty anthology of elixirs entitled *Ji jiu xian fang*. This text reiterates the *Bao pu zi*'s statement that the gaze of a dog, woman, child, or pregnant woman would ruin the concoction of elixirs, and it calls the pregnant woman "the four-eyed one."[52] Evidence of popular belief in the baleful influence of four-eyed people/pregnant women in the late nineteenth and early twentieth centuries has been collected by Nagao Ryūzō. In regions of Guangdong, people believed that someone who met such a "four-eyed person" would fall ill. In several places, including Hangzhou, these "four-eyed people" were banned from attending weddings, entering a bride's home, or coming into physical contact with items of the trousseau. In many silk-producing regions, where most of the workers involved in producing silk were women, "four-eyed people" were banned from entry into rooms where the silkworms were reared. The ideas noted in the *Bao pu zi* and *Ji jiu xian fang* also appear in more recent testimony collected by folklorists. Moreover, people in Sichuan stated that a "four-eyed person" embracing a child would cause it harm.[53] All these traditions carry forward the belief that a child or fetus was potentially a demonic or malevolent influence. The repeated emphasis on the fetus's eyes, moreover, recalls the stories of the *wu sheng* children that had appeared as early as the fourth century B.C.

These cases include examples from the full range of imperial Chinese history and the twentieth century of children who were dangerous because they were not properly incorporated into the human world. I will now examine the second theme, that of the threat posed by children who were prematurely adult or an infant son "identical" to the father. The theme of the "double" as a threat was elaborated in the *Zuo zhuan*:

> Things are produced in two's, three's, five's, and in doubles (*pei er* 陪貳). So Heaven has the three lights, Earth has the five phases, the body has left and right, and everyone has his or her mate. The king has his dukes, and the dukes their ministers, so each has his double. Heaven produced the Ji clan to assist/double the Duke of Lu, and they have done this for a long time. So is it not right for the people to submit [to the usurpation]? For generations the princes of Lu have abandoned themselves to their errors, and the Ji clan for generations has cultivated its diligence. So the people have forgotten their ruler. Even though he dies in exile, who will grieve for him? Rulers and ministers have no constant positions, and it has been thus since antiquity.[54]

In this passage the ministerial line, which is the double of the ruler, appears as a natural rebel and usurper. The character *er* 貳, which I translated here as "double," was applied in the same text to the man who assisted the chief mourner at a funeral, to sons and, above all, to rebels. This complex fusion of minister, assistant, collateral line, son, and rebel came together in the mythology of the Duke of Zhou, who was minister, dutiful son of the previous king, and rebel. In the *Xiao jing* he was celebrated as the supreme model of filial- *Mu Hijle ルbs乒* ity for having introduced the procedure of sacrificing to one's ultimate ancestor as the ritual "partner/mate" (*pei* 配) of Heaven, and to one's father as the *祀/亿* *pei* of God-on-High. He was also accused in several texts, such as the "Jin teng" chapter of the *Shang shu* and the *Han Feizi*, of being a rebel against his ward, the youthful King Cheng. Moreover, as the intellectual patron of the ducal lines and ministerial houses that claimed to represent the principle of the rule of the most worthy, he was implicated in the dismantling of the Zhou order that he was also credited with creating. This link of son, minister, and rebel was also fundamental to conventional accounts of the Spring and Autumn period, which from the *Mencius* on was described as an age in which sons murdered fathers and ministers assassinated rulers.[55]

The parallel of son and minister as the respective doubles of father and ruler in the *zong fa* kinship system that had structured the Zhou nobility, a parallel that was carried forward in the conventional correlation of family and state in Chinese political thought, suggests how the son's premature adulthood, or adulthood of any kind, might prefigure rebellion and political murder. The parallel of son and minister could never be exact, for while in the family the son routinely replaced the father, in the state the minister could replace the ruler only by becoming a rebel and assassin. Thus, to the extent that the role of the father was equated with that of the ruler, and the family with the state, the son's inevitable supplanting of the father took on overtones of rebellion and regicide.

In her book *La cité divisée*, Nicole Loraux pointed out that in ancient Greece the conventional literary formula to describe total social breakdown was that brothers killed brothers, while in ancient Rome the topos for similar situations was that sons killed their fathers. To explain this divergence in imagery Professor Loraux noted that in ancient Greece the family was theoretically excluded from the political realm, so the father–son tie remained a purely private matter. The state was constituted as a league of equals who were described as the brothers of a common mother, the earth of their native land. Consequently, social breakdown was depicted in terms of fraternal murder. In Rome, by contrast, the family was regarded as a lesser image or microcosm of the state and the foundation of political authority, so patricide was the primary image of civil conflict.[56] Chinese thought and imagery resemble the case of Rome, as evidenced in the formulaic accounts of the Spring and Autumn period that always speak of sons murdering their fathers. Consequently, in China, patricide enjoyed a central, if often repressed, role in social thought.

Although the son's actual murder of the father would be a monstrous crime that marked total social breakdown or the son's demonic nature, some evidence indicates that the son's transition to full adulthood and becoming a father in his own right, that is, becoming identical to his father, was viewed as a threat. First, an early account of the menace posed by sons born on the fifth day of the fifth month—the story of the childhood of Tian Wen, the Prince of Mengchang—clearly describes the son's maturation as a threat to the father:

> Wen was born on the fifth day of the fifth month. Ying [his father] told Wen's mother, "Do not rear him." His mother secretly reared him and kept him alive. When he had grown up, his mother made use of his brothers to gain Wen an audience with Tian Ying. Ying was angry with the mother and said, "I ordered you to abandon this child. How dare you keep him alive?" Wen bowed his head and replied, "What are your reasons for not rearing a fifth-month son?" Ying said, "Fifth-month sons if allowed to grow up so that they are the same height as the door will do their parents no good." Wen said, "Do men receive their destiny from Heaven or from the door?" Ying was silent. Wen said, "If they receive their destiny from Heaven, then you have nothing to worry about in this matter. If they receive their destiny from the door, then you can just raise the door so that no one could reach its height."[57]

While this exchange is inserted in the story to dramatize Tian Wen's debating ability, an early and hence innate talent that underlay his later successes as a diplomat, it provides valuable evidence that an "owl" son's threat to his father was specifically linked to the former's attaining physical maturity.

The idea that the son's maturity posed a threat to his parents also figures in several of the stories of the twenty-four filial children (er shi si xiao 二十四孝) who provided the classic models for filial piety throughout most of imperial Chinese history. For example, Lao Laizi demonstrated his complete filiality by the fact that even in his seventies he would dress up in baby clothes and play like an infant in front of his parents. In this way his parents were able to imagine that Lao Laizi was still a young child and consequently that they were still in their prime. Here filiality is defined precisely by the refusal to grow up in relation to one's parents, and hence to remain forever a child. Another example is the story of Guo Ju, which is recorded in the Sou shen ji and is depicted on the frequently reproduced illustrated side of a southern-dynasties coffin in the Nelson Gallery. Guo Ju was a poor peasant who was barely able to feed his mother, wife, and three-year-old son. Because the mother insisted on sharing her meager rations with the son and thereby endangering her own health, Guo Ju decided that he would have to kill the child. He took him away to bury him, but when he dug into the ground he found a pot of gold that allowed him to spare the child's life.[58] This divine intercession, however, does not overrule the lesson that loyalty to parents takes precedence over devotion to children, and that

[margin handwriting: Maintaining one's immature state = filial piety]

the son can prove his own absolute filiality in refusing to assume the role of father.

Perhaps underlying this normative rejection of the son's assumption of the role of the father is the early Chinese ritual in which the son as "corpse/impersonator (*shi* 尸)" played the role of his grandfather in order to receive and enjoy the sacrificial offerings presented by his father. In terms of this ritual, any son who in turn sired his own son thereby produced his father's corpse (as ritually played by his son) and consequently pushed his father into the exalted, but not always desired, role of a dead ancestor.

Another aspect of this phenomenon is elaborated in the discussion of filiality in Angela Zito's *Of Body and Brush: Grand Sacrifice as Text/Performance in Eighteenth-Century China*. Zito points out that within the triad formed through the roles of grandfather/father/son, the hidden superiority of the son underlies the apparent superiority of the father that is the overt ethos of *xiao*:

> Although fathers were structural necessities both biologically and ritually as passive receivers of filial actions, it was in the role of son/sacrificer that ritual power resided. . . . Insofar as *yang* was associated with masculinity, this was one thing that masculinity meant: the tremendous power to stand as the *zhuren* in sacrifice—to be a son.[59]

From the perspective of lineage, authority resided in the ancestor/father, but the true ritual center was the sacrificer/son, whose ascent to adulthood, his becoming identical with his father, entailed the latter's death.

This fear of the son becoming too close to the father and thus ultimately replacing him, which as noted earlier was imaginatively identified with regicide, was built not only into the early Chinese ritual system and but also into theories of education. As head of the family and a politicized figure, the father had to maintain a constant distance from his children and appear to them as a severe and commanding figure. This principle is worked out in the *Li ji* and other early texts in a series of ritual taboos and orders. Thus, the *Li ji* stipulates, "The true gentleman carries his grandson in his arms; he does not carry his son (*junzi bao sun, bu bao zi* 君子抱孫, 不抱子)." Here again we see the leaping across generations previously noted in the phenomenon of the impersonator, in which the son is kept distinct from the father but assimilated to the grandfather. Similarly the "Nei ze" chapter of the same text states that the father and son should dwell in separate buildings. The *Shuo yuan*, in a lengthy discussion of rulers' residences, likewise stipulates that the son should never dwell in the same building as his father.[60]

As for education, the "Li yun" chapter of the *Li ji* states that while a father sires a son, a teacher should be employed to instruct him.[61] The idea that a father should not educate his own sons because such action entailed excessive familiarity was incorporated into the later "family instruction" genre as exemplified in the *Yan shi jia xun*.[62] According to another chapter of the *Li ji*, father and son should also never hold the same official post in order to maintain proper respect.[63] This separation was carried into the ancestral temple, for under the system of alternating between *zhao* and *mu* generations the tablets of two consecutive generations could never be placed on the same side of the temple, so that in death the father and the son would not eat together. Instead the son would share offerings in the afterlife with his grandfather, whom he had played in rituals when still alive. This insistence on the separation of father and son also appeared in the mythology of Yu and his battle against the flood, for several texts state that while devoting himself to dredging and channeling the world's rivers he never entered the doorway of his own house. As a consequence, the task of rearing and educating his children was left entirely to his wife.[64] This idea of maintaining separation between fathers and sons in the process of education was also articulated in the *Mencius* and written into the rules for educating offspring that were formulated in the early Han and elaborated, as noted above, in the later genre of the family instruction.[65]

Indeed the idea of the necessary separation of father and son dated back to the beginnings of Chinese philosophy, for the locus classicus of this principle is a well-known anecdote from the *Lun yu*:

> Chen Kang asked Bo Yu [Confucius's eldest son], "Have you learned anything different [from what we have]?" Bo Yu replied, "Not yet. Once he was standing alone, and as I hastened respectfully past the courtyard he said, 'Have you studied the *Odes*?' I replied, 'Not yet.' He said, 'If you do not study the *Odes*, you will be unable to properly speak.' So I withdrew and studied the *Odes*.
>
> On another day when he was standing alone, I hastened respectfully past the courtyard and he said, 'Have you studied the *Rites*?' I replied, 'Not yet.' He said, 'If you do not study the *Rites*, you will be unable to properly stand.' So I withdrew and studied the *Rites*. I have learned these two things from him."
>
> Chen Kang withdrew and happily said, "Having asked one thing, I have learned three. I have learned about the *Odes* and the *Rites*, and I have also learned how the true gentleman keeps his son at a distance."[66]

Here Confucius as the ideal father stands in solitary majesty gazing down on his courtyard, like the Zhou ruler presiding over a court assembly. His son, by contrast, moves quickly along the edge of the courtyard as an expression of respect and avoids contact until formally addressed. The conversation eschews all sociability, moving directly from interrogation to instruction, and deals entirely with the process of education. The concluding moral derived by Chen Kang could not be more explicit. The father keeps his son at a distance, just as living people according to the famous *Lun yu* maxim should respect spirits and keep them at a distance.[67] Thus, the necessary separation between father and son is simply the downward extension of the principles that regulated relations between the living father and his own deceased parent. Each generation had to be clearly separated from those both above and below in accordance with the basic principle that the function of ritual was to separate.[68]

To summarize, the theme of the demonic child who harms its parents highlights several distinctive features of Chinese religion and family. First, it derives from the belief of the close mutual patterning of the world of the spirits or the dead and that of the living. In a world built on constant transfers between the realms of the living and the dead, where the roles of gods, ghosts, and ancestors were all filled by those who had once been living people, the idea of linking the fetus and infant with the spirits would have come easily. This was reinforced by both the repeated insistence on education and ritual as necessary to the attainment of human status, and the links of children with the sphere of women, who were in turn closely tied to the realms of animals and spirits. Second, the highly formal and authoritarian model of the Chinese family as a microcosm of the state gave the son's supplanting of the father undertones of rebellion or treason. Because the family was explained as a reduced model of the political order that served as the foundation of the state, the father–son tie became the primal pattern for that of minister and ruler. Consequently, the natural succession of generations became tainted with the idea, suppressed in formal doctrine but emerging in popular belief, of rebellion and regicide. Third, with lineage ties defined by an ancestral cult in which each individual mechanically moved through a prescribed set of generational roles, the son's resemblance to the father prefigured his subsequent adoption of the paternal role in a transfer that entailed the father's death. The centrality of ancestral worship in defining the lineage meant that the necessary fact of death became an essential element of the father–son bond.

FATHERS, SONS, AND THE COLLAPSE OF SOCIAL DIVISIONS

The tales of a regular moral reversal built into the alternation between fathers and sons in the age of the flood under Yao, Shun, and Yu can be seen as an expression of the enduring patterns in the Chinese kin system discussed earlier. The theme of wicked sons as demonic beings is already present in the *Zuo zhuan* account of wolf children and all of its derivatives. The repeated insistence that Dan Zhu and Shang Jun were uniquely impervious to all moral influence, unlike all the other people of their time, again hints at the issue of their lack of humanity. The sages likewise are marked as not entirely human, both in the repeated stories of their divine progenitors and in passages which describe their physical deformities or animal characteristics.[69] In addition to the stories of dragons, lightning, and other spirits or natural forces as progenitors, there is also an argument in the *Chun qiu fan lu* that since Yao and Shun received their office from Heaven and were the sons of Heaven, they could not transmit this gift on their own authority to anyone else. Here the "paternity" of Heaven, instituted in the fact of the mandate, supplants human paternity and places rulership outside the limits of what can be transmitted from father to son.[70] Thus the impossibility of transmission from father to son in the age of the flood is in part due to the nonhuman natures of either the parents or the offspring.

The second aspect of the demonic child in imperial China, a too close identity of the son with the father that prefigures the latter's death and replacement by the former, also appears in the myths of morally inverted generational transitions during the age of the flood. Mitarai Masaru has argued at length that in all the cases in which father and son are moral opposites, they were originally a single deity. He has attempted to demonstrate this by showing how they shared both common mythic attributes and close phonetic links in their names.[71] While the arguments regarding phonetic links are often forced, and Mitarai far too easily insists on the original identity of spirits, there is a clear pattern of mythic overlap in the functions and attributes between the bad fathers and their sage sons, and to a lesser extent between the sages and their wicked sons.

A clear example of such overly close identification of father and son is the case of Shun and Gu Sou. We have seen how Gu Sou was depicted as a wicked father who under the influence of a second wife repeatedly sought to murder his son, while Shun was accused of lacking filial piety for inheriting the worldly position of Yao and thereby rejecting his father. Similarly, the two were explicitly contrasted as a case of blindness (Gu Sou) versus one of doubled visual acuity (Shun). However, while they were rivals and opposites in all these aspects, the two were also closely linked and to a certain extent identical in their roles as practitioners or creators of music. Gu Sou's role as a musician is signaled in his name or title "gu," which in addition to the broad sense of "blind" also commonly identified the blind musicians who performed music at the courts of the early Chinese rulers or nobles.

Nor is evidence of Gu Sou's character as a musician limited to his appellation, for some passages implicitly or explicitly identify his work with music. The first, found in the *Zuo zhuan* in what is perhaps the earliest reference to Gu Sou, states: "From Mu up to Gu Sou there was none who went against the command [of Heaven, *ming* 命]. Shun doubled [*chong* 重] this with his brilliant [*ming* 明] virtue/power."[72] Taken in isolation, this passage simply reveals an early tradition of a virtuous Gu Sou who established a foundation for the subsequent achievements of Shun, and makes a veiled reference to Shun's "double acuity," that is, to the fact that each of his eyes had two pupils. However, a passage in the *Guo yu* that explains the achievements and character of their ultimate ancestor Mu shows that Gu Sou, and Shun as well, were hereditary musicians:

> As for those who achieve the greatest merit in the world, their descendants have always become eminent. Yu [虞, "forester," i.e., Shun, as discussed in chapter one], Xia [i.e., Yu], Shang, and Zhou are examples of this. Mu of Yu [ancestor of Gu Sou and Shun] was able to discern the harmonious wind [ting xie feng 聽協風] and thereby complete music so that things would be born [cheng yue wu sheng 成樂物生]. Yu of Xia was able to completely level out water and earth, and thereby properly place everything according to their categories.[73]

The exact nature of Mu's great achievement, here treated as equal in merit to Yu's taming of the flood, is explained in another passage of the Guo yu. This describes how, prior to the king's great ceremonial plowing that opened the earth to initiate the agricultural season, a blind musician (gu 瞽) had to "announce the arrival of the harmonious wind [gao xie feng zhi zhi 告協風之至]."[74] Thus, in "discerning the harmonious wind" and by completing his music, Mu had made possible the proper commencement of the agricultural season and thereby made it possible for the "things to be born," that is, for what the farmers planted to flourish and grow. He had also provided the prototype for the office of the blind musician, who with his musical skills was responsible for detecting and proclaiming the arrival of the spring.[75] The fact that his descendant Sou bore the title of "blind musician" demonstrates that Mu's work had been transmitted down through the family line in a hereditary office like that of the astrologer ancestors of Sima Qian and similar posts.

In addition to this demonstration that Gu Sou inherited from the sage creator Mu a tradition of serving as a blind musician, a position that would naturally later have passed to Shun, the Lü shi chun qiu preserves an account that specifically identifies Gu Sou as a musical innovator and Shun as his direct follower:

> When Thearch Yao came to power, he ordered Kui to create the music. Zhi then imitated the sounds of the mountain forests and the valleys to make his song. He took the untreated skin of a reindeer, bound it to an earthen jar and drummed it. Then he slapped or struck the stones to imitate the music of god-on-high's jade stone chimes, and thereby caused all the animals to dance. Gu Sou then divided the five-stringed zither and created a fifteen-stringed one. He named it the "Great Emblem" and used it in the sacrifices to god-on-high. When Shun came to power, Yang Yan divided the zither created by Gu Sou and increased it by eight strings to a twenty-three stringed one.[76]

Here Gu Sou is described as the creator of a new style of string instrument, which is carried forward into the reign of Shun.

It is noteworthy that in the *Zhou li* the holder of the office of blind musician (*gu meng* 瞽矇), identified with the same title as Gu Sou, is responsible for playing this newly invented instrument.[77] When Shun ascends to the throne he continues his father's work of adding strings to the zither. Moreover, while this is the only passage that speaks of Shun's role in the development of the zither, the tradition that he brought order to the world through playing the closely related lute (*qin* 琴) appears in more than a dozen late Warring States and Han texts. The *Li ji* credits Shun not only with playing this stringed instrument but also with its invention.[78] Moreover, the *Shan hai jing* relates that Shun had eight younger sons, reminiscent of the groups of eight good sons who figured in the *Zuo zhuan* version of the Four Maleficences. These sons originated the practice of dancing, which in early China was performed by teams of eight performers.[79] Thus, Shun's status as a musician was one of his central mythic attributes, and it overlapped directly with the defining features of his father.

In addition to sharing major mythic attributes with his wicked father, Shun also has attributes in common with his wicked son Shang Jun. As previously noted, Mu's work as a musician, which was transmitted down through the lineage all the way to Shun, focused on determining the shifting of the seasons in order to guide agriculture. Shun is also linked to agriculture, as various scholars have noted, because many texts refer to Yao's raising Shun from the agricultural fields, or entrusting his sons and daughters to serve Shun as a group in the fields. Indeed, there is a virtual consensus among Japanese scholars that Shun was, at least in one aspect, a god of agriculture.[80] This is significant because his son Shang Jun, although morally diametrically opposed to Shun, was, like his father, an agricultural spirit. The *Shan hai jing* states in several places that Shang Jun carried on the work of Hou Ji in the dissemination of grains to the common people, that he introduced the use of the plow, and that he expelled the drought demoness Ba and thereby became the ancestral spirit of agriculture (*tian zu* 田祖). The same text records that Shun and Shang Jun were buried in the same place.[81] This near identity of the father and the son is also suggested by the fact that, as Mitarai Masaru has pointed out, the son's name "Shang Jun" or "Shu Jun" could represent simply an elongated or slow pronunciation of "Shun."[82] Thus, whereas Shun as a musician shared the same inventions and actions as his father, Gu Sou, in the related role of patron of agriculture he was identical with his son Shang Jun. In the case of bad father and good son, as well as good father and bad son, both of the pair shared common mythic attributes and functions. Shun's rejection of Shang Jun, like Gu Sou's rejection of Shun, could be interpreted as a consequence of fearing a son who becomes a duplicate of the father in order to replace him and assume his position in the world.

However, the clearest example of the near identity of a morally inverted father and son is that of Gun and Yu. As we have seen in the preceding chapters, both figures in received accounts were appointed by the ruler to curb the flood, both in different stories used some of the same methods, and in many texts they were linked as those who achieved merit in the process of taming the flood, with Gun marking the beginning and Yu the completion of the process. If as some modern scholars have speculated, and the *Chu ci* might hint, there was once an account in which Gun was the hero who tamed the flood, then their links would have been even closer. Not necessarily originally a single figure, they might well have been two regional heroes who played the same role in two distinct versions of a common myth. Both credited with taming the flood by different groups of people, they could have been brought together to form a single system in which they were divided into an unsuccessful, and hence bad, father and a successful, and hence good, son. This model is essentially the one elaborated by the authors of *Gu shi bian* cited in chapter one.

The overlap between Gun and Yu, however, is not limited to their having engaged in a struggle to tame the flood. First, both appear to have been originally aquatic creatures, probably fish spirits, which accounts for their relation to the flood. This is clearest in the case of Gun, the graph for whose name 鯀 *kwen was homophonous and interchangeable with 鯤 *kwen and originally meant a large fish.[83] Moreover, according to one myth, after his death he transformed into an aquatic creature: either into a *nai* 能—which is sometimes glossed as a three-legged turtle but more likely was a kind of dragon—into a black fish or a dragon.[84] Moreover, as noted earlier, there is a tradition preserved in the "Tian wen" that Gun was assisted by birds and turtles. Thus, Gun's aquatic nature is made quite clear both in his name and mythic attributes.

Although there is no direct evidence that Yu was originally a fish or an aquatic spirit, several clear links do exist. First, Karlgren's reconstructed pronunciation of Yu, 禹 *giwo, is very close to that for "fish," 魚 *ngiwo, being distinguished only by the lack of an initial nasalisation.[85] Also Yu, like Gun, was assisted by turtles as well as dragons in his battle against the flood.[86] Even more significant are the numerous passages that record that Yu was "paralyzed on one side (*pian ku* 偏枯)," that he consequently was only able to move with a strange hopping gait, and that his legs had no hair. The hopping gait played a crucial role in the myths of Yu, for it underlay the performance of the "Pace of Yu [*yu bu* 禹步]" that was enacted as a central element in many rituals to protect travelers, cure diseases, and perform other functions (see chapter four).[87] Yu's damaging his health and ruining his limbs in the course of taming the flood are also described in one of the texts discovered at Mawangdui. Interestingly, in this text the physical deformities are linked to the disorders in his household that are suggested in other texts in the aforementioned statements that he was so busy in taming the flood that he had no time to enter his own house or help to rear his own children.[88]

The relation of these bodily attributes to the myths of the flood and to Yu's other mythic roles will be discussed in chapter four, but, given his name and mythic parentage, it is highly likely that these physical attributes of hair-lessness and a wriggling motion all derive from his original nature as a fish spirit. The links of these physical attributes to fish are strengthened by the fact that the *Shan hai jing* tells of a state inhabited by fish that are "half par-alyzed (*pian ku*)" in the same way as Yu, and this state is associated with Thearch Zhuan Xu who in many texts was Yu's grandfather.[89] Yu's aquatic origins are also suggested by the fact that in several late Warring States and Han accounts he is able to conquer the flood only after receiving a magic chart, usually the "River Chart (*he tu* 河圖)," from a spirit that is half-man and half-fish, sometimes identified as the "spirit of the Yellow River [*he jing* 河精]."[90] Thus, these accounts are variants of those in which Yu's conquest of the flood depends on the assistance of turtles, dragons, or other aquatic creatures.

While there is much evidence that Yu had aspects of a fish, like Gun he was also linked to dragons. First, as Yang Kuan has shown, the graph that represented his name was derived from the character for a type of dragon.[91] Second, several texts recount stories in which dragons assisted Yu either by dredging out river channels with their tails or carrying him across rivers.[92] Third, the rulers of the state of Bao who in the form of dragons impregnated the legendary evil beauty Bao Si are described as descendants of Yu. This indicates that Yu himself had also been a dragon.[93] Moreover, a fragment of the *Huainanzi* preserved both in com-mentaries to the "Tian wen" and the *Han shu* states that Yu, like his father Gun, turned into a bear or a *nai* dragon, most likely the latter.[94] Finally, both Yu and the son of Gong Gong, in some cases called Goulong, are identified in several texts as the mythic prototype for the spirit of the altar of the soil (*she* 社). Since Yu is the son of Gun, Goulong the son of Gong Gong, and Gun and Gong Gong are versions of the same mythic figure, there is a strong overlap if not identity between Yu and Goulong.[95] The latter's name means "Hook Dragon." This is further evidence that Yu in his capacity as the founder of the altar of the soil, a role derived from his restoration of the dry land by taming the flood, was derived from a dragon. Finally, both Gun and Yu were linked to dragons by the tradition that one clan was named "Yulong (controls dragons)" for the fact that they presented one of the Xia rulers, a descendant of Yu, with dragons to eat.[96]

In addition to the numerous references to dragons, there is also at least one story indicating that Yu, like Gun, was assisted by turtles. While this story appears in a relatively late text, it includes several direct quotations from early texts and is clearly based on themes and anecdotes already present in the Han materials. Moreover, it highlights certain central crucial aspects of the myths of Yu:

> Yu devoted all his strength to the water channels, guiding the rivers and leveling the peaks. A yellow dragon dragged its tail in front of him [to carve out channels] and a black turtle carried along blue-

green mud behind. This black turtle was the emissary of the spirit of the Yellow River [*he jing* 河精]. Beneath the turtle's chin [the plastron?] there was a seal, whose characters were all in the old seal form. These formed the graphs for [the names of] all the mountains and rivers of the Nine Provinces. Wherever Yu had dug out a channel he used the blue-green mud to seal up [*feng* 封] and record the place, then had the black turtle press down the seal on top of it. The contemporary practice of piling up earth to make boundary markers [*jie* 界] is a lingering imitation of this practice.[97]

Here the tortoise comes to Yu as a carrier of divine signs dispatched by the spirit of the Yellow River and thus linked to the "River Chart" revealed to Yu in earlier accounts. More important, the text reasserts the idea that beneath Yu's physical task of draining away the flood waters lay the essential work of reimposing divisions on the world. Notably, the imposition of such divisions is here linked with the task of naming all the defining features of the world shaped by Yu, a task that also prominently figures in accounts of Yu's work given in both the "Yu gong" and the *Shan hai jing*.

Thus, there is clear evidence that Yu like his father Gun shared features of both fish and dragon. Although the fact that each of these mythic figures appeared sometimes as a fish spirit and sometimes as a dragon might seem contradictory, several texts record the transformation of fish into dragons, or of snakes, which are closely related to dragons, into fish. Moreover, later examples of texts that speak of these transformations link them explicitly with the works of Yu.[98] Thus, the overlap between fish and dragons in the myths of Gun and Yu was part of a more general coincidence between these two categories of creatures who were both associated with life in the water.

In addition to the identity of their tasks and numerous attributes, Gun and Yu are marked as excessively close, verging on being physically identical, in the story of Yu's birth as told in the "Tian wen":

When Lord Yu came from the belly of Gun,

How did he transform?

Forcibly seizing his predecessor's task,

He completed his father's work.

An identical tradition that Yu was born from his father's belly appears in the *Shan hai jing*, and a tradition without reference to Yu that Gun's body was carved open appears in the transmitted fragments of the *Gui zang*.[99] In these passages Yu's link with his father goes to the extreme of emerging directly from his body, like Dionysus from the thigh of Zeus, without even the mediation of a mother. A direct outgrowth of his father's body, he likewise directly assumes his father's work and completes his task. In this tradition, the identity of Yu and Gun is extended to include even their physical substance.

Radically opposed in their techniques, their success, and usually in their character, Yu and his father Gun were nevertheless identical in their mythic attributes and, in this last version, in the very flesh that composed their bodies. This theme of bodies and flesh in the mythology of the flood will form a central topic in chapter four.

CONCLUSION

In early Chinese mythology the period when the world was inundated by the flood was also an age in which rulers were unable to transmit their moral character or their political position to their children. According to the stories that had developed by the Warring States period to justify this fact, both the fathers and sons of the early sages invariably had to be wicked. This generational alternation of moral character, a principle that had been noted and elaborated in Chinese texts as early as the *Guo yu* (probably fourth century B.C.), undercut the possibility of forming true lineages or dynasties that were based on the transmission of status and property from father to son. Thus, the physical chaos created by the flood's sweeping away all physical distinctions was paralleled by a moral disorder within the realm of kinship.

However, the myths of the wicked sons or wicked fathers of the sages in the epoch of the flood were not only a means of marking the moral chaos of the flood epoch, but also indicated and allowed reflection on enduring structural problems in the Chinese lineage. These problems were marked from the Warring States and early imperial periods down into the twentieth century in accounts of demonic children who would harm or kill their parents. Such children, who were already grouped together as a category in the late Eastern Han text *Feng su tong yi*, were characterized either by being too distant from the parents because by their inborn nature they were destructive spirits or animals, or else too close, lacking the clear separation demanded for proper relations between father and son. Closely related to the first case, but with an opposite moral valuation, was the idea that the sages were not true members of their own lines because they were the offspring of spirit progenitors who impregnated their human mothers.

In the case of offspring who were overly close to their parents, the tension between the two served as a human version of that absence of separation or distinction that was the recurring theme of flood mythology. Like the absence of separation between water and land or between humans and animals that figured in the accounts discussed in chapters one and two, the failure of father–son transmission in the period of the flood was at least in part a result of the absence of the full distinctions between these two kin roles that proper rituals would institute. Such distinctions were particularly important because Chinese theories of family order, as presented in texts as early as the *Lun yu* right down to the family instructions of the Age of Disunion, emphasized the necessity of maintaining a rigorous separation between the authoritarian father and his children. Consequently, the completion of the work of ending the flood, through rigorously separating land from water, paralleled the instituting of true lineage ties through sharply distinguishing fathers from sons. Only such rigorous distinctions allowed the introduction of father–son inheritance as the principle for transmitting royalty.

The mythic identification of the introduction of the lineage with the introduction of the dynasty also highlights another tension in the Chinese family that was articulated in the myths. At least from the Warring States period it became a maxim in the *ru* tradition, and later among the rulers and their agents, that the family was a microcosm of the state in which young people learned the virtues of obedience that would make them good subjects. The semantic parallels of father to ruler and son to minister had become cliches in Chinese writing by the late Warring States period. However, while ministers and sons might share the virtues of reverence and obedience, they were totally unlike in their normative careers. Ministers ideally remained ministers, while a son would in time become a father in his own right, but only through the mechanism of his father's death. Consequently, the identification of the son with the father entailed the death and supplanting of the latter, acts that in the political context by which the family was justified took on overtones of rebellion and regicide.

This issue figured in the myths of wicked sons at the time of the flood in the recurring contrast between the solitary wickedness of the heir and the groups of virtuous sons who, as discussed earlier, figured in the same tales. Apart from the two groups of eight virtuous sons mentioned in the *Zuo zhuan* as a prelude to listing the four evil heirs who were expelled to the edges of the earth, there were also the eight sons of Yao who served under Yu, the eight sons of Shun who introduced the dance, and the four sons of Fu Xi who in the Chu silk manuscript brought temporal order to the world through pacing out the seasons. Moreover, there is also an account in the *Zuo zhuan* of how each of the Five Phases, along with the altars of soil and of grain, had its patron deity who received sacrifice. Four of these are described as younger sons of Shao, while the other three are sons respectively of Zhuan Xu, Gong Gong (this is the Goulong who was linked above to Yu), and You Lieshan.[100] Finally, it is noteworthy that even the Four Maleficences become forces for order and tranquility not only by being expelled to the edges of the earth but also by becoming members of a group of four who, as a collectivity, delimited the structure of the world.

Thus, there is a recurring pattern in which numbered regularities of nature—the four directions, the four seasons, the Five Phases—as well as conventional social groups such as the teams of eight dancers (emblematic of the highest degree of coordinated action) all had their mythic origins in *groups* of sons. Whereas individual heirs blurred into the father whom they would supplant, and thus become a danger, groups of sons provided the pattern for the construction of an ordered temporal or spatial whole. They did this through being distributed among its constituent parts, which were then arrayed in space, sequenced in time, or coordinated in action to form a larger totality.

These stories could almost serve as myths of origin for the practice of parti-ble inheritance discussed in detail in chapter four of *The Construction of Space in Early China*, a practice that characterized all kin groups in imperial China with the exception of the imperial line itself. This line, due to its unique political role, remained trapped in the tension between the principle of family as embodied in the "heir," and political authority as embodied in the "sage."[101] For other families, the problem of inheritance was resolved through distrib-uting wealth and property among a group so that unitary succession featured only in the ritual transmission that defined the leadership of a lineage.

CHAPTER FOUR

FLOOD TAMING, COUPLES, AND THE BODY

As discussed in the introduction, flood myths around the world often include accounts of families, how they were formed, and the role that they played. Sometimes these families were conventional nuclear households that uniquely survived the flood, as in the story of Noah, while in others they were bizarre unions that were banned in conventional societies but were essential to the repopulation of the world after the flood. The most notable of the latter are the numerous accounts of sibling incest between a primal couple that figured *post-deluvian* prominently in Southeast Asia and appeared in medieval China. While the *incest highlights* significance of such stories is uncertain, they probably emphasize the theme *the common substance* of the shared substance out of which different beings emerged, with the *of human beings* brother–sister tie marking the extreme case of shared substance. This theme is reinforced by the fact that the offspring of the couple often take the shape of an egg or a formless blob, out of which emerge all the different peoples who later occupied the earth. In some versions, notably several in Latin America, the primal couples were formed by unions between men and animals. In several such stories the original union depended on the ability of the animals to transform into human beings, and the marriage became "normal" only when the human managed to take away the animal's powers of transformation. Such couples formed by men's unions with animals or hybrids not only marked the most extreme cases of the improper or taboo *Extreme* unions made necessary by the total devastation of the flood, but also were the *man–animal* most radical form of the man–animal cooperation that figures prominently in *"cooperation"* numerous flood myths.

Several Chinese accounts of the flood also dealt with the issues of the formation of couples and the process of childbirth. These stories likewise included the interlinked themes of incestuous or illicit unions, man and animal collaboration, and the importance of physical metamorphosis. The clearest links between the construction of the ordered world, the emergence of the nuclear family, the collaboration or union of man and animal, and the pivotal role of physical metamorphosis figured in accounts that described the role of the creator goddess Nü Gua in ending the flood. However, these accounts of the goddess were thematically and cultically tied to the tales of Yu, and the latter also included accounts of nuclear families, animal assistants, and physical metamorphosis. Consequently, no versions of the flood myths in China, even those dealing with Yu, can be fully understood without examining the role of Nü Gua in accounts of the origins of the world, the family, and the human body.[1] This chapter therefore begins with an examination of that mythology, first of Nü Gua as an individual deity and then of her role, evidenced only in art, as the female member of a primal couple that created or maintained the world. Its subsequent sections examine the role of Nü Gua as a member of a primal couple that she forms with Fu Xi, and finally the tales of Yu's birth, marriage, and fatherhood, along with the associated theme of Yu's transformation of his own body.

THE MYTHOLOGY OF NÜ GUA AND THE FLOOD

In the scattered references to her in early texts, Nü Gua appears as the fashioner of all things, but above all of human beings. She was the original creator of the human body, a major mythic prototype for the "High Matchmaker [*gao mei* 高媒]" cult that guaranteed human fertility, the controller of the progressive transformations by which the fetus became a human being, the inventor of the ritual that marked female nubility, one of the founders of the institution of marriage, and a bestower of life-giving rain. Depictions in Han art, which will be discussed in more detail in the third section, routinely portray her with the carpenter's compass in her hand to indicate her role as a fashioner of objects and of the world. Thus, Nü Gua was mainly a goddess of fertility—founder of marriage, guarantor of childbirth, guardian spirit of pregnancy, fashioner of the human body—and by extension the being who performed the broader transformations that gave shape to the world.[2] Her work in taming the flood and restoring the world was a direct extension of her general mythic character.

Two early accounts link Nü Gua to the taming of the flood, one indirectly and the other directly. The first is a passage from the *Shan hai jing*:

Two hundred *li* to the north is Mt. Fajiu. There are many *zhe* 柘 trees [a hardwood tree that can feed silkworms in the absence of mulberry] on it. There is a bird there that resembles a crow, but with a marked head, a white bill, and red claws. It is called the *jingwei* [精衛 "refined protector"]. It pronounces its own name. This daughter of the Fiery God [*yan di* 炎帝] was named Nü Gua 女娃. Nü Gua roamed freely to the Eastern Sea where she drowned and so did not return. Therefore she became the *jingwei* and is constantly carrying wood and stones from the western mountains to build a dike against the Eastern Sea.[3]

While this pathetic account of the transformed spirit of Nü Gua waging a
hopeless battle against the flood figured prominently in fiction in the final
decades of the Chinese empire, it had little influence on other early versions
of the flood myth.[4]

The most detailed early account that explicitly links Nü Gua to the
taming of the flood appears in the *Huainanzi*:

> In ancient times the four limits [of the world, *si ji* 四極] collapsed
> and the Nine Provinces split apart. Heaven did not completely cover
> the world, nor did the earth support all things. Fires raged without
> going out, and water surged on without ceasing. Fierce beasts
> devoured the simple people, and birds of prey carried off old and
> young alike. Thereupon Nü Gua smelted the five-colored stones to
> patch up the azure sky, cut off the turtle's legs to re-establish the four
> limits, and killed the black dragon to rescue Ji Province [the central
> of the Nine Provinces, which in this passage stands metonymically
> for the entirety of China]. She piled up ashes from reeds to halt the
> rampant waters. Thus the azure sky was patched, the four limits cor-
> rected, the rampant waters dried up, Ji Province restored to order,
> and the treacherous creatures died. The simple people lived, walking
> on the back of the square provinces [*fang zhou* 方州, i.e., the earth]
> and embracing the round Heaven.[5]

In its accounts of the ravages of the flood, with its references to the tipping
of the sky and the rampant presence of wild beasts in the human world, this
passage differs little from other texts of the late Warring States and early Han.
Even the inclusion of raging fires in the world of the flood is not without
precedent, for the linkage of fire and flood as parallel catastrophes was a standard image in the period.[6] What is unique in this passage are the methods
that Nü Gua uses to restore the world to order. These methods grow directly
out of the other aspects of her mythology, and these linkages in turn shed
new light on the significance of certain aspects of the tales of Yu. I will consequently discuss in turn each of the actions that Nü Gua undertakes to restore
order to the world.

The act referred to in this passage that is most frequently associated with
her in later texts is the smelting of the five-colored stones. Several scholars
have noted that these stones clearly embody the Five Phases. In fusing these
stones, Nü Gua is restoring order to the sky by bringing the phases back into
the harmony that would underlie the regular movement of the celestial lights.[7]
This indicates a role in the restoration of temporal order, for the Five Phases
above all regulated temporal sequence and the celestial bodies likewise were
the key indicators of time. The fusing of the five-colored stones might also
echo the Han practice of building an altar of five different colors of clay, each
corresponding to a direction, and enfeoffing a king by giving him a lump of

Nü linked to 社

5-colored stones as drug

soil corresponding to the direction of his state.[8] This is particularly significant, for some scholars identify this altar with the altar of the soil, and this link between the altar of the soil and Nü Gua plays an important role in the mythology of Yu's taming of the flood.[9] In the role of the blending of five-colored substances in the erection of this altar for the ritual of granting fiefs, the proper ordering of such substances becomes fundamental to the imposition of *spatial* order on the world. As yet another means of schematically encompassing the cosmos, Nü Gua's act of blending colored stones to restore proper order to time and space figured as a powerful method for rescuing the world from the chaos of the flood.

Another and more significant link is the use of the five-colored stones in the cultivation of long life, the curing of illness, and the prevention of decay in the human body that had originally been fashioned by Nü Gua.[10] The most detailed records of the use of the five-colored stones as a drug date from later centuries, specifically the Age of Disunion, when they were used for the most part as a narcotic stimulant.[11] However, there is clear textual evidence that as early as the late Warring States, and certainly in the Han, a substance known as the "five stones," undoubtedly linked to the theory of the Five Phases, was used for medical purposes. The biography of the physician Chunyu Yi in the *Shi ji* records a debate over the proper method of using the five stones to treat disease. This debate includes citations from a medical text entitled the *Bian Que yi jing*, which thus clearly existed prior to the Han.[12] Probably composed somewhat earlier, the *Zhou li* states: "In all cases of treating sores, use the five poisons [*du* 毒] to attack them, the five energies [*qi* 氣] to nourish them, the five medicines to treat them, and the five flavours to regulate them." While there is no explicit reference in this passage to the use of the five stones in medical practices, Han commentaries when used in combination with texts from the early Age of Disunion indicate a clear link between the two. Thus, in glossing this *Zhou li* passage, the second-century A.D. commentator Zheng Xuan notes that the "five poisons" refers to the active ingredients of five medicines that he identifies as the "five potent medicines [*wu du zhi yao* 五毒之藥]" used by doctors in his own day. He lists these medicines, and the list largely coincides with a list of five minerals of five different colors provided by Ge Hong writing a bit over a century later under the rubric of the "five stones."[13] In the late first century A.D., Wang Chong, in the course of writing an extended criticism of the story of Nü Gua's restoration of the world from the chaos of the flood, remarked: "As for [Nü Gua's] using the five-colored stones to patch up the sky, one might even say that these five stones are like using the five medical stones to cure illness."[14] Here the five-colored stones that appeared in Nü Gua's story are directly assimilated to the standard set of five minerals used in the Han to treat the human body. Even more significant is the fact that Wang Chong explicitly notes this analogy between Nü Gua's use of the five-colored stones to patch up the sky and doctors' use of the stones to treat the body, and he grants this analogy grudging acceptance. This passage thus shows that the state of affairs noted by Zheng Xuan and Ge Hong already existed in the first century A.D. It

is also significant because it demonstrates that certain thinkers in the Han
explicitly recognized the link between Nü Gua's twin roles as the deity who
restored the world to order after the flood, and who both originally fashioned
the human body and presided over its regular reemergence through the muta-
tions of the fetus.

It is also significant that the use of the five-colored stones both by Nü
Gua and by early physicians was only one example of the broader links
between stones and the formation, transformation, and curing of the human
body. Thus, it is almost certainly no accident that the earliest known written
account of rectifying the body through controlling the circulation of *qi*
energies is an inscription carved on a piece of jade.[15] The medium on
which the message was inscribed was itself exemplary of the process that the
inscription described. Stones also figured in a wide variety of early techniques
to produce a superior human body, such as the celebrated jade suits that
were intended to keep corpses from rotting, as well as early medical instruments. The perfected body produced by such procedures could itself be
described as a "jade body," i.e., a body made from stone and hence, as in later
Daoist alchemical practices, free from decay.[16] Many kinds of potent stones
were thus central to the fashioning of the ideal human body, so that stories
of Nü Gua's manipulation of such stones to restore the world assimilated the
process of taming the flood to the treatment or transformation of a diseased
body. These links between stones, the body, and fertility will be discussed
further.

A final important connection between the five-colored stones and Nü
Gua is to be found in the lore pertaining to metal casting. Nü Gua was a
mythical inventor of marriage as well as the prototype for a cult that aimed
to guarantee human fertility. Moreover, in Han art she was routinely depicted
as the female member of a primal couple that figured as the divine prototype
of human marriages. In early China, the relations of marriage, of which Nü
Gua was both inventor and enduring embodiment, to the casting of metal
were highly significant. As Marcel Granet has shown, accounts from the Han
and subsequent periods of fusing different metals repeatedly describe the act
of casting metal as a "marriage" between water and fire.[17] Indeed, as early as
the fourth century B.C., the *Zuo zhuan* in an astronomical divination identified water as the "male" of fire and spoke of their union.[18] These early passages generally deal with the interaction of the planets identified with the
phases "fire" and "water." Consequently, their images of a conjugal union
between the two directly link Nü Gua's mythic attribute as the founder of
marriage to the process of casting powerful metals that she used to restore
order to the Heavens.

In later accounts, the nine tripods cast by the floodtamer Yu were also
divided into *yin* and *yang* vessels on the basis of whether they contained "male
[*xiong* 雄]" or "female [*ci* 雌]" metal.[19] Moreover, in the Eastern Han, Wang
Chong in several places wrote how the masters of esoteric arts could "smelt the
five stones to produce five-colored jade [*xiao shuo wu shi, zuo wu se zhi yu*

消爍五石，作五色之玉]," and in turn "smelt the five stones to cast into the instrument [the *yangsui* bronze mirror that captured fire from the sun]."[20] In these passages the smelting of the five-colored stones produced potent metals that could capture or join with the energy of the sun and thereby link people to the powers of Heaven.

Accounts of smelting five-colored stones also figure in Han passages dealing with the casting of swords, and the latter were in some stories cast in male and female pairs that formed a married couple. The most famous of these stories appears in the *Wu yue chun qiu*, which tells of the casting of the celebrated swords Gan Jiang and Mo Ye, which were themselves the metallic equivalents of the human couple that produced them:

> The king requested that Ganjiang cast two celebrated swords. . . .
> The first would be named Ganjiang and the second Moye. Moye was Ganjiang's wife. To make the sword, Ganjiang gathered the iron essence of the Five Mountains [*wu shan zhi tie jing* 五山之鐵精] and the metal efflorescence of the three dimensions [*liu he zhi jin ying* 六合之金英]. He waited on Heaven and attended on Earth. *Yin* and *yang* shone equally on him. All the spirits came down to observe, and the celestial energies descended. However, the essences of the iron and metal would not melt, sink, or flow. Ganjiang could not understand the reason for this.
>
> Moye said, "You were recommended to the king as one skilled at making swords, but after three months you have not completed them. Is there some meaning to this?" Ganjiang said, "I do not understand its principle." Moye said, "The transformation of divine objects [*shen wu zhi hua* 神物之化, where once again the character *hua* has clear sexual overtones] needs a person so that it can be completed. Now will the completion of these swords depend on obtaining a person?" Ganjiang said, "Long ago when my master smelted metal, the categories [*lei* 類, perhaps "genders"] of metal and iron did not melt, so he and his wife together entered the smelting furnace. Only then did the metal form the object. To the present day when later generations have gone into the mountains to smelt metal they have donned sackcloth garments with a hempen band [mourning garb for the deceased couple] and only then dared to cast it. Now when I make the swords the metal does not transform. Is it related to this?" Moye said, "Your master knew how to melt the body to complete objects. How could this be difficult for me?" Then Ganjiang's wife cut her hair, clipped her nails, and threw them into the furnace. She had three hundred young boys and girls work the bellows and load the charcoal. The metal and iron then became liquid and they completed the swords.[21]

Here the swords are a male and female pair identified with the caster and his wife. They are composed of essences of metal that correspond to the temporal Five Phases, the five zones that constitute the earth (four cardinal directions and the center), and the three spatial dimensions of the universe. Ganjiang smelts them with the participation of Heaven and Earth, *yin* and *yang*, and all the celestial spirits. Nevertheless, the smelting only works with the addition of part of the body of the wife. Indeed, in a later Tang version the wife has to throw herself bodily into the furnace before the swords will finally take shape. This directly follows the earlier case of Ganjiang's master that is cited in the story as a precedent in which the human couple had to enter the furnace together to cause the metals to melt and fuse.[22] Similarly, the author's insistence on the working of the bellows by mixed teams of youths and maidens again demonstrates the sexual character of the casting process. This story, in which the fusing of ores mapped onto key components of the cosmos is identified with the processes of marriage and sexual union, dramatizes the cultural assumptions built into the accounts of Nü Gua's restoration of the cosmos after its collapse due to the flood. The technical procedure by means of which she patched up the sky was a direct extension of her role as goddess of marriage and fertility.[23]

This link between stones and fertility in the mythology of Nü Gua also figures in the cult of the High Matchmaker, through which couples sought to guarantee the birth of children. As demonstrated by Wen Yiduo in the article cited earlier, Nü Gua was one of the mythic prototypes of this deity of marriage and childbirth. This is important, because this fertility deity was also closely associated with the power of stones. Fragments preserved in the *Taiping yu lan* show that from the time of Emperor Wu of the Han a stone was placed on the altar of the High Matchmaker.[24] Indeed, every entry pertaining to the matchmaker's altar in the Song encyclopedia prominently notes this placement of a stone on it. The generative power of stones in the stories about Nü Gua has already been demonstrated, so this prominent use of a stone in a fertility cult forms a clear link between her myths and the matchmaker cult. This insistence on the fecundating power of stone also forms an important element in the mythology of Yu.

The second step in Nü Gua's work, cutting off the legs of the turtle and using them as pillars at the four limits of the earth, is even more clearly a case of restoring the world through the transformation or manipulation of bodies. Not only are the turtle legs themselves bodily parts, but there is evidence that the early Chinese sometimes imagined the earth and sky as the upper and lower elements of a turtle's shell.[25] With the round upper shell corresponding to Heaven and the *ya* 亞 -shaped plastron matching the five zones of the earth, the turtle's body provided an image for or reduced form of the cosmos. Given such a background assumption, the work of Nü Gua would have consisted in restoring the world to order by giving it a completed bodily form, a form derived from its own microcosmic image. In this way the chopping off and placing of the legs to restore the bodily form of the cosmos was a direct extension of Nü Gua's achievements as the fashioner of the human body and the patron of the sequential transformations of the fetus.

The third step of Nü Gua's work of restoring the world was to gather the accumulated ashes of reeds in order to halt the water of the floods. Again this marks a clear contrast between the organic material used by Nü Gua and the inert clay attributed to both Gun and Yu. This emphasis on Nü Gua's use of organic materials also figures in the *Shan hai jing*'s account of her death and transformation into the *jingwei* bird that carried wood and stone to build a dike against the Eastern Sea.[26] More important, the accumulation of reeds figures in Nü Gua's cultural innovations, for along with her other attributes she was the inventor of a musical instrument formed by binding together a bundle of reeds.[27] In some sources Nü Gua was said to have ruled through the power of the element wood. Consequently, her use of vegetation, whether reeds or wood, to conquer the element water is an extension of her mythic character.[28] The black dragon that she slays in the account in the *Huainanzi* would be the embodied form of the phase "water," for black is the color of water as a phase and the dragon the supreme watery creature. Thus, the mythic fashioner of the human body and patron divinity of fertility was also credited with ending the flood and restoring world order through her manipulation of marriage, bodies, and organic substances.

THE MYTHOLOGY OF NÜ GUA AND FU XI

Nü Gua was linked to the flood not only as a mythological figure in her own right but also as a member of the primal couple that she formed with the sage Fu Xi. While evidence that these two deities were a married couple does not appear in early texts, perhaps a literati suppression of an overly sexualized religious idea, their union and its functions are depicted in Han tomb art, and occurs in textual accounts preserved from the Tang dynasty on. The evidence from this art and later accounts, when combined with the scattered references to the two deities in the early texts, suggests clear links of this divine couple to the themes and stories of the flood.

In surviving literary sources Fu Xi and Nü Gua are separate deities, and they are linked in an unspecified manner in a couple of Han texts. They were, however, mythologically related in that both were credited with a fundamental role in the creation of humanity as well as the invention of the institution of marriage. These shared mythic attributes might have facilitated their forming a couple under the influence of *yin/yang* cosmology, a theme that figures prominently in their Han iconography. However, before discussing the roots and meaning of their linkage, we must examine their distinct mythological roles.[29]

By the beginning of the Han, Fu Xi appeared in several scholastic texts as the first of the sages, the creator of kingship, and progenitor of all human technology. He fulfilled this role through his invention of the trigrams of the *Yi jing*. The most important account of this invention and its impact, which was frequently cited in the Han, appears in the "Great Treatise" of the *Yi jing*:

> When Bao [Fu] Xi ruled the world in ancient times, he looked up
> to examine the images [*guan xiang* 觀象] in Heaven, and down to
> examine the models [*fa* 法] on Earth. He examined the markings
> [*wen* 文, "patterns"] of the birds and the beasts, and their suitability
> to the terrain. Near at hand he took it from himself, and at a dis-
> tance from objects. Thereupon he first created the eight trigrams in
> order to communicate with the powers of spirit intelligences [*tong
> shen ming* 通神明], and in order to categorize the natures of the
> myriad objects. He invented knotting cords [to keep records] and
> made nets and snares for hunting and fishing. He probably took [the
> idea for] this from the hexagram *li* [#30].
>
> When Bao Xi died, Shen Nong arose. He carved wood to make
> a plow, bent wood to make a plowshare, and taught the world the
> benefits of plowing. He probably took this from *yi* [#42]. At midday
> he made a market, summoned the world's people, and gathered the
> world's goods. They exchanged and then withdrew, each obtaining
> his portion [or "getting his proper place"]. He probably took this
> from *shi he* [#21].[30]

The passage continues at length in the same manner with a list of all of the
sages and their cultural innovations, suggesting how each invention was
inspired by one of the hexagrams that Fu Xi had created.
     In this account, Fu Xi is not only the first of the sage-kings, but also an
encompassing figure whose discovery of the trigrams contained the work of
all the other sages who followed in his wake. In contrast with all those who
came later, Fu Xi alone worked through the direct contemplation of natural
patterns. All the subsequent inventions—including Fu Xi's own—were
inspired by the hexagrams created in this primal act of revelation. The fact
that this first invention included all the others is also marked by its description through the play of complementary pairs used to indicate totality—
Heaven and earth, near and far, birds and beasts—and the categorization of
all things.
     A second role of Fu Xi is that as the first of the sage-kings he "initiated
leadership" and created the Way of kingship. This achievement figures prominently in the inscription appended to his image at the Wu Liang shrine,
and it appears repeatedly in the Eastern Han "apocryphal" writings (*chen wei*
讖緯).[31] Indeed, in the texts of the period the invention of the trigrams and
creation of kingship are often explicitly linked. The *Di wang shi ji* states simply that Fu Xi was the "first of the hundred kings" (*bai wang zhi xian*
百王之先), but other texts argue that all political order depends on the proper
ordering of the trigrams invented by Fu Xi.[32] In Han myth the rise of kings

was often prefigured by the presentation of magical charts by dragons, and these charts are sometimes linked with the trigrams.[33] Fu Xi himself was closely linked to the mythology of dragons. Finally, one passage traces a direct line from Fu Xi's creation of the trigrams, through King Wen's addition of the line formulas that "attach the auspicious signs of the royal mandate (*xi wang ming zhi rui* 繫王命之瑞)," to the *feng* and *shan* sacrifices that mark any king's attainment of the "Great Peace" by means of carving a stone inscription on Mount Tai.[34] This is particularly significant because in the Han dynasty the *feng* and *shan* were the highest of all imperial sacrifices and their performance was thought to be the hallmark of the succession of sages who defined the kingly way.[35] Trips to mountains were also, as noted in earlier chapters, central to accounts of Yu's taming of the flood, and the emperor's progresses to the major peaks of the four directions recapitulated the mythic work of Yu in establishing a structured space from the chaos of the flood.

Closely related both to Fu Xi's discovery of the trigrams and his creation of kingship were accounts of his receiving the "[Yellow] River Chart (*he tu* 河圖*).*" This was a document or "chart" presented to sage-rulers by a divine creature that rose out of the Yellow River. It prefigured the attainment of the Mandate of Heaven and the establishment of a new royal dynasty.[36] It also was used to mark Yu's completion of the work of ending the flood. Like the trigrams, the River Chart was a set of written signs that revealed the secret patterns of Heaven to its recipient, and thus allowed the recipient to restore the world to its proper order. By the Han dynasty, the River Chart was paired with the "Luo [River] Writing" (*luo shu* 洛書), a magic talisman of similar origins and significance but more closely linked to proto-Daoist traditions.[37] These potent, world-structuring texts that emerged from the great waters of China were clearly thematically linked to the themes of flood and the restoration of order.

At the end of the Warring States period the River Chart was cited in the "Great Commentary" in close association with the trigrams.

> Therefore the *Yi* has the Supreme Ultimate [*tai ji* 太極, i.e., the primal unity]. This produces the Two Standards [*liang yi* 兩儀, i.e., *yin* and *yang*, the broken and unbroken lines of the *Yi*]. The Two Standards produce the Four Images [*si xiang* 四象, the four possible pairs of broken and unbroken lines]. The Four Images produce the Eight Trigrams. The Eight Trigrams fix the auspicious and inauspicious. The auspicious and inauspicious produce the Great Enterprise [*da ye* 大業, i.e., the establishment of a royal dynasty]. . . .
>
> Heaven produces the numinous objects, and the sage takes them as his model. Heaven and Earth transform, and the sage imitates them. Heaven hangs down its images to reveal fate, and the sage takes them as his pattern. The Yellow River produces its chart and the Luo River its writing, and the sage takes them as his model. The *Yi* has

the Four Images in order to reveal. It appends words to them [the
images and trigrams] in order to announce. It fixes them as auspicious or inauspicious, in order to decide.[38]

The passage begins by adapting the *Dao de jing*'s account of cosmogony
through division (see chapter one) to describe the emergence of the trigrams
and the *Yi* as the foundation of royal power.[39] It concludes with a list of
the cosmic signs and patterns that served as models for the sage, including the
magical charts revealed by the rivers and culminating in the creation of the
Yi. This once again demonstrates the links between cosmogony and the imposition of divisions that were recurrent themes in the myths of the flood.

While the "Great Commentary" implicitly links Fu Xi's discovery of the
trigrams with the revelation of the River Chart and Luo Writing, several Han
texts explicitly identify the two.[40] Moreover, the *Chun qiu yuan ming bao* states
that one of the natural sources for written graphs was the markings on the
back of a tortoise. Since an Eastern Han terra-cotta tortoise has the Eight
Trigrams carved on its back, and the Luo Writing is often described as appearing on the back of a tortoise, this story likewise suggests the identity of the
Luo Writing and the trigrams.[41] It also links these accounts to tales of the
taming of the flood, in which tortoises assisted Yu in the taming of the flood.
In later accounts this aid specifically entailed using the markings on the tortoise's shell as a seal that fixed the divisions of the earth through marking
them in the mud.

Closely related to accounts of Fu Xi as the discoverer of the trigrams and
recipient of the River Chart or Luo Writing are statements and suggestions
that he was also the inventor of numbers. A passage in the *Zuo zhuan* states
that while tortoiseshell divination was associated with "image," divination by
the yarrow stalk was done through "number" (*shu* 數).[42] As the progenitor of
yarrow divination, Fu Xi was also the patron sage of numbers. The *Shi ben*
contains a reference to an otherwise unknown inventor of divination through
number, a figure who can probably be identified with Fu Xi.[43] In addition,
both the *Zhou bi suan jing* and the *Jiu zhang suan shu*, the two earliest surviving treatises on Chinese mathematics, trace the art of calculation back to
Fu Xi. The former also argues that "numbers" derived from the carpenter's
square; in Han art this tool is an iconographic feature of Fu Xi.[44]

Thus, taken in isolation, Fu Xi was the first of the sage-kings and the
initiator of man's emergence from his undifferentiated, animal state. As the
discoverer of the trigrams and the numerical underpinnings of reality, he was
consequently the father of writing and numbers, which in many versions
emerged from the waters. A final mythic role of Fu Xi, and the earliest
recorded, is as inventor of the calendar. The cosmogonic myth in the fourth-
century B.C. Chu silk manuscript discussed in chapter one relates that prior
to the existence of the sun and moon Bao (Fu) Xi and his wife engendered
four sons who measured the year by pacing it out with their feet.[45] This not
only indicates Fu Xi's role as the first regulator of time, but also anticipates

his link and that of his later wife, Nü Gua, to the sun and the moon in Han art.

Nü Gua, as noted earlier, was primarily associated with the physical creation of the world and the human race.[46] This is first signaled in the "Tian wen," which asks, "Nü Gua had a body, but who fashioned it?"[47] Taken in isolation, the sense of the question is unclear, but given later texts' accounts of Nü Gua's role in the restoration of the world after the flood and in the physical creation of the human race, it is almost certain that the author of the "Tian wen" knew these stories of Nü Gua as creator and then posed the question of who had created *her*. The *Huainanzi* contains a sentence describing Nü Gua's role in the physical creation of humanity and her power to control the transformations of a developing fetus.[48] Another version of Nü Gua's creation of humanity is presented in the late Eastern Han *Fengsu tongyi* to explain the origins of social divisions. In this story Nü Gua at first fashioned men entirely from "yellow earth." However, because the process took too much time she later dipped cords in mud. The rich and noble descended from the creatures formed of pure yellow earth, while the cord-mud hybrids were the ancestors of commoners.[49] Thus, by the end of the Han, the Warring States account of human creation had developed into a parable on the natural origins of the social hierarchy.

Nü Gua also figured as creator in the *Huainanzi*'s account of the restoration of the world after the flood. The passage dealing with the flood is followed immediately by a description of an ancient utopia under Fu Xi, a world in which all men lived at leisure and dangerous animals never showed their teeth and claws.[50] Here Nü Gua, apparently acting as an agent of Fu Xi, ends the flood and physically restores the world. At the chapter's conclusion, the two deities are cited together as exemplars of rule without reliance on written law or official measures. However, nothing in the text itself indicates that their relationship was anything other than political.

These passages are one of two Han textual sources that explicitly link Fu Xi and Nü Gua.[51] However, the next chapter begins with an account of "two spirits" (*er shen* 二神) who emerge within the primal chaos and engender the divisions between *yin* and *yang*. The two deities are not named, and the Eastern Han commentator describes them only as the "spirits of *yin* and *yang*."[52] In Han tomb art, however, Fu Xi and Nü Gua seem to have played their most important role as the spirits who embodied *yin* and *yang*. The closeness of these two passages together with the evidence from Han iconography has led some modern scholars to argue that the linking of Fu Xi and Nü Gua as a primal couple who embodied the division of the world into *yin* and *yang* began in the early Western Han.

There is also in fact one relatively early piece of evidence linking Fu Xi and Nü Gua to the later story of a sibling pair who marry in order to re-populate the earth. A fragment of the third-century A.D. *Di wang shi ji* preserved in a commentary to the "Tian wen" states that Fu Xi and Nü Gua shared the surname "Feng 風," and that since she inherited the institutions of

Fu Xi, Nü Gua took the title "Nü Xi."[53] Although this passage still treats the two as political figures, with Nü Gua being the follower and successor of Fu Xi, the idea of a common surname and the overlap in personal name do suggest closer relations, and indicate that any marriage between the two would have been incestuous. To the extent that the two figures form such a couple, as indicated in Han art, this would provide some support for Wen Yiduo's thesis that from early times Fu Xi and Nü Gua formed a primal couple tied to the flood myth through their role in restoring and repopulating the world.

Nü Gua is also linked to the myths of the flood through her relation in several accounts to Yu. The late Warring States *Shi ben* and the third-century A.D. *Di wang shi ji* identify Nü Gua as the wife of Yu.[54] Since Nü Gua later figured primarily as the wife of Fu Xi, it is possible that the latter was either a mythic transformation of Yu, or an alternative local version of the flood queller.

The link between Fu Xi and Yu is marked not only by their shared wife, but also by the fact that both of them appear to have been originally snake or dragon spirits. Indeed, virtually all the protagonists in the flood saga—Gun, Yu, Gong Gong, and Nü Gua—have names indicating aquatic origins as snakes, fish, frogs, or related creatures, and they are described as having the bodies of snakes or being transformations of dragons. Even in more human-ized versions they are often assisted by dragons.[55] That Fu Xi was likewise a snake or dragon spirit is indicated by his name, which is written with several characters indicating a phonetic cluster associated with "wriggling," "twisting," or "curving," and by the iconography of Han art in which he and Nü Gua are both depicted with human heads and the bodies of snakes. Moreover, Han apocryphal literature states explicitly that Fu Xi had the form of a dragon.[56] Being dragons or snake spirits again links both Fu Xi and Nü Gua to the issue of the flood.

That Fu Xi and Nü Gua derived from snake or dragon spirits is impor-tant not only for their links to Yu, but also because many of their cultural accomplishments are allied to the characteristics of the dragon in early Chinese thought. One important feature of the dragon in this context was its associ-ation with clouds and rain, and by extension with fertility. This is particularly noteworthy in the tales of the "spirit progenitors" of the sages or dynastic founders, for these figures were often sired by dragons. In several accounts the dragon not only impregnates the mother of the future sage but also delivers a magic chart (*tu* 圖, like the River Chart) that prophesies the rise of the sage who is about to be conceived.[57] In one of the earliest stories, dragon semen stored in a box generated its own offspring in the shape of a black tortoise that impregnated the mother of Bao Si, the concubine who brought about the fall of the Western Zhou.[58] Later popular literature contains many stories of village women being inseminated while washing clothes at the riverbank and then giving birth to dragon children.[59] The sacrificial marriage of virgins to the god of the Yellow River also indicates the dragon's links with human sexuality and fertility.

This link of dragons and snakes to fertility is important to the afore-mentioned mythology of Nü Gua as the creator of the human body, goddess of fetal transformation, and prototype of the Divine Matchmaker. However, it is noteworthy that the mythic attributes of Fu Xi were also linked to the issue of fertility. Just as the dragon was an embodiment of human fertility, so the *Yi* hexagrams invented by Fu Xi generated (*sheng* 生) the world. One text asserts that the *Yi* generates Heaven and Earth, and that the hexagrams *qian* and *kun* are the "ancestors of the myriad objects" (*wan wu zhi zu zong* 萬物之祖宗). Another states that in creating the Four Images (*si xiang* 四象, the four pairs formed from a broken and unbroken line), Fu Xi "opened the gate of generation" (*fa sheng men* 發生門). Others explain that the three lines of the trigrams correspond to the "life process"—with a beginning, a flour-ishing middle, and an end—and that *qian* and *kun* generate all things. Finally, the emergence of the trigrams is described in the same terms as that of the cosmos, moving from the nonexistence of *qi*, to the emergence of unformed *qi*, to forms (*xing* 形), substance (*zhi* 質), and finally the appearance of objects.[60] In all these ways, Fu Xi, like Nü Gua, was a patron sage of gener-ation and human fertility.

Indeed, Fu Xi's hexagrams were explicitly linked to fertility not only in accounts of cosmogony, but also in ideas about the generation of the physi-cal human form and the propagation of humankind. In one passage, each trigram is identified with a different part of the body, so that collectively they constitute a full human form. Another passage states that humans were born in response to the trigrams. The two hexagrams that begin the second half of the *Yi* are said to be "the origin of male and female, the Way of husband and wife," and from them arises the Way of man. Another passage attributes "the duties of husband and wife" to Fu Xi's invention of the trigrams. Finally, one passage states that the initial hexagram *qian* was both dragon and father.[61]

Thus, Fu Xi as inventor of the hexagrams and Fu Xi as the dragon spirit who joined with Nü Gua to generate the cosmos were two formulations of the same process. The link of dragons and hexagram divination is made explicit in a Han text that explains the powers of the yarrow. Just as turtles were employed in divination because of their great age, so yarrow was effi-cacious because it lived so long. When it reached its peak of spirit power after one thousand years, it had a purple cloud above it and a "numinous dragon and spirit turtle" (*ling long shen gui* 靈龍神龜) beneath it. Another text says that it had "five dragons" beneath it. Thus, the spirit power of the yarrow was marked by the presence of dragons at its base, or of the dragon and turtle pair associated with the divine revelation of texts.[62] The ability of tortoises and yarrow to reveal cosmic patterns was linked to their uniquely potent vital energies; the yarrow's vitality was connected to the presence of dragons at its roots.

Fu Xi and Nü Gua were also both mythologically linked to marriage and parenthood. In the Chu silk manuscript, Fu Xi was the father of the four seasons. Moreover, the *Shi ben* identifies him as inventor of the *li pi* (儷皮)

ritual, a presentation of animal skins that was part of the marriage ceremony. Later texts state that he was the creator of marriage.[63] Nü Gua was linked to marriage in two ways. First, she was the mythic inventor of the *ji* (笄), the hair ornament that marked a woman's nubility.[64] More important, due to her mythic status as bride of Yu and hence ultimate female ancestor of the Xia dynasty, Nü Gua was one of the versions of the "High Matchmaker" (*gao mei* 高媒, also called "Spirit Matchmaker" *shen mei* 神媒, "Suburban Matchmaker "*jiao mei* 校禖, and other titles), a divinity who was offered sacrifice in mid-spring as the patron of marriage and fertility.[65] Finally, the late Han writer Ying Shao stated that Nü Gua had created marriage.[66]

[margin note: Nü Gua & marriage]

    Another link to the theme of fertility is the aforementioned possibility that accounts of Fu Xi and Nü Gua were originally derived from, or provided the earliest form of, the myth of a primal couple that survived the flood and became the ultimate ancestors of humankind. As discussed in the introduction, versions of this myth appear across much of Southeast Asia, including several of the minorities of southern China.[67] The earliest literary account that makes Fu Xi and Nü Gua the primal couple is the Tang dynasty *Du yi zhi*:

[margin note: FX + NG as couple]

> Long ago when the world had just emerged, there were no people except for Nü Gua and her brother on Mount Kunlun. They thought about becoming man and wife, but were ashamed. So the brother and sister ascended Mount Kunlun [to perform a sacrifice]. He vowed, "If Heaven desires that my sister and I become man and wife, let this smoke intertwine. If not, let the smoke disperse." The smoke intertwined, so his sister mated with him.[68]

Wen Yiduo combined this account with later versions of the story of Fu Xi and Nü Gua in which they were brother and sister who survived the flood by floating in a gourd and then restored the human race through an act of primal incest that received a special imprimatur from Heaven. Wen argued that the names Fu Xi and Nü Gua both originally referred to the gourd, which is also a symbol of fecundity.[69] Western scholars such as Andrew Plaks and Norman Girardot have adopted and elaborated Wen's thesis into an argument that these tales of the flood and the primal couple were dramatized versions of the early Chinese model in which an undifferentiated chaos (the flood) divided its single substance into *yin* and *yang* (the primal couple), which in turn engendered the entire world. In this way, as Plaks argues, the union of Fu Xi and Nü Gua, and their related creation of human marriage, embodied the "structural and functional principles of an orderly universe."[70]

    While it is possible that the early accounts of Fu Xi and Nü Gua were linked to a myth of a primal couple, there is a considerable distance between their depiction in Han art and literature as snake-bodied creator deities and accounts of them as a human couple who were mythic transformations of gourds. In all likelihood, the "gourd" myth was a separate body of tales, prevalent largely among southern peoples for whom the gourd was a major plant. These tales were later conflated with the myths of Fu Xi and Nü Gua through the shared themes of the flood, the creation of humanity, and fertility.[71] Although the linking of these two myths is probably late, the fact that it could be made shows the centrality of the theme of fertility and the restoration or maintenance of world order to late Han and post-Han understanding of Fu Xi and Nü Gua. It also demonstrates how many of the themes of these myths were related to those of the flood, whether or not the flood actually figured in them.

Moreover, it is noteworthy that the theme of the gourd *is* linked to the earlier myths of Nü Gua in her role as inventor of musical instruments. Nü Gua or one of her servants was identified as the inventor of two musical instruments made from gourds, the *sheng* (笙) and the *huang* (簧).[72] The *sheng*, by reasons of homophony, was associated with birth (*sheng* 生), and the Han dynasty dictionary *Shi ming* stated that it was patterned on the image of objects growing out of the earth.[73] A late text states that Nü Gua invented the *sheng* and *huang* after the flood in order to cause humankind to multiply.[74] This once again provides some limited support for Wen Yiduo's thesis of an early version of the primal couple myth.

A final manner in which the theme of bodily fertility appears in the mythology of Fu Xi and Nü Gua is the idea that the written signs that the latter invented were capable of physical generation and growth. We have already seen this in the idea that the trigrams produced the world. In addition, in a *Zuo zhuan* passage previously cited, the creation of the "images" (*xiang* 象) that underlay written graphs led directly to "increase" or "multiplication" (*ci* 孳).[75] The clearest account of the physical or sexual generation of written graphs appears in the Eastern Han dictionary *Shuo wen jie zi* (*Explaining Patterns to Analyze Graphs*):

> When Cang Jie first made written graphs, he relied on the categories [of things] and imitated their forms. Therefore he called them "patterns" [*wen* 文]. After that the forms and sounds mutually increased, and then he called them "characters" [*zi* 字]. "Patterns" are based on resembling objects. "Characters" refers to bearing children and multiplying. When written on bamboo and silk they are called "writing." "Writing" means "to resemble." In the generations of the Five Emperors and the Three Kings they changed and had different forms. Seventy-two generations inscribed the *feng* sacrifice at Mount Tai, and none of them were identical.[76]

The gloss on the distinction between *wen* and *zi* assumes that written characters are produced through a process of generation, and this distinction is built into the title of the book. Moreover, the organization of the book, in which characters are clustered under the primal graphic form from which they derive, also assumes a genetic approach to characters. Finally, four of the six graphic structural types (*liu shu* 六書) hypothesized by Xu Shen are based on the assumption that characters are created from previously existing characters.

To summarize, in written mythology Fu Xi and Nü Gua were both snake or dragon spirits associated with the theme of creation and generation. The former was above all identified with the invention of the hexagrams that underlay all human civilization, and with the creation of kingship. The latter physically created humanity either through the process of childbirth, of which she was one of the patron spirits, or in later versions through an "artistic" fashioning that created not only the human race but also class divisions. She was also explicitly identified as the figure who restored the world to order after the chaos of the flood. Both Fu Xi and Nü Gua partook of the dragon's ability to bestow fertility on human beings and all living things. There are late traditions indicating that the two formed a primal, sibling couple who restored and repopulated the earth after the flood, and some scattered evidence that this idea existed as early as the Han. They certainly appear as a couple in Han art, and their roles there are not unrelated to the issues explored in flood mythology. Consequently, a complete analysis of these figures' relation to the flood requires an examination of their depictions in Han art.

THE ICONOGRAPHY OF NÜ GUA AND FU XI

The images of Fu Xi and Nü Gua in Han art communicate messages about these deities that are related to but distinct from those found in the texts of the period. In part this reflects the differences of the two media, but there is also clear evidence of distinctions tied to the mortuary functions of the art, as well as the interests of those who commissioned the tombs or built them. It is also possible, as argued by several modern scholars, that the artistic images preserve suggestions of an earlier version of the deities and their myths, a version that was deliberately reworked or eliminated in the scholarly texts previously discussed.

Whereas Fu Xi and Nü Gua in the texts were distinct spirits with their own mythological traits, linked only in passages from the *Huainanzi* and the *Lun heng*, as well as the shared mythology of dragon spirits, in Han art they appear as a pair (or can only be identified with certainty when they appear as such). Moreover, while the texts focus on their achievements as spirits who created the world, humanity, and civilization, or who encouraged general fertility, in the funerary art they protected the world of the tomb and maintained order therein. They did this as snake or dragon spirits, hence beings associated with the power of water, who served as the visual embodiments of the links between Heaven, Earth, and man, and of the balance between *yin* and *yang*. As a pair of elongated, highly linear figures, they also framed elements of the tomb's architecture or its art and served as "doorkeepers" or guardian figures who marked the division between inner and outer, thereby protecting the denizens of the tomb. This role as guardians of coffins or the doors to tombs might also have been suggested by their hybrid character as half-human and half-snake, an image that suggested transition from one state to another and thus the crossing of boundaries. However, as beings who maintained order through the imposition of distinctions and the guarding of boundaries, their role in the tomb *did* echo and extend the attributes of Nü Gua as a tamer of the flood.

Their character as liminal beings and as guardians of boundaries might explain in part the fact that, as Hayashi Minao has pointed out, Fu Xi and Nü Gua appear only in *funerary* art.[77] Whereas other deities such as the Queen Mother of the West or the animals of the directions also play a major role in the art of bronze mirrors and other items of daily use, Fu Xi and Nü Gua appear only in tombs and shrines. Thus, whatever might have been the significance of their depiction, it was tied above all to the well-being of the deceased and his or her transfer to another realm.

The study of the iconography of Fu Xi and Nü Gua must begin with a delimitation of the corpus. Chinese scholars tend to identify any figure with a human head and torso and the lower half of a snake or a snake's tail as Fu Xi or Nü Gua. In fact, as Jean James has pointed out, not all snake-bodied spirits can be so labeled. This is clearly demonstrated by the fact that in some images Fu Xi and Nü Gua are accompanied by other snake-bodied figures. For example, in the image from the Rear Chamber of the Wu family shrines, they are flanked by two serpent-bodied beings holding fans; similar beings frame two depictions of the Queen Mother of the West also carved in Shandong. Moreover, one Western Han tomb features a serpent-bodied creature clearly labeled as *Hou tu*, "Empress Earth."[78]

Consequently, we must establish criteria for distinguishing depictions of Fu Xi and Nü Gua from those of other snake spirits. The most reliable basis for such criteria are depictions of the pair that are clearly labeled. Assuming that these labels can be accepted, the identification can be extended to images that share similar attributes and that appear in similar contexts. On the basis of these identifications, informed speculations can be made about the significance of the images within Han funerary cult, and their relation to the issues worked out in the myths of the flood.

The best known image of Fu Xi and Nü Gua in this regard appears in the top register of the west wall of the Wu Liang shrine.[79] Here Fu Xi and Nü Gua, distinguished by their headgear, are marked by the placement of a carpenter's square in the hands of Fu Xi and a compass (lost through damage) in those of Nü Gua. Beings with the same characteristics also appear in images in other Wu family shrines, so Fu Xi and Nü Gua can be identified by the presence of the compass and square.[80]

These tools represent Fu Xi and Nü Gua's ability to regulate the world and keep all objects in their places. They clearly indicate their roles as creators of order in the world, which in the written traditions are expressed in the account of Nü Gua taming the flood and Fu Xi inventing the trigrams and kingship. From the Warring States period to the present day in China, the compass and carpenter's square have symbolized fixed standards and rules that impose order on unruly matter. As such they are clearly appropriate to deities who were credited with the invention of kingship and of social hierarchy as well as the restoration of ordered space out of the chaos of the flood. The presence of these tools in the images placed in a tomb or shrine would serve to maintain proper order, both natural and social. Many scholars also identify the tools as symbols of *yin* and *yang*. This argument, however, is not entirely persuasive, for the male Fu Xi holds the carpenter's square, which would be identified with the square earth and hence *yin*, while the female Nü Gua holds the circular compass, which would be identified with Heaven and thus *yang*.[81] However, the pairing of the tools themselves, abstracted from the question of their placement, could certainly serve as an image of *yin* and *yang*, and by extension of all correlate pairs formed through the process of division.

The carpenter's square wielded by Fu Xi has a further meaning that could account for the reversal of the logical placement of the tools. In texts the carpenter's square was linked to the trigrams that Fu Xi invented. One text states that Fu Xi lived in a time when all was chaotic and undivided, that is, a time much like that of the flood, and that he used the carpenter's square to establish divisions and create the trigrams. The "Great Commentary" of the *Yi* states that the trigrams are *square* while the yarrow are round, thus making *Yi* divination a replica of the universe.[82] The idea that the carpenter's square was fundamental to the process of creating order through the generation of lines also underlies the myths of Chui, an alternative inventor of the tool.[83] While there is no explicit discussion of a link between Nü Gua and the compass, it could reflect the fact that her primary achievement in the flood myth preserved in the *Huainanzi* was to restore the circular Heaven to its place. In any case, the allocation of the tools clearly reflects their mythological achievements rather than *yin/yang* cosmology.

A second labeled depiction of Fu Xi and Nü Gua appears on a sarcophagus of the second century A.D. from Mt. Guitou in Sichuan.[84] In this image the two snake-bodied spirits again hold their respective tools, and they frame the *xuan wu*—the directional animal of the north. The same coffin also depicts the sun and moon, although not on the same surface as the two divinities. Both features are of significance for the study of the iconography of Fu Xi and Nü Gua.

First, this label clearly proves that the pairs of snake-bodied spirits who appear on numerous Sichuan coffin lids, usually holding aloft the sun and the moon, are in fact depictions of Fu Xi and Nü Gua.[85] This identification is supported by the fact that in many examples the two spirits wield the carpenter's square and compass. Some Nü Gua figures, however, hold a set of musical pipes, of which she was the mythic inventor.[86] While in the image on the Mt. Guitou coffin Fu Xi and Nü Gua are not holding aloft the sun and the moon, the cartouches carrying their names are circles that appear in the same place in the composition as the celestial bodies on other Sichuan images.

Jean James has argued that the snake-bodied divinities on these Sichuan coffin lids are deities of the sun and moon, but, given the clear label on the Mt. Guitou example and the frequent inclusion of the carpenter's square and compass, it is almost certain that they are Fu Xi and Nü Gua. The spirits of the sun and the moon are depicted on the Mt. Guitou coffin lid, as elsewhere, as birds rather than snake-bodied creatures.[87]

These scenes of Fu Xi and Nü Gua holding up the sun and moon suggest another element of their role in Han funerary cult. The sun and the moon were important divinities; they were also the celestial embodiments of *yang* and *yin*. Similarly, Fu Xi and Nü Gua were the one pair of deities who in Han art physically met and intertwined (in contrast to the Queen Mother of the West and King Father of the East, who stood in complementary isolation at opposite ends of the earth), and as such they embodied the interaction of *yang* and *yin* in the cosmos. More explicitly, they at the same time embodied the sexual coupling necessary for the generation of the human race. With their upper halves corresponding to the human realm and their lower halves to the chthonic realm of earth, the image of Fu Xi and Nü Gua immediately below the sun and moon formed a model of the Han universe, with the balanced forces of *yin* and *yang* running through the three realms of Heaven, Man, and Earth. Moreover, there is evidence that such charts of the cosmos played a major role in Han funerary ritual.

The clearest examples are the Western Han banners from Mawangdui tombs 1 and 3, and from Mt. Jinque in Shandong.[88] These banners, placed over the coffins, depicted in successive vertical registers the three levels of the Han cosmos: the earth and its underworld, the realm of man, and the Heavens. The representation of Heaven in the banners from Mawangdui is dominated by the sun and moon, and in the Jinque banner it is represented by these two alone. Moreover, each banner contains a pair of interlaced dragons that, in the case of the examples from Mawangdui, trace lines from the underworld to the gates of Heaven. The depictions of Fu Xi and Nü Gua on the Sichuan coffin lids present a condensed version of this image of the cosmos. The paired sun and moon still mark Heaven, the human upper halves of their bodies with hallmark caps and tools signal the world of men, and the intertwined or mirrored snake bodies mark the earth and its chthonic spirits. (It is worthwhile to recall here that the one other example of a labeled snake-bodied spirit depicted the "Empress Earth.") Fu Xi and Nü Gua are not spirits of the sun and moon, but hybrids who embody the division of the universe into these three distinct levels and at the same time demonstrate the links between them. The paired deities move between the three realms, embody two of the three levels of the Han world, and lead upward to the third. Since the Sichuan images were carved on coffin lids or sides, they not only echoed the structure of the earlier banners with their dragons, but were placed in the same position within the burial and presumably performed the same function.[89] Indeed, one stone from Nanyang in Henan depicts a snake-bodied creature holding the moon aloft, and this figure—the exact equivalent of Nü Gua on the Sichuan coffins—is paralleled by a dragon lodged within a cluster of stars.

A third role of Fu Xi and Nü Gua in tomb art was that of guardian figures who protected the underworld realm of the deceased from any untoward intrusions. In this role they appear either flanking houses depicted on the walls of the tomb or on either side of entry doors to one of the chambers. In the former version they figure in several scenes in Shandong tomb carvings, in association with other paired, auspicious elements such as gate towers and trees. Jean James describes two of these scenes from the Zhang tomb and states that Fu Xi and Nü Gua signify that "good order and virtuous conduct reign within" and "watch over the Zhangs in life and in death."[90] Significantly, they also serve to instantiate the boundaries that are necessary to the preservation of order within the world of the tomb.

The identification as Fu Xi and Nü Gua of the snake-bodied guardians on the pillars of inner doorways in Nanyang and Shaanxi has been challenged by Jean James, who insists that these images depict "earth spirits."[91] However, these can be identified with Fu Xi and Nü Gua in light of the iconographic features previously established. In a Nanyang tomb one figure stands above the *xuan wu* and clutches a set of musical pipes. Fu Xi and Nü Gua are above the *xuan wu* in the Mt. Guitou coffin, and this feature appears on other Sichuanese coffins.[92] The pipes are likewise linked with Nü Gua both in myth and iconography. In one Shaanxi example, the snake-bodied guardians are surmounted directly by the sun and moon; in another they are said to hold the carpenter's square and compass, although it is not clear in the small reproduction.[93] Although the other snake-bodied guardians from Nanyang hold magical plants, these cases of iconographic overlap with the images discussed earlier show that the images of these guardian figures who marked the key division between "inside" and "outside" the tomb were read as Fu Xi and Nü Gua.[94]

Another example of Fu Xi and Nü Gua as guardians of doorways is the Yinan tomb in Shandong. This image is, however, distinctive in two ways. First, Fu Xi and Nü Gua are placed together on a single pillar, while other guardians appear on the doorway's two remaining pillars. Second, the two deities are embraced by a large figure standing behind them.[95] Other examples of this "triadic" composition have been found, producing much discussion of the identity of the third figure.[96] Suggested candidates have included the High Matchmaker, the Grand Unity, the giant Pangu, or the primal unity that preceded division into *yin* and *yang*.[97] I cite the image here primarily as evidence of the use of Fu Xi and Nü Gua as guardians on inner doorways of tombs, but will briefly discuss the issue of the third figure.

It must be noted that none of these suggestions has any basis in texts or iconography, and they ignore the settings of the images. In his article cited in the preceding note, He Fushun demonstrates that the figure does not correspond to any textual accounts of the High Matchmaker, which are our only basis for making such an identification. His own suggestion that it is the Grand

Unity ignores the fact that the iconography of this deity, as demonstrated in the clearly labeled "Spirit Chart" from Mawangdui and related images, is completely different and entails the presence of weapons.[98] Pangu is not attested in any contemporary source and the "Primal Unity" as a figure is attested nowhere at all. Although an exact identification is impossible, the depictions and their locations suggest some ideas.

The Yinan "triad" is a guardian. The images in the corresponding registers on the other two pillars are a monstrous bear or lion with jagged spikes and an archer drawing a crossbow. The former is virtually identical with the images of the war god Chi You found in the same tomb, lacking only the weapons that distinguish the latter.[99] The second figure is either the archer Yi or his divinized form "Zongbu."[100] This suggests that the third figure in the "triad," marked by his powerful arms, is another warrior or monster who was tamed and employed to crush rebels or demons.[101] Other depictions of the triad support this. In one, whose shape indicates that it was also on a pillar, the third figure has a topknot or conical cap, a loin cloth, and feet that turn upward. Such traits appear in wrestlers and in images that Chinese scholars identify as exorcists.[102] A third example of the triad appears next to a scene of a wrestling match between a man and an ox.[103] Two examples found on Shandong stones reused in later tombs emphasize the monstrous nature of the third figure. It is depicted as a giant with a mountain-like crown (?) composed of three triangles, triangular eyes and jagged, triangular teeth. It also has a tail.[104] Finally, there are at least two cases in which the generic monster face with the jade *bi* ring suspended from its mouth, the most common apotropaic guardian image in Han tomb art, is flanked by a pair of half-human, half-snake figures whose lower halves coil through the jade ring. In one of these images, at least one figure brandishes a tool that evokes the attributes of Fu Xi and Nü Gua. The links of these two images to the other "triads" are strengthened by the fact that the generic monster always has three prongs jutting from the top of its head, the central one in the shape of a triangle. All the more humanized versions of the central figure in the triad also wear triangular or conical caps. Consequently, it is likely that these images are all versions of the triad formed by Fu Xi, Nü Gua, and a guardian monster.

The theme of triads leads to another issue in the depiction of Fu Xi and Nü Gua—the question of their "children." In post-Han texts, the pair figure as the ultimate ancestors of the human race, often a pair of siblings who marry and produce children in order to repopulate the earth. Several scholars read these myths into the Han iconography, identifying small figures flanked or surmounted by Fu Xi and Nü Gua as their children. The best known example is the small figure with two snake tails that appears between the pair in the Wu Liang Shrine. In the Rear Shrine at the same site, Fu Xi and Nü Gua frame a pair of snake-tailed immortals (marked by their large ears) who form a reduced replica of the original couple. Finally, a scene from Xuzhou shows the pair with intertwining tails; at the bottom on either side appear smaller, snake-tailed beings.[105] The major problem with treating these as depictions of the myth of the human race's descent from Fu Xi and Nü Gua is that in no case are the "offspring" human, although the two tails of the Wu Liang shrine figure could be a humorous version of legs.[106] Since in several scenes Fu Xi and Nü Gua, like the Queen Mother of the West, are accompanied or flanked by smaller, snake-tailed beings, it is not at all certain that they were intended to represent progeny—and certainly not a human one. Nevertheless, the central role of marriage and fertility in their textual mythology would indicate that their intertwined bodies are images of sexual union, an act from which offspring should follow.

One final set of figures identified as Fu Xi and Nü Gua consists of pairs of snake-tailed beings carrying large mushrooms, presumably plants of immortality. These are found only in tombs in the Nanyang region. Several of these pairs figure as guardians of doorways, and others have been found on pillar-shaped stones whose original position is unclear.[107] Apart from the fact that they serve as guardians, there is no textual reason to identify these figures with Fu Xi and Nü Gua, who otherwise are not strongly linked to the realms of immortals and their magical plants. However, since the figures are snake-bodied and perform the same role in the tomb as figures that can securely be identified with Fu Xi and Nü Gua, the identification is plausible. Indeed in one of the images the figures seem to be holding the compass and the carpenter's square, although it is difficult to make out in the reproduction. Li Chenguang argues that the image of Fu Xi and Nü Gua carrying mushrooms of immortality is an innovation of artists in the Nanyang region, perhaps reflecting a distinctive local tradition.[108]

To summarize, the textual mythology of Fu Xi and Nü Gua focuses, as is typical of the period, on their role as cultural innovators. Fu Xi figured as inventor of the hexagrams and by extension of civilization, and was also credited with the creation of numbers, the calendar and the seasons. Nü Gua restored order after the flood and created the human race. Fu Xi initiated kingship, while Nü Gua established the division between noble and base. Both were credited with the invention of musical instruments and rituals pertaining to marriage. In texts, their snake or dragon nature was indicated primarily by their names, although dragons served them in the *Huainanzi*, and the dragon nature of Fu Xi figured prominently in the Eastern Han apocryphal literature. Closely linked to this dragon nature, fertility figured prominently in their myths. Apart from passages in the *Huainanzi* and the *Lun heng*, in Han texts they were either unrelated or were two figures linked by common political tasks.

In contrast to the written traditions that separated the two figures and emphasized cultural innovations and physical fecundity, the iconography of the period bound them closely together (indeed they can be identified with certainty only as a pair) and stressed their role in maintaining the world's order and assuring the underlying structure of the cosmos. It did this through the symbolism of the carpenter's square and compass; using the deities as reduced "charts" of a cosmos formed by Earth, Man, and Heaven; and employing them as guardians for the inner doorways of tombs and the houses in tomb art. Their identity as snake or dragon spirits was also fundamental, a fact that clearly linked them to the element water.

To a certain extent this distinction between the texts and images reflects the characteristics of the two media. Writing stresses the chronological element, and in the form of narrative it lends itself to emphasis on change and innovation. Visual arts, on the other hand, define themselves in space and work best in the presentation of a fixed scene. Their dynamism lies in line or color, while story or character must be epitomized in a single, defining moment. Moreover, many of the features of Fu Xi and Nü Gua in Han art can be explained in terms of conventions of visual presentation. Their twisting snake bodies, and even their human upper halves that took on a highly linear character, were admirably suited to the play of line that is a prominent feature of Chinese art from ancient times. The intertwining of their bodies echoes the emphasis on the complex weaving of lines that figured both in abstract decoration and depictions of creatures in Han art. As a symmetrical pair distinguished only by their headgear and the implements they carried, Fu Xi and Nü Gua served admirably for framing an object, as did the closely related snake-bodied figures with fans who flank higher deities in some scenes. This framing function was both decorative and of cultic significance, since placement on both sides of doorways or houses visually dramatized their protective function.

The differences between written and visual depictions also reflected the purposes of the two genres. Written mythology largely took the form of tales of origins that provided sanctions for current practices. Funerary art, on the other hand, was a major element in the project of creating a microcosm in which the dead could dwell in peace so as not to trouble the living. The role of images was thus to establish and maintain a world within the tomb, and it was for this purpose that Fu Xi and Nü Gua were repeatedly invoked to embody the linkage of the cosmic triad—Earth, Man, and Heaven—as well as the balance of yin and yang. Once established as a balanced pair of hybrid beings, they became a uniquely effective means of visually embodying fundamental cosmological principles in terms of the stylistic features of early Chinese art.

The question remains of whether there is any means of usefully combining the written accounts of the divinities and the artistic depictions produced for the funerary cult, and particularly whether this combination can shed light on the flood myths. There are several possible uses. First, despite the radical distinction between the social uses and intended messages of the written sources and the cultic art, elements of the one can in part be explained in terms of the other. Thus, the association of Fu Xi and Nü Gua with the square and compass is clearly linked to the strong political overtones revealed in the texts. Such meanings, as vividly demonstrated by the cartouches at the Wu Liang Shrine, allowed individuals to read both monarchy and class hier-

archy into the structure of the cosmos created in the tomb or shrine. Moreover, the linking of Fu Xi with the square and Nü Gua with the compass,
the inverse of what would be predicted from conventional symbolism of the
period, can only be explained through the achievements of these divinities as
revealed in texts. Similarly, the substitution of the pipes for the compass in
some images of Nü Gua echoes textual traditions. Moreover, certain tales of
Nü Gua suggest an archaic religious role as fertility goddess that, by the time
of the Eastern Han, had been forgotten or transformed.

Thus, the texts add a layer of potential meaning to the images, although
the recognition of such meanings by any individual cannot be guaranteed.
Conversely, the snake bodies of the pair and their physical union are mentioned only in post-Han texts, while their names indicate that they had snake
natures from their origins in the Warring States. Moreover, the handful of references in the *Huainanzi*, *Lun heng*, and *Di wang shi ji* indicate that they were
linked at an early stage, while casting no light on the nature of that connection. The artistic depictions thus go a long way to fill in this chronological
gap, indicating a more widespread religious tradition that was masked in the
philosophical texts of them as snake or dragon-bodied divinities who physically joined to generate the world.

These points suggest how the combination of the literary and artistic
depictions of Fu Xi and Nü Gua can shed light on the myths of the flood.
First, the texts demonstrate that Nü Gua was clearly identified as a figure who
battled the flood, both in her own right (as in the *Huainanzi* and the *Shan
hai jing*) and associated with Yu. Second, they demonstrate that both she and
Fu Xi were identified with the origins of marriage and the issue of human
fertility. This second point in turn is graphically elucidated through their
images in Han art as an intertwined couple and (perhaps) the progenitors of
offspring. Their role in the tomb as the mythic origins of the family and
human fertility is discussed at length in chapter two of *The Construction of
Space in Early China*. Third, their depictions and placement in the tomb
demonstrate that this primal couple was responsible for structuring the universe, both through embodying the vertical division into Earth, Man, and
Heaven, and through defining the horizontal distinction between inner and
outer that defined the household and ultimately the human realm. Combining their sexual pairing with that of their tools (compass and carpenter's
square) and their associated astral bodies (sun and moon), they provide an
embodied version of the fundamental *yin*/*yang* division around which the
Chinese structured their world. In short, whether or not this primal couple
directly appeared in any versions of the flood myth, the roles they played
both in the texts and in the tombs grew directly out of the issues that were
central to the flood myths. Thus, whatever their initial links to the flood, it
was no accident that as a couple they became central to many later versions.
Indeed, many of the themes suggested in the scattered myths and iconography of Fu Xi and Nü Gua appear in early textual accounts of the latter's
union with Yu.

YU, MARRIAGE, AND THE BODY

Accounts of Nü Gua's links to Yu and his feat of taming the flood took several forms. First, in a few early texts she was identified as the wife of Yu. This is explicitly stated in the late Warring States *Shi ben* and the third-century A.D. *Di wang shi ji*.[109] These passages actually state that Yu married the daughter of the Tushan clan, whose personal name was Nü Gua. The tradition that Yu married the daughter of the Tushan clan, a name that often appears in association with his assembly of the feudal lords near Kuaiji, figures in numerous early sources. Many of these list her name as beginning with the character *nü*, although the second character varies. However, Wang Xiaolien has demonstrated that all these second characters in the name are phonetically linked and that these graphs thus all refer to versions of the same figure.[110] Moreover, Wen Yiduo has pointed out that the account of Nü Gua's quelling the flood with ashes from burnt reeds also indicates an early link between her and Yu, who in rare versions also uses ash.[111] Finally, stories about this daughter of the Tushan clan also feature strong links between stones, marriage, and fertility. These elements are shared with accounts previously described of Nü Gua's taming the flood, once again demonstrating the identity of or close links between her and the daughter of the Tushan clan.

Not only is Yu linked to Nü Gua through his marriage with her in many traditions, but also through their common identification with the cult of the High Matchmaker. Nü Gua's identification as one prototype of this deity has already been noted, but Yu is also linked to the cult. First, his name in several sources is Gao Mi (高密), which Wen Yiduo has argued is simply a phonetic variant of "High Matchmaker [*gao mei* 高媒]."[112] While the phonetic links between *mi* 密 *miĕt and *mei* 媒 *mwĕg are not close, Wen Yiduo's argument at least merits consideration. Moreover, Yu's links with the High Matchmaker and cults of fertility could account for his appearing as the patron sage and primary questioner in the Mawangdui medical text "Book of the Generation of the Fetus [*tai chan shu* 胎產書]," as the eponym for the chart on the disposal of the afterbirth found in the same tomb, and in passages in other texts from Mawangdui dealing with questions of fertility and childbirth. Indeed, Yu's strong links with childbirth continued into the medieval period.[113]

Yu is also linked to the cult of the High Matchmaker through his identification as the mythic prototype of the altar of the soil (*she* 社).[114] The close links that existed between the altar of the soil and the cult of the High Matchmaker are described in several texts. First, the *Mozi* lists the sites at which different states staged the spring ritual of matchmaking. According to this list, Qi held its ritual at the altars of the soil and grain. This tradition is supported by the fact that the *Spring and Autumn Annals* likewise mentions an improper ritual that was attended by the Duke of Lu at the Qi altar of the soil. While the other commentaries do not explain what was improper about the ritual mentioned in this passage, the *Guliang zhuan* notes that it involved displaying

women.[115] The *Zhou li* also asserts a link between the cult of the High Matchmaker and the altar of the soil:

> The matchmaker is in charge of the [sexual] divisions of the people.
> All men and women from the time of their naming have the year,
> month, and day of their birth recorded there. He/she commands men
> to marry at thirty and women at twenty. . . . In the month of mid-
> spring he/she commands the assembly of men and women. At this
> time license is not prohibited. Whoever disobeys the command
> without reason will be punished. . . . All legal disputes between men
> and women over intimate matters will be listened to in the altar of
> the soil of a defeated state.[116]

As discussed in chapter one of *The Construction of Space in Early China*, several
Han commentators explain that the altar of the soil of a defeated state was to
be placed under a roof in order to cut the flow of energy that bound Heaven
to the Earth. Since it was roofed off, such an altar provided a private place
to talk about intimate matters. However, the crucial fact in this passage is that
the altar of the soil was linked to the annual ritual of matchmaking, and that
the official who served as matchmaker would even use the altar as the site
for dealing with the most intimate relations between men and women. It is
also noteworthy that the sacrifice at the altar of the soil was held in the same
month as the matchmaking ritual described here. Indeed, the account of the
matchmaking ritual in the "Monthly Ordinances" follows directly after the
ceremony at the altar of the soil.[117]

The use during the Han dynasty of the altar of the soil as a site for rituals
employed to secure the birth of offspring has been dramatically confirmed by
evidence from a set of fourteen wooden documents probably dating to A.D.
79 that contain prayers addressed to a high god.[118] These documents contain
references to the "Zhang Family's Earth Altar for Requesting Sons [*Zhang Shi
qing zi she* 張氏請子社]" as well as an "Outer Family's [i.e., relatives by mar-
riage] Earth Altar for Requesting Sons." Such family earth altars are also mentioned in at least one received literary source, although it does not specify that
their purpose was to pray for sons.[119]

Yu's links to the cult of the High Matchmaker are also indicated by the
questionable circumstances in which his own marriage to the daughter of the
Tushan clan took place. The annual ritual at the High Matchmaker's altar was
a time when sexual license was not prohibited, and the ruler's attendance at
the ritual was criticized in the commentarial tradition to the *Spring and
Autumn Annals* as a moral failing. The accounts that appear in several texts of
Yu's union with the daughter of Tushan also suggest sexual impropriety. Thus,
the "Heavenly Questions" asks:

> Yu's strength worked this great achievement,
> He descended to inspect the earth's four directions.

How did he obtain that maiden of Tushan,
Having union [*tong* 通] with her at Taisang?
The lady became his mate,
Her body produced his heir.
How, when they had different tastes,
Did they share delight in sexual pleasures?[120]

Yu can't take a break from rebuilding the world.

The account of Yu's union in this passage seems to regard as improper the fact that he paused in his world-redeeming toils to seek a liaison for himself, the manner in which that liaison was carried out, and the sexual pleasure that held it together. The *Lü shi chun qiu* likewise describes how prior to their marriage the daughter of Tushan sent out her maid to keep watch for Yu and to attract his attention. It notes that Yu had "lascivious thoughts [*you yin mian zhi yi* 有淫湎之意]" about her.[121]

To the extent that the fruit of this union, Yu's son Qi, was regarded as a sage in his own right (see chapter three), these stories would be yet another version of the numerous accounts in which sages were produced through the illicit acts of copulation performed by their mothers in the wilds.[122] The links of these stories to the general pattern are even stronger when one notes that in some accounts of the birth of his son Yu appeared to his wife in an animal guise. This would be significant because it was a common idea in the period that the early sages were produced by their mothers mating with nonhuman creatures (e.g., a dragon) or forces (e.g., a bolt of lightning). The idea that Yu's marriage to the daughter of the Tushan clan was not completely licit also links it with the questionable character of the matings that took place in association with the cult of the High Matchmaker. The absence of a true marriage would also be an extension of the idea discussed in chapter three that the age of the flood when Yu lived was a time prior to the formation of proper families.

Centrality of stones in 社 + 高禖

Perhaps the most striking link between the altar of the soil and the cult of the High Matchmaker is that both placed stones at the center of their cultic practices.[123] The emphasis on stones in the cult of the High Matchmaker as manifested in the regular placement of stones on its altar was noted earlier in the discussion of Nü Gua. Similar emphasis was placed on the religious use of stones at the altar of the soil. We have already discussed the use of five-colored soil to form the altar, echoing the five-colored rocks that Nü Gua smelted in order to patch the Heavens. However, there are also numerous records that the deity worshipped at the altar was itself made of stone:

Stone was used for the host-god [*zhu* 主] of the altar of the soil. When the Son of Heaven personally went on military expeditions, than he carried this host-god with him. Criminals were executed in front of the chariot [carrying the stone].

In the fourth month of 537 A.D. the spirit tablets [*shen zhu* 神主] of the seven previous emperors had been moved to the ancestral temple. They were about to move the stone host-god of the altar of the soil to the building that housed the altar.

According to the rites of the Yin [Shang], stone served as the deity for the altar of the soil.

The altar of the soil was not sheltered indoors. It had an altar exposed to frost, dew, wind, and rain, so that it absorbed the spirits of Heaven and Earth. Because of its hard and durable substance, stone was therefore used as the host-god on the altar.[124]

Depictions of the *she* altar in Han art also show it surmounted by a pillar of stone or, in some cases, a tree.[125] Thus, just as with the High Matchmaker, the ritual texts insist that the object worshipped in the cult at the altar of the soil was to be made from stone. The final passage quoted also insists on the altar of the soil as the place where the energies of Heaven and Earth came together. As discussed in *The Construction of Space in Early China*, this union was frequently described in sexual terms. This belief thus again links the altar of the soil to ideas of sexual union.

This convergence between the two cults in their emphasis on stone, and thus between the figures of Nü Gua and Yu who were the mythic prototypes of the cults, is particularly significant because stone played a key role at several points in the mythology of Yu. The most important of these relates to matrimony and childbirth. However, there is also a recurrent story in which Yu was given a piece of black jade. In earlier accounts either Heaven or Shun awarded him a piece of black ceremonial jade (*xuan gui* 玄圭) when he had finished his toils in bringing an end to the flood. This presentation of a stone served to "announce to the entire world the completion of his work." In another story the primal ancestor of Qin also received a black banner and a jade for assisting Yu to end the flood.[126] In several later versions of the story, Yu received the jade from a god, in what are clearly variations of tales about his receiving the "River Chart" or the "Hong fan" from a deity. In at least one account, Yu receives the jade from Fu Xi, thus once again drawing the latter into the flood myths. According to these accounts, Yu then used the jade to tame the flood.[127] Because black is the symbolic color of water in Five Phases theory, it is likely that the color of the stone bestowed on Yu is linked to the nature of his achievement. However, the fact that the symbolic presentation takes the form of *stone* is also an extension of Yu's own nature as revealed in the stories of his own birth, his marriage, and the birth of his son.

First, several texts state explicitly that Yu was born from a stone. Others include the character for "stone" in the name of his birthplace or the place where he was discovered by Shun.[128] This stone birthplace is almost certainly derived from the tradition that Yu was born from a stone. In addition, there is a version of Yu's birth in which, like all sages, his mother was impregnated not by his human father but instead by a divine source. In the case of Yu, this divine progenitor was in some texts a meteor that passed through the constellation Orion. Several Han texts explicitly note that meteors are stones or that they become stones when they fall to earth. One such text even identifies the "five stones," which were smelted by Nü Gua, as fallen meteors.[129] In other versions Yu's mother swallowed a pearl, which is likewise a stone, the seeds of a lotus fruit, or both of these together.[130] Thus, in addition to those accounts in which Yu was directly born from a stone, others have his mother impregnated by a stone or a closely related object. In any case, there are clear links between the stones placed on the altars related to fertility and the stones from which Yu was born or generated.

In addition to tales of his birth from a stone or from the body of his father (see chapter three), there are also accounts in which Yu's birth entailed his splitting open his mother's body, either the back or the side.[131] Such tales are of interest because they echo the aforementioned versions in which Yu emerged from his father's belly or was carved with a knife from his father's body. More important, the theme of the mother's body splitting open to produce the child also figures in the story of the birth of Yu's son as recorded in a fragment of the *Huainanzi* preserved in the commentary to the "Tian wen":

> When Yu was quelling the flood, he cut through Huanyuan Mountain. He turned into a bear [or "dragon"]. He said to the daughter of the Tushan clan, "When I desire to eat, you will hear the sound of the drum. Only then come." Yu hopped [*tiao* 跳, the character that describes his gait in the "Pace of Yu"] on a stone and accidentally hit the drum. The daughter of the Tushan clan arrived and saw that Yu was just then in the form of a bear. She was shocked and fled to the base of Songgao Mountain. There she turned into a stone. At that time she was about to give birth to Qi. Yu said, "Give me back my son." The stone split open and thus gave birth to Qi.[132]

This story draws together many of the ideas about Yu that have already been traced out. First, Qi's birth duplicates that of Yu, in one of those mythic doublings discussed in chapter three that highlight the tensions involved in achieving a transfer of rank from father to son. Beyond the link to Yu's own birth through the themes of birth from stone and the splitting of the mother's body, the two births are also identical in that the father transformed into a bear or dragon. Moreover, in the *Di wang shi ji* Yu's own mother also turned to stone at the time of his birth.[133] Although this last tradition is relatively late, it is also a direct expression of the belief that he was born from a stone. Furthermore, the tales of the miraculous births of Yu and Qi could be related to those of Gun's and Yu's transformation into bears, for one ode in the *Shi jing* notes that bears are the auspicious omen for the birth of a male child.[134] Finally, all the passages referring to Yu erupting out of his mother's side or back are perhaps best explained as remnants of a version in which she turned to stone and then split open.

Second, as Marcel Granet has argued, the description of hopping or dancing on a stone is linked to accounts of wading or dancing across rivers that appear in several Zhou odes dealing with the seasonal rites for fertility and rain that were later attributed to the High Matchmaker.[135] This story thus links both Yu and Nü Gua, in her guise as the daughter of the Tushan clan, back to their roles in fertility cults. Finally, the theme of Yu as a bear or a dragon, and of his wife's horror at having had sex with an animal, also link this story directly to those of sages whose mothers were impregnated by dragons or other spirit creatures.

The sources thus point out Yu's miraculous birth and immediate physical transformations, his guarantee of fecundity through embodying the fertilizing power of the magic stones found on the altars of the High Matchmaker and of the altar of the soil, and his ultimate physical metamorphosis resulting from his spirit nature and his work against the flood. All these themes converge in the microcosm of Yu's body. This is significant because the other great flood tamer Nü Gua was also identified with her creation of the human body and her mastery of all the physical transformations through which it passed.

While all the sages possessed unusual physical forms, and many myths relate to physical transformations, Yu more than any other figure found his power and his role in the manipulation of his body. This theme has already been suggested (see chapter three, note 87) in the many passages that detail how, as a result of personally toiling for decades amid the mountains and the waters, his body lost its hair and nails, he became half paralyzed, and his movement assumed the irregular hop ritually preserved in the "Pace of Yu." This idea of Yu as someone who had altered and damaged his body through toil became so conventional that when the Eastern Han heir apparent urged the aging Emperor Guangwu to work less, he couched the appeal as follows: "Your highness has the illumination of Yu and Tang, but has lost the blessing of the way of Huang-Lao and the nourishing of life. I request that you should be more cautious with your refined spirit energies [*jing shen*], enjoy leisure and give yourself some peace."[136] Here Yu figures together with Tang as the image of one who knows how to work for the people even at the expense of his own body, in contrast with the arts of preserving life through the careful husbanding of vital energies. Although the deformation of Yu's body is not mentioned, the contrast of his actions with the "way of nourishing life" clearly assumes that accounts of how he had damaged himself were common knowledge in the early Eastern Han.

The idea that Yu's sagely achievements were rooted in the manipulation of his body is also highlighted in a description of him attributed to Confucius that appears in the *Da Dai li ji* within a sequential exposition of the work of each of the sages:

> Adept in providing and able to save, he never transgressed his virtuous power. His humanity endeared him to others, and his words could be trusted. His voice formed the standard for the musical gamut, and his body formed the standard for degrees and measures. He presented these [his voice and body] to correct his tasks. Hardworking and respectful, he became the central cord and guiding thread. He toured through the nine provinces, opened the nine roads, embanked the nine marshes, and measured out the nine mountains. He became master of the spirits [a reference to the assembly at Kuaiji] and father and mother to his people. On his left was the spirit level and the straight edge; on his right the compass and carpenter's square [like Fu Xi and Nü Gua]. He paced out the four seasons [like the sons of Fu Xi], fixed in place the four seas, restored to normal the Nine Provinces, carried on his head the nine Heavens, made clear his ears and eyes, and brought order to the world.[137]

Here Yu's body and voice provided the model for all the standards that gave an intelligible order to the world, so that Yu's person became the guiding thread for the cosmos. As in so many accounts of Yu's quelling the flood and imposing order on the world, this passage insists on the manner in which this was achieved through his personal travel and toil. After spatially situating all the basic tools of construction as extensions of his person, the passage lays out all of time and space as extensions of his body. His feet demarcate the seasons, his hands the limits of the seas, his head the level of the skies, and his sense organs the order of the human world.

Closely related ideas are also developed in the text "Ten Questions" discovered at Mawangdui. In one question Yu describes how through his decade-long toil to curb the flood he had rendered his four limbs useless and left his household in disorder. The response to this question begins:

> In all cases the guiding principle for putting government in order must begin from the body. When blood and energy ought to move but do not, this is called the disaster of blockage. This is the root of [diseases of] the six extremities [both the entire body and the entire world]. So the continuity of energy and blood, the meshing of the muscles and the vessels, these cannot be forgotten.[138]

The balance of the response consists of the prescription of a regimen for Yu's bodily weakness, and a narrative of how following this regimen allowed Yu to restore his body, his household, and (by implication) his state. Thus, even in texts on medicine and the nourishing of life Yu appears as the paradigmatic figure for the derivation of political order from the cultivation of the body.

While the theme of the transformation of the body in the mythology of Yu and the flood generally deals with Yu's treatment of his own body, at least one anecdote also uses his controlling of the flood as an image for the disciplining of the senses and emotions that was so central to Chinese thought of the period (see chapter one, section two of *The Construction of Space in Early China*):

> The five grains nourish life [*yang xing* 養性] but people leave them lying on the ground. Pearls and jade have no use, but people keep them as treasures on their bodies. Therefore Shun threw away his gold on a high, steep mountain, and Yu tossed his jade and pearls into the depths of a lake. They did this in order to block up excessive, flood-like [*yin* 淫] desires and to cut off extravagant emotion.[139]

This passage begins with the Yangist topos of the body as the ultimate value and insists on the necessity of caring for it. It then proceeds to the need to constrain desires and emotions, standard themes in the literature on nourishing life. In the invocation of the figure Yu and the terms used to describe desires that must be kept under control, it associates the restraining of emotions and consequent cultivation of the body with mastery of the flood.

The emphasis in early mythology on Yu's body is also demonstrated by the aforementioned "Pace of Yu." Although this strange walk was mentioned in several early texts, and has been discussed by many scholars over the years, the earliest accounts of its character and use within the received textual tradition were in the fourth-century A.D. *Bao puzi*.[140] However, texts excavated in recent decades have revealed early uses of this practice in several contexts. First, the Qin dynasty almanacs (*ri shu* 日書) discovered at Shuihudi and at Fangmatan both contain accounts of using the "Pace of Yu" prior to setting out on a journey. In the Shuihudi text the reference to the Pace of Yu appears within a larger section on travel called the "Promptuary of Yu (*Yu xu yu* 禹須臾)." This section divides the stem and branch sexagenary cycle into five groups of twelve. It then specifies at what time of day one should depart depending on which of the five groups the day of departure would belong to. It concludes with a ritual to be performed prior to departing through the city gate:

> On reaching the bar at the capital's gate, perform the Pace of Yu three times. Advance one pace and call out, "Kegw [a reconstructed syllable that initiates many magic formulae in Chu] I dare to announce, 'Let so-and-so [filling in the traveller's name] travel without calamity. He first plays the role of Yu to clear the road.'" Then draw five lines on the ground. Pick up the soil displaced in making the central line and put it in your bosom.[141]

The Fangmatan passage follows a similar pattern, except that after performing the Pace of Yu three times the traveler is instructed to face the Dipper

constellation and draw the lines before making the oral announcement. The
oral statement in this text also indicates that the five lines are in some manner
patterned on the person or body of Yu.

Yu as the guarantor of safe travel

The ritual links of Yu to safe travel in the Warring States period are not
surprising. Both the "Yu gong" and the *Shan hai jing* claim to be the record
or product of Yu's travels throughout the world. In the course of taming the
flood, Yu journeyed to the edges of the earth and brought order to all the
lands through which he passed. Thus, it was natural that the early Chinese
would attempt to secure their own journeys by invoking the power of Yu to
guarantee the success of travel and to ward off threats. Yu already figured as
a protector of travelers in the *Zuo zhuan*, which relates the story of his casting
nine bronze vessels whose decor depicted all the menacing creatures in the
world so that travelers could identify any threats and then deal with them.[142]
What is notable or surprising in the travel ritual in the two Qin almanacs is
that the invocation of Yu took the specific form of imitating his distinctive
gait. The traveler summoned Yu as a protector through copying his bodily
movements, movements that themselves were patterned on the physical defor-
mity inflicted by his toils. This role was carried forward in the later Daoist
tradition, as demonstrated by the *Bao pu zi*'s use of the "Pace of Yu" to protect
those traveling in the mountains.

In addition to his role as the protector of travelers, a role based on the
idea that he created an ordered space through which people could move in
safety, Yu was also invoked through imitation of his limping gait as a means
of expelling demons from the body in order to cure diseases. This figures frequently in the medical texts from Mawangdui, particularly the *Wushier bing
fang* (五十二病方), but also the *Yangsheng fang* (養生方). Thus, to cure a
disease attributed to a lizard or viper spirit, one performed the Pace of Yu
three times while facing the victim, had him or her drink half a cup of silted
water, and then called on the ailment to depart. The Pace of Yu was also used
in the curing of warts, hernias or other inguinal swellings, abscesses, and diseases inflicted by the demonic child spirit mentioned earlier. It was also performed as part of a ritual to increase the speed of movement and avoid aching
feet when traveling, and formed part of a ritual to secure a camp in the mountains against hostile spirits.[143] The recently published medical strips from the
Qin tomb at Zhoujiatai also list the use of the Pace of Yu to cure a variety
of diseases such as decaying teeth, heart troubles, and sick children. Moreover,
another strip from the same tomb recounts performing the Pace of Yu after
making a sacrifice to the First Agriculturist at the New Year before proceeding out to the fields.[144] These rituals thus combined Yu's medical function with
his role in facilitating travel.

Medical uses of the 禹步

The motif of the Pace of Yu thus ties together several of the central elements of his mythology. Described as a ritual reenactment of the transformation of his body induced by his labors against the flood, it was performed
both as a means of securing safe travel through the world that he had restored

to order, and to rid the body of malevolent influences that threatened its integrity. This link between Yu's restoring the world and restoring the human body was noted by Wang Chong:

> How can one know that the world's having floods is not like the body's having ailments of excess water? How can one know that the world's having droughts is not like the body's having ailments of excess dryness? Ceremonies and prayers requesting blessings cannot heal them, and altering conduct will in the end not save anyone. If one sends for a doctor and takes the medicine, then one can hope to be cured. But if one's allotted span has reached its end, then doctors and medicine cannot help.
>
> Yao's having Yu tame [*zhi* 治, also "to heal"] the flood is like someone suffering an illness of excess water sending for a doctor. Thus Yao's flood was the world's illness of excess water. Yu's taming/curing the flood meant that he was an excellent doctor of floods. How could any disputant change this? The ritual of "attacking the altar of the soil [*gong she* 攻社, an anti-drought ceremony involving beating drums while making a sacrifice at the *she* altar]" will be of no use in the matter. The rain will not cease. Where in the *Rituals* does one see anything about sacrificing to Nü Gua? Fu Xi and Nü Gua are both sages, and the *Spring and Autumn Annals* says nothing about setting aside Fu Xi and sacrificing to Nü Gua. What basis could Dong Zhongshu have had for proposing this?[145]

It is interesting that while Wang Chong asserts the identity of Yu's roles as master of the flood and master of the body, he denies the popular practice of trying to end floods with sacrificial offerings to the altar of the soil and to Nü Gua. As we have seen, these practices were linked back to the myths in which Yu and Nü Gua were the tamers of the flood, and in which Yu was the mythic prototype for the altar of the soil. These popular beliefs marked yet another element of their mythic roles as masters of mating and fertility. With the addition of these themes of sexual liaison and paternity, indicated by the very link between Yu and Nü Gua that Wang Chong seeks to deny, this passage articulates every aspect of the myths of Yu. It reveals him as the mythic prototype for each of the forms of organized space in early China—world, region, lineage, household, and body—and for their shared meanings.

CONCLUSION

Just as early Chinese myths of the flood dealt with the issue of the origins of the state and the lineage, they also reflected on the issue of the establishment of the married couple and the consequent transformations of the human body

involved in generation and birth. The centrality of these themes in accounts
of the flood is marked by the appearance in some myths of Nü Gua, the
mythic fashioner of the human body, guiding deity of fetal development,
inventor of marriage, and patron spirit of the cult that guaranteed human fertility. The account of how she tamed the flood focuses on her manipulation
of living plants and animals, on the manner in which she restored the world
to order by reconstituting it as an organic body, and how she restored the sky
through a process of mineral smelting which in other sources was clearly
modeled on or made possible by human sexual union. In this way the taming
of the flood was assimilated to the process of generating a body, and to the
sexual union that made such generation possible.

In addition to her role as mythic hero who tamed the flood, Nü Gua
also joined with Fu Xi to form a primal couple that served to generate and
give structure to the world. In later accounts this couple was identified with
the sibling pair that appears in myths throughout southern China and Southeast Asia whose incestuous mating repopulated the world after a great flood.
While the antiquity of this version of the Fu Xi–Nü Gua pairing is uncertain, their role in Han tomb art *does* indicate a relation to the issues of the
flood. First, they are hybrid creatures with the lower bodies of snakes or
dragons and the upper bodies of humans. As such hybrid aquatic creatures,
they are mythically linked to other watery beings such as Gun and Yu who
are central in accounts of the flood. Within the tomb their intertwined bodies,
topped by the sun and the moon, provide a reduced cosmogram that traces
the structure of the world divided into the three registers of Heaven, Earth,
and the human world. In addition to thus vertically structuring the world,
they also often figure as guardian figures on doorways to the tomb, thereby
defining the division of inner and outer that constituted the tomb as a structured space and protected it from hostile forces. In providing structure and
marking divisions, the images of Fu Xi and Nü Gua played the same role in
the tomb that Nü Gua and Yu performed in the stories of the flood.

Nü Gua also appears as the sexual partner of Yu in the accounts of her
role as the daughter of the Tushan clan. This woman joined with Yu in what
the early texts treat as an illicit union, and when assisting Yu in the taming of
the flood she discovered the sage's animal nature and was consequently transformed into a stone that split apart to release Yu's son Qi. This birth myth is
linked to accounts of Yu's own birth from stone, and in turn to the central
role of stones in the fertility rituals performed at the altars of the soil and the
High Matchmaker. These altars in turn are linked back to Yu and to Nü Gua,
who are the mythic prototypes for their cults. These tales, in which the taming
of the flood converges with accounts of illicit sexual union and magical births,
are also tied to the numerous accounts of the transformation of Yu's body in
the process of taming the flood. In all these accounts Yu's body loses its human
attributes and blurs back into its original nature as a creature of the waters
or, in the tale of the daughter of Tushan, into a bear. Such accounts, along
with the tales mentioned in earlier chapters of animal assistants who helped

to tame the flood, mark the powers of nondifferentiation that provide the basis for ultimately ending the flood. They also link the manipulation or transformation of the body as essential to the successful structuring of space that is the ultimate resolution of all Chinese flood myths. The specific modifications of Yu's body produced in the course of taming the flood provided the model for a limping or hopping gait used in rituals that produced a properly ordered space as a means of protecting travelers or expelling diseases.

CONCLUSION

Early Chinese ideas about the construction of an ordered, human space were given narrative form in a set of stories dealing with the rescue of the world and its inhabitants from the chaos of a universal flood. These stories dealt primarily with the figure of Yu, although certain versions also recounted the flood-taming deeds of Gun and, more important, Nü Gua. However, even these alternative stories can best be understood in the context of the tales of Yu, and Chinese authors made this point clear by ultimately making Gun the father of Yu and Nü Gua his wife. The earliest surviving elaboration of the deeds of Yu appears in a series of chapters in the *Shang shu* culminating in the "Tribute of Yu" and subsequently in the *Shan hai jing*. Both these works claimed to give an account of Yu's work in restoring the world to order, as well as the structure of the world that he fashioned. Thus, the mythology of the flood provided a background for accounts of the structure of the world, along with the forces that made that structure possible. In narrating the *re-creation* of the world, for the taming of the flood paralleled in the period of human history the process by which the physical world had first emerged, the myths of the flood provided a charter for the institutions of Warring States and early imperial China. In this way the flood myths of China played a role similar to that of biblical and other flood accounts as discussed in the introduction.

In addition to their use in modeling the world, and thereby providing a sanction for major political institutions, the early Chinese accounts of the flood also offered a mythology of contemporary practices of water control, in both its literal and figurative uses. This mythology was oriented around the contrast between the techniques of Gun and Gong Gong, on the one hand, and those of Yu, on the other. The former two were accused of trying to block up floods by the use of walls, while the latter eliminated floods through dredging channels and guiding water to the sea. This contrast provided a classic sanction for Warring States and early imperial innovations in hydrology; it was also invoked in some contexts to criticize the failures of contemporary rulers and insist on the necessity of creating a single state that would encompass the entire world. The superiority of drainage to blocking also provided a standard image for regulating the world through the use of its own internal tendencies, as opposed to trying to impose order by the application of external force. These stories of Yu's taming of the flood were also cited in several regions of China, notably the area around the Hangzhou Bay and Sichuan, to claim Yu as the patron sage who not only physically restored the region but introduced the distinctive features of its regional culture.

While certain versions dealt with the question of water control, many also used accounts of the flood as a means of discussing social order and criminality. In these accounts, developed most elaborately in the *Mencius*, the flood served as the classic image for the collapse of all divisions and distinctions. In this context it was particularly identified with the disappearance of the fundamental distinction between men and beasts, and served as the prototype for all later periods of social collapse. Given this identification of the flood with the invasion of animals, social collapse, and rampant criminality, accounts of taming the flood dealt largely with the expulsion of beasts and reimposition of order through executing archetypal criminals or exiling them to the edges of the earth. In the most common forms of the latter version, order was restored through exiling a group of four named malefactors to the four edges of the earth, where they became forces for order. In this way accounts of the flood and its suppression provided a mythic prototype for the classic model of the world structured as a fixed center ringed by the four cardinal directions. This emphasis on criminality as a cause of the flood, and its punishment or suppression as essential to taming the deluge, is also a feature of many flood narratives found in other parts of the world.

One notable feature of the accounts of these expulsions was that the four malefactors exiled to the edges of the earth were identified as the offspring or descendants of earlier rulers. While this in part indicated the belief that a new regime had to expel the polluting traces of earlier rulers, it also indicates the key role played by father–son relations in accounts of the flood. Once again this is a feature of flood myths in many cultures, including the biblical account. The most common accounts of Yu's work indicate that he was preceded by his father, Gun, who failed in the task. Not only did Yu surpass his father, but in many accounts his father was executed for his failure prior to Yu's appointment. Moreover, accounts of Yu's toils in the flood often emphasize how he neglected his own wife and children in the decades that he devoted to his toils. Finally, one of the central roles of Yu within another body of myths was to mark the shift from the transmission of the ruler's authority from the best man in one generation to the best in the next, to that of transmission from father to son. These myths thus provided an account of the origins of the lineage system formed by the regular transfer of property and status from father to son to son, and so on down the generations.

These tales of the origins of lineages can best be explained by placing them within a broader context of early tales about fathers and sons. A set of stories, dealing above all with Yao and Shun, argued that in high antiquity the sages when they grew old yielded the throne to their finest minister, rather than transmitting it to their sons. These accounts provided a mythic form for framing the tensions between the royal succession transmitted from father to son and the bureaucratic principle of office granted on the basis of merit. However, these tales of sages not transferring the kingdom to their sons led to the idea, which figured in many stories and even in philosophical argument, that sages themselves invariably had evil parents and produced evil offspring. This pattern was noted by Warring States and Han writers, who used it either to criticize the sages as bad parents and unfilial children, to prove that virtue was not hereditary, or to show that some people—as demonstrated by the evil offspring of sages—had irremediably bad moral characters. For other writers, the absence of transmission of political authority from father to son demonstrated that families in the full sense of the term did not yet exist. In this context Yu's taming of the flood and his successful transfer of authority to his son converged as two simultaneous forms of constructing order. At the same time that he fashioned an orderly world, he also founded the true lineage based on properly defined roles of fathers and sons.

The mythological equation of the ordering of the world and that of the lineage as marked in the shift from Shun to Yu not only provided an antiquarian account of the origins of kin groups, but also served to mediate certain fundamental tensions within those groups. Specifically, the opposition between fathers and sons indicated by myths of the generational alternation of virtues at the time of the sages reflected an enduring tension in the Chinese lineage. Many beliefs in China preserved in literary sources dealt with offspring who were destined to destroy their families and consequently should be killed. These offspring fell into two categories: those who had an animal nature and hence were alien to their own families, and those who were too close a duplication of their parents. It is the latter category that is particularly important for the stories of the sages' families as prototypes for the tensions of Chinese kinship.

In the most important cases where sages had villainous parents and children, particularly the succession of Gu Sou-Shun-Shang Jun and that of Gun-Yu-Qi, the sage shared major mythic attributes with both his father and his son. Thus, the wicked Gu Sou, who repeatedly attempted to murder Shun, was a patron or spirit of music as was Shun himself. In the next generation, the irremediably wicked Shang Jun figures in several texts as an agricultural deity, a role also assigned to Shun. Gun and Yu likewise share many attributes as snake or dragon spirits, as well as being linked as tamers of the flood. Indeed, in a few accounts Yu is directly born from Gun's body. Similarly, many of the same historical enemies or achievements, such as the foundation of the Xia dynasty, are attributed alternately to Yu or Qi. Thus, the tension between the generations in the sages' families reflects the same principle as do the popular beliefs about dangerous children. In both cases, the overly close identification of father and son is translated into moral wickedness or menace.

The threat of a son who is identical to his father manifests itself primarily in the question of succession and inheritance. In the act of becoming a
father, the son must transform his own father into a dead ancestor. Furthermore, to the extent that the father–son relationship was imagined in terms of
an authority parallel to that of a ruler over his subjects, which had become a
regular cliché of early Chinese political thought, the son's inducing the death
of his father in the act of becoming an adult took on the trappings of rebellion or regicide. These problems generated in the conflation of household and
state authority are elaborated within the mythology of Yu through linking his
actions as world fashioner, ruler, and father.

A final aspect of spatial order presented within the stories of the flood
deals with the fashioning of the married couple and ultimately of the human
body that was generated by such couples. This theme is clearest in the mythology of Nü Gua, who in different texts is the fashioner of the human body,
goddess of fertility in the guise of the High Matchmaker, founder of marriage, presiding deity of the physical transformations of the human fetus, and
tamer of the flood. It is particularly striking that the best preserved account
of her role in taming the flood derives the techniques she employs for that
task from her other mythical roles. Thus, she patches up the sky with smelted
"five-colored stones" that elsewhere figure as powerful medicines or medical
implements. Versions of the same stones also appear in accounts of metallurgy
in which the casting of swords is treated as a sexual process that parallels the
generation of a body and may even incorporate bodily parts. Nü Gua also
restores the world to an even level through placing it on four giant tortoise
legs. In doing this, she not only uses bodily parts to restore the world, but
also turns the entire world into one vast tortoise body with the shell equivalent to the sky, the plastron to the five regions that make up the earth, and
the legs to support it. She also staunched the flood with burned reeds, another
organic substance that appears elsewhere as an element in her mythological
inventions of musical instruments.

While the accounts of Nü Gua as an individual create the most explicit
parallel between the formation of the world and that of the human body, the
theme of coupling and the formation of bodies also figures in Nü Gua's links
with Fu Xi in a primal pair that joined together in sexual union to generate
and maintain the world. In later accounts this couple was a sibling pair, which
is also found in tales throughout Southeast Asia and the Pacific, whose incestuous mating allowed the world to be repopulated after the human race had
been destroyed by the flood. While it is uncertain that such stories existed in
early times, or even that the couple was specifically involved in tales of the
flood, their images in Han art show how they were related to many of the
themes of the flood myth. First, they were depicted as hybrid beings whose
intertwining lower halves were snakes or dragons, while their upper bodies
were human. Compositionally linked on coffin lids to the sun and the moon,
and often shown holding the compass and the carpenter's square, they embodied the tripartite division of the world into Heaven, Earth, and human realm,

and through their tools symbolized the processes that maintained these divisions. Second, regularly placed on doorways in association with guardian figures, they served to divide "inner" from "outer." They thereby established the tomb as a distinct realm, and maintained that realm from the threatened incursions of the watery forces of pollution and chaos. It is notable in this regard that the Chinese underworld was imagined as a realm of water known as the "Yellow Springs." In these ways the conjoined images of Nü Gua and Fu Xi produced a spatial order structured in both the vertical and horizontal dimensions, an order that was generated within the sexual act that conventionally produced the human body.

These themes of coupling, the generation of bodies, and their controlled transformations also run through the myths of Yu. First, Yu and Nü Gua appear as husband and wife in several accounts of the taming of the flood. Second, Yu is described in several texts as the mythic prototype for the god of the altar of the soil. This altar had many parallels with that to the High Matchmaker, of which Nü Gua was one of the mythic prototypes. These parallels included playing a central role in rituals dealing with mating and fertility, as well as the placing of a stone or a stone figure on the altar as recipient of the sacrifice. The relation of stones to fertility in the mythology of Nü Gua was discussed earlier, and they played a similar role in tales of Yu. Specifically, several texts recount that Yu was born from a stone or in a place named for a stone. Other texts tell how Yu's son Qi was also born from a stone, or rather a mother identified with Nü Gua who had been transformed into a stone.

In addition to Yu's role in rituals of fertility, and the birth myths associated with that role, the body of Yu also figured prominently in certain tales of the flood. First, in several stories Yu's taming of the flood is associated with his transformation into a dragon or bear. More commonly, the stories emphasize the physical toil entailed in Yu's taming of the flood, and numerous accounts mark the extent of this toil with references to the alterations or deformations inflicted on his body. Some tell how his body lost its hair and nails, reverting to the fishlike condition by which he was mythically marked. Others speak of his being lamed or reduced to walking with a strange, hobbling gait. This latter was reproduced in the "Pace of Yu" that became a central element in several major ritual procedures. Significantly, these rituals figure in two of the major spatial realms with which Yu's work is associated: the ordering of the world and the formation of the body. In the former context, the "Pace of Yu" was employed in numerous rituals intended to protect travelers, often those whose journeys entailed some movement through the mountains that had figured so prominently in Yu's own structuring of the world. In the latter context, the "Pace" was employed in rituals intended to cure a variety of ailments and thus restore the body to proper order. In one medical text, this bodily treatment was also presented as a means of restoring order within the household, thus drawing in the final spatial realm of which Yu was patron and protector.

In summation, the flood myths that developed around the figures of Yu and Nü Gua provided a comprehensive mythology for the origins of virtually all the units in terms of which the early Chinese articulated their notions of a structured space. These tales elaborated in dramatic form the principles that underlay an orderly world, lineage, household/couple, and human body. While availing themselves of earlier stories and of central religious rituals of the period, the versions of these stories that developed in the Warring States and the Han turned both Yu and Nü Gua into early rulers, or ministers who became rulers. By transforming the creators of orderly space into political figures, these tales paralleled the other accounts of the sage-kings in the same period that interpreted the emergence of all aspects of human civilization as the work of early rulers. In so doing, they provided both etiologies and legitimation for the political institutions that had emerged in the Warring States and culminated in the emergence of the unitary empire. Just as the flood myths developed in the early Middle Eastern civilizations and elsewhere had justified their own society's institutions through a narrative of world destruction and re-creation, so the early Chinese found potent, wonder-working rulers at the heart of the process of imposing order and definition on a world that otherwise collapsed into chaos.

NOTES

INTRODUCTION

1. Walter Burkert, *Structure and History in Greek Mythology and Ritual* (Berkeley: University of California, 1979), p. 23; Georges Dumezil, *The Destiny of the Warrior*, tr. Alf Hiltebeitel (Chicago: University of Chicago, 1970), pp. 1–2; G. S. Kirk, *Myth: Its Meaning and Functions in Ancient and Other Cultures* (Berkeley: University of Calfornia, 1970), pp. 31–41, 251–62. On the pivotal importance of myths being "anonymous" and "traditional." see Claude Lévi-Strauss, *The Raw and the Cooked*, tr. J. Weightman and D. Weightman (New York: Harper and Row, 1970), p. 18.

2. Marcel Detienne, *L'Invention de la Mythologie* (Paris: Gallimard, 1981), esp. ch. 7, "Le mythe introuvable"; Ivan Strenski, *Four Theories of Myth in Twentieth-Century History: Cassirer, Eliade, Lévi-Strauss, and Malinowski* (Iowa City: University of Iowa, 1987); Robert Elwood, *The Politics of Myth: A Study of C. J. Jung, Mircea Eliade, and Joseph Campbell* (Albany: State University of New York, 1999); Bruce Lincoln, *Theorizing Myth: Narrative, Ideology, and Scholarship* (Chicago: University of Chicago, 1999).

3. George S. Williamson, *The Longing for Myth in Modern Germany: Religion and Aesthetic Culture from Romanticism to Nietzsche* (Chicago: University of Chicago, 2004); Richard Terdiman, *Present Past: Modernity and Memory Crisis* (Ithaca: Cornell University, 1993), pp. 3–4; Hans Blumenberg, *Work on Myth*, tr. Robert M. Wallace (Cambridge: Massachusetts Institute of Technology, 1985), Part II, ch. 2–3.

4. Lowell Edmunds, ed., *Approaches to Greek Myth* (Baltimore: Johns Hopkins University, 1990), pp. 1–20. See also Luc Brisson, *Platon, les Mots et les Mythes* (Paris: Maspero, 1982), pp. 168–73.

5. Luc Brisson, *How Philosophers Saved Myths: Allegorical Interpretations of Classical Mythology*, tr. Catherine Tihanyi (Chicago: University of Chicago, 2004).

6. Williamson, *The Longing for Myth in Modern Germany*, chs. 1, 4; Blumenberg, *Work on Myth*, Part II, chs. 2–3.

7. Christoph Jamme, *Einführung in die Philosophie des Mythos, Band 2: Neuzeit und Gegenwart* (Darmstadt, Wissenschaftliche Buchgesellschaft, 1991), pp. 10–11, 139.

8. Kurt Hübner, *Die Wahrheit des Mythos* (Munich: Verlag C. H. Beck, 1985). See also Blumenberg, *Work on Myth*, "Translator's Introduction."

9. Joseph Mali, *Mythistory: The Making of a Modern Historiography* (Chicago: University of Chicago, 2003).

10. Roman Ingarden, *The Literary Work of Art: An Investigation on the Borderlines of Ontology, Logic, and Theory of Literature*, tr. George G. Grabowicz (Evanston: Northwestern University, 1973); Wolfgang Iser, *The Implied Reader: Patterns of Communication in Prose Fiction from Bunyan to Beckett* (Baltimore: Johns Hopkins University, 1974); Iser, *The Act of Reading: A Theory of Aesthetic Response* (Baltimore: Johns Hopkins University, 1978); Hans Robert Jauss, *Toward an Aesthetic of Reception*, tr. Timothy Bahti (Minneapolis: University of Minnesota, 1981); Jauss, *Aesthetic Experience and Literary Hermeneutics*, tr. Michael Shaw (Minneapolis: University of Minnesota, 1982); Umberto Eco, *The Role of the Reader: Explorations in the Semiotics of Texts* (Bloomington: University of Indiana, 1984).

11. Blumenberg, *Work on Myth*, p. 34. Blumenberg demonstrates this capacity of myths to evolve by devoting the second half of his book to a case study of the myth of Prometheus from its earliest appearance in Hesiod to its twentieth-century versions in Kafka and Gide. It is for this reason that Wendy O'Flaherty describes myths as a "palimpsest on which generation after generation has engraved its own layer of messages." See *Women, Androgynes, and Other Mythical Beasts* (Chicago: University of Chicago, 1980), p. 4.

12. Edmunds, *Approaches to Greek Myth*, pp. 2–3, 13–15.

13. The pioneering work on collecting flood tales was James Frazer, *Folklore in the Old Testament*, vol. 1 (London: MacMillan, 1918), pp. 104–361. For a more accessible abridged version, as well as an annotated one, see *Folklore in the Old Testament: Abridged Edition* (rep. ed., New York: Avenel Books, 1988), pp. 46–143; Theodore H. Gaster, *Myth, Legend, and Custom in the Old Testament: A Comparative Study with Chapters from Sir James G. Frazer's Folklore in the Old Testament* (paperback ed., New York: Harper & Row, 1975), pp. 82–131. The most exhaustive single list, with statistical analysis of themes, is Johannes Riem, *Die Sintflut in Sage und Wissenschaft* (Hamburg: Rauhen Haus, 1934). Useful transcultural surveys also appear in Dorothy B. Vitaliano, *Legends of the Earth: Their Geologic Origins* (Bloomington: Indiana University, 1973); ch. 7; Alan Dundes, ed., *The Flood Myth* (Berkeley: University of California, 1988); Herrmann Baumann, *Schöpfung und Urzeit des Menschen im Mythus der afrikanischen Völker* (Berlin: Verlag ven Dietrich Riemer, 1936), pp. 307–19; François Berge, "Les légendes du Déluge," in *Histoire Générale des Religions*, vol. 5 (Paris: Librairie Aristide Quillet, 1951), pp. 59–101.

14. Important studies on the history of the biblical flood myth include Charles Gillispie, *Genesis and Geology: A Study in the Relations of Scientific Thought, Natural Theology, and Social Opinion in Great Britain, 1790–1850* (New York: Harper & Row, 1959); Don Cameron Allen, *The Legend of Noah* (Urbana: University of Illinois, 1963); Jack P. Lewis, *A Study of the Interpretation of Noah and the Flood in Jewish and Christian Literature* (Leiden: E. J. Brill, 1978); Paolo Rossi, *The Dark Abyss of Time: The History of the Earth and the History of Nations from Hooke to Vico*, tr. Lydia G. Cochrane (Chicago: University of Chicago, 1984); Richard Heggett, *Cataclysms and Earth History: The Development of Diluvialism* (Oxford: Oxford University, 1989); Lloyd R. Bailey, *Noah: The Person and the Story in History and Tradition* (Columbia: University of South Carolina, 1989); Norman Cohn, *Noah's Flood: The Genesis Story in Western Thought* (New Haven: Yale University, 1996).

15. On the early Mesopotamian flood myth, see Harold Peake, *The Flood: New Light on an Old Story* (London: Kegan Paul, Trench, Trubner & Co., 1930); André Parrot, *The Flood and Noah's Ark*, tr. Edwin Hudson (New York: Philosophical Library, 1955); Wilfred G. Lambert and Alan R. Millard, *Atra-hasis: The Babylonian Story of the Flood* (Oxford: Oxford University, 1969); Jeffrey H. Tigay, *The Evolution of the Gilgamesh Epic* (Philadelphia: University of Pennsylvania, 1982); Stephanie Dalley, tr., *Myths from Mesopotamia: Creation, The Flood, Gilgamesh, and Others* (revised paperback ed., Oxford: Oxford University, 2000), pp. 9–38, 109–16.

16. Alfred M. Rehwinkel, *The Flood in the Light of the Bible, Geology, and Archaeology* (St. Louis: Concordia Publishing, 1951); John C. Whitcomb, Jr. and Henry M. Morris, *The Genesis Flood: The Biblical Record and Its Scientific Implications* (Grand Rapids, Mich.: Baker Book House, 1961); Whitcomb, *The World that Perished* (Grand Rapids, Mich.: Baker Book House, 1973); Frederick A. Filby, *The Flood Reconsidered: A Review of the Evidences of Geology, Archaeology, Ancient Literature, and the Bible* (London: Pickering & Inglis, 1970). Closely related are various volumes on the search for remains of Noah's ark. See, for example, John Warwick Montgomery, *The Quest for Noah's Ark* (Minneapolis: Dimension Books, 1974). The volumes by Parrot and Peake in the preceding note argue that the Mesopotamian myth might be based on a historical flood that took place around 2800 B.C. at the Sumerian city of Shurrupak, and the biblical account was in turn based on the Mesopotomian. They do not, however, suggest a universal flood.

17. Vitaliano, *Legends of the Earth*, p. 178.

18. Dundes, "The Flood as Male Myth of Creation," reprinted in *The Flood Myth*, pp. 167–82, especially pp. 172–73. See also Mary Barnard, "Space, Time, and the Flood Myths," in *The Mythmakers* (Athens: Ohio University, 1966), p. 153; David Clines, "Noah's Flood: The Theology of the Flood Narrative," *Faith and Thought* 100 (1972), pp. 136–38.

19. For an early treatment of this theme, see Heinrich Brugsch, *Die neue Weltordnung nach Vernichtung des sündingen Menschengeschlechtes* (Leipzig, J. C. Hinrichs, 1881).

20. Frymer-Kensky, "The Atrahasis Epic and Its Significance for our Understanding of Genesis 1–9," reprinted in *The Flood Myth*, pp. 61–73, especially pp. 68–73.

21. Lewis, *The Interpretation of Noah and the Flood*, p. 119.

22. Dalley, *Myths from Mesopotamia*, p. 8. The links of the flood and human mortality also figure in the *Gilgamesh Epic*, where Utnapishtim is granted immortality for surviving the flood, but explains to Gilgamesh that this blessing can no longer be obtained. See Dalley, *Myths from Mesopotamia*, pp. 115–18. The same text also introduces other causes of death—lions, wolves, famine, and disease—in place of the flood.

23. David Shulman, "The Tamil Flood Myths and the Cankam Legend," reprinted in *The Flood Myth*, pp. 294–317.

24. Kelsen, "The Principle of Retribution in the Flood and Catastrophe Myths," reprinted in *The Flood Myth*, pp. 125–49.

25. Matthieu Casalis has argued that "noise" and "wickedness" are paradigmatic equivalents, an argument that has met with little favor elsewhere. See Casalis, "The Dry and the Wet: A Semiological Analysis of Creation and Flood Myths," *Semiotica* 17 (1976), p. 50.

26. In addition to the examples collected by Kelsen, see also Frazer, *Folklore in the Old Testament*, pp. 85, 87, 89–90, 90–91, 92, 93–94, 94–95, 96–97, 103 (2), 126; Baumann, *Schöpfung und Urzeit*, pp. 316–19, 326–27.

27. Frazer, *Folklore in the Old Testament*, pp. 101–02, 103, 106; Shulman, "The Tamil Flood Myths," pp. 310–17.

28. Leo Frobenius, *Atlantis, Volksmärchen, und Volksdichtungen Afrikus*, vol. 12, *Dichtkunst der Kassaiden* (Jena: E. Diederichs, 1928), pp. 88–89. For another version of the flood myth see pp. 90–91.

29. See Louis Ginzberg, *Legends of the Jews* (Philadelphia: Jewish Publication Society of America, 1909–1938), vol. 1, pp. 168–69; vol. 5, p. 191; Follansbee, "The Story of the Flood in the Light of Comparative Semitic Mythology," reprinted in *The Flood Myth*, pp. 75–85. Later Jewish legends on Noah are excerpted in Ginzberg, "Noah and the Flood in Jewish Legend," in *The Flood Myth*, pp. 319–35.

30. Francis Lee Utley, "The Devil in the Ark (AaTh 825)," reprinted in *The Flood Myth*, pp. 337–49; Utley, "Noah, His Wife, and the Devil," in *Studies in Biblical and Jewish Folklore*, ed. Raphael Patai, Francis Lee Utley, and Dov Noy (Bloomington: Indiana University, 1960), pp. 59–91.

31. Frazer, *Folklore in the Old Testament*, pp. 81–82, 83, 97–98, 98–99, 107; Kristina Lindell, Jan-Ojvind Swahn, and Damrong Tayanin, "The Flood: Three Northern Kammu Versions of the Story of Creation," reprinted in *The Flood Myth*, pp. 265–80.

32. Loraux, *Les enfants d'Athéna: Idées athéniennes sur la citoyenneté et la division des sexes* (Paris: La Découverte, 1984); Loraux, *Né de la terre: Mythe et politique à Athènes* (Paris: Seuil, 1996); Marcel Detienne, *Comment être autochthone: Du pur Athénien au Français raciné* (Paris: Seuil, 2003). A variant of the tale of a couple repopulating the earth by casting objects—in this case fruit—over their shoulders was told by a tribe of Mexican Indians. In a version from an island just west of Sumatra the surviving woman throws stones that strike the corpses of those drowned in the flood and thus revives them. See Frazer, *Folklore in the Old Testament*, pp. 84–85, 104.

33. Heesterman, "The Flood Story in Vedic Ritual," in *The Inner Conflict of Tradition: Essays in Indian Ritual, Kingship, and Society* (Chicago: University of Chicago, 1985), pp. 59–69. Remarks on the subject are also thinly scattered in Heesterman, *The Broken World of Sacrifice: An Essay in Ancient Indian Ritual* (Chicago: University of Chicago, 1993). As Heesterman points out, Indian tales of world origins, of which the flood is a re-creation, are replete with images of father–daughter incest. Manu himself was also the product of such a union. See Wendy Doniger O'Flaherty, *Asceticism & Eroticism in the Mythology of Siva* (Oxford: Oxford University, 1973), pp. 114–17. The links between myths of the creation/flood and the sacrificial ritual are also discussed in David Shulman, "Murukan, the Mango, and Ekāmbareśvara-Śiva: Fragments of a Tamil Creation Myth?" *Indo-Iranian Journal* 21 (1979), pp. 27–40.

34. Frazer, *Folklore in the Old Testament*, pp. 85–86, 86 (2), 100–01, 103. In a particularly bizarre version, the Haida of Queen Charlotte Island told how a being that was half-human and half-crow survived the flood. Having no companion, it wed a cockle shell. After a period of brooding, the man/crow heard the faint cry of a child from within the shell. Ultimately a girl emerged, who grew up and married the man/crow so that the country was repopulated. See Frazer, p. 125. See also Francisco Demetrio, "The Flood Motif and the Symbolism of Rebirth in Filipino Mythology," reprinted in *The Flood Myth*, p. 263.

35. Frazer, *Folklore in the Old Testament*, pp. 79, 80, 82, 83, 106; Baumann, *Schöpfung und Urzeit*, pp. 372, 383–84.

36. Leopold Walk, "Das Flut-Geschwisterparr als Ur- und Stammelternpaar der Menschheit: Ein Beitrag zur Mythengeschichte Süd- und Südostasiens," *Mitteilungen der Österreichischen Gesellschaft für Anthropologie, Ethnologie und Prähistorie* 78/79 (1949), pp. 60–115; Li Hui 李卉, "Taiwan yu Dongnanya de tongbao peiou xing hungshui chuanshuo 臺灣與東南亞的同胞配偶性洪水傳説," *Bulletin of the Ethnological Society of China* (Taipei) 1 (1955), pp. 171–206; Eveline Porée-Maspero, *Étude sur les rites agraires des Cambodgiens*, 3 vols. (Paris: Mouton, 1952–69), vol. 3, appendix 1, pp. 821–51; Ho Ting-jui, *A Comparative Study of Myths and Legends of Formosan Aborigines* (Taipei: The Orient Cultural Service, 1971), pp. 56–86. See also the myth recounted in Demetrio, "The Flood Motif and the Symbolism of Rebirth in Filipino Mythology," p. 262; Willem Koppers, "The Deluge Myth of the Bhils of Central India," reprinted in *The Flood Myth*, pp. 283–87; Emmi Kähler-Meyer, "Myth Motifs in Flood Stories from the Grassland of Cameroon," reprinted in *The Flood Myth*, pp. 251–59; Verrier Elwin, *Myths of Middle India* (Oxford: Oxford University, 1949), pp. 29–50. This last contains myths about the repopulation of the earth by both sibling marriages and those of mother and son.

37. Frazer, *Folklore in the Old Testament*, p. 83.

38. Max Kaltenmark, "La Naissance du Monde en Chine," in *La Naissance du Monde* (Paris: Seuil, 1959), pp. 458–61; Wolfram Eberhard, *The Local Cultures of South and East China*, tr. Alide Eberhard (Leiden: E. J. Brill, 1968), pp. 443–45; Andrew H. Plaks, *Archetype and Allegory in the Dream of the Red Chamber* (Princeton: Princeton University, 1976), ch. 2 "The Marriage of Nü-kua and Fu-hsi"; Norman J. Girardot, *Myth and Meaning in Early Taoism* (Berkeley: University of California, 1983), pp. 180–207.

39. Frazer, *Folklore in the Old Testament*, pp. 104–05, 108–09, 115, 125, 125–26. On myths of animal ancestors, sometimes linked to a flood, see also Ho, *Myths and Legends*, pp. 256–80; Porée-Maspero, *Rites agraires*, vol. 3, appendix, 1, pp. 821–44; 846–49.

40. Frazer, *Folklore in the Old Testament*, p. 80: a god causes the flood to drown a jackal, 85: the flood is triggered by wicked men killing and eating a huge snake, 89–90: the flood is triggered by wicked men killing and eating a huge fish, 90–91: the flood is triggered in a combat between god and his grandsons who had killed the great bird that regularly awakened him in the morning; 99–100: the flood is triggered by man who has turned into a piranha and is aided by the other fish, 101: some people kill a small crocodile, and the flood is unleashed by the lashing of its mother's tail, 102: the flood is unleashed by a curious monkey who opens the basket that contained it; 116: the flood is triggered by the wounding of water-lynxes by a human hunter; 121: the flood is caused by the lashing of the tail of a sea monster, 124 (2): the flood is triggered by a raven in an attempt to murder his human nephew or examine the bottom of the ocean, 127: the flood is triggered by the weeping of a beaver abandoned by its human wife. In one Tamil myth the flood is unleashed by the elephant-headed God Ganeśa, who, in the form of a bird, caused a magic pot containing the waters of the flood to be overturned. See Shulman, "The Tamil Flood Myths and the Cankam Legend," pp. 306–06.

41. Frazer, *Folklore in the Old Testament*, pp. 78, 105, 110, 111: in this version an eagle warns a prophet of the flood but is ignored, 114–15; Kähler-Meyer, "Flood Stories from the Grassland of Cameroon," pp. 251–52, 255, 258–59.

42. Frazer, *Folklore in the Old Testament*, pp. 79, 81, 82, 83, 85, 86 (2), 90, 91, 92, 93, 95, 102–03, 105, 108, 118, 124.

43. Frazer, *Folklore in the Old Testament*, pp. 80, 81, 82, 84–85, 86–87: in this unusual version the sea will not subside until the people can throw in an animal whose hairs are so numerous that the sea cannot count them, 103: a rat fetches corn as a sign that the flood has subsided, 105: a fox dips its tail in the water to check its receding depth, 108: the vulture and the humming bird replace the biblical raven and the dove, 109, 110, 115 (2), 116, 118–20, 120, 121, 122, 123 (2), 127. On the myths of the raven and the dove, as well as related aspects of the flood myths, see Anna Birgitta Rooth, *The Raven and the Carcass: An Investigation of a Motif in the Deluge Myth in Europe, Asia, and North America*. FF Communications no. 186 (Helsinki: Academia Scientiarum Fennica, 1962).

44. Frazer, *Folklore in the Old Testament*, pp. 87, 88–89, 89, 98–99, 107 (2), 109, 115, 122; Baumann, *Schöpfung und Urzeit*, pp. 375–76.

45. Baumann, *Schöpfung und Urzeit*, pp. 309, 329, 349.

46. Frazer, *Folklore in the Old Testament*, p. 112.

47. Frazer, *Folklore in the Old Testament*, pp. 100, 110.

48. Early Chinese ideas about fire and water as correlate substances that bring either prosperity or calamity are discussed briefly in Sarah Allan, *The Way of Water and Sprouts of Virtue* (Albany: State University of New York, 1997), pp. 57–61, 87–88.

49. Lévi-Strauss, *The Origin of Table Manners: Introduction to a Science of Mythology, 3*, tr. John and Doreen Weightman (paperback edition, New York: Harper & Row, 1979), pp. 163–69, 435–70, esp. pp. 436–37, 461–65. On a parallel ambiguity of water in Greek mythology as both primal chaos and the basis of life or fecundity, see Jean-Pierre Vernant, "Cosmogonies et mythes de souveraineté," in Vernant and Pierre Vidal-Naquet, *La Grèce ancienne*, vol. 1, *Du mythe à la raison* (paperback ed., Paris: Seuil, 1990), pp. 130–31.

50. Eliade, "Structure et Fonction du Mythe Cosmogonique," in *La Naissance du monde*, pp. 471–92, esp. 472–75, 479–80, 483–84, 487–89. Even the "cosmic egg myths" that Eliade cites usually entail a primal mass of water from which the egg emerges.

51. Baumann, *Schöpfung und Urzeit*, pp. 111, 140, 146, 160, 166, 168–69, 175, 181–82, 188–90, 202, 214, 220–21, 247, 250, 253, 342, 381.

52. The most important such writers are Athansius Kircher, Thomas Burnet, Niels Stensen (latinized as Nicolaus Stenoninus, or "Steno"), and John Woodward. See Cohn, *Noah's Flood*, pp. 44–46, 52–54, 76–78, 82; Rossi, *The Dark Abyss of Time*, pp. 17–22, 33–35, 58–59, 75–77, 80.

53. Dalley, *Myths from Mesopotamia*, pp. 233–77; Paul Garelli and Marcel Leibovici, "La naissance du monde selon Akkad," in *La Naissance du monde*, pp. 117–27, 132–45.

54. Vernant, "Cosmogonies et mythes de souveraineté," pp. 111–32. Emergence from a primal sea also figures in African mythology. See Baumann, *Schöpfung und Urzeit*, pp. 189–90.

55. Mark Edward Lewis, *Sanctioned Violence in Early China* (Albany: State University of New York, 1990), pp. 167–74.

56. Gu Jiegang 顧頡剛 et al., eds., *Gu shi bian* 古史辨, vols. 1–5 (Beijing, 1926–35), vols. 6–7 (Shanghai, 1938–41); Gu Jiegang and Yang Xiangkui 楊向奎, *San huang kao* 三皇考 (Beijing: Yenching Journal of Chinese Studies Monograph Series no. 8, 1936); Henri Maspero, "Légendes Mythologiques dans le Chou King," *Journal Asiatique* 204 (1924), pp. 1–100; Bernhard Karlgren, "Legends and Cults in Ancient China," *Bulletin of the Museum of Far Eastern Antiquities* 18 (1946), pp. 199–365; Derk Bodde, "Myths of Ancient China," in *Mythologies of the Ancient World*, ed. Samuel Noah Kramer (Garden City, N.Y.: Doubleday, 1961), pp. 367–408; K. C. Chang, "A Classification of Shang and Chou Myths," in *Early Chinese Civilization: Anthropological Perspectives* (Cambridge: Harvard University, 1976), pp. 149–73; Sarah Allan, *The Heir and the Sage: Dynastic Legend in Early China* (San Francisco: Chinese Materials Center, 1981); Allan, "Sons of Suns: Myth and Totemism in Early China," *Bulletin of the School of Oriental and African Studies* 44:2 (1981), pp. 290–326; William B. Boltz, "Kung Kung and the Flood: Reverse Euhemerism in the *Yao Tien*," *T'oung Pao* 67 (1981), pp. 141–53; Anne Birrell, *Chinese Mythology: An Introduction* (Baltimore: Johns Hopkins, 1993).

57. Julius Tsai, "In the Steps of Emperors and Immortals: Imperial Mountain Journeys and Daoist Meditation and Ritual" (Ph.D. dissertation, Stanford University, 2003.), ch. 7.

In *The Shape of the Turtle*, Sarah Allan has attempted to systematically reconstruct an earlier set of Shang myths from which the later Zhou accounts, including those of the flood, evolved. See *The Shape of the Turtle: Myth, Art, and Cosmos in Early China* (Albany: State University of New York, 1991), ch. 1. This attempt to retrieve the tales of an earlier period will not be dealt with here.

58. On the fundamental importance of tales of origins as a category of myths, see Percy Cohen, "Theories of Myth," *Man* n.s. 4 (1969), p. 350.

59. Different aspects of this process and the central role of the ruler in various features of the new order are discussed at length in Lewis, *Sanctioned Violence in Early China*; Mark Edward Lewis, *Writing and Authority in Early China* (Albany: State University of New York, 1999); Mark Edward Lewis, *The Construction of Space in Early China* (Albany: State University of New York, 2005).

CHAPTER ONE

1. The different aspects of this point are developed at much greater length in Lewis, *The Construction of Space in Early China*.

2. Noel Barnard, "The Ch'u Silk Manuscript and Other Archaeological Documents of Ancient China," in *Early Chinese Art and Its Possible Influence in the Pacific Basin*, vol. 1, *Ch'u and the Silk Manuscript*, ed. Noel Barnard (New York: Intercultural Art Press, 1972), pp. 77–101; Barnard, *The Ch'u Silk Manuscript* (Canberra: Australian National University, 1973); Li Ling, *Changsha Zidanku Zhanguo Chu bo shu yanjiu* 長沙子彈庫戰國楚帛書研究 (Beijing: Zhonghua, 1985); Li Ling, "Chu bo shu de zai renshi 楚帛書的再認識," *Zhongguo wenhua* 10 (1994), pp. 42–62; Li Ling 李零, *Zhongguo fang shu kao* 中國方術考 (Beijing: Renmin Zhongguo, 1993), pp. 178–96; Rao Tsung-yi [Zongyi], "Some Aspects of the Calendar, Astrology, and Religious Concepts of the Ch'u People as Revealed in the Ch'u Silk Manuscript," in *Early Chinese*

Art and Its Possible Influence, pp. 113–22; Rao Zongyi 饒宗頤 and Zeng Xiantong 曾憲通, *Chu bo shu* 楚帛書 (Hong Kong: Zhonghua, 1985); Hayashi Minao, "The Twelve Gods of the Chan-kuo Period Silk Manuscript Excavated at Ch'ang-sha," in *Early Chinese Art and Its Possible Influence*, pp. 123–86.

3. Hunan Sheng Bowuguan,"Changsha Zidanku Zhanguo mu guo mu 長沙子彈庫戰國木槨墓," *Wenwu* 1974 (2), pp. 36–40.

4. Li Xueqin 李學勤, "Zhanguo ti ming gaishu, part 2 戰國題名概述 (下)," *Wenwu* 1959 (9), pp. 58–61; Rao and Zeng, *Chu bo shu*, pp. 101–20.

5. Chen Mengjia 陳夢家, "Zhanguo Chu bo shu kao 戰國楚帛書考," *Kaogu xuebao* 1984 (2), pp. 137–58; Cao Jinyan 曹錦炎, "Chu bo shu 'Yue ling' pian kaoshi 楚帛書月令篇考試," *Jiang Han kaogu* 1985 (1), pp. 63–67.

6. Li Ling, *Changsha Zidanku Zhanguo Chu bo shu yanjiu*, pp. 64–75; Li Ling, *Zhongguo fang shu kao*, pp. 192–94; He Linyi 何琳儀, "Changsha bo shu tongshi 長沙帛書通釋," *Jiang Han kaogu* 1986 (2), pp. 77–82; Rao Zongyi and Zeng Xiangtong, *Chu bo shu*, pp. 4–35; Li Xueqin, "Chu bo shu zhong de gushi yu yuzhouguan 楚帛書中的故事與宇宙觀," in *Chu shi luncong* 楚史論叢, no. 1 (Wuhan: Hubei Renmin, 1982), pp. 145–54. For an English translation see Constance A. Cook and John S. Major, eds., *Defining Chu: Image and Reality in Ancient China* (Honolulu: University of Hawai'i, 1999), pp. 173–76.

7. Li Ling, *Zhongguo fang shu kao*, pp. 191–92; He Linyi, "Changsha bo shu tongshi," *Jiang Han kaogu* (1986:1), pp. 51–57; Rao Zongyi, "Chu bo shu tian xiang zai yi 楚帛書天象再議," *Zhongguo wenhua* 3 (1991), pp. 66–73; Li Xueqin, "Lun Chu bo shu zhong de tian xiang 論楚帛書中的天象," *Hunan kaogu jikan* 1 (1982), pp. 68–72.

8. Lewis, *Writing and Authority in Early China*, pp. 124–27, 198–202, 280–81; Marc Kalinowski, "Mythe, cosmogénèse et théogonie dans la Chine ancienne," *L'Homme* 137 (January–March 1996), pp. 41–60.

9. *Laozi dao de jing zhu* 老子道德經注, annotated by Wang Bi 王弼, in *Xin bian zhuzi ji cheng* 新編諸子集成, vol. 3 (Taipei: Shijie, 1974), #1, p. 1; #4, p. 3; #6, p. 4; #25, p. 14; #40, p. 26; #52, p. 32; #51, p. 31. On related passages talking about a return to the origin of all things, see #14, p. 8; #16, p. 9, #22, p. 12; #25, p. 14; #28, p. 16; #40, p. 25; #42, p. 27; #52, p. 32; #64, p. 39; #70, p. 42.

10. *Jing fa* 經法 (Beijing: Wenwu, 1976), pp. 48–49, 57, 65, 73, 85, 101–02.

11. Until recently most scholars believed that the *Wenzi* chapter was a late imitation of the *Huainanzi*. However, the discovery in an early Western Han tomb of a large number of strips containing lines from the *Wenzi* has led to considerable debate over which came first. See Barbara Kandel, *Wen Tzu—Ein Beitrag zur Problematik und zum Verständnis eines taoistischen Textes* (Frankfurt am Main: Peter Lang, 1974), pp. 323–32; "Dingzhou Xi Han Zhongshan Huai Wang mu zhu jian 'Wenzi' shiwen 定州西漢中山懷王墓竹簡文子釋文," *Wenwu* (1995:12), pp. 27–34; "Dingzhou Xi Han Zhongshan Huai Wang mu zhu jian 'Wenzi' jiaokan ji 校勘記," *Wenwu* (1995:12), pp. 35–37; "Dingzhou Xi Han Zhongshan Huai Wang mu zhu jian 'Wenzi' de zhengli he yiyi 的整理和意義," *Wenwu* (1995:12), pp. 38–40; Li Dingsheng 李定生, "'Wenzi' fei wei shu kao 文子非偽書考," in *Dao jia wenhua yanjiu* 5 (Shanghai: Guji, 1994), pp. 462–73; Zhang Dainian 張岱年, "Shi tan 'Wenzi' de niandai yu sixiang 試談文字的年代與思想," in *Dao jia wenhua yanjiu* 5, pp. 133–41. In any case both versions clearly existed in the early Western Han.

12. *Huainanzi* 淮南子, in *Xin bian zhuzi ji cheng*, vol. 7, pp. 1, 7, 9, 10; *Wenzi yao quan* 文子要詮, annotated by Li Dingsheng 李定生 and Xu Huijun 徐慧君 (Shanghai: Fudan Daxue, 1988), pp. 30–31, 43. See also Allan, *The Way of Water*, ch. 3.

13. For a discussion of the philosophical uses to which one of these cosmogonic accounts, that adapted from the *Zhuangzi* at the beginning of chapter 2, might have been put, see Michael Puett, "Violent Misreadings: The Hermeneutics of Cosmology in the *Huainanzi*," *Bulletin of the Museum of Far Eastern Antiquities* 72 (2000), pp. 29–46.

14. Lewis, *Sanctioned Violence*, pp. 165–74; Lewis, *Writing and Authority*, pp. 127–29.

15. For a discussion of some early Western accounts of the generation of political states and a human world through processes of division out of a world that was originally without limits or distinctions, see Michel Serres, *Les origines de la géométrie* (Paris: Flammarion, 1993).

16. *Li ji zhu shu* 禮記注疏, in *Shi san jing zhu shu* 十三經注疏, vol. 5 (Taipei: Yiwen, 1976), ch. 37, "Yue ji," pp. 11b–12a; *Shi ji* 史記, written by Sima Qian 司馬遷 (Beijing: Zhonghua, 1959) 24, p. 1187. *Li ji zhu shu*, ch. 37, p. 14a: "Ritual differentiates types of service but joins together the reverent"; p. 19a: "Heaven is high and Earth low. The myriad objects having dispersed and divided, the ritual institutions are carried out. Flowing without cease, joining together in identity and transforming, music arises. . . . Music makes harmony sincere. Guiding the spirits, it follows Heaven. Ritual distinguishes local characteristics [*bie yi* 別宜]. Giving ghosts a place to dwell, it follows Earth. . . . Ritual is the separation of Heaven and Earth."

17. *Xunzi ji jie* 荀子集解, in *Xin bian zhuzi ji cheng*, vol. 2, ch. 2, "Rong ru," p. 44: here the statement that former kings created ritual and duty to divide people and hierarchize them leads to a discussion of the division of labor as the basis of social order; ch. 5, "Wang zhi," p. 96: here the text argues that if people are equal in position and desires there will be chaos, so they must be divided by rituals into hierarchies; ch. 13, "Li lun 禮論," p. 231: this states that ritual was created to divide people in order to maintain order; p. 232: states that rituals devoted to ancestors are the origins of *lei* 類 "categories." On the separation of men from beasts being due to rituals and duty, see ch. 1, "Quan xue," p. 7; ch. 3, "Fei xiang," p. 50; ch. 5, "Wang zhi," p. 104. In addition to general statements, the *Xunzi* also describes specific social divisions created by ritual, including those between husband and wife. See, for example, ch. 6, "Fu guo," p. 114. See also *Guanzi jiao zheng* 管子郊正, annotated by Dai Wang 戴望, in *Xin bian zhu zi ji cheng*, vol. 5 (Taipei: Shijie, 1974), ch. 17, "Jin zang," p. 290; *Huainanzi*, ch. 11, "Qi su," p. 169. Discussions of the role of ritual in creating divisions are even more common in *Li ji*. For those dealing specifically with the separation between husband and wife, or man and woman, see *Li ji zhu shu*, ch. 13, "Wang zhi 王制," p. 23b; ch. 26, "Jiao te sheng," pp. 18b, 19a: "The marriage ritual is the origin of the myriad generations. One takes a wife from a different surname in order to bring close those who are distant and to emphasize the separation [*bie*, of men and women]"; this page also states that without separation (*bie*) humans are beasts; ch. 32, "Sang fu xiao ji 喪服小記," p. 11a: here the separation of men and women is described as the greatest principle of the human Way; ch. 34, "Da zhuan," pp. 3b, 4a: here the separation of men and women is one of the unchangeable principles of the sage; ch. 37, "Yue ji," p. 11a; ch. 49, "Ji tong," pp. 10b, 14b; ch. 50, "Jing jie," p. 5a; ch. 51, "Ai Gong wen," pp. 7a, 9b; "Fang ji," pp. 24b, 25a; ch. 61, "Hun li 昏禮," p. 6b: here the separation of men and women is described as the essence (*da ti* 大體) of ritual, and

betrothal rites as the root of all ritual. See also *Mozi jian gu* 墨子間詁, in *Xin bian zhuzi ji cheng*, vol. 6, ch. 1, "Ci guo," p. 18; *Huainanzi*, ch. 20, "Tai zu," p. 350. The *Zuo zhuan* asserts that "the distinction of the surnames of men and women [i.e., no marriage between people of the same surnames] is the great rule of ritual." See [*Chun qiu*] *Zuo zhuan zhu* 春秋左傳注, annotated by Yang Bojun 楊伯峻 (Beijing: Zhonghua, 1983), Zhao year 1, pp. 1220–21.

18. *Huainanzi*, ch. 11, p. 169: "Therefore when benefit and duty are established then the Way and its virtuous power depart. When ritual and music are ornamented then uncarved simplicity disperses. When judgments of right and wrong take shape, than the common people grow bewildered. When pearls and jade are valued then the whole world fights over them. These four are all the creations of declining ages and the tools of latter days. Ritual is the means of separating (*bie*) honored from humble, or noble from base."

19. Robin D. S. Yates, "Body, Space, Time and Bureaucracy: Boundary Creation and Control Mechanisms in Early China," in *Boundaries in China*, ed. John Hay (London: Reaktion Books, 1994), pp. 56–80; Yates, "Cosmos, Central Authority, and Communities in the Early Chinese Empire," in *Empires*, ed. Susan E. Alcock et al. (Cambridge: Cambridge University, 2000), pp. 360–68; Yates, "Purity and Pollution in Early China," in *Integrated Studies of Chinese Archaeology and Historiography*, Symposium Series of the Institute of History and Philology, Academia Sinica 4 (July 1997), pp. 479–536.

20. Lothar von Falkenhausen, "Grabkult und Ahnenkult im Staat Qin: Der religiöse Hintergrund der Terrakotta-Armee," in *Jenseits der Grossen Mauer: Der Erste kaiser von China und seine Terrakotta-Armee*, ed. Lothar Ledderose and Adele Schlombs (Munich: Bertelsmann Lexikon Verlag, 1990), pp. 35–48; von Falkenhausen, "Sources of Taoism: Reflections on Archaeological Indicators of Religious Change in Eastern Zhou China," *Taoist Resources* 5.2 (1994), pp. 1–12; Pu Muzhou [Poo Mu-chou] 蒲慕州, *Muzang yu shengsi: Zhongguo gudai zongjiao zhi xingsi* 墓葬與生死: 中國古代宗教之省思 (Taipei: Lianjing, 1993), pp. 139–91, 198–201; Wang Zhongshu, *Han Civilization*, tr. K. C. Chang and collaborators (New Haven: Yale University, 1982), pp. 206–10.

21. *Xunzi ji shi*, ch. 13, "Li lun," pp. 243–46; *Li ji zhu shu*, ch. 8, "Tan gong shang," p. 5b: "To treat the dead as dead would be inhuman; it cannot be done. To treat the dead as living would be unwise; it cannot be done. Thus the bamboo utensils cannot be used, the clay utensils have no lustre, wooden utensils are not carved, the lutes are strung but not in balance, the pipes are complete but not harmonized, there are bells and musical stones, but no frame on which to hang them. They are called *ming qi* [brilliant vessels] in order to treat the dead as spirit brilliance [*shen ming*];" ch. 9, "Tan gong xia 下," p. 20a: "Confucius said, 'The one who created *ming qi* understood the Way of funerals. All objects were present, but they could not be used [by the living]. If the dead used the vessels of the living, would there not be a danger of introducing human sacrifice [to accompany the dead]? They are called brilliant vessels in order to treat the dead as spirit brilliance.'"

22. *Li ji zhu shu*, ch. 9, "Tan gong xia," p. 18b.

23. Anna Seidel, "Post-mortem Immortality—or the Taoist Resurrection of the Body," in *Gilgul: Essays on Transformation, Revolution and Permanence in the History of Religions* (Leiden: E. J. Brill, 1987), pp. 223–37; Seidel, "Traces of Han Religion in Funeral

Texts Found in Tombs," in *Dōkyō to shūkyō bunka* 道教と宗教文化, ed. Akizuki Kan'ei 秋月觀暎 (Tokyo: Hirakawa, 1987), pp. 21–57.

24. Ikeda On 池田溫, "Chūgoku rekidai boken ryakkō 中國歷代墓券略考," *Tōyō bunka kenkyūsho kiyō* 86 (1981), p. 273, no. 7.

25. "Jiangsu Gaoyou Shaojiagou Han dai yizhi de qingli 江蘇高郵邵家沟 漢代遺址的清理," *Kaogu* (1960:10), pp. 20–21.

26. Wu Hung, "Beyond the 'Great Boundary': Funerary Narrative in the Cang-shan Tomb," in *Boundaries in China* (London: Reaktion Books, 1994), pp. 93–98.

27. *Han shu* 漢書 (Beijing: Zhonghua, 1962) 53, pp. 2428–30. A similar story tells how in the seventh century A.D. the Empress Wu killed two erstwhile rivals, chopped up their bodies, and pickled their bones, but was still haunted by their ghosts. This story is related in *Zi zhi tong jian* 資治通鑑, compiled by Sima Guang 司馬光 (Beijing: Zhonghua, 1956), pp. 6294–95.

28. Like all modern studies of Chinese myth, those analyzing the tales of the flood and of Yu began with Gu Jiegang and the collective critical enterprise that he assembled in *Gu shi bian*. The most important of these are Gu Jiegang 顧頡剛, "Jiu zhou zhi Rong yu 'Rong Yu' 九州之戎與戎禹," *Gu shi bian* 古史辨 (reprint ed., Shang-hai: Guji, 1982), vol. 7c, pp. 117–42; Gu Jiegang and Tong Shuye 童書業, "Gun Yu de chuanshuo 鯀禹的傳說," in *Gu shi bian*, vol. 7c, pp. 142–95; Yang Kuan, "Zhongguo shanggu shi daolun 中國上古史導論," in *Gu shi bian*, vol. 7a, pp. 329–45, 353–65; Lü Simian 呂思勉, "San huang wu di kao 三皇五帝考," in *Gu shi bian*, vol. 7b, pp. 350–60. Some of these studies have been summarized and extended in Liu Qiyu 劉起釪, *Gu shi xu bian* 古史續辨 (Beijing: Zhongguo Shehui Kexue, 1991), pp. 6–7, 9–11, 129–31, 182–85, 477–500, 602–06; Zhang Guangzhi 張光直, "Zhongguo chuang shi shenhua zhi fenxi yu gu shi yanjiu 中國創世神話之分析與古史研究," *Bulletin of the Institute of Ethnology, Academia Sinica* 8 (1959), pp. 47–79. An extended discussion of the con-tribution of the *Gu shi bian* group to modern myth analysis, along with an analysis of the flood myths, appears in Mitarai Masaru 御手洗勝, *Kodai Chūgoku no kamigami* 古代中國の神神 (Tokyo: Sōbunsha, 1984), pp. 5–97, 101–37, 408–76, 532–605. A modern retelling of the myths, with relevant sources cited in the notes, is Yuan Ke 袁珂, *Zhongguo shenhua chuanshuo* 中國神話傳説 (Taipei: Liren, 1987), pp. 465–572. Other useful studies in Chinese and Japanese include Wen Yiduo 聞一多, "Fu Xi kao 伏羲考," in *Wen Yiduo quan ji*, vol. 1, pp. 3–68; Shirakawa Shizuka 白川靜, *Chūgoku no shinwa* 中國の神話 (Tokyo: Chūō Kōron, 1975), pp. 17, 59–69; Mori Yasutarō 森安太郎, *Kōtei densetsu: kodai Chūgoku shinwa no kenkyū* 黃帝傳説: 古代中國 神話の研究 (Kyoto: Kyōto Joshi Daigaku Jinbun Gakkai, 1970), pp. 41–62; Izushi Yoshihiko 出石誠彥, *Shina shinwa densetsu no kenkyū* 支那神話傳説の研究 (2nd ed. rev., Tokyo: Chūō Kōron, 1973), pp. 267–98. Useful studies in European languages include Granet, *Danses et légendes de la China ancienne* (1926, rev. ed. Paris: Presses Uni-versitaires de France, 1994), pp. 236–73, 316–20, 466–579; Wolfram Eberhard, *Lokalkul-turen im Alten China*, vol. 1, *Nordens und Westens* (Leiden: E. J. Brill, 1942), pp. 256–66, 326–29, 338–40, 354–65; Eberhard, *The Local Cultures of South and East China*, pp. 59–60, 66, 74, 71–79, 125–26, 210–11, 279, 307, 349–363, 393; Bernhard Karlgren, "Legends and Cults in Ancient China," *Bulletin of the Museum of Far Eastern Antiqui-ties* 18 (1946), pp. 218–20, 227–31, 247–55, 301–11; William G. Boltz, "Kung Kung and the Flood: Reverse Euhemerism in the *Yao Tien*," *T'oung Pao* 67 (1981), pp. 141–53; Rémi Mathieu, "Yu le Grand et le mythe de déluge dans la Chine ancienne,"

T'oung Pao 78 (1992), pp. 162–90; Deborah Lynn Porter, *From Deluge to Discourse: Myth, History, and the Generation of Chinese Fiction* (Albany: State University of New York, 1996), ch. 2; Anne Birrell, "The Four Flood Myth Traditions of Classical China," *T'oung Pao* 83 (1997), pp. 213–59.

29. Boltz, "Kung Kung," pp. 144–45; Allan, *The Way of Water*, pp. 39–41; Shirakawa, *Chūgoku no shinwa*, pp. 59–69. On flood stories as conventional accounts of the creation of order from a primal chaos, see Heinrich Zimmer, *Myths and Symbols in Indian Art and Civilization*, ed. Joseph Campbell (Princeton: Princeton University/Bollingen Paperback, 1972), pp. 16–17, 37, 83–90; Mircea Eliade, *The Sacred and the Profane*, tr. Willard R. Trask (New York: Harcourt, Brace & World, 1959), pp. 129–36.

30. Gu Jiegang, "Taolun gu shi da Liu, Hu er xiansheng 討論古史答劉胡二先生," in *Gu shi bian*, vol. 1, pp. 106–14. For the references to Yu, see *Mao shi zheng yi* 毛詩正義, in *Shi san jing zhu shu*, vol. 2, ch. 13.2, #201, "Xin Nanshan," p. 17a; ch. 16.5, #244, "Wen Wang you sheng," p. 13a; ch. 18.4, #261, "Han yi," p. 2a; ch. 20.2, #300, "Bi gong," p. 2a; ch. 20.4, #304, "Chang fa," p. 2b; ch. 20.4, #305, "Yin wu," p. 10b. For discussions of the relevant bronzes, see Gu Jiegang and Tong Shuye, "Gun Yu de chuanshuo," pp. 147–48. Versions of these phrases are also incorporated into several later compositions that purport to be early Zhou or pre-Zhou documents. See, for example, *Shang shu zheng yi* 尚書正義, in *Shi san jing zhu shu*, vol. 1, ch. 17, "Li zheng 立政," p. 25a; ch. 19, "Lü xing 呂刑," p. 22a; *Yi Zhou shu hui jiao ji zhu* 逸周書彙校集注, annotated by Huang Huaixin 黃懷信, Zhang Maorong 張懋鎔, and Tian Xudong 田旭東 (Shanghai: Shanghai gu ji, 1995), ch. 5, "Shang shi 商誓," p. 481.

On the newly acquired bronze with the inscription referring to Yu, see Li Xueqin 李學勤, "Lun X gong xu ji qi zhongyao yiyi 論X公盨及其重要意義," *Zhongguo lishi wenwu* (2002:6), pp. 5–12; Qiu Xigui 裘錫圭, "X gong xu mingwen kaoshi X公盨銘文考釋," *Zhongguo lishi wenwu* (2002:6), pp. 13–27; Zhu Fenghan 朱鳳瀚, "X gong xu mingwen chushi X公盨銘文初釋," *Zhongguo lishi wenwu* (2002:6), pp. 28–34; Li Ling 李零, "X gong xu faxian de yiyi X公盨發現的意義," *Zhongguo lishi wenwu* (2002:6), pp. 35–45; Xing Wen, ed., "The X Gong Xu: A Report and Papers from the Dartmouth Workshop," *International Research on Bamboo and Silk Documents Newsletter: Special Issue* (2003).

31. On the early myths whose traces run through the "Yao dian," see Allan, *The Shape of the Turtle*, ch. 3.

32. *Shang shu zheng yi*, ch. 2, pp. 6a–10b. On Yao as a solar deity see Mitarai Masaru, *Kodai Chūgoku no kamigami*, pp. 437–41. On the meanings of the graph "yao 堯" and related characters that cluster around the senses of "lofty," "bright," or "ablaze," see Boltz, "Kung Kung," pp. 149–50.

33. *Shang shu zheng yi*, ch. 2, pp. 19a–24b.

34. *Shang shu zheng yi*, ch. 3, pp. 1b–14b.

35. *Shang shu zheng yi*, ch. 3, pp. 21a–28a. A related account, in which Yu's taming of the flood is followed by Hou Ji's introduction of agriculture and then Qie's institution of proper human relations, appears in *Mengzi zheng yi* 孟子正義, annotated by Jiao Xun 焦循, in *Xin bian zhuzi ji cheng*, vol. 1, IIIA "Teng Wen Gong shang," pp. 221–26.

36. For a reference to the flood in the "Da Yu mo," see *Shang shu zheng yi*, ch. 4, p. 8b.

37. On the dating of the chapter, see Shi Nianhai 史念海, *He shan ji* 河山集 (Beijing: Sanlian, 1981), pp. 391–434.

38. The word that I here translate as "province" is *zhou* 州, which in the *Shi jing* and as glossed in the Eastern Han dictionary *Shuo wen jie zi* meant a "river island" or a "place amidst water where one can dwell (*shui zhong ke ju zhe* 水中可居者)." *Mao shi zhengyi*, ch. 1.1, #1, "Guan ju 關雎," p. 20a; *Shuo wen jie zi zhu* 説文解字注, compiled by Xu Shen 許慎, annotated by Duan Yucai 段玉裁 (Taipei: Yiwen, 1974), ch. 11b, p. 4b. The current version of the *Mao shi* uses the graphic equivalent 洲, but the *Shuo wen* quotes it with the form without the water signific. It also states, "Long ago Yao encountered the flood, and the people lived on higher land amidst the waters. Therefore they speak of the 'Nine Provinces/Islands'." Thus, Xu Shen explicitly linked the term to the story of the flood. On the evolution of this term see Gu Jiegang 顧頡剛, "Zhou yu yue de yanbian 州與嶽的演變," *Shixue nianbao* 1:5 (1933), pp. 11–33.

For a discussion of the significance of the model of the "Nine Provinces" and its later developments in early China, see Lewis, *The Construction of Space in Early China*, ch. 5. For a full-length monograph on the topic, see Xin Shuzhi 辛樹幟, *Yu gong xin jie* 禹貢新解 (Hong Kong: Zhonghua, 1973).

39. *Shang shu zheng yi*, in *Shi san jing zhu shu* (Beijing: Beijing Daxue, 1999), ch. 6, "Yu gong," pp. 159, 167, 169, 170, 176, 181, 183.

40. *Shang shu zheng yi*, ch. 6, "Yu gong," pp. 183, 185.

41. *Shang shu zheng yi*, ch. 6, "Yu gong," pp. 188–90.

42. For examples of flood myths that involve people climbing mountains to escape, or boats coming to rest on mountains, see Frazer, *Folklore in the Old Testament*, pp. 56, 78, 80–81, 84, 85, 86, 86–87, 89, 90–91, 92 (2), 93, 96, 97, 98 (2), 100, 101, 104 (2), 105, 107, 109, 111, 112, 123, 126, 128. Several of these myths also involve trees that are associated with mountains because they grow there, as in the account of Yu, or act as parallel images of great heights—see pp. 81(2), 84, 85, 90, 91, 96, 97 (2), 98 (2), 99, 100, 101, 102, 107, 121–22, 126. On the links between trees and mountains in early China see Lewis, *The Construction of Space*, ch. 2.

43. *Shang shu zheng yi*, ch. 6, "Yu gong," pp. 163, 166, 172, 173, 177.

44. *Shang shu zheng yi*, ch. 6, "Yu gong," p. 170. Since the character *yi* 乂 originally meant to "cut down" grasses or weeds (later written as 刈), the semantic parallel between the two lines is even closer than is indicated in the translation. See also p. 183: "The [hills of] Min and Po being brought under cultivation, the Tuo and Qian [rivers] were guided [into their channels]."

45. For a discussion of the links between regions, customs, tribute, and the structure of the world, see Lewis, *The Construction of Space in Early China*, ch. 4.

46. On models of the world based on five or nine zones, see *Shang shu zheng yi*, ch. 6, "Yu gong," pp. 30a–32b; *Han shu* 28a, p. 1537. The *Zhou li* expanded this model to nine zones. See *Zhou li zhu shu* 周禮注疏, in *Shi san jing zhu shu*, vol. 3, ch. 33, "Zhi fang shi 職方氏," pp. 15a–b; ch. 37, "Da xing ren 大行人," pp. 18b–20b. For a discussion of the five-zone version, see Yü Ying-shih, "Han Foreign Relations," in *The Cambridge History of China, Volume 1: The Ch'in and Han Empires* (Cambridge: Cambridge University, 1986), pp. 379–81; Lewis, *The Construction of Space*, ch. 5.

47. *Shang shu zheng yi*, ch. 6, "Yu gong," pp. 164, 169, 170, 172, 175, 181, 183, 184, 187.

48. *Shang shu zheng yi*, ch. 6, "Yu gong," pp. 191–97.

49. *Shang shu zheng yi*, ch. 6, "Yu gong," pp. 195–96.

50. On the contents and impact of the "Hong fan," see Michael Nylan, *The Shifting Center: The Original "Great Plan" and Later Readings*, Monumenta Serica Monograph Series no. 24 (Nettetal: Steyler Verlag, 1992).

51. *Shang shu zheng yi*, ch. 12, p. 2b.

52. *Mengzi zheng yi* IIIB "Teng Wen Gong xia," pp. 263–64.

53. *Mengzi zheng yi* VIIA "Jin xin shang," p. 531. Shun's life in the wilds is also suggested in a passage that refers to him eating uncooked food and wild vegetables. See *Mengzi zheng yi* VIIB "Jin xin xia," p. 568.

54. *Mengzi zheng yi* IVb "Li Lou xia," pp. 334, 350–51.

55. *Shang shu zheng yi*, ch. 3, pp. 24b–25a.

56. *Zhou li zhu shu*, ch. 16, pp. 10b–12a, 13b–14a. Writing in the Eastern Han, Zheng Xuan also glossed the *yu ren* or forester as the official "in charge of the mountains and the wastes/marshes". See *Li ji zhu shu*, ch. 10, "Tan gong xia," p. 21b.

57. *Shang shu zheng yi*, ch. 3, p. 2b. The Han dictionary *Shuo wen jie zi* glosses the character *lu* as the title of the official in charge of preserving mountain forests, citing the *Zuo zhuan* as its authority. It then adds, "Some say that forests that pertain to mountains are called *lu*." See *Shuo wen jie zi zhu* ch. 6a, pp. 67b–68a. Shun's entering the mountain forest is also described in *Lun heng ji jie* 論衡集角, written by Wang Chong 王充, annotated by Liu Pansui 劉盼遂 (Beijing: Guji, 1957), ch. 18, "Gan lei 感類," p. 374.

58. *Li ji zhu shu*, ch. 46, "Ji fa," p. 15a; *Lun heng ji jie*, ch. 25, "Ji yi 祭意," p. 516.

59. *Huainanzi*, ch. 9, "Zhu shu," p. 149; *Shuo yuan* 説苑, in *Han Weicongshu* (Taipei: Xinxing, 1977), ch. 20, p. 5b; *Di wang shi ji ji cun* 帝王世紀輯存, compiled by Xu Zongyuan 徐宗元 (Beijing: Zhonghua, 1964), p. 40.

60. *Shi ji* 1, pp. 21–22. See also p. 38, where the "Shun dian" passage is quoted directly. A version of this story also appears in *Di wang shi ji ji cun*, p. 41. The role of the *yu ren* as one who can find his way in the wilds is suggested in one passage from the *Yi jing*:

> Going into the mountain forest [*lu* 麓] without a forester [*yu* 虞]. One would only get lost in the woods. The gentleman is in peril, it is best to abandon it. If one goes, there will be regret. The *Image* commentary says, "'Going into the mountain forest without a forester' in order to pursue game. The gentleman abandons it. 'If one goes, there will be regret' and one will be in desperate straits."

See *Zhou yi zheng yi* 周易正義, in *Shi san jing zhu shu* 十三經注疏, vol. 1 (Taipei: Yiwen, 1976), ch. 1, pp. 30a–b.

The theme of Shun as a man of the wilds who is recruited by Yao also figures in a Warring States account of Yao discovering Shun in the "grasses and reeds." See *Zhanguo ce* 戰國策 (Shanghai: Guji, 1978), ch. 21, "Zhao si," p. 757.

61. These successive units as fundamental elements of early China defined by recurring structural patterns form the topic of Lewis, *The Construction of Space in Early China*. The reference to the ritual at the "four gates" probably alludes to the accounts of the "Bright Hall (*ming tang* 明堂)" as the scene of great assemblies that defined the social structure. See Lewis, *Construction of Space*, ch. 5.

62. For a broader treatment of this theme, see Roel Sterckx, *The Animal and the Daemon in Early China* (Albany: State University of New York, 2002), ch. 1–2.

63. *Shan hai jing jiao zhu*, ch. 9, "Da huang dong jing," pp. 344, 346, 347, 348, 355, 367, 371, 371–72; ch. 12, "Da huang bei jing," p. 419. On the identity of Shun and the figure Jun (俊) referred to in some of these passages, see Guo Moruo 郭沫若, *Buci tongzuan* 卜辭通纂 (Tokyo: Bunkyodo, 1933), *kaoshi*, pp. 55–56; Mitarai Masaru, *Kodai Chūgoku no kamigami*, pp. 552–57. On the animal officials see *Shang shu zheng yi*, ch. 3, p. 25a. For a discussion of the Yellow Thearch's commanding of animals to form his armies, see Lewis, *Sanctioned Violence*, pp. 175–76, 200–01. On Kui commanding the animals with music, see *Shang shu zheng yi*, ch. 3, p. 26a; ch. 5, pp. 14b–15a; *Shi ji* 1, p. 39; *Liezi ji shi* 列子集釋, annotated by Yang Bojun 楊伯峻 (Beijing: Zhonghua, 1979), ch. 2, p. 84. On the intellectual context of this story see Roel Sterckx, "Transforming the Beasts: Animals and Music in Early China," *T'oung Pao* 86 (2000), pp. 1–46.

64. *Yue jue shu jiao zhu gao ben* 越絕書校注稿本 (Taipei: Shijie, 1967), ch. 8, p. 110; *Lun heng ji jie*, ch. 4, "Shu xu 書虛," pp. 82–83; *Shi ji* 1, p. 44, *ji jie* 集解 commentary quoting *Huang lan* 皇覽; *Di wang shi ji ji cun*, pp. 40, 46. Interestingly the same story is applied once to Yu, although in most cases his tomb is associated with flocks of birds who helped people weed their fields. See *Di wang shi ji ji cun*, pp. 46, 50; *Yue jue shu jiao zhu gao ben*, ch. 8, pp. 109–10.

65. *Shi ji* 1, p. 45, note 4; *Di wang shi ji ji cun*, p. 45; *Bo hu tong de lun* 白虎通德論, in *Han Wei cong shu* 漢魏叢書, vol. 1 (Taipei: Xinxing, 1977), ch. 1, "Feng gong hou 封公候," p. 31b.

66. *Wen Yiduo quan ji* 聞一多全集 (rep. ed. Beijing: Sanlian, 1982), vol. 2, *Gu dian xin yi* 古典新義, "Shi you 釋囿," pp. 549–50, 555 note 17. For the relevant passages, see *Han shu* 63, p. 2770; *Hou Han shu*, compiled by Fan Ye 范曄 (Beijing: Zhonghua, 1965) 42, p. 1435; *Hou Han shu* 74b, p. 2413; p. 2413 note 2: this last quotes a passage from the *Mencius* with the graph *bi* 鼻, which varies from the received text but appears in most commentaries as shown in *Mengzi zheng yi* VA "Wang Zhang xia," p. 371; *Shui jing zhu*, ch. 38, p. 473.

67. The story appears in the Tang dynasty *zheng yi* 正義 commentary to *Shi ji*, where it is attributed to a work called the "Universal History [*tong shi* 通史]." See *Shi ji* 1, pp. 34–35 notes 9, 11. A similar story is recorded in *Song shu* 宋書, written by Shen Yue 沈約 (A.D. 441–513) (Beijing: Zhonghua, 1974) 27, p. 762, but it says nothing about the advice of the two wives. Instead it is Shun himself who possesses the ability to adopt the powers of birds and dragons. However, both versions depict Shun as a man who takes on the attributes of animals.

68. On this early and less specific account of the contribution of the two wives of Shun, see *Gu lie nü zhuan* 古列女傳 (Si bu cong kan ed.), ch. 1, "You Yu er fei 有虞二妃," pp. 1b–2a. This story also includes a third attempt at murdering Shun by first getting him drunk. The two wives provide him with an elixir that prevents intox-

ication and thus save him. On the role of women as prescient counselors in early China, see Lisa Raphals, *Sharing the Light: Representations of Women and Virtue in Early China* (Albany: State University of New York, 1998), ch. 2. References to the story of the two wives of Shun appear on p. 35; p. 218 note 11; p. 226 note 50.

69. *Mozi jian gu*, ch. 2, "Shang xian xia 尚賢下," p. 40.

70. *Shan hai jing jiao zhu*, ch. 10, "Da huang nan jing," pp. 367, 371.

71. *Shan hai jing jiao zhu*, ch. 13, "Hai nei jing," p. 459; *Guo yu* (Shanghai: Guji, 1978) ch. 19, "Wu yu," p. 598. This second passage states that King Ling of Chu exhausted the wealth of his state building a great tower ringed with water diverted from the Han River "in order to imitate Shun." If this story is true, it would indicate that the idea of Shun as a being ringed by water had spread throughout much of the Chinese realm at a very early date.

72. Mitarai Masaru, *Kodai Chūgoku no kamigami*, pp. 582–87; Katō Jōken 加藤常賢, *Kanji no hakkutsu* 漢字の發掘 (Tokyo: Kadokawa, 1973), pp. 19–20.

73. *Di wang shi ji ji cun*, p. 39.

74. *Shi ji* 5, p. 173. This passage identifies Da Fei with Bo Yi, who figures as "forester (*yu* 虞)" and trainer of wild animals in the *Shang shu*. See *Shang shu zheng yi*, ch. 3, pp. 24b–25a. This argument assumes the identity of Bo Yi 伯益 and Bo Yi 伯 (柏) 翳, which has been demonstrated by a series of Chinese scholars. See Mitarai Masaru, *Kodai Chūgoku no kamigami*, pp. 304–05 note 10. The free interchange of the two names already appears between *Han shu* 28c, p. 1641 (two different forms), and *Hou Han shu* 60b, p. 1987.

75. *Mengzi zheng yi* VIB, "Gaozi xia," p. 507.

76. *Mengzi zheng yi* IIIA, "Teng Wen Gong shang," p. 221. The same idea under-lies the argument in *Mengzi zheng yi* IVB, "Li Lou xia," pp. 244–45: "The world's dis-cussions of human nature are nothing but self-will (*gu* 故). Self-will is based on what profits [oneself]. What I dislike about these clever men is that they force their argu-ments (*zuo* 鑿). If the clever ones were like Yu guiding water, then there would be nothing to dislike in them. As for Yu's guiding of water, he guided it to do that which required no work [on his part]. If the clever ones also guided things in a way that required no work, their cleverness would be great indeed." Here Yu's methods of guiding water serve as an image for proper modes of thought and argument.

77. *Mengzi zheng yi* VIA, "Gaozi shang," pp. 433–34.

78. *Chu ci bu zhu* 楚辭補注, annotated by Hong Xingzu 洪興祖 (Si bu cong kan ed.), ch. 3, "Tian wen," p. 6a. The sense of *ze* 則 in the passage on the "square earth" as indicating division is noted in all early glosses and dictionaries. On this as a primary early sense of this character, see Katō Jōken 加藤常賢, *Kanji no kigen* 漢字の起原 (Tokyo: Kadokawa, 1972), pp. 1681–82. The Han commentary to the question about the Responding Dragon states that the dragon used its tail to carve out the course of the rivers for Yu. This is another element of the topos of Yu's guiding rivers into their channels. See "Tian wen," p. 5b.

79. *Guo yu* 國語, "Zhou yu xia 周語下", ch. 3, pp. 103–04. The execution of Gun, attributed to Shun, and the employment of Yu is also mentioned in "Jin yu wu 晉語五." ch. 11, p. 393. The identification of Yu with correct treatment of water—strikingly in contrast with Shun, King Ling of Chu, and King Fuchai of Wu—is also

cited in "Wu yu 吳語," ch. 19, pp. 598–99. On the relation of Yu to Gun, see also "Lu yu shang," ch. 4, p. 166. The linkage of Gun's blocking the flood and his execution also appears in *Li ji zhu shu*, ch. 46, "Ji fa 祭法," p. 15a.

80. On the relations between theories of *qi* and those of the human body, see Lewis, *The Construction of Space in Early China*, ch. 1.

81. The reference to making "images of all the things in the world" as one step in the re-creation of order alludes to an earlier myth in which Yu had images of all the creatures of the world cast on the nine tripods which he cast and which became the embodiments of sovereignty. See *Zuo zhuan zhu*, Xuan year 3, pp. 699–71. For a discussion of this myth, and references to other passages in which it appears, see Lewis, *Writing and Authority*, pp. 268–71. See also Chang Kwang-chih, *Art, Myth, and Ritual: The Path to Political Authority in Ancient China* (Cambridge: Harvard University, 1983), pp. 95–100.

82. Mitarai, *Kodai Chūgoku no kamigami*, pp. 122–23. *Mengzi zheng yi* IIIB "Teng Wen Gong xia," p. 271; *Shan hai jing jiao zhu*, ch. 17, "Da huang bei jing," p. 428; *Huainanzi*, ch. 4, "Di xing," pp. 56–57.

83. The relevant passages from the *Mencius* have been cited earlier. For other passages in the *Huainanzi* that contrast Yu with Gun and insist on Yu as someone who broke down barriers and guided waters to the sea, see *Huainanzi*, ch. 1, "Yuan dao," p. 5: "Long ago Gun of Xia built ninety-foot walls, so the feudal lords rebelled against him and to the most distant parts of the earth people had treacherous minds. Yu understood the world's rebellion, so he destroyed the walls and filled in the moats. . . . So Yu's dredging out of the water channels followed the nature of the water so he could establish his teachings"; ch. 8, "Ben jing," p. 118: "At this time Gong Gong stirred up the great flood, so that it reached to Kongsang. The Dragon Gate [of the Yellow River] was not yet opened, nor was the Lü Bridge. The Jiang and Huai Rivers completely flowed together, and the Four Seas were boundless. The people ascended mountains or climbed trees. Shun then sent Yu to dredge out the three rivers and five lakes. He opened up Mt. Yinque to guide out the Chan and Jian Rivers. He levelled out and opened up the channels and the dry land, so the waters flowed out to the Eastern Sea. The flood drained away, and the Nine Provinces were dry"; ch. 9, "Zhu shu," pp. 134–35: "Yu dredged out the Jiang and the Yellow River, thinking that the world could raise up irrigation works but could not cause the waters to flow west"; ch. 11, "Qi su," pp. 171–72: "When Yao ruled the world, Shun was minister of the masses, Qie was minister of war, Yu was minister of works, Hou Ji was the great master of the fields, and Xi Zhong the chief craftsman. As for the way they guided the people, those on the water fished, those in the mountains gathered wood, those in valleys herded flocks, and those on land practiced agriculture. The land was appropriate to the work, the work to the tools, the tools to their uses, and the uses to the people"; ch. 14, "Quan yan," p. 243: "The Way of the Three Dynasties was to accord. Thus Yu's dredging out of the Jiang and the Yellow River accorded with [the nature of] water"; ch. 18, "Ren jian," p. 310: "In ancient times the ditches were blocked up and not repaired, so the waters harmed people. Yu bored out the Dragon Gate and opened up Mt. Yinque. He levelled and regulated the water and land, so that the people had land on which to dwell"; ch. 19, "Xiu wu," pp. 331–32: "Yu bathed in the streams and the pouring rain. He combed his hair with the raging wind. He dredged out the Jiang and the Yellow River, bored out the Dragon Gate, opened Mt. Yinque, and repaired

the embankment around the Pengli Marsh. He rode the four types of conveyance, following the mountains to cut down the trees, and thereby levelled and regulated the water and land to establish 1,800 states"; ch. 19, "Xiu wu," p. 333: "The earth's topography leads water to flow east, but only after people work at it will the water bubblingly flow down the valleys. Grain is born in the spring, but only after people work at it will the five grains be able to grow. If you allow it to flow of itself, or wait for it to grow of itself, then the great Yu's achievements would never have been, and Hou Ji's wisdom would be of no use"; ch. 20, "Tai zu," p. 350: "So if you accord you will be great, but if you create you will be petty. Yu bored out the Dragon Gate, opened up Mt. Yinque, dredged the Jiang and the Yellow River, and led them east to the sea. This accorded with the flowing of water"; ch. 21, "Yao lüe," p. 375: "In the time of Yu the world was one vast body of water. Yu personally grasped his tools to take the lead among the people. He dug out the Yellow River, guided its nine branches, bored the Jiang, and linked up the nine roads. He opened the five lakes and fixed the [limits of the] Eastern Sea."

For other references to Yu's work identified as dredging or clearing out, see *Mozi jian gu*, ch. 4, "Jian ai zhong 兼愛中," pp. 67–69; *Zhuangzi ji shi* 莊子集釋, annotated by Guo Qingfan 郭慶藩, in *Xin bian zhuzi ji cheng*, vol. 3, ch. 33, "Tian xia 天下," p. 466; *Lü shi chun qiu jiao shi* 呂史春秋校釋, annotated by Chen Qiyou (Shanghai: Xuelin, 1984), ch. 5, "Gu yue 古樂, p. 286; ch. 14, "Shen ren 慎人," p. 802; ch. 16, "Le cheng 樂成," p. 989; ch. 21, "Ai lei," p. 1463; *Xin yu* 新語, written by Lu Jia 陸賈, in *Xin bian zhu zi ji cheng*, vol. 2 (Taipei: Shijie, 1974), ch. 1, "Dao ji," p. 2; *Shi ji* 6, p. 271; 28, p. 1391; *Han shi wai zhuan ji shi* 韓氏外傳集釋, annotated by Xu Weiyu 許維遹 (Beijing: Zhonghua, 1980), ch. 2, p. 42; *Shuo yuan*, ch. 5, "Gui de 貴德," pp. 2a–b; *Lun heng ji jie*, ch. 12, "Cheng cai 程材," p. 250; *Feng su tong yi jiao shi* 風俗通義校釋, written by Ying Shao 應劭, annotated by Wu Shuping 吳樹平 (Tianjin: Renmin, 1980), p. 380.

84. *Shan hai jing jiao zhu,* ch. 8, "Hai wai bei jing," p. 233; ch. 5, "Zhong shan jing," pp. 179–80.

85. On the importance of this contrast in the intellectual sphere, see Lewis, *Writing and Authority*, ch. 7. On its applications to physical space and the social order, see Lewis, *The Construction of Space*.

86. The most famous example is Zhi Bo's diversion of a river to flood the capital of the rival Zhao clan. See *Zhanguo ce*, ch. 3, "Qin yi," p. 110; ch. 6, "Qin 4," p. 230; *Han Feizi ji shi* 韓非子集釋, annotated by Chen Qiyou 陳奇猷 (Shanghai: Remin, 1974), ch. 3, "Shi guo," p. 199. Qin also diverted a river to flood the Chu city Yan, as recounted in *Shui jing zhu* 水經注, compiled by Li Daoyuan 李道元 (Shanghai: Shijie, 1936), ch. 28, p. 364.

87. On the rise of literary topoi and genres devoted to regional cultures, see Lewis, *The Construction of Space*, ch. 4.

88. *Qin Han bei shu* 秦漢碑述, ed. Yuan Weichun 袁維春 (Beijing: Gongyi meishu, 1990), pp. 123–26.

89. On the Han mountain inscriptions as evidence for the relation of the court to the localities and for the forms of local culture, see Lewis, *The Construction of Space*, ch. 4.

90. *Li shi* 隸釋, compiled by Hong Gua 洪适, in *Shike shiliao congshu* 石刻史料叢書, vol. 1–3 (Taipei: Yiwen, 1966), ch. 2, pp. 7b–9b. The account of Yu is on p. 9a.

91. *Qin Han bei shu*, pp. 258, 471; *Li shi*, ch. 2, pp. 7b, 9a, 13a, 14b; ch. 3, pp. 5a, 15a; ch. 4, pp. 4b, 9b, 11b–12, 14b, 15a; ch. 7, p. 4b; ch. 10, p. 19a; 11, p. 9b; ch. 12, p. 14b: this simply claims descent from Yu; ch. 16, p. 1b: this records the cartouche from the Wu Liang shrine, which specifies that Yu was "supreme in the structure of the land (*chang yu di li* 長於地理)"; ch. 17, p. 6b; ch. 19, pp. 9a, 13a; *Quan shanggu sandai Qin Han Sanguo Liuchao wen* 全上古三代秦漢三國六朝文, ed. Yan Kejun 嚴可均 (Beijing: Zhonghua, 1965), *Quan Hou Han wen* 全後漢文, ch. 64, p. 5a; *Qin Han bei shu*, pp. 123–26: this section of the inscription to Yu's wife recounts the sage's feats in controlling floods, regulating rivers, and establishing mountain sacrifices, p. 511: here a mountain sacrifice is justified because the peak is numbered among the "nine mountains" of Yu.

92. *Li shi*, ch. 3, p. 5a; ch. 4, pp. 4b, 9b, 11b–12a, 14b, 15a; ch. 7, p. 4b; 10, p. 19a; ch. 11, p. 9b; ch. 12, p. 14b; ch. 17, p. 6; *Mengzi zheng yi* IVB, "Li Lou xia," p. 351.

93. On the dating of the two works, see the entries by John Lagerwey on the *Wu Yue chun qiu*, and Axel Schuessler and Michael Loewe on the *Yue jue shu* in Michael Loewe, ed., *Early Chinese Texts: A Bibliographic Guide* (Berkeley: Society for the Study of Early China and the Institute of East Asian Studies, 1993), pp. 473–76, 490–93.

94. *Yue jue shu* 越絕書 (Shanghai: Shangwu, 1956), ch. 8, "Wai zhuan ji [Yue] di zhuan 外傳記越地傳," pp. 1a–b Another reference to Yu's tour of inspection appears in ch. 15, "Pian xu wai zhuan ji 篇敘外傳記," p. 4b. The *Wu Yue chun qiu*, for its part, devotes an entire chapter to the story of Yu, including all the details from the *Yue jue shu* and much more. Like the *Yue jue shu*, it also explains that the state of Yue was founded to provide sacrifices at Yu's grave, and later Yue kings refer to their descent from Yu. See *Wu Yue chun qiu* 吳越春秋 (Si bu bei yao ed.), ch. 6, "Yue wang Wuyu wai zhuan 越王吳余外傳," ch. 10, "Goujian fa Wu wai zhuan 勾踐伐吳外傳," p. 10b. Yu's burial at Kuaiji, its modesty, and his attempts not to burden the peasants are also mentioned in *Lü shi chun qiu jiao shi*, ch. 10, "An si 安死," p. 536; *Huainanzi*, ch. 11, "Qi su," p. 176; *Shi ji* 2, p. 83.

95. *Yue jue shu*, ch. 8, p. 5b.

96. *Guo yu*, ch. 5, "Lu yu xia," p. 213. On the significance of stories in which Confucius identifies prodigies see Lewis, *Writing and Authority*, pp. 34–35. Yu's assembling the spirits in a court assembly [*chao* 朝] at Kuaiji and his execution of Fangfeng are also mentioned in *Han Feizi ji shi*, ch. 5, "Shi xie 飾邪," p. 310. Interestingly, Yu's execution of Fangfeng is paired with Shun's execution of Gun, although the latter is not explicitly named. The fact of the assembly, with no mention of Fangfeng, appears in *Lun heng ji jie*, ch. 7, "Dao xu 道虛," p. 146.

97. For a list of several of these, see Yuan Ke, *Zhongguo shenhua chuanshuo*, p. 489, notes 7–10. For the account of the cult to Fangfeng in the *Shu yi ji*, see *Shu yi ji* 述異記, compiled by Ren Fang 任昉 (A.D. 460–508), in *Bai zi quan shu* 百子全書 (Hangzhou: Zhejiang guji, 1998), p. 1320b.

98. *Zuo zhuan zhu*, Ai year 7, p. 1642.

99. For a survey of the local traces of Yu's career and related cults, see Kudō Moto'o 工藤元男, "U no iseki to sono minzokuteki denshō o motomete 禹の遺跡とその民族的傳承を求めて," *Tōyō no shisō to shūkyō* (Waseda University) 12 (March 1995), pp. 132–48.

100. *Han shu* 28c, p. 1669.

101. *Taiping yu lan* 太平御覽 (Taipei: Shangwu, 1935), ch. 82, pp. 3b–4a.

102. *Huayang guo zhi jiao zhu* 華陽國志校注, compiled by Chang Qu 常璩, annotated by Liu Lin 劉琳 (Taipei: Xin Wen Feng, 1988), pp. 1–2, 10, 424. This last reference describes the general purge of shrines and the preservation of those dedicated to Yu.

103. On Li Bing's historical accomplishments and the significance of Dujiangyan, see Steven Sage, *Ancient Sichuan and the Unification of China* (Albany: State University of New York, 1992), pp. 148–51; Yang Kuan, *Zhanguo shi*, pp. 39–41; Yang Xiangkui 楊向奎, "Zhongguo gudai de shuilijia—Li Bing 中國古代的水利家—李冰," *Wen shi zhe* 1961 (3), pp. 23–61, 92; Deng Zixin 鄧自欣 and Tian Shang 田尚, "Shi lun Dujiangyan jing jiu bu shuai de yuanyin 試論都江堰經久不衰的原因," *Zhongguo shi yanjiu* 1986 (3), pp. 101–10; Tian Shang and Deng Zixin, "Tuo Jiang Mo Shui, Li Dui kaobian 沱江, 沫水, 離堆考辨," *Lishi dili* 1987 (5), pp. 70–75; Zhang Xunliao 張勛燎, "Li Bing zuo Li Dui de weizhi he Baoping Kou xingcheng de niandai xin tan 李冰鑿離堆的位置和寶瓶口形成的年代新探," *Zhongguo shi yanjiu* 1982 (4), pp. 87–101. For the argument that Dujiangyan actually was begun well before Li Bing, an argument convincingly refuted by Tian Shang and Deng Zixin in the article cited earlier, see Yu Quanyu 喻權域, "Baoping Kou he Tuo Jiang shi Li Bing zhi qian kai zuo de 寶瓶口和沱江是李冰之前開鑿的," *Lishi yanjiu* 1978 (1), pp. 95–96; Yu Quanyu, "Erlang qin long de shenhua yu Kaiming zuo Ping Kou de shishi 二郎禽龍的神話與開明鑿瓶口的事實," *Sichuan wenwu* 1988 (2), pp. 38–44.

104. On the Han sculptural depictions of Li Bing and his reception of cult, see Sichuan sheng Guan xian Wenjiaoju, "Dujiangyan chutu Dong Han Li Bing shixiang 都江堰出土東漢李冰石," *Wenwu* 1974 (7), pp. 27–28; Wang Wencai 王文才, "Dong Han Li Bing shixiang yu Dujiangyan shui ce 東漢李冰石像與都江堰水測," *Wenwu* 1974 (7), pp. 29–33. For an Eastern Han account of Li Bing's battle with the river god, see *Fengsu tong yi jiaoshi*, pp. 448–49. This story did not survive in the received *Fengsu tong yi*, but it is quoted in *Shui jing zhu*, ch. 33, p. 415; *Taiping yu lan*, ch. 262, p. 5a; ch. 882, pp. 4a–b. The historical significance of this and related stories is discussed in Jean Levi, *Les fonctionnaires divins: Politique, despotisme, et mystique en Chine ancienne* (Paris: Seuil, 1989), pp. 234–69, esp. pp. 239–41.

105. Max Kaltenmark, "Le Dompteur des flots," *Han Hiue* 3 (1948), pp. 37–39, 42; Jean Levi, *Les fonctionnaires divins*, pp. 240–41; Huang Zhigang 黃芝崗, "Da Yu yu Li Bing zhi shui de guanxi 大禹與李冰治水的關係," *Shuo wen yue kan* 1943 (9), pp. 69–76; Huang Zhigang, *Zhongguo de shui shen* 中國的水神 (1968 rep., Taipei: Chinese Association for Folklore, 1934), pp. 7–43; Lin Mingjun, "Sichuan zhishuizhe yu shui shen 四川治水者與水神," *Shuo wen yue kan* 1943 (9), pp. 77–86; Luo Kaiyu 羅開玉, "Lun Dujiangyan yu Shu wenhua de guanxi 論都江堰與蜀文化的關係," *Sichuan wenwu* 1988 (2), pp. 32–37.

106. Versions of these stories recorded in local histories and collected by folklorists are presented in Yuan, *Zhongguo shenhua chuanshuo*, vol. 2, pp. 569–72.

CHAPTER TWO

1. *Mengzi zheng yi* IIIA "Ten Wen Gong shang," pp. 219–29.

2. *Mengzi zheng yi* 3B "Teng Wen Gong xia," pp. 263–72.

3. *Shang shu zheng yi*, ch. 1, p. 19b; ch. 4, pp. 12a–14b.

4. On the Miao and the origins of criminality in the most extended account of this subject in the *Shang shu*, the chapter entitled "Lü xing (The Punishments of Lü)," see Lewis, *Sanctioned Violence*, pp. 196–99. For other accounts in which the Miao appear as the archetypal rebels, see *Shang shu zheng yi*, ch. 3, pp. 14a–b, 28b: here the evaluation and ranking of all officials culminate in the expulsion of the Miao; ch. 5, p. 11a.

5. *Mozi jiangu*, ch. 5, "Fei gong xia 非攻下," pp. 92–93.

6. *Zuo zhuan zhu*, Xuan year 3, pp. 669–71. For accounts of the tripods see also *Mozi jian gu*, ch. 11, "Geng Zhu," pp. 255–57; *Shi ji* 40, p. 1700. On the tripods as a symbol of dynastic power in Han art and literature, see Wu Hung, *The Wu Liang Shrine* (Stanford: Stanford University Press, 1989), pp. 59, 92–96, 236.

7. *Hou Han shu* 24, p. 838; *Baopuzi nei pian jiao shi* 抱扑子內篇校釋, compiled by Ge Hong 葛洪, annotated by Wang Ming 王明 (Beijing: Zhonghua, 1980), p. 375.

8. Martin W. Huang, *Desire and Fictional Narrative in Late Imperial China* (Cambridge: Harvard University Asia Center, 2001), pp. 26–28.

9. For a preliminary inventory of the myths associated with Gong Gong, see Yuan Ke, *Zhongguo shenhua chuanshuo zidian* 中國神話傳說字典 (Shanghai: Shanghai Zishu, 1985), pp. 144–45.

10. *Shang shu zheng yi*, ch. 2, pp. 19a–b.

11. Boltz, "Kung Kung," pp. 142–43. It is interesting that "flooding up to Heaven" (in this case *yi tian* 溢天) recurs as a characteristic of doomed objects and doomed rulers in the silk manuscript found in association with the *Laozi* at Mawangdui. See *Jing fa*, pp. 41–42.

12. *Shang shu zheng yi*, ch. 3, p. 14a.

13. *Guo yu*, ch. 3, "Zhou yu," pp. 101–03.

14. In fact the graph 湛 by itself could mean "flood." See, for example, *Lun heng ji jie*, ch. 15, "Shun gu 順鼓," pp. 322, 323.

15. *Huainanzi*, ch. 3, "Tian wen," p. 35. In the *Shan hai jing* this mountain is called Mt. Buzhoufuzi. It is significantly located next to a mountain entitled "Yu attacked the state of Gong Gong (*Yu gong Gong Gong guo shan* 禹攻共工國山)." In the "Tian wen" the tipping of the earth is blamed on a figure named Kang Hui who also toppled it out of anger. Not surprisingly the Eastern Han commentator Wang Yi identified this figure with Gong Gong. See *Chu ci bu zhu*, ch. 3, "Tian wen," p. 6a. There are no other traditions pertaining to the mysterious Kang Hui.

16. *Huainanzi*, ch. 1, "Yuan dao," p. 7.

17. *Huainanzi*, ch. 8, "Ben jing," p. 118. On the links of the Hollow Mulberry with myths of magical births, see Lionel Jensen, "Wise Man of the Wilds: Fatherlessness, Fertility, and the Mythic Exemplar, Kongzi," *Early China* 20 (1995), pp. 428–34. On its association with the flood, see Yves Bonnefoy, ed., *Asian Mythologies*, tr. under the direction of Wendy Doniger (Chicago: University of Chicago, 1991), p. 251.

18. *Lü shi chun qiu jiao shi*, ch. 21, "Ai lei," p. 1463; *Shizi* 尸子 (Si bu bei yao ed.), ch. 1, p. 16b.

19. *Huainanzi*, ch. 15, "Bing lüe," p. 251. There is also in the *Huainanzi* a reference to Gong Gong's birth from one of the directional winds, but the passage indicates nothing about his character or conduct. See *Huainanzi*, ch. 3, "Di xing," p. 65.

20. On the relation in early Chinese myths between accounts of flood and drought and those of the origins of warfare, see Lewis, *Sanctioned Violence*, pp. 179–85.

21. *Xunzi ji jie*, ch. 10, "Yi bing," p. 185; *Zhanguo ce*, ch. 3, "Qin yi," p. 81.

22. *Xunzi ji jie*, ch. 6, "Fu guo," pp. 126–27; *Mozi jian gu*, ch. 1, "Qi huan 七患," p. 16; *Zhuangzi ji shi*, ch. 17, "Qiu shui," p. 265; *Guanzi jiao zheng* 管子校正, annotated by Dai Wang 戴望, in *Xin bian zhuzi ji cheng*, vol. 5, ch. 22, "Shan quan 山權," p. 365; *Huainanzi*, ch. 19, "Xiu wu," p. 332; *Jiazi xin shu jiao shi* 賈子新書校釋, annotated by Qi Yuzhang 祁玉章 (Taipei: Qi Yuzhang, 1974), ch. 3.9, "You min 憂民," p. 391; memorial from Jia Yi quoted in *Han shu* 24a, p. 1129; memorial from Chao Cuo quoted in *Han shu* 24a, p. 1130; question set by Emperor Wu and Gongsun Hong's response in *Han shu* 58, pp. 2614, 2617; *Han shi wai zhuan ji shi*, ch. 3, p. 102; *Chun qiu fan lu yi zheng* 春秋繁露義證, annotated by Su Yu 蘇輿 (Beijing: Zhonghua, 1992), ch. 12, "Nuan qing shu duo 暖清孰多," pp. 348–49; *Yan tie lun* 鹽鐵論 (Shanghai: Renmin, 1974), ch. 1, "Li geng 力耕," p. 4; ch. 6, "Shui han 水旱," p. 78; *Bo hu tong de lun*, ch. 1, "Zai bian 災變," pp. 60a–b; *Lun heng ji jie*, ch. 14, "Ming yu 明雩," p. 314; ch. 15, "Shun gu," p. 322; Cai Yong quoted in *Hou Han shu* 60b, p. 1987; *Yue jue shu*, ch. 4, "Ji ni nei jing 計倪內經," p. 3a.

23. *Shi ji* 40, p. 1689.

24. *Lun heng ji jie*, ch. 11, "Tan tian," pp. 215–17; ch. 15, "Shun gu," p. 325.

25. *Guanzi jiao zheng*, ch. 23, "Kuei duo 揆度," p. 384.

26. *Zuo zhuan zhu*, Zhao year 17, p. 1386. Another passage that describes Gong Gong as a Thearch associated with water appears in *Han shu* 21b, p. 1012. This cites a work that lists the sanctioned sacrifices to early sages or founding ancestors. Gong Gong is also described as a king in a chapter from the *Yi Zhou shu*. In this account he was a ruler who regarded himself alone as truly worthy and consequently refused to appoint any high officials. He thus left himself completely isolated, aroused discontent among his officials, and was finally attacked and overthrown by Yao. See *Yi zhou shu hui jiao ji zhu*, ch. 8, "Shi ji 史記," pp. 1024–25. While this account concurs with the conventional portrayal of Gong Gong as a criminal or a degenerate ruler, it has no relation to the flood myth and is thus only tangentially relevant here.

27. *Guo yu*, ch. 4, "Lu yu shang," p. 166; *Li ji zhu shu*, ch. 46, "Ji fa," p. 14b. The *Zuo zhuan* also states that Gong Gong's son, whom it names Goulong 句龍, became Lord Earth and god of the earth altar. Although it does not state that he ruled the world, it places him in a list with several world rulers. See *Zuo zhuan zhu*, Zhao year 29, p. 1503.

28. Boltz, "Kung Kung," pp. 150–51. A similar argument is given in Mitarai Masaru, *Kodai Chūgoku no kamigami*, pp. 124–25.

29. There is also one brief mention of a figure named Gong Gong in the Chu silk manuscript. This figure, however, is credited simply with the division of the day into four segments and has no visible connection with the flood myths. See Li Ling, *Zhongguo fang shu kao*, pp. 193–94.

30. Using Karlgren's reconstructions in *Grammata Serica Recensa*, Gong Gong 共工 would be *kiung kung, while Gun 鯀 would be *kwen.

31. Yang Kuan, *Gu shi bian*, vol. 7, part 1, pp. 329–35.

32. *Guo yu*, ch. 3, "Lu yu xia," p. 103. It is on p. 108 that Gong Gong's ruin and that of Gun are paired.

33. *Mozi jian gu*, ch. 2, "Shang xian zhong," p. 36.

34. *Shang shu zheng yi*, ch. 2, pp. 19b–20a; ch. 3, pp. 14a–b; ch. 12, p. 2b. In *Han Feizi ji shi*, ch. 13, "Wai chu shuo zuo shang," p. 741 both Gun and Gong Gong oppose Yao's decision to yield the world to Shun and are consequently executed. This is thus linked to the stories of their being punished along with San Miao and Huan Dou. In other accounts it is Gun alone who opposes Yao's yielding of his authority. See *Lü shi chun qiu jiao shi*, ch. 20, "Xing lun 行論," p. 1389; *Lun heng ji jie*, ch. 2, "Shuai xing 率性," p. 37.

35. As for stories of transformations, many texts relate that Gun was transformed into a yellow bear (*xiong* 熊), a giant turtle (*nai* 能), or a dragon. See *Zuo zhuan zhu*, Zhao year 7, p. 1290: this states that Gun changed into a bear *xiong* 熊, probably a graphic confusion of *nai*; *Guo yu*, ch. 14, "Jin yu ba," p. 478; *Chu ci bu zhu*, ch. 3, "Tian wen," p. 13b; *Gui zang* 歸藏, in *Quan shanggu sandai Qin Han Sanguo liu chao wen* 全上古三代秦漢三國六朝文, compiled by Yan Kejun 嚴可均 (A.D. 1762–1843) (Beijing: Zhonghua, 1958), ch. 15, p. 3a: this refers to a yellow dragon; *Shuo yuan*, ch. 18, "Bian wu 辨物," p. 14a; *Lun heng ji jie*, ch. 2, "Wu xing 無形," p. 30: this refers to a yellow *nai*; ch. 21, "Si wei," pp. 432–33: this refers to a yellow bear; *Wu yue chun qiu*, ch. 6, "Yue wang Wuyu wai zhuan," pp. 1b–2a: this version is relatively late and much more elaborate, and the presenter is described as a messenger from a certain river; *Shi yi ji* 拾遺記, by Wang Jia 王嘉, annotated by Qi Zhiping 齊治平 (Beijing: Zhonghua, 1981), ch. 2, p. 33: this refers to a black fish, later observed leaping about with dragons. This reference to a black fish appears to be simply a division of the two elements that make up the character for Gun. While less widespread, there is also a tradition recorded in the texts discovered in the tomb of a king of Wei buried in 299 B.C. that a minister of Gong Gong executed by Zhuan Xu turned into a "red bear [*chi xiong* 赤熊]" and like Gun descended into a body of water. See *Taiping yu lan*, ch. 908, pp. 2b–3a. Both stories feature Duke Ping of Jin falling ill, dreaming of a red or yellow bear, and Zi Chan explaining the historical background. Thus, they are clearly two versions of the same story, with Gong Gong and Gun substituting one for the other.

36. For discussions of evidence of an independent mythology pertaining to Gun, a mythology that often parallels that of Gong Gong, see Tong Shuye, *Gu shi bian*, vol. 7, pt. 1, pp. 329–45. For a discussion of the drawing together of the myths of Gun and Yu into a single narrative, see Gu Jiegang and Tong Shuye, *Gu shi bian*, vol. 7, part 3, pp. 142–95, esp. pp. 159–72, 180–95. For the argument that both Gun and Gong Gong were originally mythic heroes among the people of Chu and the Eastern Yi, see Yang Kuan, *Gu shi bian*, vol. 7, part 1, pp. 336–37. Anne Birrell adopts this idea of alternative traditions in which Gun and Gong Gong were heroes in her article on the flood myth. See Birrell, "Four Flood Myth Traditions," pp. 228–41. For a summary of the positions of Yang Kuan and Gu Jiegang, and a critique thereof, see Mitarai Masaru, *Kodai Chūgoku no kamigami*, pp. 109–15. As I have argued, there are no passages that suggest any positive valuation of Gong Gong as a hero. However, several passages discussed next could be read as evidence for a positive reading of Gun.

37. *Li ji zhu shu*, ch. 46, "Ji fa," p. 1a; *Guo yu*, ch. 4, "Lu yu shang," p. 166. For a presentation of both these lists of sacrifices in the form of tables that help to clarify

their similarities and differences, see Mitarai Masaru, *Kodai Chūgoku no kamigami*, p. 558.

38. This reference to the owl and turtle is of interest, because the former is a creature of ill omen. These two creatures acting as assistants may contrast with the Responding Dragon who assists Yu in the passage quoted in chapter one, at note 78. For links between the dragon and turtle in the work of Yu, see "Li han wen jia 禮含文嘉," in *Gu wei shu* 古緯書, ch. 17, p. 5a, in *Wei shu ji cheng* 緯書集成 (Shanghai: Guji, 1994), p. 250; *Shi yi ji*, ch. 2, p. 33.

39. The first line here reads, "*Shun yu cheng gong* 順裕成功," which Anne Birrell translates, "If he completed his task according to His [the Thearch's] wishes." This translation is grammatically possible. However, since the excerpt from the same poem quoted in chapter one repeatedly points out that it was Yu who completed the task begun by Gun, such a translation assumes that the authors of the poem were incoherent and self-contradictory. The translation I have given is both grammatically possible and accords with the rest of the poem.

40. *Chu ci bu zhu*, ch. 3, "Tian wen," pp. 4b–5a. On the basis of a version of the same story recorded in the *Gui zang*, as preserved in Guo Pu's commentary to the *Shan hai jing*, Anne Birrell and David Hawkes translate the final line as asking why he did not "decompose" or "rot." See *Shan hai jing jiao zhu*, ch. 13, p. 473. However, there is no reason to assume that the *Gui zang* and the "Tian wen" versions would be in all ways identical, and I have found no evidence of any edition of the "Tian wen" that followed the *Gui zang*'s version. The version actually found in the text is in itself coherent, and it should be followed even though it is not as dramatic or entertaining as the *Gui zang* variant. I will discuss the possible significance of the *Gui zang*'s variation to our interpretation of the figure of Gun and his relations to Yu.

41. See *Chu ci bu zhu*, ch. 1, "Li sao," p. 15b: "Stubbornly upright [*xing zhi* 婞直], Gun forgot his own person, and in the end he died in the fields at Feather Mountain"; ch. 4, "Jiu zhang 九章, Xi song 惜誦" p. 5b: "In his conduct stubbornly upright [*xing zhi* 婞直] and not satisfied, Gun's work was thus not completed."

42. *Shan hai jing jiao zhu*, ch. 13, "Hai nei jing," p. 472. The story of Yu's use of the "swelling soil" to control the flood is also mentioned in *Huainanzi*, ch. 4, "Di xing," p. 56.

43. *Lü shi chun qiu jiao shi*, ch. 17, "Jun shou 君守," p. 1051; ch. 20, "Xing lun," p. 1389; *Huainanzi*, ch. 1, "Yuan dao," p. 5; *Shi ben* 世本, in *Shi ben ba zhong* 八種 (Shanghai: Shangwu, 1957), Wang Mo 王謨 edition, p. 40; *Wu Yue chun qiu*, quoted in *Taiping yu lan*, ch. 193, p. 5b. This last, an Eastern Han passage, is valuable because it refers to both the inner and outer walls of the city, thus making it clear that it is speaking of cities and not just walls.

44. The third-century A.D. *Bo wu zhi* attributes the invention of city walls to Yu, but also treats them as a destructive invention that leads to social breakdown and war. See *Bo wu zhi jiao zheng* 博物志校證, compiled by Zhang Hua 張華, annotated by Fan Ning 范寧 (Beijing: Zhonghua, 1980), ch. 8, "Shi bu 史補," pp. 93, 98 note 3.

45. *Lü shi chun qiu jiao shi*, ch. 17, "Jun shou 君守," p. 1051. This story is also presented in *Lun heng ji jie*, ch. 2, "Shuai xing," p. 37. Shun's execution of Gun, although the latter is not explicitly named, is also mentioned in *Han Feizi ji shi*, ch. 5, "Shi xie," p. 310.

46. Thus, several texts refer to "the achievements of Gun and Yu [*Gun Yu zhi gong* 鯀禹之功]" or otherwise pair Gun and Yu as two men who together restored spatial order to China. See, in addition to the passages from the "Tian wen" quoted earlier, *Guo yu*, ch. 4, "Lu yu shang," p. 166; ch. 19, "Wu yu 吳語," p. 599; *Huainanzi*, ch. 19, "Xiu wu," p. 333: however, in this passage in some editions the characters *Gun Yu* 鯀禹 appear as *da Yu* 大禹; *Han Feizi ji shi*, ch. 19, "Wu du 五蠹," p. 1040; *Shan hai jing jiao zhu*, ch. 18, "Hai nei jing," p. 469; *Li ji zhu shu*, ch. 46, "Ji fa," p. 15a; *Lun heng ji jie*, ch. 25, "Ji yi," p. 516; *Liezi ji shi*, ch. 7 "Yang Zhu 楊朱," p. 231: this refers to Yu carrying on Gun's work. However, all these passages clearly indicate that Gun had no achievements apart from Yu, that he represented at best a first step toward work that was completed by his son. The third century A.D. *Bo wu zhi* tells how Gun divined about his attempts to channel the flood and the prognostication said, "Inauspicious. There will be a beginning but nothing will follow." This accurately summarizes the conventional depiction of Gun in earlier texts. See *Bo wu zhi jiao zheng*, ch. 9, "Za shuo shang 雜說上," p. 105.

47. The secondary literature on the *Shan hai jing* consists largely of brief articles on aspects of the work or ideas extracted from it. Many try to identify modern equivalents of the places named, a futile task given the mythical core of the text. Among the few book-length treatments that deal with the work as a whole are Matsuda Minoru 松田稔, *Sangaikyō no kisoteki kenkyū* 三海經の基礎的研究 (Tokyo: Rikkan Shoin, 1995); Xu Xianzhi 徐顯之, *Shan hai jing tan yuan* 山海經探原 (Wuhan: Wuhan Chubanshe, 1991); Yun Ruxin 惲茹辛, ed., *Shan hai jing yanjiu lunji* 山海經研究論集 (Hong Kong: Zhongshan Tushu, 1974). There is also a useful dissertation: Suh Kyung Ho, "A Study of 'Shan-hai-ching': Ancient Worldviews Under Transformation" (Ph.D. diss., Harvard University, 1993). Dealing with spatial organization, there are several valuable articles by Véra V. Dorofeeva-Lichtmann: "Conception of Terrestrial Organization in the *Shan Hai Jing*," *Bulletin de l'École Française d'Extrême Orient* 82 (1995), pp. 57–110; Dorofeeva-Lichtmann, "Mapping a "Spiritual" Landscape: Representations of Terrestrial Space in the *Shanhaijing*," in *Political Frontiers, Ethnic Boundaries, and Human Geographies in Chinese History*, ed. Nicola Di Cosmo and Don J. Wyatt (London: Rutledge/Curzon, 2003), pp. 35–79; Dorofeeva-Lichtmann, "Text as a Device for Mapping a Sacred Space: A Case of the Wu Zang Shan Jing ('Five Treasuries: The Itineraries of Mountains')," in *Göttinger Beiträge zur Asienforschung* 2–3 (2003), ed. Tatyana Gardner and Daniela Moritz, Special Double Issue "Creating and Representing Sacred Spaces," pp. 147–210. There is also a translation: Rémi Mathieu, tr., *Étude sur la mythologie et l'ethnologie de la Chine ancienne: Traduction annotée du Shanhai jing*, 2. vols. (Paris: Collège de France, Institut des Hautes Études Chinoises, 1983). The second volume is an index to the work. For a survey of textual history, editions, and major studies, see the article by Riccardo Fracasso in *Early Chinese Texts: A Bibliographical Guide*, pp. 357–67.

48. Lestrignant, "Fortunes de la singularité à la Renaissance: le genre de l'Isolario'," in *Écrire le monde à la Renaissance* (Caen: Paraligme, 1993), pp. 17–48.

49. Dorofeeva-Lichtmann, "Conception of Terrestrial Organization in the *Shan hai jing*," pp. 58, 60, 86.

50. *Shan hai jing jiao zhu*, p. 477.

51. *Shan hai jing jiao zhu*, pp. 179–80.

52. *Shan hai jing jiao zhu*, p. 472.

53. This point is discussed at length in Lewis, *The Construction of Space in Early China*, ch. 5.

54. *Shan hai jing jiao zhu*, pp. 198, 372. Zuochi figures little in other texts. Granet constructs a model in which Yi sequentially kills destructive beings associated with each of the directions, and Zuochi is associated with the south. See Granet, *Danses et légendes*, pp. 378–81. Another passage indicates that, at least in the *Shan hai jing*, Yi acted as the agent of the god Jun. See p. 466.

55. *Shan hai jing jiao zhu*, p. 214.

56. *Shan hai jing jiao zhu*, pp. 218, 253 (2), 307, 311: these last two refer to a corpse described as a rebel whose name consists of two characters [*er fu* 貳負] that can both mean "treason" or "to rebel," 314: this corpse is described as an executed criminal, 319: this corpse has been torn to pieces, 351, 355, 375, 400, 411: this figure like Xingtian is a beheaded rebel who clutches a lance and shield, 435, 462: this corpse is a criminal with bound hands, wearing a cangue, but still carrying a lance in apparent defiance of the forces of order.

57. On their tombs see *Shan hai jing jiao zhu*, pp. 202 (2), 244, 273 (2), 291, 364, 380, 419, 445. The fact that divinities have tombs is not surprising, as the Yellow Thearch also had a tomb in the Han despite having ascended to Heaven as an immortal. The fact that the same *di* is buried in more than one tomb in the *Shan hai jing*, and that other tombs are noted elsewhere, also suggest that many different traditions existed as to the natures of these beings. On their towers, and that of the God-on-High, see pp. 141, 167, 233 (2), 313 (4), 380, 399, 428, 430.

58. Lewis, *Sanctioned Violence*, ch. 5. In his commentary on the *Shan hai jing*, Yuan Ke interprets all the tales of combat in the text as folk memories of battles between early, tribal peoples. Such an interpretation, although common in China, is unlikely, for it presupposes a cultural memory which entirely transcends the cultural units that supposedly produced it.

59. On the Yellow Thearch's use of thunder and the drum, see *Shan hai jing jiao zhu*, pp. 361, 442, 448. On the battle with Chi You and the agents of the Yellow Thearch, see pp. 359, 427, 430. In one account the killing of Chi You is paired with the killing of Kuafu, a rebel who pursued the sun. See p. 238.

60. *Shan hai jing jiao zhu*, p. 233. The variant story appears on p. 428. In addition to the changes noted earlier, the creature also has a different second character in its name and eats the "nine soils [*jiu tu* 九土]" rather than the nine mountains. References to the towers mentioned here are collected in note 235 of this edition.

61. *Xunzi ji jie*, ch. 18, "Cheng xiang," p. 308.

62. *Shan hai jing jiao zhu*, pp. 376, 387.

63. *Shan hai jing jiao zhu*, p. 472. In my translation I have amended the character *fu* 復 "further, later; again" to *fu* 腹 "stomach, belly" on the basis of a version of this story found in the poem "Tian wen." See *Chu ci bu zhu*, ch. 3, "Tian wen," p. 5a. For the reading of this passage I follow Wen Yiduo, *Chu ci jiao bu* 楚辭校補, in *Wen Yiduo quan ji*, vol. 2, p. 391.

64. Anthony Pagden, *The Fall of Natural Man: The American Indian and the Origins of Comparative Ethnology* (Cambridge: Cambridge University, 1982); Antonello Gerbi, *The Dispute of the New World: The History of a Polemic, 1750–1900*, tr. Jeremy Moyle (Pittsburgh: University of Pittsburgh, 1973); Gerbi, *Nature in the New World: From*

Christopher Columbus to Gonzalo Fernández de Oviedo, tr. Moyle (Pittsburgh: University of Pittsburgh, 1985).

65. Johannes Fabian, *Time and the Other: How Anthropology Makes Its Object* (New York: Columbia University, 1983).

66. François Hartog, *Le Miroir d'Hérodote: Essai sur la représentation de l'autre* (Paris: Gallimard, 1980); Hartog, *Mémoire d'Ulysse: Récits sur la frontière en Grèce ancienne* (Paris: Gallimard, 1996); Jean-Pierre Vernant, "Le mythe hésiodique des races, essai d'analyse structurale," "Le mythe hésiodique des races; sur un essai de mise au point," *Mythe et pensée chez les Grecs* (Paris: Maspero, 1965), pp. 13–79.

67. Lewis, *Sanctioned Violence*, pp. 180, 191–92, 307 note 53.

68. *Shi ji* 7, p. 338.

69. *Xunzi ji jie*, ch. 3, "Fei xiang," pp. 46–48; *Huainanzi*, ch. 19, "Xiu wu," p. 337; *Lun heng ji jie*, ch. 2, "Gu xiang," pp. 52–53.

70. On some of the ramifications of the idea of physiognomy in early China, see Lewis, *The Construction of Space in Early China*, ch. 1.

71. Lewis, *Sanctioned Violence*, pp. 155–57, 165–74; Lewis, *Writing and Authority*, pp. 109–29, 197–98.

72. *Shan hai jing jiao zhu*, pp. 465, 466, 468 (2), 469.

73. *Mengzi zheng yi* IA, "Liang Hui Wang shang," p. 54; IIIB, "Teng Wen Gong xia," p. 271: here the commanding of the barbarians follows immediately after Yu's controlling the flood and is linked directly to the expulsion of the animals; *Mozi jian gu*, ch. 5, "Fei gong zhong 非攻中," p. 86; "Fei gong xia," pp. 94, 95; *Li ji zhu shu*, ch. 52, "Zhong yong 中庸," pp. 20b (2), 21b; *Lü shi chun qiu jiao shi*, ch. 2, "Gong ming 功名," p. 110; ch. 17, "Zhi du 知度," p. 1092; ch. 19, "Wei yu 為欲," pp. 1293–94; *Guanzi jiao zheng*, ch. 5, "Ba guan 八觀," p. 73; ch. 8, "Xiao kuang 小匡," p. 126; ch. 11, "Xiao cheng 小稱," p. 181; ch. 23, "Qing zhong jia 輕重甲," p. 395; *Huainanzi*, ch. 11, "Qi su," p. 173; *Jiazi xin shu jiao shi*, ch. 3.11 "Wei bu xin," p. 417; ch. 9.3 "Xiu zheng yu shang," p. 1033: this refers to the Yellow Thearch traveling to the extremities of the earth before assuming rulership, pp. 1044–45. The idea also figured in the stone inscriptions of the First Emperor. See *Shi ji* 6, p. 243 (2): this refers to the emperor visiting distant lands where none failed to submit, and to his "illuminating inner and outer," p. 245: this refers to his authority reaching wherever the sun shines and human tracks reach, so that diverse customs are all corrected, p. 250: here he shakes "the four extremities," p. 262: here he unites "the entire universe."

74. *Shi ji* 117, pp. 3044, 3047, 3049, 3051 (4), 3065, 3067, 3071; *Han shu* 22, pp. 1052, 1054, 1056, 1060–61, 1067, 1069. On these poems and their relation to earlier temple hymns, see Martin Kern, *Die Hymnen der chinesischen Staatsopfer: Literatur und Ritual in der politischen Repräsentation von der Han-zeit bis zu ende den Sechs Dynastien* (Stuttgart: Franz Steiner Verlag, 1997), pp. 174–303.

75. Granet, *Danses et légendes*, pp. 236–97.

76. *Zuo zhuan zhu*, Wen year 18, pp. 638–42.

77. On evil demons who are conquered and used to expel or guard against other demons, see Lewis, *Sanctioned Violence*, pp. 183–95, 201–04. Ruling the world through the distribution of four men to each of the four directions also figures in the mythology of the Yellow Thearch. See *Shizi* 尸子, quoted in *Taiping yu lan*, ch. 79, p. 6a.

78. *Zuo zhuan zhu*, Zhao year one, pp. 1217–18.

79. *Zhuangzi ji shi*, ch. 7, "Ying di wang 應帝王," p. 139: "The Thearch of the south was Shu, the Thearch of the north was Hu, and the Thearch of the center was Hundun. Shu and Hu at times [or "seasonally"] met in Hundun's territory. Hundun treated them very generously. Shu and Hu planned together how to repay Hundun's generosity. They said, 'Men all have seven orifices in order to see, hear, eat, and breath. [Hundun] alone has none. Let us try to bore [orifices]. Each day they bored one opening, and on the seventh day Hundun died." Related stories apply the name *hundun* to a sack that was filled with blood, hung in a tree, and shot with arrows. This act is said to be "shooting at Heaven," thus equating the liquid-filled sack with the original, undivided source of life. See Granet, *Danses et légendes*, pp. 540–44; Eberhard, *The Local Cultures of South and East China*, pp. 441–42. See also *Zhuangzi ji shi*, ch. 12, "Tian di 天地," p. 195: "Confucius said, 'That man [a gardener/hermit who had dazzled Zi Gong] falsely cultivates the methods of Master Hundun. He knows one part of it but not the other. He regulates his interior but not his exterior. Now one who knew how to enter the distinctionless [*su* 素 "without attributes"], be without contrivance, return to the uncarved [*fu pu* 復樸], to embody his true nature, to hold onto his spirit energies, and thereby wander freely through the common world, [if you saw such a person] you would certainly be frightened! How are you or I worthy to recognize anything of the methods of Master Hundun?'" In this passage Hundun again stands for the uncarved, primal state prior to the introduction of all distinctions and divisions, the state that only the true perfected man of the Daoist tradition could reenter.

For a monograph on the myths related to the primal *hundun* and their role in Daoist philosophy and religion, see Girardot, *Myth and Meaning in Early Taoism*.

80. *Mengzi zheng yi* VA, p. 360; *Shi ji* 1, p. 33. A version of this story also appears in *Shizi*, ch. 2, p. 9b. See also *Jin louzi* 金樓子, in *Si ku quan shu zhen ben bie ji* 四庫全書珍本別輯, vol. 207 (Taipei: Shangwu, 1975), ch. 1, "Xing wang 興王," pp. 5a–b.

81. *Lü shi chun qiu jiao shi*, ch. 1, "Qu si 去私," p. 55; ch. 22, "Qiu ren 求人," p. 1514.

82. *Lun heng ji jie*, ch. 25, "Jie chu," p. 505. A shorter version of this story preserved in the same text states that the third demon lived not only in the corner of houses but also in stables, and that the demon was given to frightening children. See *Lun heng ji jie*, ch. 22, "Ding gui," p. 450. A fragment of the *Han jiu yi* 漢舊儀 preserved in the commentary to the ritual monograph of the *Xu Han shu* states that the third demon also lived in granaries. See *Hou Han shu*, "Li yi zhong 禮儀中," p. 3128 note 2. On the *wangliang* demon and its role in the Great Exorcism at the New Year, see Derk Bodde, *Festivals in Classical China: New Year and Other Annual Observances During the Han Dynasty* (Princeton: Princeton University, 1975), pp. 79–80, 84, 101, 103–04, 106–08, 112–14, 117, 124.

83. In addition to the *Shang shu*, see *Mengzi zheng yi*, VA, "Wan Zhang shang," p. 371; *Zhuangzi ji shi*, ch. 11, "Zai You," p. 169—the *Zhuangzi*, as one would expect, argues that these punishments were ineffective; *Huainanzi*, ch. 19, "Xiu wu," p. 331; *Shi ji* 1, p. 28: in this account each of the four miscreants is said to transform (*bian* 變) the barbarians of the region to which he is exiled; *Da Dai li ji jie gu* 大戴禮記解詁, annotated by Wang Pinzhen 王聘珍, rep. ed. (Beijing: Zhonghua, 1964), ch. 7, "Wu di de 五帝德," p. 121: this tells the same story of "transformation" as the *Shi ji*. Other texts

refer to only one or two of the punishments, such as those of Gong Gong and Gun. In addition to those cited, see also *Zuo zhuan zhu*, Xi year 33, p. 502 Zhao year 7, p. 1290 *Lü shi chun qiu jiao shi*, ch. 21, "Kai chun 開春," p. 1427.

84. Lewis, *Sanctioned Violence*, pp. 196–205.

85. *Shang shu zheng yi*, ch. 3, pp. 9a–b; *Shi ji* 1, p. 24. In a version of the story in the *Xunzi*, three of the four malefactors expelled by Shun are sequentially attacked by Yao, Shun, and Yu. In this same passage the criminals identified with the flood are paired with the overthrow of evil rulers by the founders of the Shang and Zhou, just as in the second flood account in the *Mencius*. See *Xunzi ji jie*, ch. 10, "Yi bing," pp. 185–86.

CHAPTER THREE

1. Gu Jiegang and Tong Shuye argued that Yao and Shun originally had nothing to do with myths of the flood, and that it was only with the development of the myth of the consecutive yielding of the kingship from Yao to Shun to Yu that the first two explicitly became actors in the flood myths. See Gu Jiegang and Tong Shuye, "Gun Yu de chuanshuo," *Gu shi bian*, vol. 7, part 3, pp. 189–90. This is possible, but, as I pointed out earlier, the mythic attributes of Shun, which run throughout stories of his career without always being explicitly thematized, indicate many links to the themes articulated in tales of the flood. Consequently it is likely that Shun had been involved in flood stories prior to being drawn into accounts of the royal succession, and that his involvement in the former made possible or necessary his inclusion in the latter.

2. The most detailed and sophisticated study of these myths and their meanings is Sarah Allan, *The Heir and the Sage*.

3. *Shi ji* 1, p. 45.

4. For a discussion by leading Eastern Han scholars of the principle that the sages were the offspring of spirit progenitors, see *Bo wu jing yi yi* 駁五經異義, by Xu Shen 許慎 and Zheng Xuan 鄭玄, in *Hou zhi bu zu zhai congshu* 後知不足齋叢書 (n.p.: Chang Shubao, 1884), *tao* 1, ch. 1, pp. 19a–b. For a study by a modern scholar of the same theme, see Yasui Kōzan 安居香山, *Isho no seiritsu to sono tenkai* 緯書の成立とその展開 (Tokyo: Kokusho Kankō, 1981), pp. 413–44. On the myth of the spiritual progenitor of Confucius and its ramifications in the early accounts of his life, see Lewis, *Writing and Authority in Early China*, p. 219. In the same book, pp. 447–48, note 117 provides references to primary sources on accounts of the spirit progenitors of the early sages, dynastic founders, Confucius, and even Mencius. Many of these are recorded in the *chen wei* prophetic texts that flourished during the Eastern Han. The account of the divine paternity of the Han founder appears in *Shi ji* 8, p. 341.

5. Mori Mikisaburō 森三樹三郎, *Shina kodai shinwa* 支那古代神話 (reprint of 1944 ed., Tokyo: Kiyomizu Kōbundō, 1969), p. 62; Mitarai Masaru, *Chūgoku kodai no kamigami*, pp. 117, 123, 125, 127–28, 411–12, 444–45, 546–47.

6. *Guo yu*, ch. 17, "Chu yu shang 楚語上," p. 527. The principle of wicked fathers having good sons, as demonstrated above all by the relation of Gun and Yu, is also articulated in the late Eastern Han text *Qian fu lun jian*, ch. 4, "Lun rong 論榮," p. 35.

7. *Han Feizi ji shi*, ch. 17, "Shuo yi 説疑," p. 924; *Shang Jun shu zhu yi* 商君書注譯, annotated by Gao Heng 高亨 (Beijing: Zhonghua, 1974), ch. 7, "Kai se 開塞," pp. 182–83. The dating of this latter text remains disputed among modern scholars, but most would agree that it had been compiled no later than the Western Han period.

8. Thus, references to Wu Guan (also called Wu Zi) as a son of Qi who causes disorder appear in *Chu ci bu zhu*, ch. 1, "Li sao," pp. 17a–b; *Yi Zhou shu hui jiao ji zhu*, ch. 6, "Chang mai 嘗麥," pp. 786–87; "Zong zheng qing zhen 宗正卿箴," by Yang Xiong 揚雄, in Yan Kejun, ed., *Quan shanggu sandai Qin Han Sanguo Liuchao wen*, "Quan Han wen," ch. 54, pp. 5b–6a. This myth may have derived from a seventh-century B.C. historical event recorded in the *Zuo zhuan*, in which five sons (which in Chinese would be "wu zi") of Lord Huan of Qi struggled over the succession. This event was later than the supposed date of the mythic events but probably took place before the formation of the myth. See *Zuo zhuan zhu*, Xi year 17, pp. 373–76. The *Gui zang* text discovered in the Warring States tomb at Wangjiatai also contains several stories that celebrate Qi as a great sage.

9. The "Wu (五)" of "Wu Guan" is reconstructed as *ngo or *ngag. The "Hu (扈)" of "Guan Hu" is *go or *gag, that is, the former is distinguished only by an initial nasal. The other character is identical. On the tradition of a battle between Qi and Hu or Guan Hu, a battle that was supposedly the occasion for the battle oath at Gan ("Gan shi" 甘誓)," see *Shang shu zheng yi*, ch. 7, "Gan shi," pp.1b–2a; *Zuo zhuan zhu*, Zhao year 1, p. 1206; *Yi Zhou shu hui jiao ji zhu*, ch. 8, "Shi ji," p. 1017; *Lü shi chun qiu jiao shi*, ch. 3, "Xian ji 先己," pp. 145, 155 note 43; *Huainanzi*, ch. 15, "Yi bing," p. 251; *Shi ji* 2, p. 84. On the Hu as offspring of Yu, see *Shi ji* 2, p. 89; *Shi ben*, in *Shi ben ba zhong*, Sun Pingyi 孫馮翼 edition, p. 14; *Huainanzi*, ch. 11, "Qi su," p. 179: Gao You's Eastern Han commentary states that Hu was Qi's elder brother, i.e., Yu's son; *Hou Han shu* 28b, pp. 992, 993 note 6; Li Daoyuan 酈道元, *Shui jing zhu* 水經注 (Shanghai: Shijie, 1936), ch. 26, p. 337 quoting the *Ji zhong shu*. See also the passages assembled by Sun Yirang in *Mozi jian gu*, ch. 8, "Fei yue shang 非樂上," p. 161.

10. Some texts accuse Qi of giving himself up to excessive pleasure in music and drink. See, for example, *Mozi jian gu*, ch. 8, "Fei yue shang," pp. 161–62: this passage quotes what appears to be a lost chapter from the *Shang shu* pertaining to Wu Guan; *Chu ci bu zhu*, ch. 1, "Li sao," pp. 17a–b. As the next note will show, many accounts of Qi focus on the theme of music. Other texts accuse Qi of rebelling against his father's designated successor and seizing the throne. See *Chu ci bu zhu*, ch. 3, "Tian wen," pp. 11a–b: this follows Zhu Xi's reading of the passage in *Chu ci bian zheng* 楚辭辨證, which quotes the *Ji zhong shu*; *Han Feizi ji shi*, ch. 14, "Wai chu shuo you xia," pp. 775, 776; *Zhan guo ce*, ch. 29, "Yen yi," p. 1059; *Shi ji* 34, p. 1556; *Han shu* 21a, p. 978. The *Mencius* argues against this version, insisting that Qi was elevated because the people followed him rather than Yu's chosen successor, but this moralizing account demonstrates that stories of Qi's criminality were widespread. See *Mengzi zheng yi* VA, "Wan Zhang shang," pp. 381–85. The *Gu ben zhu shu ji nian* states that "Yi violated [or 'interfered with' *gan* 干] Qi's position, so Qi killed him." See [*Jin ben*] *zhu shu ji nian shu zheng* 今本竹書紀年疏證, annotated by Wang Guowei 王國維, in [*Gu ben*] *zhu shu ji nian ji zheng* 古本竹書紀年輯證, annotated by Fang Shiming 方詩銘 and Wang Xiuling 王修齡 (Shanghai: Shanghai Gu Ji, 1981), p. 2. This indicates that the authors considered Qi legitimate and Yi a rebel.

11. In addition to the passages cited earlier, in which Qi appeared in the list of sages with his own wicked son(s), he figures in the *Shan hai jing* as a sage hero who rides to Heaven on dragons and brings back the "Nine Songs." See *Shan hai jing jiao zhu*, ch. 7, "Hai wai xi jing," p. 209, p. 210 note 6 quoting the *Gui zang*; ch. 16, "Da huang xi jing," p. 414; [*Gu ben*] *zhu shu ji nian ji zheng*, p. 2.

12. *Mozi jian gu*, ch. 8, "Ming gui xia," pp. 148–49: this passage calls the "Gan shi" the "Yu shi"; *Zhuangzi ji shi*, ch. 4, "Ren jian shi," p. 64; *Lü shi chun qiu jiao shi*, ch. 20, "Zhao lei," p. 1360; *Shuo yuan*, ch. 7, "Zheng li 政理," p. 4a.

13. See, for example, *Lü shi chun qiu jiao shi*, ch. 1, "Qu si," p. 55; ch. 3, "Huan dao 圜道," p. 173; *Xunzi ji jie*, ch. 12, "Zheng lun," p. 224; ch. 18, "Cheng xiang," pp. 307–08.

14. *Zhuangzi ji shi*, ch. 29, "Dao Zhi 盜跖," pp. 430, 434; *Lü shi chun qiu jiao shi*, ch. 11, "Dang wu 當務," p. 596; ch. 19, "Ju nan 舉難," p. 1309; *Xunzi ji jie*, ch. 12, "Zheng lun 正論," p. 224; *Huainanzi*, ch. 13, "Fan lun," p. 226; *Yue jue shu*, ch. 3, "Yue jue Wu nei zhuan," p. 3b; ch. 15, "Pian xu wai zhuan ji," p. 3a. Emperor Wen of the Han referred to Yao and Shun exiling their own kin. See *Shi ji* 118, p. 3080. This tradition of the sages being poor fathers is also suggested by the passages that describe how during his labors Yu repeatedly passed the door of his house without entering it. See, for example, *Mengzi zheng yi*, IVB, "Li Lou xia," p. 351; [*Gu*] *lie nü zhuan* 古列女傳 (Si bu cong kan ed.), ch. 1, p. 3a: this text says that due to Yu's dereliction, the burden of educating his sons fell entirely on his wife; *Shang shu zheng yi*, ch. 5, "Yi Ji," p. 11a: this text specifies that Yu heard the sound of his son weeping but ignored it in order to devote himself to taming the flood; *Shi ji* 2, p. 51; *Wu Yue chun qiu*, ch. 16, "Yue wang Wuyu wai zhuan," p. 1b.

15. *Huainanzi*, ch. 19, "Xiu wu," p. 336. In reading this passage I have followed some emendations suggested by Wang Niansun 王念孫 collected in *Huainanzi ji shi* 集釋 (Beijing: Zhonghua, 1998), p. 1329.

16. *Lun heng ji jie*, ch. 2, "Ming yi 命義," p. 27; ch. 3, "Ou hui 偶會," p. 48: "Yao was destined to yield his position to Shun, so Dan Zhu acted criminally. Shun was destined to yield his position to Xia [Yu], so Shang Jun was deviant. It was not the case that Shun and Yu being suitable to obtain the world could cause the two sons to be wicked. Goodness and badness, right and wrong, will always just work out [as dictated by destiny]"; ch. 3, "Ben xing 本性," pp. 63, 64: the third passage previously quoted follows a discussion of human nature that divides people into the "supremely good [*ji shan* 極善]" who act correctly without teaching, the middling types who are guided by instruction and influence, and the "supremely wicked [*ji e* 極惡]" who act badly no matter what, of which Dan Zhu and Shang Jun are the definitive examples; ch. 16, "Jiang rui 講瑞," p. 345: "Some say, 'The unicorn's relation to beasts, the phoenix's relation to birds, Mt. Tai's relation to hills, the Yellow River's and the sea's relation to pools are all categories/species [*lei* 類].' Thus the phoenix and unicorn are of the same category/species as birds or beasts. It is just that their forms and colors are completely different. How could they be of a completely different type? They are in the same category, but are remarkable [*qi* 奇]. Being remarkable is not hereditary. Not being hereditary, it is difficult to judge. How do we know this? Yao sired Dan Zhu, and Shun sired Shang Jun. So Shang Jun and Dan Zhu were of the same breed as Yao and Shun. However, their natures were completely different. Gun sired Yu, and Gu Sou sired Shun, so Shun and Yu were of the same breed as Gun and Gu Sou.

However, their knowledge and virtue were distinct." Dan Zhu also appears in isolation as the very type of uneducable humanity in ch. 2, "Shuai xing," p. 38. The formula about even neighboring houses being enfeoffed—*bi wu er feng* 比屋而封—also appears in *Xin yu*, ch. 4, "Wu wei 無為," p. 7.

The idea that the bad sons of good fathers and good sons of bad fathers demonstrated that some people were bad or good by nature and not liable to the influence of education or experience already appears as a position to be refuted in the *Mencius*. See *Mengzi zheng yi*, VIA, "Gaozi shang," p. 441. Dan Zhu's animal nature, upon which these passages insist, was also noted in the *Shang shu zheng yi*, ch. 5 "Yi Ji 益稷," pp. 10b–11a: this passage lists the various forms of Dan Zhu's misconduct; *Yue jue shu*, ch. 3, p. 3b.

On the story of Yangshe Shiwo [= Yang Shiwo] as a figure with a bestial nature who was thus irremediably wicked, as well as other examples of the same belief, see *Zuo zhuan zhu*, Xuan year 4, p. 629; Zhao year 28, pp. 1493. For a brief discussion, see Lewis, *Sanctioned Violence*, p. 304 note 25.

17. *Shizi*, ch. 1, pp. 13a–b.

18. On Dan Zhu and chess, see *Shi ben*, in *Shi ben ba zhong*, Zhang Shu edition, p. 22; *Jin louzi*, ch. 1, "Xing wang," p. 5a: this passage seems to suggest that Dan Zhu was corrupted by the ornate character of the *go* board and pieces. On *go* and chess as substitutes for warfare given as presents to lure bellicose people into more civil pursuits, see Lewis, *Sanctioned Violence in Early China*, p. 147.

19. Guo Pu's commentary to the *Shan hai jing* quotes the *Zhu shu ji nian* to this effect. See *Shan hai jing jiao zhu*, ch. 10, "Hai nei nan jing," p. 274 note 2. This Dan River, which is toponymically linked to Dan Zhu, also figures as the site of Yao's battle with some unnamed southern barbarians (*man* 蠻). See *Shang shu yi pian*, cited in *Taiping yu lan*, ch. 63; *Lü shi chun qiu jiao shi*, ch. 20, "Zhao lei," p. 1360. As Yuan Ke has pointed out, elsewhere Yao fights this battle against the San Miao who figured as archetypal rebels and one of the four malefactors in the *Shang shu* and other texts. One passage in the *Shan hai jing* also links Dan Zhu to Huan Dou, another of the evil figures who appear in these lists of archetypal criminals. See *Shan hai jing jiao zhu*, ch. 6, "Hai wai nan jing," pp. 189, 190 notes 1–2. Thus, there is some evidence for linking the tradition of Dan Zhu as an evil son to the criminal figures expelled by Shun. The now conventional identification of Dan Zhu with Huan Dou, however, has been disputed at some length by Mitarai Masaru. See *Kodai Chūgoku no kamigami*, pp. 410–17.

20. *Mengzi zheng yi*, VA "Wan Zhang shang," pp. 359–73. References to the wickedness of Shun's parents and brother, without any specific details, also appear in *Shang shu zheng yi*, ch. 2, "Yao dian," pp. 24a–b. The version from the *Mencius* is followed in *Shi ji* 1, pp. 31–34, and in *Lun heng ji jie*, ch. 2, "Ji yan 吉驗," p. 40; ch. 26, "Zhi shi," p. 531; *Shang shu da zhuan* 尚書大傳 (Si bu bei yao ed.), ch. 2, p. 4a; *Xin xu shu zheng* 新序疏證, annotated by Zhao Shanyi 趙善詒 (Shanghai: Huadong Shifan Daxue, 1989), ch. 1, "Za shi 雜事," p. 1; *Shuo yuan*, ch. 3, "Jian ben 建本," pp. 4a–b; *Yue jue shu*, ch. 3, "Yue jue Wu nei zhuan," p. 3b; ch. 15, "Pian xu wai zhuan ji," p. 3a. The story is also assumed in *Lun heng ji jie*, ch. 16, "Jiang rui," p. 345, which states that Gun and Gu Sou were of the same kind, and ch. 27, "Ding xian 定賢," pp. 541–42. This last passage makes the interesting argument that just as true heroism can only be demonstrated when one is born in a time of crisis, so true filial piety can

only be demonstrated when one's parents are wicked. This turns the pattern of wicked parents of sages into a logical necessity, since only someone with wicked parents can be truly filial. The *Han Feizi* refers to the story, but it states that Shun ultimately exiled his wicked father and killed his brother, thus demonstrating that he was not the moral exemplar celebrated in the *Mencius* and other texts in the *ru* tradition. See *Han Feizi ji shi*, ch. 20, "Zhong xiao 忠孝," p. 1108 (2).

21. On Shun's doubled pupils, see *Shizi*, ch. 2, p. 2a: this text specifically states that his two pupils indicated his "double acuity"; *Xunzi ji jie*, ch. 3, "Fei xiang," p. 47; *Di wang shi ji ji cun*, p. 40; *Huainanzi*, ch. 19, "Xiu wu," p. 337: this passage also states that the double pupils indicate double acuity; *Shang shu da zhuan*, ch. 5, p. 2a; *Lun heng ji jie*, ch. 3, "Gu xiang," pp. 52; ch. 16, "Jiang rui," p. 340; *Chun qiu fan lu yi zheng*, ch. 7, "San dai gai zhi zhi wen 三代改制質文," p. 212: this passage again links Shun's double pupils to his acuity.

22. For an example of such an attack, see *Lun heng ji jie*, ch. 30, "Zi ji 自紀," p. 591. In this final chapter that gives some of the author's personal history and justifies the writing of the text, Wang Chong cites Gun and Gu Sou as the villainous fathers of sages in an extended demonstration that good fathers have bad sons and vice versa. This argument serves to refute those who used Wang Chong's origins in a family of merchants and local bullies to dismiss his aspirations to office and his claims to literary excellence. In this way it is linked to Wang Chong's more general attack on the increasingly hereditary character of the Han elite.

23. *Zuo zhuan zhu*, Xuan year 4, p. 629; Zhao year 28, p. 1493.

24. *Feng su tong yi jiao shi*, pp. 434–35. The belief that children born in the first and fifth months would kill their parents is also recorded in the *Lun heng ji jie*, ch. 23, "Si hui," pp. 470–71.

25. *Shi ji* 75, p. 2352. On the textual evidence for Han beliefs about the fifth day of the fifth month and the closely related summer solstice, see Bodde, *Festivals in Classical China*, pp. 289–316. For evidence of these and related beliefs from archaeologically recovered texts, see Anne Behnke Kinney, *Representations of Childhood & Youth in Early China* (Standford: Standford University, 2004), pp. 18–19, 104, 173–174.

26. See, for example, *Yi yuan* 異苑, in *Xue jin tao yuan* 學津討源, fragments compiled by Zheng Pengyi 張鵬一 [Qing dynasty] (Shanghai: Shangwu, n.d.), ch. 8, pp. 9a, 9b.

27. *Zuo zhuan zhu*, Yin year 1, p. 10.

28. *Shi liu guo chun qiu* 十六國春秋, quoted in the commentary to *San guo zhi* 三國志, compiled by Chen Shou 陳壽 (Beijing: Zhonghua, 1959) 30, p. 845.

29. *Lie xian zhuan* 列仙傳, in *Zheng tong Dao zang* 正統道藏, vol. 8 (rep. ed., Taipei: Yiwen, 1976), ch. 2, p. 6128.

30. The idea that children who harmed their parents belonged to these two categories also appeared in ancient Greece. See Marie Delcourt, *Stérilités mystérieuses et naissances maléfiques dans l'Antiquité classique*, Bibliothèque de la Faculté de Philosophie et Lettres de l'Université de Liège, Fascicule LXXXIII (1938), reissued in Paris, 1986, pp. 47–48.

31. Lewis, *Sanctioned Violence in Early China*, pp. 167–73.

32. On the relevant ritual regulations see, for example, *Yi li zhu shu* 儀禮注疏, in *Shi san jing zhu shu*, vol. 4 (Taipei: Yiwen, 1974), ch. 31, pp. 14a–b; *Li ji zhu shu*, ch. 19, "Zengzi wen 曾子問," pp. 14b–20b; ch. 32, "Sang fu xiao ji," p. 9b; ch. 43, "Za ji xia," p. p. 2b. On the relevant regulation in the Qin code, see *Shuihudi Qin mu zhu jian* 睡虎地秦慕竹簡 (Beijing: Wensu, 1978), p. 181. On the disputed practice of infanticide see Kinney, *Representations*, ch. 4.

33. *Han shu* 72, pp. 3075, 3079; *Hou Han shu* 7, p. 301; *Li ji zhu shu*, ch. 28, p. 20a.

34. *Li shi*, ch. 6, p. 17b.

35. This inscription is translated and the images from the stone reproduced in Wu Hung, "Private Love and Public Duty: Images of Children in Early Chinese Art," in *Chinese Views of Childhood*, ed. Anne Behnke Kinney (Honolulu: University of Hawaii, 1995), pp. 79–81.

36. *Li ji zhu shu*, ch. 27, p. 5a; ch. 28, p. 13b; *Chūgoku kodai fukushoku*, p. 35.

37. Lewis, *Sanctioned Violence in Early China*, pp. 190–91.

38. *Chun qiu yuan ming bao* 春秋元命包, cited in *Tai ping yu lan*, ch. 363, p. 6a.

39. *Yunmeng Shuihudi Qin mu* 雲蒙睡虎地秦墓 (Beijing: Wenwu, 1981), illustrations p. 132, strip 867 verso. The "innocent ghost [*bu gu gui* 不辜鬼]" who repeatedly kills children may well also be a child spirit. See p. 134, strip 844 verso. On the *qi* spirit, see *Shuo wen jie zi zhu*, ch. 9a, p. 41b; Ma Jixing 馬繼興, *Mawangdui gu yi shu kaoshi* 馬王堆古醫書考釋 (Changsha: Hunan kexue jishu, 1992), pp. 635–38; Donald Harper, *Early Chinese Medical Literature* (London: Kegan Paul, 1998), p. 302. See also J. J. M. de Groot, *The Religious System of China*, 6 vols. (Leiden, 1892–1910), vol. 5, pp. 696–97.

40. [*Bei ji*] *Qian jin yao fang* 備急千金要方, written by Sun Simiao 孫思邈, in *Zhengtong dao zang*, vol. 43, ch. 11, p. 6.

41. *Shan hai jing jiao zhu*, pp. 6, 14, 76, 77, 82, 86, 109, 115, 124, 130.

42. *Shan hai jing jiao zhu*, pp. 15, 18, 72, 115.

43. *Baopuzi nei pian jiao shi*, p. 277.

44. *Bai ze tu* 白澤圖, in Ma Guohan 馬國翰, ed., *Yu han shan fang ji yi shu* 玉函山房輯佚書 (Changsha: 1883), ch. 77, pp. 58a, 58b–59a, 59a, 60a, 60b–61a. For a description of the *Bai ze tu* based on the surviving fragments, and a comparison of it with the Shuihudi demonography, see Donald Harper, "A Chinese Demonography of the Third Century B.C.," *Harvard Journal of Asiatic Studies* 45 (1985), pp. 491–94.

45. *Baopuzi nei pian jiao shi*, p. 76.

46. *Lun heng ji jie*, ch. 23, "Si hui," p. 468. On the threatening pollution of childbirth. See also Kinney, *Representations*, pp. 167–69.

47. Hu Puan 胡朴安, *Zhonghua quan guo fengsu zhi* 中華全國風俗志 (Zhengzhou: Zhengzhou guji, 1990, rept. of 1936 ed.), p. 287; Nagao Ryūzō 永尾龍造, *Shina minzoku shi* 支那民俗誌 (Tokyo: Dai Nippon, 1940–42), vol. 6, p. 161.

48. *Yi yuan*, ch. 8, p. 9b.

49. Patricia Buckley Ebrey, *The Inner Quarters: Marriage and the Lives of Chinese Women in the Sung Period* (Berkeley: University of California, 1993), pp. 174–75.

50. Arthur P. Wolf, "Gods, Ghosts, and Ancestors," in *Religion and Ritual in Chinese Society* (Stanford: Stanford University, 1974), pp. 147–48.

51. *Qi min yao shu jin shi* 齊民要術今釋, written by Jia Sixie 賈思勰, annotated by Shi Shenghan 石聲漢 (Beijing: Kexue, 1957), vol. 3, pp. 524, 541; *Si shi zuan yao jiao shi* 四時纂要校釋, written by Han E 韓鄂, annotated by Miu Qiyu 繆啟愉 (Beijing: Nongye, 1981), pp. 128, 178.

52. *Ji jiu xian fang* 急救仙方, in *Zhengtong dao zang* 正統道藏, vol. 44, ch. 6, p. 35626.

53. Nagao Ryūzō, *Shina minzoku shi*, vol. 6, pp. 224–28; Sun Jiujun 孫鳩軍 et al., *Sichuan minsu da guan* 四川民俗大觀 (Chengdu: Sichuan Renmin, 1989), pp. 384–85; *Zhejiang minsu tong zhi* 浙江民俗通志 (Hangzhou: Zhejiang Renmin, 1986), p. 43. The Ming dynasty carpenter's manual *Lu ban jing* 魯班經 also contains a reference to spells being spoiled if looked at by "four eyes," but in the context it seems to refer only to the two eyes of any observer, in addition to those of the person performing the spell. See Klaas Ruitenbeek, *Carpentry and Building in Late Imperial China: A Study of the Fifteenth-Century Carpenter's Manual Lu Ban Jing* (Leiden: E. J. Brill, 1996), reproduction of "Secret Charms and Magical Devices," p. 42, with a translation on p. 305.

54. *Zuo zhuan zhu*, Ding year 1, pp. 1519–20. See also Xiang year 14, pp. 1016–17. On the double as a threat, see Lewis, *Writing and Authority in Early China*, pp. 215–16.

55. On the mythology of the Duke of Zhou, see Lewis, *Writing and Authority in Early China*, pp. 209–18. The theme of the tension between a ruler and his heir over the issue of survival and the manner in which it sometimes turns to bloodshed is discussed in Elias Canetti, *Crowds and Power*, tr. Carol Stewart (New York: Seabury Press, 1978), pp. 242–46. On the manner in which the killing of imperial heirs was almost routine in the Han see Kinney, *Representations*, pp. 69–84.

56. Nicole Loraux, *La cité divisée: L'oubli dans la mémoire d'Athènes* (Paris: Payot, 1997), pp. 216–21.

57. *Shi ji* 75, p. 2352.

58. *Sou shen ji* 搜神記, compiled by Gan Bao 干寶, annotated by Wang Shaoying 汪紹楹 (Beijing: Zhonghua, 1979), p. 136. For a reproduction of the side of the coffin, see Laurence Sickman and Alexander Soper, *The Pelican History of Art: The Art and Architecture of China* (paperback edition; Harmondsworth, Middlesex: Penguin Books, 1971), p. 138.

59. Angela Zito, *Of Body and Brush: Grand Sacrifice as Text/Performance in Eighteenth-Century China* (Chicago: University of Chicago, 1997), pp. 202–06. The quotation is found on page 204.

60. *Shuo yuan*, ch. 19, "Xiu wen 脩文," p. 5b.

61. *Li ji zhu shu*, ch. 3, "Qu li shang 曲禮上," p. 2a; ch. 22, "Li yun," p. 1a; ch. 27, "Nei ze," p. 5b.

62. *Yan shi jia xun hui zhu* 顏氏家訓彙注, written by Yan Zhitui 顏之推, annotated by Zhou Fagao 周法高 (Taipei: Zhongyang Yanjiuyuan Lishi Yuyan Yanjiusuo, 1960), ch. 2, "Jiao zi 教子," p. 4a. While only this particular passage argues that a father should not engage in the teaching of his son, the entire chapter argues that fathers, and indeed both parents, must remain stern and distant from their offspring.

63. *Li ji zhu shu*, ch. 51, "Fang ji 坊記," p. 17a.

64. [*Gu*] *lie nü zhuan*, ch. 1, p. 3a: this discusses the question of maternal responsibility for education. Other references to Yu not entering his house appear in *Shang shu zheng yi*, ch. 5, "Yi Ji," p. 11a: this specifies that Yu heard the sound of his son weeping but ignored it in order to devote himself to taming the flood; *Shi ji* 2, p. 51; *Wu Yue chun qiu*, ch. 16, "Yue wang Wuyu wai zhuan," p. 1b.

65. *Mengzi zheng yi*, IVA, "Li Lou shang," pp. 207–08. On early Han advocacy of the ruler not educating his own son, see *Han shu* 48, p. 2248. As an example of the idea in the later family instructions that fathers should not educate their own sons, and always keep them at a distance, see the aforementioned Chapter Two of the *Yan shi jia xun*.

66. *Lun yu zheng yi* 論語正義, annotated by Liu Baonan 劉寶楠 and Liu Gongmian 劉恭冕, in *Xin bian zhu zi ji cheng*, vol. 1 (Taipei: Shijie, 1974), ch. 20, "Yang Huo 陽貨," pp. 363–64.

67. *Lun yu zheng yi*, ch. 7, "Yong ye 雍也," p. 126.

68. On the principle that the function of ritual is to separate, often placed in parallel opposition to the idea that the role of music is to unite, see Lewis, *The Construction of Space in Early China*, introduction.

69. See, for example, *Xunzi ji jie*, ch. 3, "Fei xiang," p. 47; *Shizi*, ch. 1, pp. 16b–17a; ch. 2, pp. 2a, 5b, 10b (2); *Jing fa*, p. 45; *Lü shi chun qiu jiao shi*, ch. 14, "Ben wei 本味," p. 740; *Di wang shi ji ji cun*, pp. 3, 9, 10–13, 27, 28, 29, 31, 34, 40, 49; *Huainanzi*, ch. 19, "Xiu wu," p. 337; *Shang shu da zhuan ji jiao*, ch. 5, p. 2a; *Han shi wai zhuan ji shi*, ch. 9, p. 323; *Lun heng ji jie*, ch. 3, "Gu xiang," pp. 52–53; ch. 16, "Jiang rui," p. 340; ch. 30, "Zi ji," p. 587; *Chun qiu fan lu yi zheng*, ch. 7, "San dai gai zhi zhi wen," pp. 212–13.

70. *Chun qiu fan lu yi zheng*, ch. 7, "Yao Shun bu shan yi, Tang Wu bu zhuan sha 堯舜不擅移, 湯武不專殺," pp. 219–20.

71. Mitarai Masaru, *Kodai Chūgoku no kamigami*, pp. 115–31, 417–57, 541–51.

72. *Zuo zhuan zhu*, Zhao year 8, p. 1305. The passage is quoted virtually verbatim in *Shi ji* 36, p. 1581.

73. *Guo yu*, ch. 16, "Zheng yu 鄭語," p. 511.

74. *Guo yu*, ch. 1, "Zhou yu shang," p. 18.

75. On the linkage of music, winds, and the seasons in early China, and the role of musical specialists in properly harmonizing them, see Lewis, *Sanctioned Violence in Early China*, pp. 214–21.

76. *Lü shi chun qiu jiao shi*, ch. 5, "Gu yue 古樂," p. 284. Shun is also credited with the invention of the *xiao* 簫 pipes. See *Shi ben*, in *Shi ben ba zhong*, Zhang Shu edition, p. 23.

77. *Zhou li zhu shu*, ch. 23, p. 18a. In the *Guo yu*, the two characters that make up this title appear on a list of officials who submit music or verse to remonstrate with the ruler, and the same list includes the second character of Gu Sou's name, 瞍, as yet another office of the same type. See *Guo yu*, ch. 1, "Zhou yu shang," pp. 9–10.

78. *Mengzi zheng yi*, VA, "Wan Zhang shang," pp. 366–68: in this passage Shun's brother Xiang demands to be given Shun's lute after he is killed, and then finds Shun

sitting in his room playing his lute and thinking of the state; VIIB, "Jin xin xia 盡心下," p. 568: in this passage playing the lute is used as one of Shun's defining activities during his period as ruler; *Lü shi chun qiu jiao shi*, ch. 22, "Cha chuan 察傳," p. 1526: this passage speaks of Shun's using music to transmit his teaching throughout the world; *Shizi*, ch. 1, p. 12b; *Huainanzi*, ch. 14, "Quan yan," p. 245: this and all subsequent passages refer to Shun's bringing order to the world through strumming the lute; *Li ji zhu shu*, ch. 38, "Yue ji," p. 1a; *Di wang shi ji ji cun*, p. 45; *Shang shu da zhuan ji jiao*, ch. 2, p. 6b; *Shi ji* 24, pp. 1197, 1235; *Han shi wai zhuan ji shi*, ch. 4, p. 135; *Xin yu*, ch. 4, "Wu wei 無為," p. 6; *Shuo yuan*, ch. 19, "Xiu wen," p. 19a; *Yue jue shu*, ch. 13, "Wai zhuan zhen zhong 外專枕中," p. 1a. Although it does not refer to his strumming the lute, one of the temple hymns composed under the Han founder also cites Shun's music as a mode of causing the entire world to submit. See *Han shu* 22, p. 1047. On this point see Kern, *Die Hymnen der chinesischen Staatsopfer*, pp. 124, 170.

79. *Shan hai jing jiao zhu*, ch. 18, "Hai nei jing," p. 468. The text speaks of Thearch Jun, but the identity of Jun and Shun has been demonstrated by several scholars, and another version of the story quoted in the commentary refers explicitly to Shun. Shun is also linked to dancing through the tradition that he caused the San Miao to submit by means of a dance. See, for example, *Shang shu zhu shu*, ch. 4, "Da Yu mo," pp. 14a–b; *Jiazi xin shu jiao shi*, ch. 4.1, "Xiongnu 匈奴," p. 430; *Shi ji* 43, p. 1807. This tradition of the sons of Shun forming a team of dancers could be a distant echo of the four sons of Fu Xi who paced out the patterns of the seasons in the Chu silk manuscript as described in chapter one.

80. On Shun being located in the agricultural fields, see *Mengzi zheng yi*, VA, "Wan Zhang shang," pp. 359, 360; VB, "Wan Zhang xia," p. 424; VIB, "Gaozi xia 告子下," p. 510; *Xunzi ji jie*, ch. 18, "Cheng xiang," p. 308; *Zhanguo ce*, ch. 11, "Qi si," p. 409; ch. 21, "Zhao si," p. 757; *Shizi*, ch. 1, pp. 11a, 16a; ch. 2, p. 9b; *Han Feizi ji shi*, ch. 15, "Nan yi 難一," p. 795; *Lü shi chun qiu jiao shi*, ch. 14, "Shen ren 慎人," p. 802 (2); *Guanzi jiao zheng*, ch. 21, "Ban fa jie 版法解," p. 342; *Huainanzi*, ch. 1, "Yuan dao," p. 7; ch. 2, "Chu zhen," p. 33; *Xin xu shu zheng*, ch. 1, "Za shi," p. 1; *Lun heng ji jie*, ch. 30, "Zi ji," pp. 581–82.

For Japanese scholars' arguments that Shun was a spirit of agriculture, see Mori Yasutarō, *Kōtei no densetsu*, pp. 63–87; Mitarai Masaru, *Kodai Chūgoku no kamigami*, pp. 541–46, 591–92; Katō Jōken, *Kanji no hakkutsu*, pp. 19–20.

81. On the shared place of burial, see *Shan hai jiao zhu*, ch. 15, "Da huang nan jing," p. 364. The text names the second figure as Shu Jun 叔均, rather than Shang Jun 商均, but given their shared links with Shun and the phonetic relation of the two initial characters—叔 *siak and 商 *siang, distinguished only by the nasalization of the latter—they are certainly the same figure. On the phonetic links of the two character see Zhu Junsheng 朱駿聲, *Shuo wen tong xun ding sheng* 説文通訓定聲 (Taipei: Yiwen, 1974), ch. 6, p. 105. On Shu/Shang Jun as a spirit of agriculture, see *Shang hai jing jiao zhu*, ch. 16, "Da huang xi jing," p. 392: in this passage he is a grandson of Shun, rather than a son, who carries on the work of disseminating grains begun by Hou Ji and who introduces plowing; ch. 17, "Da huang bei jing," p. 430: here he helps to expel the drought demoness Ba and becomes the field spirit (*tian zu* 田祖, literally "field ancestor"); ch. 18, "Hai nei jing," p. 469: here he is again the successor of Hou Ji and the inventor of the plow. On the *tian zu* as an agricultural spirit, see *Mao shi zheng yi*, ch. 14.1, #211, "Fu tian 甫田," p. 6a; #212, "Da tian 大田," p. 15b; *Zhou li*

zhu shu, ch. 24, "Yue zhang 籥章," p. 7b: this passage states that the state prayed to the *tian zu* for a good harvest.

82. Mitarai Masaru, *Kodai Chūgoku no kamigami*, p. 545.

83. See Bernhard Karlgren, *Grammata Serica Recensa* (1957, reprint edition; Stockholm: Museum of Far Eastern Antiquities, 1964), pp. 117, 118; *Zhuangzi ji shi*, ch. 1, "Xiao yao you 逍遙遊," p. 1. For an extended discussion of Gun's and Yu's common aquatic nature, a discussion making frequent appeal to phonetic analysis, see Mori Yasutarō, *Kōtei no densetsu*, pp. 41–62.

84. See chapter two, note 35 for a list of the relevant passages. While several passages indicate that Gun turned into a "bear [*xiong* 熊]," the fact that these same passages say that the transformed Gun then dove into a watery abyss suggest that the character 熊 is a mistake for 能 "*nai*," a turtle or dragon. As the latter character became rare, which was already the case in the Warring States, it is not surprising that scribes would replace it with the better-known 熊, although the actions of a "bear" do not fit the story.

85. Karlgren, *Grammata Serica Recensa*, pp. 40, 45.

86. On traditions of his being aided by the Responding Dragon see chapter one, note 78. On the manner in which turtles and dragons worked together to assist Yu in his work, see *Li han wen jia* 禮含文嘉, quoted in *Taiping yu lan*, ch. 82, p. 3b; *Chun qiu Kong yan tu* 春秋孔演圖, quoted in *Taiping yu lan*, ch. 82, p. 3b.

87. On Yu as half paralyzed, see *Zhuangzi ji shi*, ch. 29, "Dao Zhi," p. 430; *Shizi*, ch. 1, p. 16b; *Di wang shi ji ji cun*, pp. 50, 51 (2): this links the tradition of Yu's partial paralysis to the fact that his hands and feet were calloused due to toil, the first character of the compound meaning calloused (*pian* 胼) also meaning "webbed" and hence perhaps hinting at his aquatic character; *Huainanzi*, ch. 19, "Xiu wu," p. 333; *Chun qiu fan lu yi zheng*, ch. 7, "San dai gai zhi zhi wen," p. 212; *Liezi ji shi*, ch. 7 "Yang Zhu," pp. 230, 231. On Yu's one-sided, hopping gait, see *Xunzi ji jie*, ch. 3, "Fei xiang," p. 47; *Lü shi chun qiu jiao shi*, ch. 20, "Xing lun," p. 1389: this also describes how Yu's skin was burned black in the sun; ch. 22, "Qiu ren 求人," pp. 1514–15; *Shizi*, ch. 1, p. 16b; *Huainanzi*, quoted in the commentary to *Chuci bu zhu*, ch. 3, "Tian wen," p. 11a; *Shang shu da zhuan ji jiao*, ch. 5, p. 2a; *Han shu* 6, p. 190 note 2; *Di wang shi ji ji cun*, pp. 50, 51; *Chun qiu fan lu yi zheng*, ch. 7, "San dai gai zhi zhi wen," p. 212. On Yu's legs' lack of hair, see *Shizi*, ch. 2, p. 10b: this also refers to his fingers having no nails; *Han Feizi ji shi*, ch. 19, "Wu du," p. 1041; *Zhuangzi ji shi*, ch. 33, "Tian xia 天下," p. 466; *Shi ji* 6, p. 27; *Fuzi* 符子, quoted in *Taiping yu lan*, ch. 82, p. 4a: this also refers to his having no hair on his head. The image of hairlessness also appears in *Zhuangzi ji shi*, ch. 11, "Zai You 在宥," p. 169, but it is applied to Yao and Shun as a general image of how the ancient sages destroyed their bodies in the service of the world. An account of how in the course of laying out the world's rivers and establishing all living things in their proper places Yu exposed his body to the elements, without any mention of the body's consequent deformations, appears in *Xin yu*, ch. 1, p. 1.

88. Ma, *Mawangdui gu yi shu kaoshi*, p. 940; Harper, *Early Chinese Medical Literature*, p. 404.

89. *Shan hai jing jiao zhu*, ch. 16, "Da huang xi jing," p. 416. On Zhuan Xu as Yu's grandfather, see *Da Dai li ji jie gu*, ch. 7, "Di xi 帝繫," p. 126; *Shi ji* 2, p. 49; *Shi*

ben, in *Shi ben ba zhong*, Zhuang Shu edition, p. 90 (this contains two versions, one in which Yu is Zhuan Xu's grandson and one in which he is a sixth-generation descendant); *Lun heng ji jie*, ch. 25, "Ji yi 祭意," p. 513. *Di wang shi ji ji cun*, p. 39 and *Han shu* 21b, p. 1013 describe Gun not as Zhuan Xu's son but his fifth-generation descendant.

90. *Shizi*, ch. 2, p. 14a; *Shi ji* 38, p. 1611: here Yu receives the "Hong fan" as a magic text bestowed by Heaven; *Di wang shi ji ji cun*, pp. 40, 43: in these passages it is Shun who receives the texts, p. 50: here it is Yu who receives it; *Lun heng ji jie*, ch. 26, "Zheng shuo 正說," pp. 555–56; *Shang shu zhong hou* 尚書中侯, in *Gu wei shu*, ch. 2, pp. 5a–b, 5b–6a, in *Wei shu ji cheng*, p. 165; *He tu wo ju qi* 河圖握拒起, quoted in *Taiping yu lan*, ch. 82, p. 2b; *Wu yue chun qiu* [zhu zi suoyin] ch. 6, p. 28; *Shi yi ji*, ch. 2, p. 38; *Bo wu zhi jiao zheng*, ch. 7, p. 83; *Shui jing zhu*, quoted in He Yixing's commentary to the *Shan hai jing*, see *Shan hai jing jiao zhu*, ch. 2, "Xi shan jing," p. 50 note 2. A version of this story appears in the *Shi yi ji*, where a black turtle described as the "emissary of the spirit of the Yellow River" assists Yu by pressing the names of all the mountains and rivers into the earth with the seal of his plastron. See *Shi yi ji*, ch. 2, p. 37. Since the "River Chart" is often revealed on the shell of a turtle, and here its signs are used to impose divisions and order on the world, this story is closely related to accounts of the revelation of a magic text that allows Yu to end the flood. On turtles and the "River Chart" as elements in the mythology of the origins of writing, see Lewis, *Writing and Authority in Early China*, pp. 200–01.

91. Yang Kuan, "Shang gu shi dao lun," in *Gu shi bian*, vol. 7, part 1, p. 358.

92. *Chu ci bu zhu*, ch. 3, "Tian wen," pp. 5b–6a; *Lü shi chun qiu jiao shi*, ch. 20, "Zhi fen 知分," p. 1346; *Huainanzi*, ch. 7, "Jing shen," p. 106; *Lun heng ji jie*, ch. 5, "Yi xu 異虛," p. 103; *Shi yi ji*, ch. 2, pp. 33, 37. The tradition that Yu was assisted in his work by dragons is also recorded in local histories from late imperial China and in oral traditions still circulating in the Three Gorges region. See Yuan, *Zhongguo shenhua chuanshuo*, p. 492 note 22; Yuan Ke, *Zhongguo gudai shenhua* 中國古代神話 (Shanghai: Shangwu, 1957), p. 19.

93. On the legends of Bao Si's dragon origins, see *Guo yu*, ch. 16, "Zheng yu," p. 519; *Shi ji* 4, p. 147. On the descent of the Bao from Yu, see *Shi ji* 2, p. 89; *Qian fu lun jian* 潛夫論箋, by Wang Fu 王符, annotated by Wang Jipei 汪繼培 (Beijing: Zhonghua, 1979), ch. 8, "Wu de zhi 五德志," p. 396; *Shi ben*, in *Shi ben ba zhong*, Zhang Shu edition, p. 59.

94. *Chu ci bu zhu*, ch. 3, "Tian wen," p. 11a; *Han shu* 6, p. 190 note 2. It is most likely that the original character referred to the *nai* dragon; since this character became very rare, later authors or editors did not recognize it and it was consequently rewritten as the more common graph meaning "bear."

95. For statements that Yu was the prototype of the altar of the soil, see *Huainanzi*, ch. 13, "Fan lun," p. 233; *Shi ji* 28, p. 1357; *Han shu* 25b, p. 1269; *Lun heng ji jie*, ch. 25, "Ji yi," p. 514; [*Jiao zheng*] *San fu huang tu* 校正三輔黃圖, annotated by Zhang Zongxiang 張宗祥 (Shanghai: Gudian, 1958), ch. 5, p. 44. For statements that the son of Gong Gong was the prototype of the altar of the soil, see *Zuo zhuan*, Zhao year 29, p. 1503: this identifies as Goulong the son of Gong Gong who becomes god of the *she*; *Guo yu*, ch. 4, "Lu yu shang," p. 166: this describes an unnamed son of Gong Gong as "able to level the nine lands [*neng ping jiu tu* 能平九土]," which is exactly Yu's achievement; *Han shu* 25a, p. 1191: this applies the same phrase as the *Guo yu*,

but specifically names the son as Goulong; *Du duan* 獨斷, by Cai Yong 蔡邕, in *Han Wei cong shu*, vol. 1 (Taipei: Xin xing, 1977), ch. 1, p. 12b. For modern discussions of the identity of Yu and Goulong, see Yang Kuan, "Shang gu shi dao lun," *Gu shi bian*, vol. 7, part 1, pp. 353–62. Yang Kuan cites earlier work on this topic by Gu Jiegang. See also Mitarai Masaru, *Kodai Chūgoku no kamigami*, pp. 127–28.

96. *Zuo zhuan zhu*, Zhao year 29, p. 1501. The clan presented dragons to the Xia king Kong Jia who enjoyed eating them. He consequently granted them the name "Yulong 御龍." One meaning of *yu* 御 is to present as food.

97. *Shi yi ji*, ch. 2, p. 37. The opening sentence is a direct quote from the *Lun yu*. See *Lun yu zheng yi*, ch. 9, "Tai Bo 泰伯," p. 169. The account of the dragon carving channels with its tail refers to a story derived from the "Tian wen." See *Chu ci bu zhu*, ch. 3, "Tian wen," p. 5b. The reference to the turtle as emissary of the spirit of the Yellow River who used signs on its shell to name and thus impose order on the world refers back to the numerous stories cited in note 90 of the text revealed to Yu. Most of these stories are preserved in several of the "apocryphal" texts produced in the Eastern Han, and thus date back at least to the Han dynasty.

98. *Shan hai jing jiao zhu*, ch. 6, "Hai wai nan jing," p. 186; ch. 16, "Da huang xi jing," p. 416; *Shuo yuan*, ch. 9, "Zheng jian 正諫," p. 18b (2). Fragments of texts from the Age of Disunion record that the "Dragon Gate [*long men* 龍門]" opened by Yu took its name from the fact that any fish who could swim upstream through it would become a dragon. See Yuan, *Zhongguo shenhua chuanshuo*, p. 491 note 17. For early reference to the idea that Yu opened the Dragon Gate, see *Lü shi chun qiu jiao shi*, ch. 2, "Gu yue," p. 286; ch. 21, "Ai lei," p. 1463; *Huainanzi*, ch. 8, "Ben jing," p. 118; *Shuo yuan*, ch. 5, "Gui de," pp. 2a–b.

99. *Chu ci bu zhu*, ch. 3, "Tian wen," p. 5a. *Shan hai jing jiao zhu*, ch. 18, "Hai nei jing," p. 472. The *Gui zang*, in *Quan shang gu san dai wen*, ch. 15, p. 3a, describes how Gun's body was carved up with a knife from Wu (the southeast being celebrated for its blades in the Warring States period), but it says nothing about Yu's emerging from it.

100. *Zuo zhuan zhu*, Zhao year 29, p. 1503.

101. On the tension between these two principles and the manner in which this is expressed in myth and philosophy, see Allan, *The Heir and the Sage*. For a discussion of the manner in which contradictory claims of inheritance and virtue were worked out in the principles of succession under the Tang dynasty, see Howard Wechsler, *Offerings of Jade and Silk: Ritual and Symbol in the Legitimation of the T'ang Dynasty* (New Haven: Yale University, 1985), ch. 4, "Merit and Virtue Conjoined: The Early T'ang Accession Ceremonies."

CHAPTER FOUR

1. Tales of Nü Gua are collected in Anne Birrell's inventory of Chinese myths. See Birrell, *Chinese Mythology: An Introduction*, pp. 33–35, 69–72, 163–65. See also Lewis, *Writing and Authority*, pp. 202–08. More systematic discussion of Nü Gua's role in the flood myths appear in Birrell, "The Four Flood Myth Traditions," pp. 221–28; Zhang Zhenli, *Zhongyuan gudian shenhua liu bian lunkao* 中原古典神話流變論考 (Shanghai: Shanghai Wenyi, 1991), pp. 45, 63–88, 209–36. For a useful exposition of the mythology of Nü Gua that leads directly into the tales of Yu, see Jing Wang, *The*

Story of Stone: Intertextuality, Ancient Chinese Stone Lore, and the Stone Symbolism of Dream of the Red Chamber, Water Margin, and the Journey to the West (Durham: Duke University, 1992), pp. 44–66.

2. On these features of Nü Gua, see *Chu ci bu zhu*, ch. 3, "Tian wen," p. 16a; *Huainanzi*, ch. 6, "Lan ming 覽冥," p. 95; ch. 17, "Shuo lin 説林," p. 292; *Shan hai jing jiao zhu*, ch. 16, "Da huang xi jing," p. 389; *Lun heng ji jie*, ch. 15, "Shun gu 順鼓," p. 323; *Feng su tong yi jiao shi*, p. 449: this contains the passages on both Nü Gua's instituting marriage and her original fashioning of the human body from the soil of the earth; *Lu shi* 路史, written by Luo Bi, 羅泌 (d. ca. 1176 A.D.), *Hou ji* 後紀 (Si bu bei yao edition), ch. 2, p. 2a; *Shuo wen jie zi zhu*, ch. 12b, p. 11a: this passage describes Nü Gua as the ancient goddess who "transformed all things [*hua wan wu* 化萬物]," that is, who caused all things to grow and develop into their proper shapes. The use here of the term *hua* echoes the passage that describes her role in the development of the human fetus.

On Nü Gua as a mythic prototype for the "High Matchmaker," see Wen Yiduo, "Gao Tang shen nü chuanshuo zhi fenxi 高唐神女傳説之分析," in *Wen Yiduo quan ji*, vol. 1, pp. 97–107; Chen Mengjia 陳蒙家, "Gao mei jiao she zu miao tong kao 高媒校社祖廟通考," *Qinghua xuebao* 12.3 (1937): 445–72; Chow Tse-tsung, "The childbirth myth and ancient Chinese medicine," in *Ancient China: Studies in Early Civilization*, ed. David T. Roy and Tsuen-hsuin Tsien (Hong Kong: Chinese University, 1978), pp. 56, 65; Ikeda Suetoshi 池田末利, *Chūgoku kodai shūkyō shi kenkyū* 中國古代宗教史研究 (Tokyo: Tōkai Daigaku, 1983), pp. 602–22; Bodde, *Festivals in Classical China*, pp. 243–61.

3. *Shan hai jing jiao zhu*, p. 92.

4. In the late imperial period, largely due to the influence of her brief appearance in the celebrated novel *Hong lou meng* (*The Dream of the Red Chamber*), Nü Gua became closely linked to romantic passion and to the idea of total devotion to difficult or lost causes. In this role she, and her mythic transform Jingwei, became recurrent figures in fiction and theater in the last decades of the empire. See Xiaobing Tang, *Chinese Modern: The Heroic and the Quotidian* (Durham: Duke University, 2000), pp. 18–21.

5. *Huainanzi*, ch. 6, "Lan ming 覽冥," p. 95. This tradition is also recorded in *Lun heng ji jie*, ch. 11, "Tan tian," pp. 215–17; ch. 15, "Shun gu," p. 325; *Liezi ji shi*, ch. 5, "Tang wen 湯問," pp. 150–51. In these texts, however, the story of Nü Gua's work is always linked to the tale of Gong Gong battling with Zhuan Xu and knocking over Mt. Buzhou.

6. See the discussion in chapter two, in the passages that include notes 16–19 along with the references in those notes.

7. See Andrew H. Plaks, *Archetype and Allegory in the Dream of the Red Chamber* (Princeton: Princeton University, 1976), p. 39; Jing Wang, *The Story of Stone*, pp. 48–49; Granet, *Danses et légendes*, pp. 485, 498–99.

8. The relevant primary sources are collected in Edouard Chavannes, *Le Tai Chan: Essai de monographie d'un culte chinois* (Paris: Leroux, 1910), pp. 450–59.

9. On the *she* altar as composed of five colors of soil, see, for example, the "Wai zhuan" chapter of the *Li ji* as quoted in *Taiping yu lan*, ch. 532, p. 2b.

10. Li Ling, *Zhongguo fangshu xu kao* 續考 (Beijing: Dongfang, 2000), pp. 341–49; Li Ling, "Wu shi kao 五石考," *Xueren* 13 (1998), pp. 397–404.

11. Rudolph Wagner, "Lebenstil und Drogen in chinesischen Mittelalter," *T'oung Pao* 59 (1973), pp. 79–178; Yu Jiaxi 余嘉錫, "Han shi san kao 寒食散考," in *Yu Jiaxi lun xue za zhu* 論學雜著 (Beijing: Zhonghua, 1963), pp. 181–226.

12. *Shi ji* 105, pp. 2810–11.

13. *Zhou li zhu shu*, ch. 5, "Yang yi 瘍醫," p. 7b; *Baopuzi nei pian jiao shi*, ch. 4, "Jin dan 金丹," p. 69.

14. *Lun heng ji jie*, ch. 11, "Tan tian," p. 217.

15. Li, *Zhongguo fang shu kao*, pp. 342–46 provides a good introduction to this celebrated "Inscription on Moving Qi" along with references to the most important earlier work dealing with this topic.

16. Vivienne Lo, "Spirit of Stone: Technical Considerations in the Treatment of the Jade Body," *Bulletin of the School of Oriental and African Studies* 65:1 (2002), pp. 99–128.

17. Granet, *Danses et légendes*, pp. 485–88, 498–503, On smelting as a marriage, see *Shi ji* 27, p. 1320; *Yue jue shu*, ch. 11, "Wai zhuan ji bao jian 外傳記寶劍," p. 1a. Granet cites a late tradition collected by de Groot, who recorded that people in Yunnan believed that the bodies of people buried in accidents in those mines that produced the "five varieties of metal" did not decay. They lived on as spirits nourished by the emanations of the mixed metals, and could enter into social relations with living miners if the latter approached them properly. Here again the five types of metals when properly combined took on organic properties and generated life.

18. *Zuo zhuan zhu*, Zhao year 17, p. 1391.

19. *Shi yi ji*, ch. 2, p. 36.

20. *Lun heng ji jie*, ch. 2, "Shuai xing," p. 36. Nearly identical accounts appear in ch. 16, "Luan long 亂龍," p. 328; ch. 27, "Ding xian," p. 539.

21. *Wu yue chun qiu*, ch. 4, "He Lü nei zhuan 闔閭內傳," pp. 1b–2a. Moye's cutting off her hair and fingernails is the standard preparation of one who is about to offer up his or her own life, as in the Shang founder Tang's self-sacrifice to end the drought that his rebellion had brought about. See *Shang shu da zhuan*, ch. 2, p. 14a. In the story immediately following that of Ganjiang and Moye the successful casting of some metal hooks requires that the man add the blood of his two sons to the metal so that it will properly fuse. References to Ganjiang and the swords also figure in *Yue jue shu*, ch. 11, "Wai zhuan ji bao jian," p. 2b; *Shi yi ji*, ch. 10, "Kunwu shan 昆吾山," pp. 233–34. For a discussion of stories about the casting of swords in Wu and Yue, placed in the context of evidence for early metallurgy, see Donald B. Wagner, *Iron and Steel in Ancient China* (Leiden: E. J. Brill, 1993), pp. 100–15.

22. See *Wu di ji* 吳地記, annotated by Cao Lindi 曹林娣 (Nanjing: Jiangsu Guji, 1986), p. 24.

23. In an extension of the ideas underlying the tales of Nü Gua and Ganjiang, the smelting of metals and of human bodies was explicitly linked in later Daoist alchemy. See, for example, *Bao puzi nei pian jiao shi*, ch. 4, "Jin dan," p. 62.

24. *Taiping yu lan*, ch. 529, pp. 4a–5a. The fragments come from a Jin dynasty (third century A.D.) essay about the altar to the High Matchmaker, from Xu Shen's *Wu jing yi yi* 五經異義 composed in the Eastern Han, and from the ritual monograph of the *Sui shu*. Sun Zuoyun wrote an article on the worship of stones in ancient China that includes a list of the references to stones on the altar of the High Matchmaker

from the Han through the Song. This article is cited in Yang Kuan, "Zhongguo shang gu shi daolun," pp. 360–61.

25. Sarah Allan, *The Shape of the Turtle*, ch. 4.

26. *Shan hai jing jiao zhu*, p. 92.

27. *Shi ben*, Qin Jiamo edition, ch. 9, pp. 358–59; *Li ji zhu shu*, ch. 31, "Ming tang wei," p. 16b; *Shuo wen jie zi zhu*, ch. 5a, pp. 17a–b; *Feng su tong yi jiao shi*, ch. 6, p. 246; *Zhonghua gu jin zhu* 中華古今注, written by Ma Gao 馬縞 (rep. ed., Shanghai: Shangwu, 1956).

28. "San huang ben ji 三皇本紀," written by Sima Zhen 司馬貞, in *Shi ji hui zhu kao zheng* 史記會注考證 (rep. ed., Taipei: Hongye, 1976), p. 2.

29. For a detailed examination of one aspect of the mythology of Fu Xi see Lewis, *Writing and Authority in Early China*, pp. 197–209.

30. *Zhou yi zheng yi*, ch. 8 "Xi ci zhuan xia 繫辭傳下," pp. 4b–8a. For a later, abbreviated account that attributes the creation of civilization to Fu Xi, see *Bo hu tong de lun*, ch. 1, pp. 9a–b. For an early passage that describes the work of the sages and the *Yi* in terms identical to those applied to Fu Xi, see *Zhou yi zheng yi* 7 "Xi ci xia," p. 9a.

31. Wu Hung, *The Wu Liang Shrine*, p. 156. The apocryphal literature states that the *Yi* or the trigrams serve to "make clear the Way of kings" (*ming wang dao* 明王道) or "fix the royal enterprise" (*ding wang ye* 定王業) and that through them "the royal transformations [of the people] are completed" (*wang hua quan* 王化全). They also serve to cause the "royal teachings to arise" (王教興). See [*Zhou*] *yi qian zao du* 周易乾鑿度, in *Qi wei* 七緯 2, 2a (twice), 10a (twice); 11b; in *Wei shu ji cheng* 緯書集成 (Shanghai: Guji, 1994), pp. 798, 790, 791.

32. *Di wang shi ji ji cun*, p. 3. On the trigrams as the basis of political order, see *Yi tong gua yan* 易通卦驗, in *Qi wei* 七緯 6, p. 7b; in *Wei shu ji cheng*, p. 823; *Bo hu tong de lun* 1, p. 9b.

33. *Yi qian zao du* 易乾鑿度, in *Qi wei* 2, p. 18a; in *Wei shu ji cheng*, p. 794.

34. *Yi tong gua yan*, in *Qi wei* 6, pp. 4a–b; in *Wei shu ji cheng*, p. 821; a passage from the same work on p. 3a, *Wei shu ji cheng*, p. 820 also links the *Yi* to the *feng* and *shan* sacrifices.

35. Mark Edward Lewis, "The *Feng* and *Shan* Sacrifices of Emperor Wu of the Han," in *State and Court Ritual in China*, ed. Joseph P. McDermott (Cambridge: Cambridge University, 1999), pp. 50–80; Stephen Bokenkamp, "Record of the Feng and Shan Sacrifices," in *Religions of China in Practice*, ed. Donald S. Lopez, Jr. (Princeton: Princeton University, 1996), pp. 251–60; *Shuo wen jie zi zhu*, ch. 15, p. 3a.

36. Probably the earliest reference to the River Chart appears in the "Gu ming" chapter of the *Shang shu*, in which it seems to have been a jade object placed on display at the funeral of King Cheng. As such, it was apparently a central element of royal regalia with no suggestion of supernatural origins, and it may have had no relation to later accounts except for providing a name. See *Shang shu zheng yi*, ch. 18 "Gu ming 顧命," p. 20a. In a passage from the second period of the *Lun yu*'s composition, the master laments, "The phoenix does not arrive. The river does not put forth its chart. I am done for!" See *Lun yu zheng yi* 9 "Zi han," p. 179. Here the River Chart had become an auspicious omen in the same category as the phoenix, and it was sup-

posed to emerge directly from the Yellow River. The *Mozi* clarifies the significance of this omen in a passage indicating that it emerged from the river immediately prior to King Wu's establishment of the Zhou as the royal line. See *Mozi jiangu*, ch. 19 "Fei gong xia," p. 95. In this passage the chart is described as "green," perhaps referring back to its original character as an object made of jade. The passage from the *Huainanzi* cited earlier also describes the chart as green. The idea that the appearance of the River Chart and Luo Writing indicated the transfer of dynastic power and the imminent rise of a sage also appears in *Lun heng ji jie*, ch. 5 "Gan xu," p. 113; ch. 22 "Ji yao" p. 447.

37. On the rival scholastic origins of the River Chart and Luo Writing, see Schuyler Cammann, "Some Early Chinese Symbols of Duality," *History of Religions* 24.3 (February 1985), pp. 227–31. For a more general treatment, see Michael Saso, "What is the Ho-t'u?" *History of Religions* 17.3/4 (February–May 1978), pp. 399–416. The earliest exclusive reference to the Luo Writing appears in the *Zhuangzi*. See *Zhuangzi ji shi*, ch. 14, "Tian yun," p. 220. This passage refers to it as the "Nine[-fold] Luo." Another piece of evidence indicating the Daoist provenance of the Luo Writing is the fact that the *Huainanzi* lists it prior to the River Chart, whereas most sources give precedence to the latter. See *Huainanzi*, ch. 2 "Chu zhen," p. 32.

38. *Zhou yi zheng yi* 7 "Xi ci shang," pp. 28b–30a. In the Eastern Han, Wang Chong argued that the trigrams were identical with the River Chart, and that the Luo Writing was identical with the "Hong fan" chapter of the *Shang shu*. See *Lun heng ji jie*, "Zheng shuo 正説," pp. 271–72. He also argued that the coming forth of the Chart and the Writing was identical to the invention of writing. See *Lun heng ji jie*, ch. 5, "Gan xu," p. 113. One Eastern Han apocryphal text lists the River Chart and Luo Writing as the "signs" provided by the Earth, parallel to the markings on birds and animals, which were the signs provided by Heaven. Fu Xi created the *Yi* by copying these signs. See *Li wei han wen jia* 禮緯含文嘉, in *Gu wei shu* 17, pp. 3a–b; in *Wei shu ji cheng*, p. 249.

39. See *Laozi dao de jing zhu*, pp. 26–27. The account was also adapted in *Huainanzi* 3 "Tian wen xun," p. 46; 7 "Jing shen xun," p. 99.

40. *Lun heng ji jie*, "Zheng shuo," pp. 271–72; *Li wei han wen jia*, in *Gu wei shu* 17, pp. 3a–b; in *Wei shu ji cheng*, p. 249.

41. *Chun qiu yuan ming bao* 春秋元命包, in *Qi wei* 七緯 24, p. 24b; in *Wei shu ji cheng*, p. 924; Michèle Pirazzoli-t'Serstevens, *The Han Dynasty*, tr. Janet Seligman (New York: Rizzoli, 1982), p. 188 fig. 147; *Bo hu tong de lun* 2 "Feng shan 封禪," p. 1b; *Shang shu zhong hou* 尚書中侯, in *Gu wei shu* 古緯書 4, pp. 1b, 2b–3a, 3b (twice), 14a (three times), reprinted in *Wei shu ji cheng*, pp. 163, 164, 169; Zheng Xuan's commentary in *Zhou yi zhengyi* 7 "Xi ci shang," p. 30a. The version in the *Shuo fu* of the passage from the *Li han wen jia* refers to the Luo Writing as the "Turtle Writing" (*gui shu* 龜書). See *Wei shu ji cheng*, p. 116. A story in the *Shi yi ji* depicts Fu Xi not receiving the River Chart, but revealing the hexagrams as a River Chart to the sage Yu. See *Shi yi ji*, p. 38. The turtle was not the only animal cited as a natural source for writing, since Fu Xi also examined the patterns (*wen*) of birds and beast. Texts on "insect graphs" (*chong shu* 蟲書) and "bird graphs" (*niao shu* 鳥書) existed in the Han. See *Han shu* 30, pp. 1721, 1722.

42. *Chun qiu Zuo zhuan zhu*, Xi 15, p. 365.

43. Mori Yasutarō, *Kōtei densetsu: kodai Chūgoku shinwa no kenkyū*, pp. 187–93. The argument for the identification is based on phonetic links of the two names. Mori also argues that the appearance of the character for "hexagram" (*yao* 爻) in the graphs meaning "to teach" and "to study" refers not to instruction in divination, of which there is no record as part of a general curriculum, but rather to that in arithmetic. See pp. 191–92. This would also indicate that Fu Xi and the *Yi* were closely tied to the use of numbers.

44. *Zhou bi suan jing* 周髀算經, in *Suan jing shi shu* 算經十書, ed. Qian Baozong 錢寶綜 (Beijing: Xinhua, 1963), p. 13; *Jiu zhang suan shu* 九章算書, in *Suan jing shi shu*, p. 91. On the datings of these texts, see Joseph Needham, *Science and Civilisation in China*, vol. 3, *Mathematics and the Sciences of the Heavens and the Earth* (Cambridge: Cambridge University, 1970), pp. 19–20, 24–25. See also the article on the *Jiu zhang suan shu* in *Early Chinese Texts*. The link between the origin of numbers and the carpenter's square is also noted in *Huainanzi* 2 "Chu zhen," p. 25.

45. See the transcription in Li Ling, *Zhongguo fang shu kao*, pp. 180–81.

46. Discussions of Fu Xi and Nü Gua as a couple appear in English in Plaks, *Archetype and Allegory*, ch. 2; and in Girardot, *Myth and Meaning in Early Taoism*, pp. 202–07 and passim (see index under "Fu-hsi," "Nü-kua," and "Primordial Couple"). See also Hayashi, *Kan dai no kamigami*, pp. 287–99, 306–08; Mitarai, *Kodai Chūgoku no kamigami*, pp. 627–36; Shirakawa, *Chūgoku no shinwa*, pp. 69–74; Yuan Ke, *Zhongguo gudai shenhua*, pp. 40–60.

47. *Chu ci bu zhu* 3 "Tian wen 天問," p. 16a.

48. *Huainanzi* 17 "Shuo lin 説林," p. 292. Nü Gua's powers of transformation, closely linked to her role as creator, are also mentioned in *Shang hai jing jiao zhu*, 16 "Da huang xi jing," p. 389: this passage is followed by a lengthy note on Nü Gua; *Shuo wen jie zi zhu* 12b, p. 11a. Yuan Ke argues that the "seventy transformations" worked by Nü Gua refer to the changes undergone by the fetus in the womb. See Yuan Ke 袁珂, *Zhongguo shenhua tong lun* 中國神話通論 (Chengdu: Bashu, 1991), pp. 76–77.

49. *Fengsu tongyi jiao shi*, p. 449. The story was lost in the transmitted text, but it was preserved in quotation in two later works. These two versions have some textual variations, but they do not affect the content of the story.

50. In the *Huainanzi*, as in the *Zhuangzi*, Fu Xi sometimes represents the ideal state of primitive man and sometimes the beginning of the work of the sages who destroyed that state. See *Zhuangzi ji shi* 4 "Ren jian shi 人間世," p. 69: Fu Xi along with other sages embodies the trance state of one in harmony with the Way; 6 "Da zong shi 大宗師," p. 112: Fu Xi is one who attained the Way, and thereby joined with the "mother of breath/energy" (*qi mu* 氣母); 10 "Qu qie 胠篋," p. 162: Fu Xi, once again identified with the knotting of cords, is the penultimate ruler of the "age of supreme virtue," when men lived at peace in perfect simplicity; 16 "Shan xing 繕性," pp. 243–44: Fu Xi emerges as ruler because of the decline of primitive virtue; 21 "Tianzi Fang 田子方," p. 317: Fu Xi is no match for a "perfected man" (*zhen ren* 真人); *Huainanzi* 2 "Chu zhen," p. 28: Fu Xi embodies the break with primal virtue; 6 "Lan ming," pp. 95–96, 98: Fu Xi is linked with Nü Gua as embodiment of the primitive paradise, and they are said to rule without laws or measures; 9 "Zhu shu 主術," pp. 129–30: Fu Xi and Shen Nong are exemplary teachers who command without words and have audience without being seen; 13 "Fan lun 氾論," p. 215: Fu Xi and

Shen Nong rule without rewards or punishments, but the people do no wrong. The *Fengsu tongyi*, in a fragment preserved in the Song dynasty *Lu shi*, identifies Nü Gua as Fu Xi's younger sister. See *Fengsu tongyi jiao shi*, p. 449.

51. The other passage appears in the *Lun heng*, in which Wang Chong denounces certain rainmaking rituals employed in his day: "Where in the ritual texts does it say that if rain does not stop one should sacrifice to Nü Gua? Fu Xi and Nü Gua were both sages. The *Spring and Autumn Annals* never speaks of setting aside Fu Xi and sacrificing to Nü Gua. So why does Dong Zhongshu discuss [such a practice]?" See *Lun heng ji jie*, ch. 15, "Shun gu," p. 212. Here Wang Chong appears to follow the *Huainanzi* in viewing Fu Xi and Nü Gua as two early sages whose work was closely linked. Interestingly, however, the rituals of his day made Nü Gua an independent deity.

52. *Huainanzi* 7 "Jing shen xun," p. 99.

53. *Shan hai jing jian shu* 山海經箋疏 (Taipei: Yiwen, 1974), ch. 16, p. 1b.

54. *Shi ben ji bu* 世本輯補, annotated by Qin Jiamo 秦嘉謨, in *Shi ben ba zhong* 世本八種 (Shanghai: Shangwu, 1957) 1 "Di xi 帝繫," p. 15; *Di wang shi ji ji cun*, p. 52. On this point see Katō Jōken, "Shina ko sei shi no kenkyū—Ka U Shi sei kō 支那古姓氏の研究—夏禹姒姓考," in *Chūgoku kodai bunka no kenkyū*, pp. 454–55.

55. See Katō, "Shina ko sei shi," pp. 437–49; Edward H. Schafer, *The Divine Woman: Dragon Ladies and Rain Maidens in T'ang Literature* (Berkeley: University of California, 1973), pp. 30–31; Shirakawa, *Chūgoku no shinwa*, pp. 60–69; Mitarai Masaru, *Kodai Chūgoku no kamigami*, pp. 117–21, 124–25, 131–32.

56. On the significance of Fu Xi's name, see Mitarai Masaru, *Kodai Chūgoku no kamigami*, pp. 631–36; Katō Jōken, "Futsu ki kō 弗忌考," in *Chūgoku kodai bunka no kenkyū*, pp. 303–22. For examples of the depictions of Fu Xi and Nü Gua in Han tomb art, see Käte Finsterbusch, *Verzeichnis und Motivindex der Han-Darstellungen:Band II Abbildungen und Addenda* (Wiesbaden: Otto Harrowitz, 1971), illustrations 32a, 45, 101–02, 106, 127, 137, 150, 158, 161, 167, 172, 261j, 274, 282, 347, 507c, 508m, 570, 696, 789, 947; Plaks, *Archetype and Allegory*, pp. 238–39; Hayashi, *Kan dai no kamigami*, pp. 288, 289, 290, 291, 292, 293; Mori, *Kōtei densetsu*, p. 203; Shirakawa, *Chūgoku no shinwa*, p. 71; Wu Hung, *The Wu Liang Shrine*, pp. 47, 157. For the statement that Fu Xi had the form of a dragon see, for example, *Chun qiu yuan ming bao*, in *Qi wei* 七緯, p. 26b, in *Wei shu ji cheng*, p. 923; *Chun qiu he cheng tu* 春秋合誠圖, in *Gu wei shu* 8, p. 7b, in *Wei shu ji cheng*, p. 192. A variety of dragons and snakes accompany Fu Xi in the account of his reign in the *Huainanzi*. See 6 "Lan Ming," p. 95.

57. One of the earliest datable accounts of a dragon sire is that of the conception of the Han founder. See *Shi ji* 6, p. 341. For tales in the Han apocryphal texts of dragons fathering sage kings see, for example, *Chun qiu yuan ming bao*, in *Gu wei shu* 古緯書 6, pp. 6b–7a, in *Wei shu ji cheng*, pp. 179–80; *Chun qiu he cheng tu* 春秋合誠圖 8, in *Gu wei shu* 6, pp. 9a–b, in *Wei shu ji cheng*, p. 193. In this second story the dragon presents a chart to Yao's future mother before impregnating her. The same story is also mentioned in *Chun qiu yuan ming bao*, in *Qi wei* 24, p. 7b; in *Wei shu ji cheng*, p. 931.

58. *Guo yu* 16, p. 519; *Shi ji* 4, p. 147.

59. Wolfram Eberhard, *Typen chinesischer Volksmärchen* (Helsinki: F F Communications No. 120, 1937), pp. 102–04; Eberhard, *The Local Cultures of South and East China*, pp. 39–40, 231–33; Schafer, *The Divine Woman*, pp. 22–23. The first chapter of the

Divine Woman is devoted to the themes of women, dragons, rain, and fertility. It contains a section devoted to Nü Kua (Gua). See pp. 29–32.

60. *Yi qian kun zao du* 易乾坤鑿度, in *Qi wei* 1, p. 6b–7a; *Yi qian zao du* 易乾鑿度, in *Qi wei* 2, pp. 2b, 5b–6a, 12a–b, 13a, 14a; in *Wei shu ji cheng*, pp. 779, 788, 792. See Yasui Kōzan and Nakamura Shōhachi 中村璋八, *Isho no kisoteki kenkyū* 緯書の基礎的研究 (Kyoto: Kokusho Kankō, 1978), pp. 171–200.

61. *Yi qian kun zao du*, in *Qi wei* 1, pp. 8a, 16b; *Yi qian zao du*, in *Qi wei* 2, pp. 2a, 3b, 6a; in *Wei shu ji cheng*, pp. 780, 784, 786, 787, 788.

62. *Yi qian kun zao du*: *kun zao du*, in *Qi wei* 1, pp. 9a–b; in *Wei shu ji cheng*, p. 780. This text quotes the *Wan xing jing* 萬形經 and the *Xuanyuan ben jing* 軒轅本經, for the two versions of the links between dragons and yarrow. On the age of turtles as crucial to their role in divination, see *Bo hu tong de lun* 2, pp. 14b, 15a.

63. *Shi ben ji bu* 9 "Zuo," p. 355; *Bo hu tong de lun* 1, p. 9a; *Di wang shi ji ji cun*, p. 3.

64. *Lu shi*, *Hou ji* 後紀, ch. 2, p. 2a.

65. Wen Yiduo, "Gao Tang shen nü chuanshuo zhi fenxi, pp. 97–107; Chen Mengjia, "Gao mei jiao she zu miao tong kao," pp. 445–72; Chow, "The childbirth myth and ancient Chinese medicine," pp. 56, 65; Ikeda Suetoshi, *Chūgoku kodai shūkyō shi kenkyū*, pp. 602–22; Derk Bodde, *Festivals in Classical China*, pp. 243–61. Recently, Liu Dunyuan and Zheng Yan have interpreted depictions of embracing couples in two second-century A.D. tombs as evidence of the practice of this rite. See Liu Dunyuan 劉敦願, "Han huaxiangshi shang yin shi nan nü—Pingyin Mengzhuan Han mu shizhu jisi gewu tuxiang fenxi 汉画像石上饮食男女—平阴孟庄汉墓石柱祭祀各物图像分析," *Gu Gong wen wu yuekan* 古宮文物月刊, 141 (December 1994), pp. 122–35; Zheng Yan, "Anqiu Dongjiazhuang li zhu diaoke tuxing kao 安丘董家庄立柱雕刻图形考," *Jinian Shangdong Daxue kaogu zhuanye chuangjian ershi zhounian wenji* 紀念山東大學考古專業創建二十周年文集, (Ji'nan: Shandong Daxue, 1992), pp. 397–413. The theme of fertility, without any reference to the *gao mei* ritual, as depicted in the latter tomb is also discussed in Li Liyang 李黎陽, "Shi lun Shandong Anqiu Han mu ren xiang zhu yishu 试论山东安丘汉墓人像柱艺术," *Zhongyuan wen wu* (1991: 3), pp. 86–87, 85.

66. *Fengsu tongyi jiao shi*, p. 449. This passage is missing in the received version of the *Fengsu tongyi* but was preserved in quotations in later texts.

67. See note 36 of the Introduction for references to the books and articles on this theme.

68. *Du yi zhi* 獨異志, written by Li Rong 李冗, in *Bai hai* 稗海 (Taipei: Xinxing, 1965), ch. *xia*, p. 19a.

69. Wen Yiduo, "Fu Xi kao 伏羲考," in *Wen Yiduo quan ji*, vol. 1, pp. 3–68. The multiple manifestations of ancient gourd myths in China is the subject of Norman Girardot, *Myth and Meaning in Early Taoism*. On page 206 of his book he provides two late versions of southern myths in which Fu Xi and Nü Gua are a sibling pair who repopulate the earth after a flood has wiped out the human race. In both versions their original offspring are shapeless blobs who must be carved into pieces to form human beings. In one version this act is anticipated by the fact that Fu Xi cuts into pieces the bamboo and the tortoise who first advise him to marry his sister. These two beings then reassemble, but bear the traces of the act in the lines that mark their

bodies. Wen Yiduo's arguments are also analyzed and developed in Plaks, *Archetype and Allegory in the Dream of the Red Chamber*, ch. 2.

70. Plaks, *Archetype and Allegory*, p. 38.

71. See Maspero, "Légendes mythologiques dans le Chou King," *Journal Asiatique* 214 (1924), pp. 74–75; Yuan Ke, *Zhongguo gudai shenhua*, p. 46, note 15; Edward H. Schafer, *The Vermilion Bird: T'ang Images of the South* (Berkeley: University of California, 1967), p. 13; Mitarai Masaru, *Kodai Chūgoku no kamigami*, pp. 627–30.

72. *Shi ben ji bu* 9 "Zuo," pp. 358–59; *Li ji zhu shu* 31 "Ming tang wei 明堂位," p. 16b; *Shuo wen jie zi zhu* 5A, pp. 17a–b; *Fengsu tongyi jiao shi*, p. 246.

73. *Shi ming shu zheng bu* 釋名疏證補, written by Liu Xi 劉熙, annotated by Wang Xianqian 王先謙 (rep. ed.: Shanghai: Guji, 1984) 7 "Shi yue qi 釋樂器," pp. 7a–b. See also *Shuo wen jie zi zhu* 5A, pp. 17a–b.

74. *Zhonghua gu jin zhu* 中華古今注, written by Ma Gao 馬縞 (rep. ed.: Shanghai: Shangwu, 1956).

75. *Zuo zhuan zhu* Xi 15, p. 365.

76. *Shuo wen jie zi zhu* 15A, pp. 2a–3a. For the gloss on *zi*, see 14B, p. 25a. A similar gloss also appears in *Shi ming shu zheng bu* 4 "Shi yan yu 釋言語," p. 2a. One passage in the apocryphal literature links the relation of *wen* to *zi* with that of the hexagrams to primal energy. "In high antiquity they transformed patterns into characters, changed energy into the *Yi*, and drew the hexagrams into images (*xiang* 象). When the images were completed they established their positions." See *Yi qian kun zao du*, in *Qi wei* 1, p. 4b; in *Wei shu ji cheng*, p. 778.

77. Hayashi, *Kan dai no kamigami*, p. 294.

78. Jean James, *A Guide to Tomb and Shrine Art of the Han Dynasty, 206 B.C.–A.D. 220* (Lewiston, New York: Edwin Mellen, 1996), pp. 88, 96–101. In all three depictions of Fu Xi and Nü Gua in the Wu family shrines, the central deities are accompanied by other serpent-bodied beings. See Wu, *The Wu Liang Shrine*, pp. 246–47. On the serpent-bodied beings wielding fans who frame the Queen Mother of the West, see *Shandong Han huaxiang shi xuan ji* 山東漢畫像石選集 (Ji'nan: Qi Lu, 1982), figures 219, 281; Li Falin 李发林, *Shandong Han huaxiang shi yanjiu* 山东汉画像石研究 (Ji'nan: Qi Lu, 1982), figure 12; James, *Tomb and Shrine Art*, figures 51, 52.

79. For a discussion of this image in context, see Wu, *The Wu Liang Shrine*, pp. 156–61.

80. Jean James, who is skeptical of many of the identifications, accepts that these two objects distinguish Fu Xi and Nü Gua from other snake-bodied spirits.

81. For a typical formulation of the appeal to *yin/yang* symbolism, see Lü Pin 吕品, "Henan Han hua suo jian tuteng yi su kao 河南汉画所见图腾遗俗考," *Zhongyuan wen wu* 1991:3, p. 48. For the counter-argument, see James, *Tomb and Shrine Art*, pp. 97–98.

82. On Fu Xi using the carpenter's square to create the trigrams, see *Yi tong gua yan* 易通卦驗, in *Qi wei* 6, p. 1b, in *Wei shu ji cheng*, p. 820. On the trigrams as square and the yarrow as round, see *Zhou yi zheng yi* 7 "Xi ci shang," p. 26b.

83. Perhaps the earliest references to Chui is in *Shang shu zheng yi* 3 "Shun dian 舜典," p. 24b. In this account Chui is appointed chief of the craftsmen (*gong gong* 共工) by Shun. His title or function is identical with the name of the rebel who causes

the flood and the tipping of the heavens in many versions of the flood myth, including the one in which Nü Gua appears. The meaning of this link is unclear. On Chui as the inventor of the carpenter's square and the inked cord used as a straightedge, see *Shi ben ji bu* 9 "Zuo 作," p. 360. On Chui as a figure who represents the dangers or uselessness of crafts, see *Zhuangzi ji shi* 10 "Qu qie," p. 161; 19 "Da sheng," p. 290; *Lü shi chun qiu jiaoshi* 18 "Li wei," p. 1179; *Huainanzi* 8 "Ben jing," p. 117; 12 "Dao ying," p. 208.

84. "Sichuan Jianyang xian Guitou shan Dong Han ya mu 四川简阳县鬼头山东汉崖墓," *Wenwu* (1991:3), p. 23 (figure 10); Wu Hung, "Beyond the 'Great Boundary': Funerary Narrative in the Cangshan Tomb," in John Hay, ed., *Boundaries in China* (London: Reaktion Books, 1994), pp. 88–90.

85. For examples of such images, see Finsterbusch, *Verzeichnis und motivindex*, figures 32a, 45, 101–2, 106, 127, 137, 150, 158, 161, 167, 172, Hebei appendix 3–4; "Sichuan Pi xian Dong Han zhuan mu de shi guan huaxiang 四川郫县东汉砖墓的石棺画象," *Kaogu* (1979:6), pp. 497, 499: the article also refers to two other coffin-lid images of Fu Xi and Nü Gua that are not reproduced; Li Fuhua 李复华 and Guo Ziyou 郭子游, "Pi Xian chutu Dong Han huaxiang shi guan tuxiang lüe shuo 郫县出土东汉画象石棺图象略说," *Wenwu* (1975:8), p. 63; "Hechuan Dong Han huaxiang shi mu 合川东汉画象石墓," *Wenwu* (1977:2), p. 67 (figures 15 and 16); Xie Li 谢荔 and Xu Lihong 徐利红, "Sichuan Hejiang xian Dong Han zhuan shi mu qingli jian bao 四川合江县东汉砖室墓清理简报," *Wenwu* (1992:4), p. 47; "Sichuan Changning 'qi ge dong' Dong Han jinian huaxiang ya mu 四川长宁七个洞东汉纪年画像崖墓," *Kaogu yu wenwu* (1985:5), p. 47; Cui Chen 崔陈, "Yibin diqu chutu Han dai huaxiang shi guan 宜宾地区出土汉代画像石棺," *Kaogu yu wenwu* (1991:1), p. 37 (figures 3 and 5); Gao Wen 高文 and Gao Chengying 高成英, "Han hua guibao—Sichuan xin chutu de ba ge huaxiang shi guan 汉画瑰宝—四川新出土的八个画像石棺," *Wenwu tian di* (1988:3), p. 4, fig. 11. While the image of a pair of snake-bodied creatures with the sun and moon is most common on Sichuan coffins, it also appears on stones from the walls of Shandong tombs. See, for example, "Shandong Zao zhuang huaxiang shi diaocha ji 山东枣庄画像石调查记," *Kaogu yu wenwu* (1983:3), p. 28 (figures 13 and 14).

86. In the images cited in the preceding note, the square and compass, or the pipes, are clearly visible in Finsterbusch, figures 45, 101–02, 106, 172 (102, 106, and perhaps 172 look like pipes), Hebei appendix, 3–4; *Kaogu* (1979:6), p. 497; *Wenwu* (1973:6), p. 30; *Wenwu* (1977:2), p. 67 (both plates); *Wenwu* (1991:4), p. 47; *Kaogu yu wenwu* (1991:1), p. 37 (figure 3); *Wenwu tian di* (1988:3). Although they do not hold the compass and carpenter's square, the snake-bodied spirits who accompany the sun and moon in the wall paintings of the late Western Han tomb of Bu Qianqiu are also generally accepted as Fu Xi and Nü Gua. This would strengthen the case for identifying the Sichuan images with these two spirits. See "Luoyang Xi Han Bu Qianqiu bihua mu fajue jianbao 洛阳西汉卜千秋壁画发掘简报," *Wenwu* (1977:6), pp. 1–12; Chen Shaofeng 陈少丰 and Gong Dazhong 宫大中, "Luoyang Xi Han Bu Qianqiu mu bihua yishu 洛阳西汉卜千秋墓壁画艺术," *Wenwu* (1977:6), pp. 13–16; Sun Zuoyun 孙作云," Luoyang Xi Han Bu Qianqiu mu bihua kaoshi 洛阳西汉卜千秋墓壁画考释," *Wenwu* (1977:6), pp. 17–22.

87. While the paired snake-bodied spirits holding the sun and moon are certainly Fu Xi and Nü Gua, there are a handful of images in which a single snake-bodied spirit holding the moon is paired with the sun being carried by a bird spirit. See, for

example, "Xuzhou Qingshan quan Baiji Dong Han huaxiang shi mu 徐州青山泉白集东汉画象石墓," *Kaogu* (1981:2), p. 146 (figures 11:3 and 11:4); Su Zhaoqing 苏兆庆 and Zhang Anli 张安礼 "Shandong Ju xian Chenliu zhuang Han huaxiang shi mu 山东莒县沉刘庄汉画像石墓," *Kaogu* (1988:9), p. 793. In the first article, the author identifies the snake-bodied spirit as Nü Gua. In the second, they identify it as Fu Xi with the sun, even though it is paired with the bird and sun and no clear indication exists whether the circle is sun or moon. The exact identity of this creature is uncertain, but the staff of the Nanyang City Museum has suggested that such a figure represents Chang Xi 常羲 (or "Chang Yi 常仪"), who appears as mother of the moon(s) in the *Shan hai jing*. See "Nanyang shi Wang zhuang Han huaxiang shi mu 南阳市王庄汉画像石墓," *Zhongyuan wenwu* (1985:3), pp. 31–32. While the identification remains questionable, and there is no textual evidence that Chang Xi had a serpent body, it could account for the pairing of a serpent-bodied spirit linked to the moon with the bird of the sun. See also Finsterbusch, *Verzeichnis und Motivindex*, figures 873, 996c.

There are also examples of a human figure with a snake tail holding aloft the sun. In one case this figure occupies one pillar of the entrance to the rear chamber of the tomb; there is no decoration on the other pillar. In theory, there should have been a matching figure with the moon, in which case these would be identifiable as Fu Xi and Nü Gua. In the absence of the second element of the pair, however, this identification remains uncertain. See "Hechuan Dong Han huaxiang shi mu," p. 66 (figure 12). On the location of the image and the gap where the "partner" should have been, see p. 65. A similar image in another tomb is described as Xi He (羲和) holding aloft the sun. See Qiu Yongsheng 邱永生, "Xuzhou Qing shan quan shui ni er chang yi, er hao Han mu fajue jianbao 徐州青山泉水泥二厂一、二号汉墓发掘简报," *Zhongyuan wenwu* (1992:1), p. 94 (figure 10). *Xuzhou Han huaxiang shi* (Nanjing: Jiangsu meishu, 1985), figures 28 and 104 are also images of snake-bodied spirits lifting the sun and the moon. The editors identify these as Fu Xi and Nü Gua, but no arguments are given. A similar figure appears in *Jiangsu Xuzhou Hanhuaxiang shi* 江蘇徐州漢畫象石 (Beijing: Kexue, 1959), figure 90.

88. These three banners are discussed in James, *Tomb and Shrine Art*, pp. 10–18, 24–27.

89. See also An Zhimin 安志敏, "Changsha xin faxian de Xi Han bo hua shi tan 长沙新发现的西汉帛画试探," *Kaogu* 1973:1, pp. 43–53.

90. Finsterbusch, *Verzeichnis und Motivindex*, figures 261, 274, 275; James, *Tomb and Shrine Art*, pp. 93–98; Zhou Dao 周到 and Li Jinghua 李京华 "Tanghe Zhenzhi chang Han huaxiang shi mu de fajue 唐河针织厂汉画像石墓的发掘," *Wenwu* (1973:6), p. 35 (figure 3:1, lower right panel).

91. James, *Tomb and Shrine Art*, p. 59.

92. Zhou and Li, "Tanghe Zhenzhi chang Han huaxiang shi mu de fajue," pp. 30, 34 (figure 2B); Finsterbusch, *Verzeichnis und Motivindex*, figure 161.

93. Wu Lan 吴兰, Zhi An 志安, and Chun Ning 春宁, "Suide Xindian faxian de liang zuo huaxiang shi mu 绥德辛店发现的两座画像石墓," *Kaogu yu wenwu* (1993:1), p. 17; Wu Lan and Xue Yong 学勇, "Shaanxi Mizhi xian Guan zhuang Dong Han huaxiang shi mu 陕西米脂县官庄东汉画像石墓," *Kaogu* (1987:11), p. 998 (figure 2). The reproduction is too small to make out the nature of the tools held by the snake-bodied guardians, but they are identified in the text on the same page.

94. For examples of pairs of snake-bodied doorway guardians holding magical plants, see "Henan Nanyang Junzhang ying Han huaxiang shi mu 河南南阳军帐营汉画像石墓," *Kaogu yu wenwu* (1982:1), pp. 40 (figure 1, bottom), 41 (figure 2:1); "Henan Nanyang xian Ying zhuang Han huaxiang shi mu 河南南阳县英庄汉画像石墓," *Wenwu* (1984:3), p. 33.

95. Zeng Zhaoyu 曾昭燏, Jiang Baogeng 蒋宝庚, and Li Zhongyi 黎忠义, *Yinan gu huaxiang shi mu fajue baogao* 沂南古画像石墓发抉报告 (Shanghai: Wenhuabu Wen Wu Guanliju, 1956), figure 25, (rubbing 2); Finsterbusch, *Verzeichnis und Motivindex*, figure 282.

96. For other examples, see Finsterbusch, *Verzeichnis und Motivindex*, figure 947; Zhou Dao and Li Jinghua, "Tanghe Zhenzhi chang Han huaxiang shi mu de fajue," *Wenwu* 1973:6, p. 33 (figure 1:2); Zhu Xilu 朱義禄, ed., *Jiaxiang Han huaxiang shi* 嘉祥汉画像石 (Ji'nan: Shangdong meishu, 1992), figures 105 (right), 126.

97. The different theories are listed in James, *Tomb and Shrine Art*, pp. 63–64, 101. For the theory that the figure is the High Matchmaker, see Chen Changshan 陈长山, "Gaomei huaxiang xiao kao 高禖画像小考," *Kaogu yu wenwu* (1987:5), pp. 82–83, 6. For the "Grand Unity," see He Fushun 贺福顺, "'Gaomei huaxiang xiao kao' yi wen shangque ·高禖画像小考·一文商榷," *Kaogu yu wenwu* (1992:1), pp. 57–59. For Pangu, see Sun Wenqing 孫文青, *Nanyang Han huaxiang hui cun* 南陽漢畫像彙存 (Nanjing, 1937), p. 68. For the primal unity, see Martin Powers, "An Archaic Bas-relief and the Chinese Moral Cosmos in the First Century A.D.," *Ars Orientalis* 12 (1981), p. 34.

98. On the iconography of the Grand Unity, see Li Ling, "An Archaeological Study of Taiyi 太一 (Grand One) Worship," tr. Donald Harper, *Early Medieval China* 2 (1995–1996), pp. 1–39.

99. See *Yinan*, figure 28 (rubbing 8), figure 33 (rubbing 14); Finsterbusch, *Verzeichnis und Motivindex*, figures 288 (left), 294.

100. On the myth of Yi and Zongbu in Han art, see Chen Jiangfeng 陈江风, "Han huaxiang 'shen gui shijie' de siwei xingtai ji qi yishu 汉画像·神鬼世界·的思维形态及其艺术," *Zhongyuan wenwu* (1991:3), pp. 15, 16. For images of the archer loading his crossbow, see Finsterbusch, *Verzeichnis und Motivindex*, figures 62a, 62b, 448, 601, 998; *Jiangsu Xuzhou Han huaxiang shi*, figure 58; "Tanghe xian Zhenzhi chang er hao Han huaxiang shi mu 唐河县针织厂二号汉画像石墓," *Zhongyuan wenwu* (1985:3), p. 18 (figure 11:2); "Nanyang shi Liuwa cun Han huaxiang shi mu 南阳市刘洼村汉画像石墓," *Zhongyuan wenwu* (1991:3), p. 111 (figure 19).

101. On this recurring type in Chinese civilization, with special reference to Chi You and Yi, see Lewis, *Sanctioned Violence in Early China*, pp. 183–208.

102. Finsterbusch, *Verzeichnis und Motivindex*, figure 712, 922; Zhang Xiaojun 张晓军, "Qian tan Nanyang Han huaxiang shi zhong niu de yishu xingxiang 浅谈南阳汉画像石中牛的艺术形象," *Zhongyuan wenwu* (1985: 3), pp. 77 (figure 5), 78 (figures 8–10); "Tanghe xian Zhenzhi chang er hao Han huaxiang shi mu," p. 17 (figure 7); Yang Hong 杨泓, "Gu wen wu tuxiang zhong de xiangpu 古文物图像中的相扑," *Wenwu* (1980:10), p. 89 (figures 2, 3).

103. Zhou Dao and Li Jinghua, "Tanghe Zhenzhi chang Han huaxiang shi mu de fajue," *Wenwu* (1973:6), p. 33 (figure 1:2, lower left panel). Finsterbusch, *Verzeichnis und Motivindex*, figures 896–99 depict figures who are clothed and wear unusual headgear

reminiscent of this image, also wrestling animals. Two of them also have monstrous faces like that of the images in the next note.

104. Zhu Xilu, ed., *Jiaxiang Han huaxiang shi*, figures 105 (right), 126. The strange headgear composed of three triangles also appears on a monster in a register just above a depiction of Chi You found on a stone from Jiangsu. See Finsterbusch, *Verzeichnis und Motivindex*, Jiangsu appendix, figure 16.

105. *Jiangsu Xuzhou Han huaxiang shi*, figure 85; Finsterbusch, *Verzeichnis un Motivindex*, figure 570.

106. In one image a small human figure stands below Fu Xi and Nü Gua, but it is separated from them by a tree under which it stands, and it appears to be a distinct scene in a separate register. See "Lun Xuzhou Han huaxiang shi 论徐州汉画像石," *Wenwu* (1980:2), p. 53 (figure 9).

107. In addition to the pairs cited in note 92, see also Finsterbusch, *Verzeichnis und Motivindex*, figures 934–942, Honan appendix, figure 25; "Nanyang shi Wang zhuang Han huaxiang shi mu," *Zhongyuan wenwu* 1985:3, pp. 27 (figure 3), 29 (figures 10–11); Lü Pin, "Henan Han hua suo jian tuteng yi su kao," *Zhongyuan wenwu* (1991:3), p. 47 (figures 5–6); *Nanyang Han dai huaxiang shi* 南阳汉代画像石 (Beijing: Wenwu, 1985), figures 42, 143, 315, 323; "Nanyang Han huaxiang shi gaishu 南阳汉画像石概述," *Wenwu* (1973:6), p. 25 (figure 13); "Nanyang xian Wang Zhai Han huaxiang shi mu 南阳县王寨汉画像石墓," *Zhongyuan wenwu* (1982:1), p. 15; "Deng xian Changzhong-dian Han huaxiang shi mu 邓县长冢店汉画像石墓," *Zhongyuan wenwu* (1982:1), p. 19.

108. Li Chenguang 李陈广, "Han hua Fu Xi Nü Gua de xingxiang tezheng ji qi yiyi 汉画伏羲女娲的形象特征及其意义," *Zhongyuan wenwu* (1992:1), p. 36.

109. *Shi ben*, in *Shi ben ba zhong*, Qin Jiamo edition, p. 15; *Di wang shi ji ji cun*, p. 52; Katō Jōken, "Shina ko seishi no kenkyū—Ka U Shi sei kō, pp. 454–55.

110. On the daughter of the Tushan clan as Yu's wife, see *Shang shu zheng yi*, ch. 5, "Yi ji," p. 11a; *Chu ci bu zhu*, ch. 3, "Tian wen," p. 10b; *Lü shi chun qiu jiao shi*, ch. 6, "Yin chu 音初," pp. 334–35; *Shang shu da zhuan*, quoted in the *suo yin* commentary to *Shi ji* 2, p. 81 note 3; *Huainanzi*, quoted in *Chu ci bu zhu*, ch. 3, "Tian wen," p. 11a; *Shi ji* 2, pp. 80, 84; 49, p. 1967; 128, p. 3223; *Da Dai li ji jie gu*, ch. 7, "Di xi," p. 130; *Xin xu shu zheng*, ch. 1, "Za shi," p. 4; *Gu lie nü zhuan*, ch. 1, p. 3a; Yang Xiong, *Shu wang ben ji* 蜀王本紀, quoted in *Taiping yu lan*, ch. 82, p. 3b; *Yue jue shu*, ch. 8, "Wai zhuan ji Yue di," p. 9a; *Wu yue chun qiu*, ch. 6, "Yue wang Wuyu wai zhuan," p. 2b; *Han shu* 20, p. 880; *Di wang shi ji ji cun*, p. 52; *Shui jing zhu*, ch. 6, p. 84. On the different personal names of this woman, see the previous passages from *Da dai li ji*; *Wu yue chun qiu*; *Han shu*; *Shi ji* 2, p. 81 note 3; *Di wang shi ji ji cun*; "San huang ben ji," p. 3. There is a reference to a woman with a closely related name in *Guo yu*, ch. 10, "Jin yu si," p. 356, but she is described as the mother of the Yellow Thearch and the Fiery Thearch.

For the argument that all these names refer to one and the same figure, see Wang Xiaolian 王孝廉, *Zhongguo de shenhua yu chuanshuo* 中國的神話與傳說 (Taipei: Lian-jing, 1977), p. 66.

111. Wen Yiduo, "Gao Tang shen nü chuanshuo zhi fenxi," pp. 115–16.

112. See *Shi ben*, quoted in *Shi ji* 2, p. 49 note 2; *Wu Yue chun qiu*, ch. 6, "Yue wang Wuyu wai zhuan," p. 1a; *Di wang shi ji ji cun*, pp. 49, 50. For a discussion of this, see Wen Yiduo, "Gao Tang shen nü chuanshuo zhi fenxi," pp. 98–99.

113. Ma, *Mawangdui gu yi shu kaoshi*, pp. 744, 763, 779–821; Harper, *Early Chinese Medical Literature*, pp. 358, 367, 372–84. On the evidence of Yu being linked to childbirth in the medieval Chinese period, see footnote 2 on p. 367 of Harper, *Early Chinese Medical Literature*.

114. See the passages listed in chapter three, note 95.

115. *Mozi jian gu*, ch. 8, "Ming gui xia 明鬼下," p. 142; *Guliang zhuan zhu shu*, Zhuang year 23, ch. 6, p. 5a. In this passage I gloss the character *shi* 尸 as *chen* 陳 "to lay out, to display." This follows *Shuo wen jie zi zhu*, ch. 8a, p. 70a. On the significance of the *Mozi* passage, see Guo Moruo 郭沫若, *Jiagu wenzi yanjiu* 甲骨文字研究 (Hong Kong: Zhonghua, 1976), "Shi zu bi 釋祖妣," pp. 19–24.

116. *Zhou li zhu shu*, ch. 14, "Mei shi 媒氏," pp. 13b–17a.

117. *Li ji zhu shu*, ch. 15, "Yue ling," pp. 3a–4a.

118. For discussions of these documents, their authenticity, transcriptions, and color reproductions, see Rao Zhongyi 饒宗頤, "Zhongwen Daxue Wenwuguan cang Jianchu si nian 'Xuning jian' yu 'Baoshan jian': lun Zhanguo Qin, Han jieji daoci zhi zhu shen yu gushi renwu 中文大學文物館藏建初四年序寧簡與包山簡：論戰國, 秦, 漢解疾禱辭之諸神與古史人物," *Hua Xia wenming yu chuanshi cangshu: Zhongguo guoji Hanxue yantaohui lunwenji* 華夏文明與傳世藏書：中國國際漢學研討會論文集 (Beijing: Zhongguo Shehui Kexue Chubanshe, 1996), pp. 662–72; Chen Songchang 陳松長, *Xianggang Zhongwen Daxue Wenwuguan cang jiandu* 香港中文大學文物館藏簡牘 (Hong Kong: Xianggang Zhongwen Daxue Wenwuguan, 2001), pp. 97–108; Lian Shaoming 連劭名, "Dong Han Jianchu si nian wu dao quanshu yu gudai de cezhu 東漢建初四年巫禱券書與古代的冊祝," *Chuantong wenhua yu xiandaihua* 傳統文化與現代化 (1996:6), pp. 28–33. A detailed study, translation, and analysis will appear in Donald Harper, "Contracts with the Spirit World in Han Common Religion: The Xuning Prayer and Sacrifice Documents of A.D. 79," *Cahiers d'Extrême-Asie*, forthcoming.

119. *Han shu* 27B, p. 1413. For a study of references to *she* altars found in the Han strips discovered at Juyan, along with a summary of the evidence from the received sources, see Lao Gan 勞榦, *Juyan Han jian: kaoshi zhi bu* 居延漢簡：考釋之部 (Taipei: Zhongyang Yanjiuyuan Lishi Yuyan Yanjiusuo, 1960), pp. 66–67.

120. *Chu ci bu zhu*, ch. 3, "Tian wen," pp. 10b–11a.

121. *Lü shi chun qiu jiao shi*, ch. 6, "Yin chu," pp. 334–35; ch. 11, "Dang wu 當務," p. 596. The *Wu Yue chun qiu* recounts the words of the suggestive song supposedly composed by the maid on this occasion. See "Yue wang Wuyu wai zhuan," p. 2b. This accusation in early texts against Yu for his supposed sexual license is discussed by Wen Yiduo. See "Gao Tang shen nü chuanshuo," p. 86. Wen also notes that Ma Xulun has argued that a reference in the "Robber Zhi" chapter of *Zhuangzi* to Yu's "half paralysis" originally referred to his "lascivious thoughts." This argument is based on the fact that the rest of the list in which it appears deals with suspicions regarding the sages' moral character, not with their physical defects. For the relevant passage, see *Zhuangzi ji shi*, ch. 29, "Dao Zhi," p. 430.

122. On this pattern, see Lewis, *Writing and Authority*, pp. 219, 447 note 117.

123. This overlap has previously been discussed in Jing Wang, *The Story of Stone*, pp. 49–62.

124. Quoted from the "Li ji wai zhuan," in *Taiping yu lan*, ch. 532, p. 3a; quoted from *Hou Wei shu* 後魏書, in *Taiping yu lan*, ch. 532, p. 5b; *Huainanzi*, ch. 11, "Qi su," p. 176; *Song shu* 102, p. 2484. The account in the *Song shu* of the *she* being exposed to the elements, without the final passage on the use of stone, derives from a passage in the *Li ji*. See *Li ji zhu shu*, ch. 25, "Jiao te sheng 郊特牲," pp. 20a–b. The focus in the *Li ji* passage is on the links of the *she* altar to the swearing of an oath, to which the use of stone was closely linked.

125. On the depictions of the *she* in Han art, see Kominami Ichirō 小南一郎, "Sha no saiji no shokeitai to sono kigen 社の祭祀の諸形態とその起源," *Koshi shunjū* 4 (1987), pp. 17–37.

126. *Shang shu zheng yi*, ch. 6, "Yu gong," p. 33b; *Shi ji* 2, p. 77; 5, pp. 173, 174 note 6; *Shang shu xuan ji qian* 尚書旋璣鈐, quoted in *Taiping yu lan*, ch. 82, p. 2b: this apocryphal text says that the black ceremonial jade was inscribed "Heaven-bestowed Pendant of Joy-extending Jade Received by the Virtuous *yan xi yu shou de tian ci pei* 延喜玉受德天賜佩"; *Di wang shi ji ji cun*, p. 52.

127. *Shi yi ji*, ch. 2, p. 38: in this story the god, who is identified as Fu Xi, gives Yu both the "River Chart" with the hexagrams he has invented and a strip of jade that allows Yu to restore order to land and water; *Shui jing zhu*, quoted in He Yixing commentary to the *Shan hai jing*, see *Shan hai jing jiao zhu*, ch. 2, "Xi shan jing," p. 50 note 2. The god in this story is the ruler of a mountain noted for its abundance of jade and green stones; *Dun jia kai shan tu* 遁甲開山圖, quoted in *Taiping yu lan*, ch. 82, p. 3b.

128. The statement that Yu was born from a stone first appears in *Huainanzi*, ch. 19, "Xiu wu," p. 337. The same tradition was elaborated in the later *Sui chaozi* 隨巢子, along with the story that Yu's son Qi was also born from a stone. See *Taiping yu lan*, ch. 51, p. 5b. The graph for "stone" in the name of Yu's birthplace appears in a lost passage of *Mencius* quoted by Huangfu Mi and preserved in the *ji jie* 集解 commentary to the *Shi ji* 15, p. 686 note 1. While this passage does not appear in the current version of *Mencius*, it fits exactly into the first sentence of chapter IVB "Li Lou xia," p. 317, which gives the birthplaces of Shun and King Wen, and then states that they were respectively "eastern" and "western" barbarians. The passage given by Huangfu Mi states that Yu was born at Shiniu (石紐 "Stone Knot") and that he was a "western barbarian." The tradition that Yu was born at Shiniu also appears in a "Chronicle of the Kings of Shu" written by Yang Xiong: see *Shi ji* 2, p. 49 note 2; *Taiping yu lan*, ch. 82, p. 3b; *Wu Yue chun qiu*, ch. 6, "Yue wang Wuyu wai zhuan," p. 1a: in this story Yu was not only born at Shiniu, but his mother conceived him by swallowing the seeds of a lotus fruit while wandering in the wilds at "Whetstone Mountain (*di shan* 砥山)"; *Di wang shi ji ji cun*, pp. 49, 51. In a passage from the *Di wang shi ji* that is quoted in the Song-dynasty *Lu shi*, the name is given as "Stone Hollow [*shi ao* 石坳]." The Eastern Han divinatory text *Yi lin* contains the tradition that Shun found Yu at a place called "Stone Level [or 'Stone Barbarian', *shi yi* 石夷]." See *Jiao Shi Yi lin* 焦氏易林 (Si bu cong kan edition), ch. 16, p. 38b.

129. *Lun heng ji jie*, ch. 7, "Yu zeng," p. 164; ch. 8, "Ru zeng 儒增," p. 173; "Yi zeng 藝增" pp. 179–80; ch. 11, "Shuo ri 説日" pp. 235–36; ch. 22, "Ji yao 紀妖," p. 442. For discussions in the secondary sources of early Chinese ideas about the nature of meteors, see Joseph Needham, *Science and Civilisation in China*, vol. 3, *Mathematics and the Sciences of the Heavens and the Earth* (Cambridge: Cambridge University, 1970),

pp. 433–34; Edward H. Schafer, *Pacing the Void: T'ang Approaches to the Stars* (Berkeley: University of California, 1977), pp. 101–03.

130. Yang Xiong, "Shu wang ben ji," quoted in *Taiping yu lan*, ch. 82, p. 3b: this refers to her swallowing a pearl; *Lun heng ji jie*, ch. 3, "Qi guai 奇怪," p. 73: here she swallows the seeds of a lotus fruit; *Qian fu lun jian*, ch. 8, "Wu de zhi," p. 393: here she is impregnated by the sight of a meteorite; *Xiao jing gou ming jue* 孝經鉤命決, quoted in *Taiping yu lan*, ch. 82, p. 3b: this refers to the story of the meteorite; *Shang shu di ming yan* 尚書帝命驗, quoted in *Taiping yu lan*, ch. 82, p. 2b: this refers to the story of the meteorite; *Di wang shi ji ji cun*, pp. 49, 50: in these passages she is rendered pregnant by the sight of the meteorite, but also swallows a pearl in one version and both a pearl and the seed of a lotus fruit in the other.

131. Yang Xiong, "Shu wang ben ji," quoted in *Taiping yu lan*, ch. 82, p. 3b: Yang Xiong's description in this passage of Yu's birth is exactly the opposite of that of Hou Ji in the ode "Sheng min 生民" (See *Mao shi zheng yi*, ch. 17.1, #245, p. 6b.); *Lun heng ji jie*, ch. 3, "Qi guai," p. 73: this relates that he burst out of his mother's back; *Chun qiu fan lu yi zheng*, ch. 7, "San dai gai zhi zhi wen," p. 212: this also says that he came out of her back; *Wu yue chun qiu*, ch. 6, "Yue wang Wuyu wai zhuan," p. 1a: this states that he burst out of her side; *Di wang shi ji ji cun*, p. 50: in this case Yu bursts out of his mother's chest; Gan Bao, quoted in the *ji jie* commentary to *Shi ji* 40, p. 1690 note 1: this says that he came out of her back.

132. *Huainanzi*, quoted in the commentary to *Chuci bu zhu*, ch. 3, "Tian wen," p. 11a. A reference from 110 B.C. shows that this story was well known during the Western Han, and the Tang commentator Yan Shigu confirms that it was recorded in the *Huainanzi*. See *Han shu* 6, p. 190 note 2. This story is also preserved in the later *Sui chaozi*, without the incident of hopping on the stone.

133. *Di wang shi ji ji cun*, p. 51.

134. *Mao shi zheng yi*, ch. 11.2, #189, "Si gan 斯干," pp. 9a–b.

135. Marcel Granet, *Fêtes et chansons anciennes de la Chine* (2nd ed., Paris: Leroux, 1929), pp. 134, 155–74.

136. *Hou Han shu* 1b, p. 85.

137. *Da Dai li ji jie gu*, ch. 7, "Wu di de," pp. 124–25.

138. Ma, *Mawangdui gu yi shu*, p. 940; Harper, *Early Chinese Medical Literature*, pp. 404–05.

139. *Xin yu*, ch. 2, p. 4. Several other texts tell the story of Yu's throwing away precious objects to teach simplicity to the people, but they do not employ the theme of the body or the imagery of the flood. These themes also structure Chao Cuo's memorial on agriculture in 178 B.C. See *Han shu* 24a, pp. 1130–34.

140. The most detailed account is that of Marcel Granet, *Danses et légendes*, pp. 549–79. More broadly construed, one could also include pp. 503–48, which deal with mythic tales related to Yu's drumming. More recently the use of the "Pace of Yu" in religious Daoism has been examined in Poul Andersen, "The Practice of *Bugang*," *Cahiers d'Extrême-Asie* 5 (1989–90), pp. 15–33. See also Granet, "Remarques sur le Taoisme ancien," *Asia Major* 2 (1925), pp. 146–51; Eberhard, *The Local Cultures of South and East China*, pp. 74–75; Schafer, *Pacing the Void*, pp. 238–40. For the passages in the *Bao pu zi*, see *Bao pu zi nei pian jiao shi*, ch. 11, "Xian yao 仙樂," p. 190; ch. 15, "Za

ying 雜應," p. 251: here the use of the "Pace of Yu" appears as an alternative to the use of five-colored jade; ch. 17, "Deng she 登涉," pp. 276, 279.

141. *Shuihudi Qin mu zhu jian*, pp. 222–23. This practice anticipates the later *nayin* 納音 hemerological system described in the *Bao pu zi*. See Marc Kalinowski, "Les traités de Shuihudi et l'hémérologie chinoise," *T'oung Pao* 72 (1986), pp. 200–04. On early Chinese rituals pertaining to travel see Lewis, *Sanctioned Violence*, pp. 23, 182, 187–94; Jiang Shaoyuan 江紹源, *Zhongguo gudai lüxing zhi yanjiu* 中國古代旅行之研究 (Shanghai: Shangwu, 1935).

142. *Zuo zhuan zhu*, Xuan year 3, pp. 669–70. On the tripods, their relation to the *Shan hai jing*, and other accounts of Yu, see Lewis, *Writing and Authority*, pp. 34, 268–69; Robert Ford Campany, *Strange Writing: Anomaly Accounts in Early Medieval China* (Albany: State University of New York, 1996), pp. 102–06. The tripods as a source for the names of wicked spirits who can thus be fended off are also mentioned in *Bao pu zi nei pian jiao shi*, ch. 17, "Deng she," p. 282. The same page also mentions facing the Dipper while performing a ceremony to ward off spirits when traveling, just as in the earlier Fangmatan almanac.

143. Ma, *Mawangdui gu yi shu kaoshi*, "Wushier bing fang," pp. 414, 421, 474, 477, 483, 592, 635: this refers to warding off the child sprite; "Yangsheng fang," pp. 736: this gives a magic formula for securing a campsite for the night when traveling in the mountains, 738: this offers the formula for walking swiftly without hurting the feet. The formula for securing the campsite appears in a closely related version in the later *Bao pu zi nei pian jiao shi*, ch. 17, "Deng she," p. 287. For a brief discussion of the "Pace of Yu" in the Mawangdui materials, and translations of the relevant passages, see Harper, *Early Chinese Medical Literature*, pp. 148, 160, 167–69, 243, 244–45, 259, 261, 264, 290, 302, 354, 355. Harper also suggests that two missing characters in one passage are *Yu bu* 禹步. See p. 253.

144. *Guanju Qin Han mu jiandu* 關沮秦漢墓簡牘 (Beijing: Zhonghua, 2001), pp. 129, 130 (2), 131 (3), 132.

145. *Lun heng ji jie*, ch. 15, "Shun gu," p. 323. Wang Chong's linking of the *she* altar to rituals for rain, or rather his attribution of such a linkage to Dong Zhongshu, is supported by other sources. See Wang Xiaolian, *Zhongguo de shenhua yu chuanshuo*, p. 51.

WORKS CITED

PRIMARY SOURCES

Bai ze tu 白澤圖. In Ma Guohan 馬國翰, ed. *Yu han shan fang ji yi shu* 玉函山房輯佚書. Changsha: 1883.

Baopuzi nei pian jiao shi 抱朴子內篇校釋. Written by Ge Hong 葛洪. Annotated by Wang Ming 王明. Beijing: Zhonghua, 1980.

Bo hu tong de lun 白虎通德論. In *Han Wei cong shu* 漢魏叢書. Vol. 1. Taipei: Xinxing, 1977.

Bo wu jing yi yi 駁五經異義. Written by Xu Shen 許慎 and Zheng Xuan 鄭玄. In *Hou zhi bu zu zhai congshu* 後知不足齋叢書. N.p.: Chang Shubao, 1884.

Bo wu zhi jiao zheng 博物志校證. Compiled by Zhang Hua 張華. Annotated by Fan Ning 范寧. Beijing: Zhonghua, 1980.

Chu ci bu zhu 楚辭補注. Annotated by Hong Xingzu 洪興祖. Si bu cong kan edition.

Chun qiu fan lu yi zheng 春秋繁露義證. Annotated by Su Yu 蘇與. Beijing: Zhonghua, 1992.

Chun qiu he cheng tu 春秋合誠圖. In *Gu wei shu* 古緯書. In *Wei shu ji cheng* 緯書集成. Shanghai: Guji, 1994.

Chun qiu yuan ming bao 春秋元命包. In *Gu wei shu*. In *Wei shu ji cheng*. Shanghai: Guji, 1994.

Da Dai li ji jie gu 大戴禮記解詁. Annotated by Wang Pinzhen 王聘珍. Reprint ed. Beijing: Zhonghua, 1964.

Di wang shi ji ji cun 帝王世紀輯存. Compiled by Xu Zongyuan 徐宗元. Beijing: Zhonghua, 1964.

Du duan 獨斷. Written by Cai Yong 蔡邕. In *Han Wei cong shu*. Vol. 1. Taipei: Xinxing, 1977.

Du yi zhi 獨異志. Written by Li Rong 李冗. In *Bai hai* 稗海. Taipei: Xinxing, 1965.

Feng su tong yi jiao shi 風俗通義校釋. Written by Ying Shao 應劭. Aannotated by Wu Shuping 吳樹平. Tianjin: Renmin, 1980.

Guanju Qin Han mu jiandu 關沮秦漢墓簡牘. Beijing: Zhonghua, 2001.

Guanzi jiao zheng 管子郊正. Annotated by Dai Wang 戴望. In *Xin bian zhu zi ji cheng* 新編諸子集成. Vol. 5. Taipei: Shijie, 1974.

Gui zang 歸藏. In *Quan shanggu sandai Qin Han Sanguo liu chao wen* 全上古三代秦漢三國六朝文. Compiled by Yan Kejun 嚴可均. Beijing: Zhonghua, 1958.

Guliang zhuan zhu shu 穀梁傳注疏. In *Shi san jing zhu shu* 十三經注疏. Vol. 7. Taipei: Yinen, 1976.

Guo yu 國語. Yiwen: Guji, 1978.

Han Feizi ji shi 韓非子集釋. Annotated by Chen Qiyou 陳奇猷. Shanghai: Renmin, 1974.

Han shi wai zhuan ji shi 韓氏外傳集釋. Annotated by Xu Weiyu 許維遹. Beijing: Zhonghua, 1980.

Han shu 漢書. Compiled by Ban Gu 班固. Beijing: Zhonghua, 1962.

Hou Han shu 後漢書. Compiled by Fan Ye 范曄. Beijing: Zhonghua, 1965.

Huainanzi 淮南子. Annotated by Gao You 高誘. In *Xin bian zhuzi ji cheng*. Vol. 7. Taipei: Shijie, 1974.

Huainanzi ji shi 集釋. Annotated by Wang Niansun 王念孫. Beijing: Zhonghua, 1998.

Huayang guo zhi jiao zhu 華陽國志校注. Compiled by Chang Qu 常璩. Annotated by Liu Lin 劉琳. Taipei: Xin wen feng, 1988.

Ji jiu xian fang 急救仙方. In *Zhengtong dao zang* 正統道藏. Vol. 44. Reprint ed. Taipei: Yiwen, 1976.

Jiao Shi Yi lin 焦氏易林. Si bu cong kan edition.

Jiazi xin shu jiao shi 賈子新書校釋. Annotated by Qi Yuzhang 祁玉章. Taipei: Qi Yuzhang, 1974.

Jin louzi 金樓子. In *Si ku quan shu zhen ben bie ji* 四庫全書珍本別輯. Vol. 207. Taipei: Shangwu, 1975.

Jing fa 經法. Beijing: Wenwu, 1976.

Jiu zhang suan shu 九章算書. In *Suan jing shi shu* 算經十書. Ed. Qian Baozong 錢寶綜. Beijing: Xinhua, 1963.

Laozi dao de jing zhu 老子道德經注. Annotated by Wang Bi 王弼. In *Xin bian zhuzi ji cheng*. Vol. 3. Taipei: Shijie, 1974.

Li han wen jia 禮含文嘉. In *Gu wei shu*. In *Wei shu ji cheng*. Shanghai: Guji, 1994.

Li ji zhu shu 禮記注疏. In *Shi san jing zhu shu*. Vol. 5. Taipei: Yiwen, 1976.

Li shi 隸釋. Compiled by Hong Gua 洪适. In *Shike shiliao congshu* 石刻史料叢書. Vol. 1–3. Taipei: Yiwen, 1966.

[*Gu*] *Lie nü zhuan* 古列女傳. Si bu cong kan edition.

Lie xian zhuan 列仙傳. In *Zheng tong Dao zang* 正統道藏. Vol. 8. Reprint ed. Taipei: Yiwen, 1976.

Liezi ji shi 列子集釋. Annotated by Yang Bojun 楊伯峻. Beijing: Zhonghua, 1979.

Lu shi 路史. Written by Luo Bi 羅泌. Si bu bei yao edition.

Lü shi chun qiu jiao shi 呂氏春秋校釋. Annotated by Chen Qiyou 陳奇猷. Shanghai: Xuelin, 1984.

Lun heng ji jie 論衡集解. Written by Wang Chong 王充. Annotated by Liu Pansui 劉盼遂. Beijing: Guji, 1957.

Lun yu zheng yi 論語正義. Annotated by Liu Baonan 劉寶楠 and Liu Gongmian 劉恭冕. In *Xin bian zhu zi ji cheng*. Vol. 1. Taipei: Shijie, 1974.

Mao shi zheng yi 毛詩正義. In *Shi san jing zhu shu*. Vol. 2. Taipei: Yiwen, 1976.

Mengzi zheng yi 孟子正義. Annotated by Jiao Xun 焦循. In *Xin bian zhuzi ji cheng*. Vol. 1. Taipei: Shijie, 1974.

Mozi jian gu 墨子間詁. Annotated by Sun Yirang 孫詒讓. In *Xin bian zhuzi ji cheng*. Vol. 6. Taipei: Shijie, 1974.

Qi min yao shu jin shi 齊民要術今釋. Written by Jia Sixie 賈思勰. Annotated by Shi Shenghan 石聲漢. Beijing: Kexue, 1957.

Qian fu lun jian 潛夫論箋. Written by Wang Fu 王符. Annotated by Wang Jipei 汪繼培. Beijing: Zhonghua, 1979.

[*Bei ji*] *Qian jin yao fang* 備急千金要方. Written by Sun Simiao 孫思邈. In *Zhengtong dao zang*. Vol. 43. Reprint ed. Taipei: Yiwen, 1976.

Qin Han bei shu 秦漢碑述. Ed. Yuan Weichun 袁維春. Beijing: Gongyi meishu, 1990.

Quan shanggu sandai Qin Han Sanguo Liuchao wen 全上古三代秦漢三國六朝文. Ed. Yan Kejun 嚴可均. Beijing: Zhonghua, 1965.

[*Jiao zheng*] *San fu huang tu* 校正三輔黃圖. Annotated by Zhang Zongxiang 張宗祥. Shanghai: Gudian, 1958.

San guo zhi 三國志. Compiled by Chen Shou 陳壽. Beijing: Zhonghua, 1959.

"*San huang ben ji* 三皇本紀." Written by Sima Zhen 司馬貞. In *Shi ji hui zhu kao zheng* 史記會注考證. Reprint ed. Taipei: Hongye, 1976.

Shan hai jing jian shu 山海經箋疏. Taipei: Yiwen, 1974.

Shan hai jing jiao zhu 山海經校注. Annotated by Yuan Ke 袁珂. Shanghai: Guji, 1980.

Shang Jun shu zhu yi 商君書注譯. Annotated by Gao Heng 高亨. Beijing: Zhonghua, 1974.

Shang shu da zhuan ji jiao 尚書大傳輯校. Annotated by Chen Shouqi 陳壽祺. In *Huang Qing jing jie xu bian* 皇清經解續編. n.p.: Nanqing shuyuan, 1888.

Shang shu zheng yi 尚書正義. In *Shi san jing zhu shu*. Vol. 1. Taipei: Yiwen, 1974.

Shang shu zhong hou 尚書中侯. In *Gu wei shu*. In *Wei shu ji cheng*. Shanghai: Guji, 1994.

Shi ben ba zhong 世本八種. Shanghai: Shangwu, 1957.

Shi ben ji bu 世本輯補. Annotated by Qin Jiamo 秦嘉謨. In *Shi ben ba zhong* 世本八種. Shanghai: Shangwu, 1957.

Shi ji 史記. Written by Sima Qian 司馬遷. Beijing: Zhonghua, 1959.

Shi ming shu zheng bu 釋名疏證補. Written by Liu Xi 劉熙. Annotated by Wang Xianqian 王先謙. Reprint ed. Shanghai: Guji, 1984.

Shi yi ji 拾遺記. Compiled by Wang Jia 王嘉. Annotated by Qi Zhiping 齊治平. Beijing: Zhonghua, 1981.

Shizi 尸子. Si bu bei yao edition.

Shu yi ji 述異記. Compiled by Ren Fang 任昉. In *Bai zi quan shu* 百子全書. Hangzhou: Zhejiang guji, 1998.

Shuihudi Qin mu zhu jian 睡虎地秦慕竹簡. Beijing: Wenwu, 1978.

Shui jing zhu 水經注. Compiled by Li Daoyuan 李道元. Shanghai: Shijie, 1936.

Shuo wen jie zi zhu 説文解字注. Compiled by Xu Shen 許慎. Annotated by Duan Yucai 段玉裁. Taipei: Yiwen, 1974.

Shuo yuan 説苑. In *Han Wei cong shu*. Vol. 1. Taipei: Xinxing, 1977.

Si shi zuan yao jiao shi 四時纂要校釋. Written by Han E 韓鄂. Annotated by Miu Qiyu 繆啓愉. Beijing: Nongye, 1981.

Song shu 宋書. Compiled by Shen Yue 沈約. Beijing: Zhonghua, 1974.

Sou shen ji 搜神記. Compiled by Gan Bao 干寶. Annotated by Wang Shaoying 汪紹楹. Beijing: Zhonghua, 1979.

Taiping yu lan 太平御覽. Taipei: Shangwu, 1935.

Wenzi yao quan 文子要詮. Annotated by Li Dingsheng 李定生 and Xu Huijun 徐慧君. Shanghai: Fudan Daxue, 1988.

Wu di ji 吳地記. Annotated by Cao Lindi 曹林娣. Nanjing: Jiangsu guji, 1986.

Wu Yue chun qiu 吳越春秋. Si bu bei yao edition.

Xin xu shu zheng 新序疏證. Compiled by Liu Xiang 劉向. Annotated by Zhao Shanyi 趙善詒. Shanghai: Huadong Shifan Daxue, 1989.

Xin yu 新語. Written by Lu Jia 陸賈. In *Xin bian zhu zi ji cheng*. Vol. 2. Taipei: Shijie, 1974.

Xunzi ji jie 荀子集解. Annotated by Wang Xianqian 王先謙. In *Xin bian zhuzi ji cheng*. Vol. 2. Taipei: Shijie, 1974.

Yan shi jia xun hui zhu 顏氏家訓彙注. Written by Yan Zhitui 顏之推. Annotated by Zhou Fagao 周法高. Taipei: Zhongyang Yanjiuyuan Lishi Yuyan Yanjiusuo, 1960.

Yan tie lun 鹽鐵論. Shanghai: Renmin, 1974.

Yi li zhu shu 儀禮注疏. In *Shi san jing zhu shu*. Vol. 4. Taipei: Yiwen, 1974.

Yi qian kun zao du 易乾坤鑿度. In *Qi wei* 七緯. In *Wei shu ji cheng*. Shanghai: Guji, 1994.

Yi qian zao du 易乾鑿度. In *Qi wei*. In *Wei shu ji cheng*. Shanghai: Guji, 1994.

Yi tong gua yan 易通卦驗. In *Qi wei*. In *Wei shu ji cheng*. Shanghai: Guji, 1994.

Yi yuan 異苑. In *Xue jin tao yuan* 學津討源. Fragments compiled by Zhang Pengyi 張鵬一 [Qing dynasty]. Shanghai: Shangwu, n.d.

Yi Zhou shu hui jiao ji zhu 逸周書彙校集注. Annotated by Huang Huaixin 黃懷信, Zhang Maorong 張懋鎔, and Tian Xudong 田旭東. Shanghai: Shanghai Guji, 1995.

Yue jue shu 越絕書. Shanghai: Shangwu, 1956.

Yue jue shu jiao zhu gao ben 越絕書校注稿本. Taipei: Shijie, 1967.

Yunmeng Shuihudi Qin mu 雲蒙睡虎地秦墓. Beijing: Wenwu, 1981.

Zhanguo ce 戰國策. Shanghai: Gu ji, 1978.

Zhonghua gu jin zhu 中華古今注. Written by Ma Gao 馬縞. Reprint ed. Shanghai: Shangwu, 1956.

Zhou bi suan jing 周髀算經. In *Suan jing shi shu* 算經十書. Ed. Qian Baozong 錢寶琮. Beijing: Xinhua, 1963.

Zhou yi zheng yi 周易正義. In *Shi san jing zhu shu*. Vol. 1. Taipei: Yiwen, 1976.

[*Gu ben*] *zhu shu ji nian ji zheng* 古本竹書紀年輯證. Annotated by Fang Shiming 方詩銘 and Wang Xiuling 王修齡. Shanghai: Shanghai Guji, 1981.

Zhuangzi ji shi 莊子集釋. Annotated by Guo Qingfan 郭慶藩. In *Xin bian zhuzi ji cheng*. Vol. 3. Taipei: Shijie, 1974.

Zi zhi tong jian 資治通鑑. Compiled by Sima Guang 司馬光. Beijing: Zhonghua, 1956.

"Zong zheng qing zhen 宗正卿箴." Written by Yang Xiong 揚雄. In *Quan shanggu sandai Qin Han Sanguo Liuchao wen*. Ed. Yan Kejun. Beijing: Zhonghua, 1965.

[*Chun qiu*] *Zuo zhuan zhu* 春秋左傳注. Annotated by Yang Bojun 楊伯峻. Beijing: Zhonghua, 1983.

SECONDARY WORKS IN CHINESE AND JAPANESE

An, Zhimin 安志敏. "Changsha xin faxian de Xi Han bo hua shi tan 长沙新发现的西汉帛画试探." *Kaogu* (1973:1), pp. 43–53.

Cao, Jinyan 曹錦炎. "Chu bo shu 'Yue ling' pian kaoshi 楚帛書月令篇考試." *Jiang Han kaogu* (1985:1), pp. 63–67.

Chen, Changshan 陈长山. "Gaomei huaxiang xiao kao 高禖画像小考." *Kaogu yu wenwu* (1987:5), pp. 82–83, 6.

Chen, Jiangfeng 陈江风. "Han huaxiang 'shen gui shijie' de siwei xingtai ji qi yishu 汉画像'神鬼世界'的思维形态及其艺术." *Zhongyuan wenwu* (1991:3), pp. 10–17.

Chen, Mengjia 陳夢家. "Gao mei jiao she zu miao tong kao 高媒校社祖廟通考." *Qinghua xuebao* 12.3 (1937), pp. 445–72.

Chen, Mengjia 陳夢家. "Zhanguo Chu bo shu kao 戰國楚帛書考." *Kaogu xuebao* (1984: 2), pp. 137–58.

Chen, Shaofeng 陈少丰, and Gong, Dazhong 宮大中. "Luoyang Xi Han Bu Qianqiu mu bihua yishu 洛阳西汉卜千秋墓壁画艺术." *Wenwu* (1977:6), pp. 13–16.

Chen, Songchang 陳松長. *Xianggang Zhongwen Daxue Wenwuguan cang jiandu* 香港中文大學文物館藏簡牘. Hong Kong: Xianggang Zhongwen Daxue Wenwuguan, 2001.

Cui, Chen 崔陈. "Yibin diqu chutu Han dai huaxiang shi guan 宜宾地区出土汉代画像石棺." *Kaogu yu wenwu* (1991:1), pp. 34–40.

"Deng xian Changzhongdian Han huaxiang shi mu 邓县长冢店汉画像石墓." *Zhongyuan wenwu* (1982:1), pp. 17–23.

Deng, Zixin 鄧自欣, and Tian, Shang 田尚. "Shi lun Dujiangyan jing jiu bu shuai de yuanyin 試論都江堰經久不衰的原因." *Zhongguo shi yanjiu* (1986:3), pp. 101–10.

"Dingzhou Xi Han Zhongshan Huai Wang mu zhu jian 'Wenzi' de zhengli he yiyi 的整理和意義." *Wenwu* (1995:12), pp. 38–40.

"Dingzhou Xi Han Zhongshan Huai Wang mu zhu jian 'Wenzi' jiaokan ji 校勘記." *Wenwu* (1995:12), pp. 35–37.

"Dingzhou Xi Han Zhongshan Huai Wang mu zhu jian 'Wenzi' shiwen 定州西漢中山懷王墓竹簡文子釋文." *Wenwu* (1995:12), pp. 27–34.

Gao, Wen 高文, and Gao, Chengying 高成英. "Han hua guibao—Sichuan xin chutu de ba ge huaxiang shi guan 汉画瑰宝——四川新出土的八个画像石棺." *Wenwu tian di* (1988:3), pp. 47–49.

Gu, Jiegang 顧頡剛 et al., eds. *Gu shi bian* 古史辨. 1926–41. Reprint ed. Shanghai: Guji, 1982.

Gu, Jiegang. "Jiu zhou zhi Rong yu 'Rong Yu' 九州之戎與戎禹." In *Gu shi bian*. Vol. 7c. Reprint ed. Shanghai: Guji, 1982.

Gu, Jiegang. "Zhou yu yue de yanbian 州與嶽的演變." *Shixue nianbao* 1:5 (1933), pp. 11–33.

Gu, Jiegang, and Tong, Shuye 童書業. "Gun Yu de chuanshuo 鯀禹的傳說." In *Gu shi bian*. Vol. 7c. Reprint ed. Shanghai: Guji, 1982.

Gu, Jiegang, and Yang, Xiangkui 楊向奎. *San huang kao* 三皇考. Beijing: Yenching Journal of Chinese Studies Monograph Series no. 8, 1936.

Guo, Moruo 郭沫若. *Buci tongzuan* 卜辭通纂. Tokyo: Bunkyodo, 1933.

Guo, Moruo. *Jiagu wenzi yanjiu* 甲骨文字研究. Hong Kong: Zhonghua, 1976.

Hayashi, Minao 林巳奈夫. *Kan dai no kamigami* 漢代の神神. Kyoto: Nozokawa, 1989.

He, Fushun 贺福顺. "'Gaomei huaxiang xiao kao' yi wen shangque 高禖画像小考一文商榷." *Kaogu yu wenwu* (1992:1), pp. 57–59.

He, Linyi 何琳儀. "Changsha bo shu tongshi 長沙帛書通釋." *Jiang Han kaogu* (1986:1), pp. 51–57.

"Hechuan Dong Han huaxiang shi mu 合川东汉画象石墓." *Wenwu* (1977:2), pp. 63–69.

"Henan Nanyang Junzhang ying Han huaxiang shi mu 河南南阳军帐营汉画像石墓." *Kaogu yu wenwu* (1982:1), pp. 40–43.

"Henan Nanyang xian Ying zhuang Han huaxiang shi mu 河南南阳县英庄汉画像石墓." *Wenwu* (1984:3), pp. 25–37.

Hu, Puan 胡朴安. *Zhonghua quan guo fengsu zhi* 中華全國風俗志. 1936. Reprint ed. Zhengzhou: Zhengzhou guji, 1990.

Huang, Zhigang 黃芝崗. "Da Yu yu Li Bing zhi shui de guanxi 大禹與李冰治水的關係." *Shuo wen yue kan* (1943:9), pp. 69–76.

Huang, Zhigang. *Zhongguo de shui shen* 中國的水神. 1968 reprint ed. Taipei: Chinese Association for Folklore, 1934.

Hunan Sheng Bowuguan. "Changsha Zidanku Zhanguo mu guo mu 長沙子彈庫戰國木槨墓." *Wenwu* (1974:2), pp. 36–40.

Ikeda, On 池田温. "Chūgoku rekidai boken ryakkō 中國歷代墓券略考." *Tōyō bunka kenkyūsho kiyō* 86 (1981), pp. 193–278.

Ikeda, Suetoshi 池田末利. *Chūgoku kodai shūkyō shi kenkyū* 中國古代宗教史研究. Tokyo: Tokai Daigaku, 1983.

Izushi, Yoshihiko 出石誠彥. *Shina shinwa densetsu no kenkyū* 支那神話傳説の研究. 2nd ed. rev. Tokyo: Chūō Kōron, 1973.

Jiang, Shaoyuan 江紹源. *Zhongguo gudai lüxing zhi yanjiu* 中國古代旅行之研究. Shanghai: Shangwu, 1935.

"Jiangsu Gaoyou Shaojiagou Han dai yizhi de qingli 江蘇高郵邵家泃漢代遺址的清理." *Kaogu* (1960:10), pp. 18–23, 44.

Jiangsu Xuzhou Hanhuaxiang shi 江蘇徐州漢畫象石. Beijing: Kexue, 1959.

Katō Jōken 加藤常賢, "Futsu ki kō 弗忌考." In *Chūgoku kodai bunka no kenkyū* 中國古代文化の研究. Tokyo: Nishō Gakusha Daigaku, 1980.

Katō, Jōken. *Kanji no hakkutsu* 漢字の發掘. Tokyo: Kadokawa, 1973.

Katō, Jōken. *Kanji no kigen* 漢字の起原. Tokyo: Kadokawa, 1972.

Katō, Jōken. "Shina ko seishi no kenkyū—Ka U Shi sei kō 支那古姓氏の研究—夏禹姒姓考." In *Chūgoku kodai bunka no kenkyū*. Tokyo: Nishō Gakusha Daigaku, 1980.

Kominami, Ichirō 小南一郎. "Sha no saiji no shokeitai to sono kigen 社の祭祀の諸形態とその起源." *Koshi shunjū* 4 (1987), pp. 17–37.

Kudō, Moto'o 工藤元男. "U no iseki to sono minzokuteki denshō o motomete 禹の遺跡とその民族的傳承を求めて." *Tōyō no shisō to shūkyō* (Waseda University) 12 (March 1995), pp. 132–48.

Lao, Gan 勞榦. *Juyan Han jian: kaoshi zhi bu* 居延漢簡：考釋之部. Taipei: Zhongyang Yanjiuyuan Lishi Yuyan Yanjiusuo, 1960.

Li, Chenguang 李陈广. "Han hua Fu Xi Nü Gua de xingxiang tezheng ji qi yiyi 汉画伏羲女娲的形象特征及其意义." *Zhongyuan wenwu* (1992:1), pp. 33–37.

Li, Dingsheng 李定生. "'Wenzi' fei wei shu kao 文子非偽書考." In *Dao jia wenhua yanjiu* 道家文化研究 5 Shanghai: Guji, 1994.

Li, Falin 李发林. *Shandong Han huaxiang shi yanjiu* 山东汉画像石研究. Ji'nan: Qi Lu, 1982.

Li, Fuhua 李复华, and Guo, Ziyou 郭子游. "Pi Xian chutu Dong Han huaxiang shi guan tuxiang lüe shuo 郫县出土东汉画象石棺图象略说." *Wenwu* (1975:8), pp. 60–67.

Li, Hui 李卉. "Taiwan yu Dongnanya de tongbao peiou xing hungshui chuanshuo 臺灣與東南亞的同胞配偶性洪水傳説." *Bulletin of the Ethnological Society of China* (Taipei) 1 (1955), pp. 171–206.

Li, Ling 李零. *Changsha Zidanku Zhanguo Chu bo shu yanjiu* 長沙子彈庫戰國楚帛書研究. Beijing: Zhonghua, 1985.

Li, Ling. "Chu bo shu de zai renshi 楚帛書的再認識." *Zhongguo wenhua* 10 (1994), pp. 42–62.

Li, Ling. "X gong xu faxian de yiyi X公盨發現的意義." *Zhongguo lishi wenwu* (2002:6), pp. 35–45.

Li, Ling. "Wu shi kao 五石考." *Xueren* 13 (1998), pp. 397–404.

Li, Ling. *Zhongguo fang shu kao* 中国方术考. Beijing: Renmin Zhongguo, 1993.

Li, Ling. *Zhongguo fangshu xu kao* 續考. Beijing: Dongfang, 2000.

Li, Liyang 李黎阳. "Shi lun Shandong Anqiu Han mu ren xiang zhu yishu 试论山东安丘汉墓人像柱艺术." *Zhongyuan wenwu* (1991: 3), pp. 86–87, 85.

Li, Xueqin 李學勤. "Lun Chu bo shu zhong de tian xiang 論楚帛書中的天象." *Hunan kaogu jikan* 1 (1982), pp. 68–72.

Li, Xueqin. "Lun X gong xu ji qi zhongyao yiyi 論 X 公盨及其重要意義." *Zhongguo lishi wenwu* (2002:6), pp. 5–12.

Li, Xueqin. "Zhanguo ti ming gaishu, part 2 戰國題名概述（下）." *Wenwu* (1959:9), pp. 58–61.

Lian, Shaoming 連劭名. "Dong Han Jianchu si nian wu dao quanshu yu gudai de cezhu 東漢建初四年巫禱券書與古代的册祝." *Chuantong wenhua yu xiandaihua* 傳統文化與現代化 (1996:6), pp. 28–33.

Lin, Mingjun 林明君. "Sichuan zhishuizhe yu shui shen 四川治水者與水神." *Shuo wen yue kan* (1943:9), pp. 77–86.

Liu, Dunyuan 劉敦願. "Han huaxiangshi shang yin shi nan nü—Pingyin Mengzhuang Han mu shizhu jisi gewu tuxiang fenxi 汉画像石上饮食男女——平阴孟庄汉墓石柱祭祀各物图像分析." *Gu Gong wenwu yue kan* 古宫文物月刊 141(December 1994), pp. 122–35.

Liu, Qiyu 劉起釪. *Gu shi xu bian* 古史續辨. Beijing: Zhongguo shehui kexue, 1991.

Lü, Pin 吕品. "Henan Han hua suo jian tuteng yi su kao 河南汉画所见图胜遗俗考." *Zhongyuan wenwu* (1991:3), pp. 42–49, 74.

Lü, Simian 吕思勉. "San huang wu di kao 三皇五帝考." In *Gu shi bian*. Vol. 7b. Reprint ed. Shanghai: Guji, 1982.

"Lun Xuzhou Han huaxiang shi 論徐州漢畫像石." *Wenwu* (1980:2), pp. 44–55.

Luo, Kaiyu 羅開玉. "Lun Dujiangyan yu Shu wenhua de guanxi 論都江堰與蜀文化的關係." *Sichuan wenwu* (1988:2), pp. 32–37.

"Luoyang Xi Han Bu Qianqiu bihua mu fajue jianbao 洛阳西汉卜千秋壁画发掘简报." *Wenwu* (1977:6), pp. 1–12.

Ma, Jixing 馬繼興. *Mawangdui gu yi shu kaoshi* 馬王堆古醫書考釋. Changsha: Hunan kexue jishu, 1992.

Matsuda, Minoru 松田稔. *Sangaikyō no kisoteki kenkyū* 山海經の基礎的研究. Tokyo: Rikkan shoin, 1995.

Mitarai, Masaru 御手洗勝. *Kodai Chūgoku no kamigami* 古代中國の神神. Tokyo: Sōbunsha, 1984.

Mori, Mikisaburō 森三樹三郎. *Shina kodai shinwa* 支那古代神話. 1944. Reprint ed. Tokyo: Kiyomizu kōbundō, 1969.

Mori, Yasutarō 森安太郎. *Kōtei densetsu: kodai Chūgoku shinwa no kenkyū* 黄帝傳説：古代中國神話の研究. Kyoto: Kyōto Joshi Daigaku Jinbun Gakkai, 1970.

Nagao, Ryūzō 永尾龍造. *Shina minzoku shi* 支那民俗誌. Tokyo: Dai Nippon, 1940–42.

Nanyang Han dai huaxiang shi 南阳汉代画像石. Beijing: Wenwu, 1985.

"Nanyang Han huaxiang shi gaishu 南阳汉画像石概述." *Wenwu* (1973:6), pp. 25–27.

"Nanyang shi Liuwa cun Han huaxiang shi mu 南阳市刘洼村汉画像石墓." *Zhongyuan wenwu* (1991:3), pp. 107–11.

"Nanyang shi Wangzhuang Han huaxiang shi mu 南阳市王庄汉画像石墓." *Zhongyuan wenwu* (1985:3), pp. 26–35.

"Nanyang xian Wangzhai Han huaxiang shi mu 南阳县王寨汉画像石墓." *Zhongyuan wenwu* (1982:1), pp. 12–16.

Pu, Muzhou [Poo Mu-chou] 蒲慕州, *Muzang yu shengsi: Zhongguo gudai zongjiao zhi xingsi.* 墓葬與生死：中國古代宗教之省思 Taipei: Lianjing, 1993.

Qiu, Xigui 裘錫圭. "X gong xu mingwen kaoshi X 公盨銘文考釋." *Zhongguo lishi wenwu* (2002:6), pp. 13–27.

Qiu, Yongsheng 邱永生. "Xuzhou Qing shan quan shui ni er chang yi, er hao Han mu fajue jianbao 徐州青山泉水泥二厂一，二号汉墓发掘简报." *Zhongyuan wenwu* (1992:1), pp. 91–96.

Rao, Zongyi 饒宗頤. "Chu bo shu tian xiang zai yi 楚帛書天象再議." *Zhongguo wenhua* 3 (1991), pp. 66–73.

Rao, Zongyi 饒宗頤. "Zhongwen Daxue Wenwuguan cang Jianchu si nian 'Xuning jian' yu 'Baoshan jian': lun Zhanguo Qin, Han jieji daoci zhi zhu shen yu gushi renwu 中文大學文物館藏建初四年序寧簡與包山簡：論戰國，秦，漢解疾禱辭之諸神與古史人物." *Hua Xia wenming yu chuanshi cangshu: Zhongguo guoji Hanxue yantaohui lunwenji* 華夏文明與傳世藏書：中國國際漢學研討會論文集. Beijing: Zhongguo shehui kexue, 1996.

Rao, Zongyi 饒宗頤 and Zeng, Xiantong 曾憲通. *Chu bo shu* 楚帛書. Hong Kong: Zhonghua, 1985.

Shandong Han huaxiang shi xuan ji 山東漢畫像石選集. Ji'nan: Qi Lu, 1982.

"Shandong Zao zhuang huaxiang shi diaocha ji 山東枣庄画像石调查记." *Kaogu yu wenwu* (1983:3), pp. 24–30, 23.

Shi, Nianhai 史念海. *He shan ji* 河山集. Beijing: Sanlian, 1981.

Shirakawa, Shizuka 白川靜. *Chūgoku no shinwa* 中國の神話. Tokyo: Chūō Kōron, 1975.

"Sichuan Changning 'qi ge dong' Dong Han jinian huaxiang ya mu 四川长宁七个洞东汉纪年画像崖墓." *Kaogu yu wenwu* (1985:5), pp. 43–55, 34.

"Sichuan Hejiang xian Dong Han zhuan shi mu qingli jian bao 四川合江县东汉砖室墓清理简报." *Wenwu* (1992:4), pp. 45–48.

"Sichuan Jianyang xian Guitou shan Dong Han ya mu 四川简阳县鬼头山东汉崖墓." *Wenwu* (1991:3), pp. 20–25.

"Sichuan Pi xian Dong Han zhuan mu de shi guan huaxiang 四川郫县东汉砖墓的石棺画象." *Kaogu* (1979:6), pp. 495–503.

Sichuan sheng Guan xian Wenjiaoju. "Dujiangyan chutu Dong Han Li Bing shixiang 都江堰出土東漢李冰石像." *Wenwu* (1974:7), pp. 27–28.

Su, Zhaoqing 苏兆庆, and Zhang, Anli 张安礼. "Shandong Ju xian Chenliu zhuang Han huaxiang shi mu 山东莒县沉刘庄汉画像石墓." *Kaogu* (1988:9), pp. 788–99.

Sun, Jiujun 孙鸠军 et al. *Sichuan minsu da guan* 四川民俗大觀. Chengdu: Sichuan renmin, 1989.

Sun, Zuoyun 孙作云. "Luoyang Xi Han Bu Qianqiu mu bihua kaoshi 洛阳西汉卜千秋墓壁画考释." *Wenwu* (1977:6), pp. 17–22.

"Tanghe xian Zhenzhi chang er hao Han huaxiang shi mu 唐河县针织厂二号汉画像石墓." *Zhongyuan wenwu* (1985:3), pp. 14–20.

Tian, Shang 田尚, and Deng, Zixin 鄧自欣. "Tuo Jiang, Mo Shui, Li Dui kaobian 沱江，沫水，離堆考辨." *Lishi dili* (1987:5), pp. 70–75.

Wang, Wencai 王文才. "Dong Han Li Bing shixiang yu Dujiangyan shui ce 東漢李冰石像與都江堰水測." *Wenwu* (1974:7), pp. 29–33.

Wang Xiaolian 王孝廉. *Zhongguo de shenhua yu chuanshuo* 中國的神話與傳説. Taipei: Lianjing, 1977.

Wen, Yiduo 聞一多. *Wen Yiduo quan ji* 全集. 4 vols. Reprint. ed. Beijing: Sanlian, 1982.

Wu, Lan 吴兰, and Xue Yong 学勇. "Shaanxi Mizhi xian Guan zhuang Dong Han huaxiang shi mu 陝西米脂县官庄东汉画像石墓." *Kaogu* (1987:11), pp. 997–1001.

Wu, Lan , Zhi, An 志安, and Chun, Ning 春宁. "Suide Xindian faxian de liang zuo huaxiang shi mu 绥德辛店发现的兩座画像石墓." *Kaogu yu wenwu* (1993:1), pp. 17–22.

Xie, Li 谢荔, and Xu, Lihong 徐利红. "Sichuan Hejiang xian Dong Han zhuan shi mu qingli jian bao 四川合江县东汉砖室墓清理简报." *Wenwu* (1992:4), pp. 45–48.

Xin, Shuzhi 辛樹幟. *Yu gong xin jie* 禹貢新解. Hong Kong: Zhonghua, 1973.

Xu, Xianzhi 徐顯之. *Shan hai jing tan yuan* 山海經探原. Wuhan: Wuhan chubanshe, 1991.

"Xuzhou Qingshan quan Baiji Dong Han huaxiang shi mu 徐州青山泉白集东汉画象石墓." *Kaogu* (1981:2), pp. 145–51.

Yang, Hong 杨泓. "Gu wenwu tuxiang zhong de xiangpu 古文物图像中的相扑." *Wenwu* (1980:10) , pp. 88–90, 85.

Yang, Kuan 樣寬. "Zhongguo shanggu shi daolun 中國上古史導論." In *Gu shi bian*. Vol. 7a. Reprint ed. Shanghai: Guji, 1982.

Yang, Xiangkui 楊向奎. "Zhongguo gudai de shuilijia—Li Bing 中國古代的水利家—李冰." *Wen shi zhe* (1961:3), pp. 23–61, 92.

Yasui, Kōzan 安居香山. *Isho no seiritsu to sono tenkai* 緯書の成立とその展開. Tokyo: Kokusho kankō, 1981.

Yasui, Kōzan, and Nakamura, Shōhachi 中村璋八. *Isho no kisoteki kenkyū* 緯書の基礎の研究. Kyoto: Kokusho kankō, 1978.

Yu, Jiaxi 余嘉錫. "Han shi san kao 寒食散考." In *Yu Jiaxi lun xue za zhu* 論學雜著. Beijing: Zhonghua, 1963.

Yu, Quanyu 喻權域. "Baoping Kou he Tuo Jiang shi Li Bing zhi qian kai zuo de 寶瓶口和沱江是李冰之前開鑿的." *Lishi yanjiu* (1978:1), pp. 95–96.

Yu, Quanyu. "Erlang qin long de shenhua yu Kaiming zuo Ping Kou de shishi 二郎禽龍的神話與開明鑿瓶口的事實." *Sichuan wenwu* (1988:2), pp. 38–44.

Yuan, Ke 袁珂. *Zhongguo gudai shenhua* 中國古代神話. Revised ed. Shanghai: Shangwu, 1957.

Yuan, Ke. *Zhongguo shenhua chuanshuo* 中國神話傳説. Taipei: Liren, 1987.

Yuan, Ke. *Zhongguo shenhua chuanshuo zidian* 中國神話傳説字典. Shanghai: Shanghai zishu, 1985.

Yuan Ke. *Zhongguo shenhua tong lun* 中國神話通論. Chengdu: Bashu, 1991.

Yun, Ruxin 惲茹辛, ed. *Shan hai jing yanjiu lunji* 山海經研究論集. Hong Kong: Zhongshan tushu, 1974.

Zeng, Zhaoyu 曾昭燏, Jiang, Baogeng 蔣宝庚 and Li, Zhongyi 黎忠义. *Yinan gu hua-xiang shi mu fajue baogao* 沂南古画像石墓发抉报告. Shanghai: Wenhuabu Wen Wu Guanliju, 1956.

Zhang, Dainian 張岱年. "Shi tan 'Wenzi' de niandai yu sixiang 試探文子的年代與思想." In *Dao jia wenhua yanjiu* 5. Shanghai: Guji, 1994.

Zhang, Guangzhi [Chang Kwang-chih] 張光直. "Zhongguo chuang shi shenhua zhi fenxi yu gu shi yanjiu 中國創世神話之分析與古史研究." *Bulletin of the Institute of Ethnology, Academia Sinica* 8 (1959), pp. 47–79.

Zhang, Xiaojun 張晓军. "Qian tan Nanyang Han huaxiang shi zhong niu de yishu xingxiang 浅谈南阳汉画像石中牛的艺术形象." *Zhongyuan wenwu* (1985: 3), pp. 75–80.

Zhang, Xunliao 張勛燎. "Li Bing zuo Li Dui de weizhi he Baoping Kou xingcheng de niandai xin tan 李冰鑿離堆的位置和寶瓶口形成的年代新探." *Zhongguo shi yanjiu* (1982:4), pp. 87–101.

Zhang, Zhenli. *Zhongyuan gudian shenhua liu bian lunkao* 中原古典神話流變論考. Shanghai: Shanghai wenyi, 1991.

Zhejiang minsu tong zhi 浙江民俗通志. Hangzhou: Zhejiang renmin, 1986.

Zheng, Yan. "Anqiu Dongjiazhuang li zhu diaoke tuxing kao 安丘董家庄立柱雕刻图形考." *Jinian Shangdong Daxue kaogu zhuanye chuangjian ershi zhounian wenji* 紀念山東大學考古專業創建二十周年文集. Ji'nan: Shandong Daxue, 1992.

Zhou, Dao 周到, and Li, Jinghua 李京华. "Tanghe Zhenzhi chang Han huaxiang shi mu de fajue 唐河针织厂汉画像石墓的发掘." *Wenwu* (1973:6), pp. 26–40.

Zhu, Fenghan 朱鳳瀚. "X gong xu mingwen chushi X 公盨銘文初釋." *Zhongguo lishi wenwu* (2002:6), pp. 28–34.

Zhu, Junsheng 朱駿聲. *Shuo wen tong xun ding sheng* 説文通訓定聲. Taipei: Yiwen, 1974.

Zhu, Xilu 朱羲祿, ed. *Jiaxiang Han huaxiang shi* 嘉祥汉画像石. Ji'nan: Shangdong meishu, 1992.

SECONDARY WORKS IN WESTERN LANGUAGES

Allan, Sarah. *The Heir and the Sage: Dynastic Legend in Early China.* San Francisco: Chinese Materials Center, 1981.

Allan, Sarah. *The Shape of the Turtle: Myth, Art, and Cosmos in Early China.* Albany: State University of New York, 1991.

Allan, Sarah. "Sons of Suns: Myth and Totemism in Early China." *Bulletin of the School of Oriental and African Studies* 44:2 (1981), pp. 290–326.

Allan, Sarah. *The Way of Water and Sprouts of Virtue.* Albany: State University of New York, 1997.

Allen, Don Cameron. *The Legend of Noah.* Urbana: University of Illinois, 1963.

Andersen, Poul. "The Practice of *Bugang*." *Cahiers d'Extrême-Asie* 5 (1989–90), pp. 15–33.

Bailey, Lloyd R. *Noah: The Person and the Story in History and Tradition*. Columbia: University of South Carolina, 1989.

Barnard, Mary. "Space, Time, and the Flood Myths." In *The Mythmakers*. Athens: Ohio University, 1966.

Barnard, Noel. *The Ch'u Silk Manuscript*. Canberra: Australian National University, 1973.

Barnard, Noel. "The Ch'u Silk Manuscript and Other Archaeological Documents of Ancient China." In *Early Chinese Art and Its Possible Influence in the Pacific Basin*, vol. 1, *Ch'u and the Silk Manuscript*. Ed. Noel Barnard. New York: Intercultural Art Press, 1972.

Baumann, Herrmann. *Schöpfung und Urzeit des Menschen im Mythus der afrikanischen Völker*. Berlin: Verlag ven Dietrich Riemer, 1936.

Berge, François. "Les légendes du Déluge." In *Histoire Générale des Religions*. Vol. 5. Paris: Librairie Aristide Quillet, 1951.

Birrell, Anne. *Chinese Mythology: An Introduction*. Baltimore: Johns Hopkins, 1993.

Birrell, Anne. "The Four Flood Myth Traditions of Classical China." *T'oung Pao* 83 (1997), pp. 213–59.

Blumenberg, Hans. *Work on Myth*. Tr. Robert M Wallace. Cambridge: Massachusetts Institute of Technology, 1985.

Bodde, Derk. *Festivals in Classical China: New Year and Other Annual Observances During the Han Dynasty*. Princeton: Princeton University, 1975.

Bodde, Derk. "Myths of Ancient China." In *Mythologies of the Ancient World*. Ed. Samuel Noah Kramer. Garden City, N.Y.: Doubleday, 1961.

Boltz, William B. "Kung Kung and the Flood: Reverse Euhemerism in the *Yao Tien*." *T'oung Pao* 67 (1981), pp. 141–53.

Bokenkamp, Stephen. "Record of the Feng and Shan Sacrifices." In *Religions of China in Practice*. Ed. Donald S. Lopez, Jr. Princeton: Princeton University, 1996.

Bonnefoy, Yves, ed. *Asian Mythologies*. Tr. under the direction of Wendy Doniger. Chicago: University of Chicago, 1991.

Brisson, Luc. *How Philosophers Saved Myths: Allegorical Interpretations of Classical Mythology*. Tr. Catherine Tihanyi. Chicago: University of Chicago, 2004.

Brisson, Luc. *Platon, les mots et les mythes*. Paris: Maspero, 1982.

Brugsch, Heinrich. *Die neue Weltordnung nach Vernichtung des sündingen Menschengeschlechtes*. Leipzig: J. C. Hinrichs, 1881.

Burkert, Walter. *Structure and History in Greek Mythology and Ritual*. Berkeley: University of California, 1979.

Cammann, Schuyler. "Some Early Chinese Symbols of Duality." *History of Religions* 24.3 (February 1985), pp. 227–31.

Campany, Robert Ford. *Strange Writing: Anomaly Accounts in Early Medieval China*. Albany: State University of New York, 1996.

Canetti, Elias. *Crowds and Power*. Tr. Carol Stewart. New York: Seabury Press, 1978.

Casalis, Matthieu. "The Dry and the Wet: A Semiological Analysis of Creation and Flood Myths." *Semiotica* 17 (1976), pp. 35–67.

Chang Kwang-chih. *Art, Myth, and Ritual: The Path to Political Authority in Ancient China*. Cambridge: Harvard University, 1983.

Chang, Kwang-chih. "A Classification of Shang and Chou Myths." In *Early Chinese Civilization: Anthropological Perspectives*. Cambridge: Harvard University, 1976.

Chavannes, Edouard. *Le Tai Chan: Essai de monographie d'un culte chinois*. Paris: Leroux, 1910.

Chow, Tse-tsung. "The Childbirth Myth and Ancient Chinese Medicine." In *Ancient China: Studies in Early Civilization*. Ed. David T. Roy and Tsuen-hsuin Tsien. Hong Kong: Chinese University, 1978.

Clines, David. "Noah's Flood: The Theology of the Flood Narrative." *Faith and Thought* 100 (1972), pp. 136–38.

Cohen, Percy. "Theories of Myth." *Man* n.s. 4:3 (September 1969), pp. 337–53.

Cohn, Norman. *Noah's Flood: The Genesis Story in Western Thought*. New Haven: Yale University, 1996.

Cook, Constance A., and Major, John S., eds. *Defining Chu: Image and Reality in Ancient China*. Honolulu: University of Hawai'i, 1999.

Dalley, Stephanie, tr. *Myths from Mesopotamia: Creation, The Flood, Gilgamesh, and Others*. Revised paperback ed. Oxford: Oxford University, 2000.

Delcourt, Marie. *Stérilités mystérieuses et naissances maléfiques dans l'Antiquité classique*. Bibliothèque de la Faculté de Philosophie et Lettres de l'Université de Liège. Fascicule LXXXIII (1938). Reissued in Paris, 1986.

Demetrio, Francisco. "The Flood Motif and the Symbolism of Rebirth in Filipino Mythology." In *The Flood Myth*. Ed. Alan Dundes. Berkeley: University of California, 1988.

Detienne, Marcel. *Comment être autochthone: Du pur Athénien au Français raciné*. Paris: Seuil, 2003.

Detienne, Marcel. *L'Invention de la mythologie*. Paris: Gallimard, 1981.

Dorofeeva-Lichtmann, Véra V. "Conception of Terrestrial Organization in the *Shan Hai Jing*." *Bulletin de l'École Française d'Extrême Orient* 82 (1995), pp. 57–110.

Dorofeeva-Lichtmann, Véra V. "Mapping a 'Spiritual' Landscape: Representations of Terrestrial Space in the *Shanhaijing*." In *Political Frontiers, Ethnic Boundaries, and Human Geographies in Chinese History*. Ed. Nicola Di Cosmo and Don J. Wyatt. London: Rutledge/Curzon, 2003.

Dorofeeva-Lichtmann, Véra V. "Text as a Device for Mapping a Sacred Space: A Case of the Wu Zang Shan Jing ('Five Treasuries: The Itineraries of Mountains')." *Göttinger Beiträge zur Asienforschung* 2–3 (2003). Ed. Tatyana Gardner and Daniela Moritz. Special Double Issue. "Creating and Representing Sacred Spaces," pp. 147–210.

Dumezil, Georges. *The Destiny of the Warrior*. Tr. Alf Hiltebeitel. Chicago: University of Chicago, 1970.

Dundes, Alan. "The Flood as Male Myth of Creation." In *The Flood Myth*. Berkeley: University of California, 1988.

Dundes, Alan, ed. *The Flood Myth*. Berkeley: University of California, 1988.

Eberhard, Wolfram. *The Local Cultures of South and East China*. Tr. Alide Eberhard. Leiden: E. J. Brill, 1968.

Eberhard, Wolfram. *Lokalkulturen im Alten China*, vol. 1, *Nordens und Westens*. Leiden: E. J. Brill, 1942.

Eberhard, Wolfram. *Typen chinesischer Volksmärchen*. Helsinki: F F Communications No. 120, 1937.

Ebrey, Patricia Buckley. *The Inner Quarters: Marriage and the Lives of Chinese Women in the Sung Period*. Berkeley: University of California, 1993.

Eco, Umberto. *The Role of the Reader: Explorations in the Semiotics of Texts*. Bloomington: University of Indiana, 1984.

Edmunds, Lowell, ed., *Approaches to Greek Myth*. Baltimore: Johns Hopkins University, 1990.

Eliade, Mircea. *The Sacred and the Profane*. Tr. Willard R. Trask. New York: Harcourt, Brace & World, 1959.

Eliade, Mircea. "Structure et fonction du mythe cosmogonique." In *La Naissance du monde*. Paris: Seuil, 1959.

Elwin, Verrier. *Myths of Middle India*. Oxford: Oxford University, 1949.

Elwood, Robert. *The Politics of Myth: A Study of C. J. Jung, Mircea Eliade, and Joseph Campbell*. Albany: State University of New York, 1999.

Fabian, Johannes. *Time and the Other: How Anthropology Makes Its Object*. New York: Columbia University, 1983.

Filby, Frederick A. *The Flood Reconsidered: A Review of the Evidences of Geology, Archaeology, Ancient Literature, and the Bible*. London: Pickering & Inglis, 1970.

Finsterbusch, Käte. *Verzeichnis und Motivindex der Han-Darstellungen: Band II Abbildungen und Addenda*. Wiesbaden: Otto Harrowitz, 1971.

Follansbee, Eleanor. "The Story of the Flood in the Light of Comparative Semitic Mythology." In *The Flood Myth*. Berkeley: University of California, 1988.

Frazer, James. *Folklore in the Old Testament: Abridged Edition*. Rep. ed. New York: Avenel Books, 1988.

Frobenius, Leo. *Atlantis, Volksmärchen, und Volksdichtungen Afrikus*, vol. 12, *Dichtkunst der Kassaiden*. Jena: E. Diederichs, 1928.

Frymer-Kensky, Tikva. "The Atrahasis Epic and Its Significance for our Understanding of Genesis 1–9." In *The Flood Myth*. Berkeley: University of California, 1988.

Garelli, Paul, and Leibovici, Marcel. "La naissance du monde selon Akkad." In *La Naissance du monde*. Paris: Seuil, 1959.

Gaster, Theodore H. *Myth, Legend, and Custom in the Old Testament: A Comparative Study with Chapters from Sir James G. Frazer's Folklore in the Old Testament*. Paperback ed. New York: Harper & Row, 1975.

Gerbi, Antonello. *The Dispute of the New World: The History of a Polemic, 1750–1900*. Tr. Jeremy Moyle. Pittsburgh: University of Pittsburgh, 1973.

Gerbi, Antonio. *Nature in the New World: From Christopher Columbus to Gonzalo Fernández de Oviedo*. Tr. Jeremy Moyle. Pittsburgh: University of Pittsburgh, 1985.

Gillispie, Charles. *Genesis and Geology: A Study in the Relations of Scientific Thought, Natural Theology, and Social Opinion in Great Britain, 1790–1850*. New York: Harper & Row, 1959.

Ginzberg, Louis. *Legends of the Jews*. Vols. 1–5. Philadelphia: Jewish Publication Society of America, 1909–1938.

Ginzberg, Louis. "Noah and the Flood in Jewish Legend." In *The Flood Myth*. Berkeley: University of California, 1988.

Girardot, Norman J. *Myth and Meaning in Early Taoism*. Berkeley: University of California, 1983.

Granet, Marcel. *Danses et légendes de la China ancienne*. 1926. Revised ed. Paris: Presses Universitaires de France, 1994.

Granet, Marcel. *Fêtes et chansons anciennes de la Chine*. 2nd ed. Paris: Leroux, 1929.

Granet, Marcel. "Remarques sur le Taoisme ancien." *Asia Major* 2 (1925), pp. 145–51. Reprinted in *Études sociologiques sur la Chine*. Paris: Presses Universitaires de France, 1953.

Harper, Donald. "A Chinese Demonography of the Third Century B.C." *Harvard Journal of Asiatic Studies* 45:2 (1985), pp. 459–98.

Harper, Donald. "Contracts with the Spirit World in Han Common Religion: The Xuning Prayer and Sacrifice Documents of A.D. 79." *Cahiers d'Extrême-Asie*. Forthcoming.

Harper, Donald. *Early Chinese Medical Literature*. London: Kegan Paul, 1998.

Hartog, François. *Mémoire d'Ulysse: Récits sur la frontière en Grèce ancienne*. Paris: Gallimard, 1996.

Hartog, François. *Le Miroir d'Hérodote: Essai sur la représentation de l'autre*. Paris: Gallimard, 1980.

Hayashi, Minao. "The Twelve Gods of the Chan-kuo Period Silk Manuscript Excavated at Ch'ang-sha." In *Early Chinese Art and Its Possible Influence in the Pacific Basin*, vol. 1, *Ch'u and the Silk Manuscript*. Ed. Noel Barnard. New York: Intercultural Art Press, 1972.

Heesterman, J. C. *The Broken World of Sacrifice: An Essay in Ancient Indian Ritual*. Chicago: University of Chicago, 1993.

Heesterman, J. C. "The Flood Story in Vedic Ritual." In *The Inner Conflict of Tradition: Essays in Indian Ritual, Kingship, and Society*. Chicago: University of Chicago, 1985.

Heggett, Richard. *Cataclysms and Earth History: The Development of Diluvialism*. Oxford: Oxford University, 1989.

Ho, Ting-jui. *A Comparative Study of Myths and Legends of Formosan Aborigines*. Taipei: The Orient Cultural Service, 1971.

Huang, Martin W. *Desire and Fictional Narrative in Late Imperial China*. Cambridge: Harvard University Asia Center, 2001.

Hübner, Kurt. *Die Wahrheit des Mythos*. Munich: Verlag C. H. Beck, 1985.

Ingarden, Roman. *The Literary Work of Art: An Investigation on the Borderlines of Ontology, Logic, and Theory of Literature.* Tr. George G. Grabowicz. Evanston, Ill.: Northwestern University, 1973.

Iser, Wolfgang. *The Act of Reading: A Theory of Aesthetic Response.* Baltimore: Johns Hopkins University, 1978.

Iser, Wolfgang. *The Implied Reader: Patterns of Communication in Prose Fiction from Bunyan to Beckett.* Baltimore: Johns Hopkins University, 1974.

James, Jean. *A Guide to Tomb and Shrine Art of the Han Dynasty, 206 B.C.–A.D. 220.* Lewiston, New York: Edwin Mellen, 1996.

Jamme, Christoph. *Einführung in die Philosophie des Mythos, Band 2: Neuzeit und Gegenwart.* Darmstadt: Wissenschaftliche Buchgesellschaft, 1991.

Jauss, Hans Robert. *Aesthetic Experience and Literary Hermeneutics.* Tr. Michael Shaw. Minneapolis: University of Minnesota, 1982.

Jauss, Hans Robert. *Toward an Aesthetic of Reception.* Tr. Timothy Bahti. Minneapolis: University of Minnesota, 1981.

Jensen, Lionel. "Wise Man of the Wilds: Fatherlessness, Fertility, and the Mythic Exemplar, Kongzi." *Early China* 20 (1995), pp. 407–37.

Kähler-Meyer, Emmi. "Myth Motifs in Flood Stories from the Grassland of Cameroon." In *The Flood Myth.* Ed. Alan Dundes. Berkeley: University of California, 1988.

Kalinowski, Marc. "Mythe, cosmogénèse et théogonie dans la Chine ancienne." *L'Homme* 137 (January–March 1996), pp. 41–60.

Kalinowski, Marc. "Les traités de Shuihudi et l'hémérologie chinoise." *T'oung Pao* 72 (1986), pp. 175–228.

Kaltenmark, Max. "Le Dompteur des flots." *Han Hiue* 3 (1948), pp. 1–112.

Kaltenmark, Max. "La Naissance du monde en China." In *La Naissance du monde.* Paris: Seuil, 1959.

Kandel, Barbara. *Wen Tzu—Ein Beitrag zur Problematik und zum Verständnis eines taoistischen Textes.* Frankfurt am Main: Peter Lang, 1974.

Karlgren, Bernhard. *Grammata serica recensa.* 1957. Reprint ed. Stockholm: Museum of Far Eastern Antiquities, 1964.

Karlgren, Bernhard. "Legends and Cults in Ancient China." *Bulletin of the Museum of Far Eastern Antiquities* 18 (1946), pp. 199–365.

Kelsen, Hans. "The Principle of Retribution in the Flood and Catastrophe Myths." In *The Flood Myth.* Berkeley: University of California, 1988.

Kern, Martin. *Die Hymnen der chinesischen Staatsopfer: Literatur und Ritual in der politischen Repräsentation von der Han-zeit bis zu ende den Sechs Dynastien.* Stuttgart: Franz Steiner Verlag, 1997.

Kinney, Anne Behnke. *Representations of Childhood and Youth in Early China.* Stanford: Stanford University, 2004.

Kirk, G. S. *Myth: Its Meaning and Functions in Ancient and Other Cultures.* Berkeley: University of Calfornia, 1970.

Koppers, Willem. "The Deluge Myth of the Bhils of Central India." In *The Flood Myth*. Berkeley: University of California, 1988.

Lambert, Wilfred G., and Millard, Alan R. *Atra-hasis: The Babylonian Story of the Flood*. Oxford: Oxford University, 1969.

Lestrignant, Frank. "Fortunes de la singularité à la Renaissance: le genre de l'Isolario'." In *Écrire le monde à la Renaissance: Quinze études sur Rabelais, Postel, Bodin et la littérature géographique*. Caen: Paradigme. 1993.

Levi, Jean. *Les fonctionnaires divins: Politique, despotisme, et mystique en Chine ancienne*. Paris: Seuil, 1989.

Lévi-Strauss, Claude. *The Origin of Table Manners: Introduction to a Science of Mythology, 3*. Tr. John and Doreen Weightman. New York: Harper & Row, 1979.

Lévi-Strauss, Claude. *The Raw and the Cooked: Introduction to a Science of Mythology, 1*. Tr. J. Weightman and D. Weightman. New York: Harper & Row, 1970.

Lewis, Jack P. *A Study of the Interpretation of Noah and the Flood in Jewish and Christian Literature*. Leiden: E. J. Brill, 1978.

Lewis, Mark Edward. *The Construction of Space in Early China*. Albany: State University of New York, 2005.

Lewis, Mark Edward. "The *Feng* and *Shan* Sacrifices of Emperor Wu of the Han." In *State and Court Ritual in China*. Ed. Joseph P. McDermott. Cambridge: Cambridge University, 1999.

Lewis, Mark Edward. *Sanctioned Violence in Early China*. Albany: State University of New York, 1990.

Lewis, Mark Edward. *Writing and Authority in Early China*. Albany: State University of New York, 1999.

Li, Ling. "An Archaeological Study of Taiyi 太一 (Grand One) Worship." Tr. Donald Harper. *Early Medieval China* 2 (1995–1996), pp. 1–39.

Lincoln, Bruce. *Theorizing Myth: Narrative, Ideology, and Scholarship*. Chicago: University of Chicago, 1999.

Lindell, Kristina, Swahn, Jan-Ojvind, and Tayanin, Damrong. "The Flood: Three Northern Kammu Versions of the Story of Creation." In *The Flood Myth*. Berkeley: University of California, 1988.

Lo, Vivienne. "Spirit of Stone: Technical Considerations in the Treatment of the Jade Body." *Bulletin of the School of Oriental and African Studies* 65:1 (2002), pp. 99–128.

Loewe, Michael, ed. *Early Chinese Texts: A Bibliographic Guide*. Berkeley: Society for the Study of Early China and the Institute of East Asian Studies, 1993.

Loraux, Nicole. *La cité divisée: L'oubli dans la mémoire d'Athènes*. Paris: Payot, 1997.

Loraux, Nicole. *Les enfants d'Athéna: Idées athéniennes sur la citoyenneté et la division des sexes*. Paris: La Découverte, 1984

Loraux, Nicole. *Né de la terre: Mythe et politique à Athènes*. Paris: Seuil, 1996.

Mali, Joseph. *Mythistory: The Making of a Modern Historiography*. Chicago: University of Chicago, 2003.

Maspero, Henri. "Légendes mythologiques dans le Chou King." *Journal Asiatique* 204 (1924), pp. 1–100.

Mathieu, Rémi, tr. Étude sur la mythologie et l'ethnologie de la Chine ancienne: Traduction annotée du Shanhai jing. 2. vols. Paris: Collège de France, Institut des Hautes Études Chinoises, 1983.

Mathieu, Rémi. "Yu le Grand et le mythe de déluge dans la Chine ancienne." T'oung Pao 78 (1992), pp. 162–90.

Montgomery, John Warwick. The Quest for Noah's Ark. Minneapolis: Dimension Books, 1974.

Needham, Joseph. Science and Civilisation in China, vol. 3, Mathematics and the Sciences of the Heavens and the Earth. Cambridge: Cambridge University, 1970.

Nylan, Michael. The Shifting Center: The Original "Great Plan" and Later Readings. Monumenta Serica Monograph Series no. 24. Nettetal: Steyler Verlag, 1992.

O'Flaherty, Wendy Doniger. Asceticism & Eroticism in the Mythology of Siva. Oxford: Oxford University, 1973.

O'Flaherty, Wendy Doniger. Women, Androgynes, and Other Mythical Beasts. Chicago: University of Chicago, 1980.

Pagden, Anthony. The Fall of Natural Man: The American Indian and the Origins of Comparative Ethnology. Cambridge: Cambridge University, 1982.

Parrot, André. The Flood and Noah's Ark. Tr. Edwin Hudson. New York: Philosophical Library, 1955.

Peake, Harold. The Flood: New Light on an Old Story. London: Kegan Paul, Trench, Trubner & Co., 1930.

Pirazzoli-t'Serstevens, Michèle. The Han Dynasty. Tr. Janet Seligman. New York: Rizzoli, 1982.

Plaks, Andrew H. Archetype and Allegory in the Dream of the Red Chamber. Princeton: Princeton Unversity, 1976.

Porée-Maspero, Eveline. Étude sur les rites agraires des Cambodgiens. 3 vols. Paris: Mouton, 1952–69.

Porter, Deborah Lynn. From Deluge to Discourse: Myth, History, and the Generation of Chinese Fiction. Albany: State University of New York, 1996.

Powers, Martin. "An Archaic Bas-relief and the Chinese Moral Cosmos in the First Century A.D." Ars Orientalis 12 (1981), pp. 25–40.

Puett, Michael. "Violent Misreadings: The Hermeneutics of Cosmology in the Huainanzi." Bulletin of the Museum of Far Eastern Antiquities 72 (2000), pp. 29–46.

Rao, Tsung-yi [Zongyi]. "Some Aspects of the Calendar, Astrology, and Religious Concepts of the Ch'u People as Revealed in the Ch'u Silk Manuscript." In Early Chinese Art and Its Possible Influence in the Pacific Basin, vol. 1, Ch'u and the Silk Manuscript. Ed. Noel Barnard. New York: Intercultural Art Press, 1972.

Raphals, Lisa. Sharing the Light: Representations of Women and Virtue in Early China. Albany: State University of New York, 1998.

Rehwinkel, Alfred M. The Flood in the Light of the Bible, Geology, and Archaeology. St. Louis: Concordia Publishing, 1951.

Riem, Johannes. Die Sintflut in Sage und Wissenschaft. Hamburg: Rauhen Haus, 1934.

Rooth, Anna Birgitta. *The Raven and the Carcass: An Investigation of a Motif in the Deluge Myth in Europe, Asia, and North America.* FF Communications no. 186. Helsinki: Academia Scientiarum Fennica, 1962.

Rossi, Paolo. *The Dark Abyss of Time: The History of the Earth and the History of Nations from Hooke to Vico.* Tr. Lydia G. Cochrane. Chicago: University of Chicago, 1984.

Ruitenbeek, Klaas. *Carpentry and Building in Late Imperial China: A Study of the Fifteenth-Century Carpenter's Manual Lu Ban Jing.* Leiden: E. J. Brill, 1996.

Sage, Steven. *Ancient Sichuan and the Unification of China.* Albany: State University of New York, 1992.

Saso, Michael. "What is the Ho-t'u?" *History of Religions* 17:3/4 (February–May 1978), pp. 399–416.

Schafer, Edward H. *The Divine Woman: Dragon Ladies and Rain Maidens in T'ang Literature.* Berkeley: University of California, 1973.

Schafer, Edward H. *Pacing the Void: T'ang Approaches to the Stars.* Berkeley: University of California, 1977.

Schafer, Edward H. *The Vermilion Bird: T'ang Images of the South.* Berkeley: University of California, 1967.

Seidel, Anna. "Post-mortem Immortality—or the Taoist Resurrection of the Body." In *Gilgul: Essays on Transformation, Revolution and Permanence in the History of Religions.* Leiden: E. J. Brill, 1987.

Seidel, Anna. "Traces of Han Religion in Funeral Texts Found in Tombs," in *Dōkyō to shūkyō bunka* 道教と宗教文化. Ed. Akizuki Kan'ei 秋月觀暎. Tokyo: Hirakawa, 1987.

Serres, Michel. *Les origines de la géométrie.* Paris: Flammarion, 1993.

Shulman, David. "Murukan, the Mango, and Ekāmbareśvara-Śiva: Fragments of a Tamil Creation Myth?" *Indo-Iranian Journal* 21 (1979), pp. 27–40.

Shulman, David. "The Tamil Flood Myths and the Cankam Legend." In *The Flood Myth.* Berkeley: University of California, 1988.

Sterckx, Roel. *The Animal and the Daemon in Early China.* Albany: State University of New York, 2002.

Strenski, Ivan. *Four Theories of Myth in Twentieth-Century History: Cassirer, Eliade, Lévi-Strauss, and Malinowski.* Iowa City: University of Iowa, 1987.

Suh, Kyung Ho. "A Study of 'Shan-hai-ching': Ancient Worldviews Under Transformation." Ph.D. dissertation, Harvard University, 1993.

Tang, Xiaobing. *Chinese Modern: The Heroic and the Quotidian.* Durham: Duke University, 2000.

Terdiman, Richard. *Present Past: Modernity and Memory Crisis.* Ithaca: Cornell University, 1993.

Tigay, Jeffrey H. *The Evolution of the Gilgamesh Epic.* Philadelphia: University of Pennsylvania, 1982.

Tsai, Julius. "In the Steps of Emperors and Immortals: Imperial Mountain Journeys and Daoist Meditation and Ritual." Ph.D. dissertation, Stanford University, 2003.

Utley, Francis Lee. "The Devil in the Ark (AaTh 825)." In *The Flood Myth*. Berkeley: University of California, 1988.

Utley, Francis Lee. "Noah, His Wife, and the Devil," in *Studies in Biblical and Jewish Folklore*. Ed. Raphael Patai, Francis Lee Utley, and Dov Noy. Bloomington: Indiana University, 1960.

Vernant, Jean-Pierre. "Cosmogonies et mythes de souveraineté." In Vernant and Pierre Vidal-Naquet, *La Grèce ancienne*, vol. 1, *Du mythe à la raison*. Paris: Seuil, 1990.

Vernant, Jean-Pierre. "Le mythe hésiodique des races, essai d'analyse structurale." "Le mythe hésiodique des races; sur un essai de mise au point." *Mythe et pensée chez les Grecs*. Paris: Maspero, 1965.

Vitaliano, Dorothy B. *Legends of the Earth: Their Geologic Origins*. Bloomington: Indiana University, 1973.

Von Falkenhausen, Lothar. "Grabkult und Ahnenkult im Staat Qin: Der religiöse Hintergrund der Terrakotta-Armee." In *Jenseits der Grossen Mauer: Der Erste kaiser von China und seine Terrakotta-Armee*. Ed. Lothar Ledderose and Adele Schlombs. Munich: Bertelsmann Lexikon Verlag, 1990.

Von Falkenhausen, Lothar. "Sources of Taoism: Reflections on Archaeological Indicators of Religious Change in Eastern Zhou China." *Taoist Resources* 5.2 (1994), pp. 1–12.

Wagner, Donald B. *Iron and Steel in Ancient China*. Leiden: E. J. Brill, 1993.

Wagner, Rudolph. "Lebenstil und Drogen in chinesischen Mittelalter." *T'oung Pao* 59 (1973), pp. 79–178.

Walk, Leopold. "Das Flut-Geschwisterparr also Ur- und Stammelternpaar der Menschheit: Ein Beitrag zur Mythengeschichte Süd- und Südostasiens." *Mitteilungen der Österreichischen Gesellschaft für Anthropologie, Ethnologie und Prähistorie* 78/79 (1949), pp. 60–115.

Wang, Jing. *The Story of Stone: Intertextuality, Ancient Chinese Stone Lore, and the Stone Symbolism of Dream of the Red Chamber, Water Margin, and the Journey to the West*. Durham: Duke University, 1992.

Wang, Zhongshu. *Han Civilization*. Tr. K. C. Chang and collaborators. New Haven: Yale University, 1982.

Wechsler, Howard. *Offerings of Jade and Silk: Ritual and Symbol in the Legitimation of the T'ang Dynasty*. New Haven: Yale University, 1985.

Whitcomb, John C. *The World that Perished*. Grand Rapids, Mich.: Baker Book House, 1973.

Whitcomb, John C., Jr., and Morris, Henry M. *The Genesis Flood: The Biblical Record and Its Scientific Implications*. Grand Rapids, Mich.: Baker Book House, 1961.

Williamson, George S. *The Longing for Myth in Modern Germany: Religion and Aesthetic Culture from Romanticism to Nietzsche*. Chicago: University of Chicago, 2004.

Wolf, Arthur P. "Gods, Ghosts, and Ancestors." In *Religion and Ritual in Chinese Society*. Stanford: Stanford University, 1974.

Wu, Hung. "Beyond the 'Great Boundary': Funerary narrative in the Cangshan Tomb." In *Boundaries in China*. Ed. John Hay. London: Reaktion Books, 1994.

Wu, Hung. "Private Love and Public Duty: Images of Children in Early Chinese Art." In *Chinese Views of Childhood*. Ed. Anne Behnke Kinney. Honolulu: University of Hawaii, 1995.

Wu, Hung. *The Wu Liang Shrine*. Stanford: Stanford University Press, 1989.

Xing, Wen, ed. "The X Gong Xu: A Report and Papers from the Dartmouth Workshop." *International Research on Bamboo and Silk Documents Newsletter: Special Issue* (2003).

Yates, Robin D. S. "Body, Space, Time and Bureaucracy: Boundary Creation and Control Mechanisms in Early China." In *Boundaries in China*. Ed. John Hay. London: Reaktion Books, 1994.

Yates, Robin D. S. "Cosmos, Central Authority, and Communities in the Early Chinese Empire." In *Empires*. Ed. Susan E. Alcock et al. Cambridge: Cambridge University, 2000.

Yates, Robin D. S. "Purity and Pollution in Early China." In *Integrated Studies of Chinese Archaeology and Historiography*. Symposium Series of the Institute of History and Philology, Academia Sinica 4 (July 1997), pp. 479–536.

Yü, Ying-shih. "Han Foreign Relations." In *The Cambridge History of China, Volume 1: The Ch'in and Han Empires*. Ed. Michael Loewe. Cambridge: Cambridge University, 1986.

Zimmer, Heinrich. *Myths and Symbols in Indian Art and Civilization*. Ed. Joseph Campbell. Princeton: Princeton University/Bollingen Paperback, 1972.

Zito, Angela. *Of Body and Brush: Grand Sacrifice as Text/Performance in Eighteenth-Century China*. Chicago: University of Chicago, 1997.

INDEX

Abraham, 6
Acawaoios, 8
Adam, 6
Africa, 7, 11
agriculture, 6, 93
 by animals, 36, 45
 creation of, 28–31, 36, 44, 50–51, 59,
  72, 77, 169 n. 83
 opening of season, 101
 regional, 31, 47
 Shun and, 102
alcohol,
 invention of wine, 8–9
altars,
 and enfeoffment, 111–112, 136
 to High Matchmaker, 115
 for requesting sons, 135
 to Shun, 37
 soil, 134–137, 139, 143, 144, 151, 174
  n. 27
 to Yu, 45
altars of grain and soil, 60
 and droughts, 143
 and enfeoffment, 112
 and fertility, 134–137, 139
 Goulong and, 104, 107
 on intimate relations, 135–136
 stones at, 139
 Yu and, 104, 134–135, 151
ancestors, 10, 23, 89, 122
 and corpse, 92, 99, 150
 of humanity, 10–12, 18–19, 23, 70,
  120, 123, 130

of lineage, 17–18, 101, 123
 mythic, 61, 120, 137, 189 n. 81
 of royal houses, 22, 29, 38, 101, 123,
  137
 sacrifices to, 95, 97, 161 n. 17, 174
  n. 26
ancient Greece,
 fratricide, 95
 myths, 2, 3–4, 6, 7, 10, 15, 158 n. 49,
  185 n. 30
Anhui, 93
animals, 6, 40, 41, 123, 144, 186 n. 38
 as assistants, 12–13, 40, 144, 145, 168
  n. 74
 and children, 86–87, 88, 89, 90–93,
  99
 of directions, 126, 127
 expulsion of, 13, 29, 30, 33, 34–35,
  37, 42, 50–51, 53, 66, 71–72
 mating with people, 11–12, 109, 136,
  138–139
 mingling with people, 25, 26, 28, 34,
  36, 38, 45, 49, 50, 51, 52, 119–120,
  149
 rebellions of, 8, 12, 63–64
 relations to people, 5, 8, 49, 101
 sages and, 71, 100, 136, 138–139
 and Shun, 35–38, 184 n. 16
 transformations of, 11–12, 19, 53, 61,
  71, 104–105, 110
Arawaks, 8
Aristophanes, 2
Aristotle, 2